Creating Citizenship in the Nineteenth-Century South

UNIVERSITY PRESS OF FLORIDA

Florida A&M University, Tallahassee
Florida Atlantic University, Boca Raton
Florida Gulf Coast University, Ft. Myers
Florida International University, Miami
Florida State University, Tallahassee
New College of Florida, Sarasota
University of Central Florida, Orlando
University of Florida, Gainesville
University of North Florida, Jacksonville
University of South Florida, Tampa
University of West Florida, Pensacola

# CREATING CITIZENSHIP IN THE NINETEENTH-CENTURY SOUTH

Edited by William A. Link, David Brown,
Brian Ward, and Martyn Bone

University Press of Florida
Gainesville · Tallahassee · Tampa · Boca Raton
Pensacola · Orlando · Miami · Jacksonville · Ft. Myers · Sarasota

This book may be available in an electronic edition.

23  22  21  20  19  18    6  5  4  3  2  1

First cloth printing, 2013
First paperback printing, 2018

A record of cataloging-in-publication data is available from the Library of Congress.
ISBN 978-0-8130-4413-2 (cloth)
ISBN 978-0-8130-6483-3 (pbk.)

The University Press of Florida is the scholarly publishing agency for the State
University System of Florida, comprising Florida A&M University, Florida Atlantic
University, Florida Gulf Coast University, Florida International University, Florida
State University, New College of Florida, University of Central Florida, University of
Florida, University of North Florida, University of South Florida, and University of
West Florida.

University Press of Florida
15 Northwest 15th Street
Gainesville, FL 32611-2079
http://upress.ufl.edu

# Contents

# Preface

## Understanding the South

In 2008, the Arts and Humanities Research Council in the United Kingdom agreed to fund an international research network dedicated to the theme "Understanding the South, Understanding America: The American South in Regional, National and Global Perspectives." The network was based at the University of Manchester, with the Universities of Copenhagen, Cambridge, and Florida as partners. Between May 2008 and August 2010 each of these institutions hosted a network conference. These meetings brought together scholars from a range of disciplines and allowed them to explore together the current state and future prospects for the study of that section of the North American continent that eventually became known, with all due disclaimers about the definitional slipperiness of the term, as the American South.

This series of books from the University Press of Florida extends the work of the network, initially in three volumes grouped around the themes of creating citizenship in the nineteenth-century South, the South and the Atlantic world, and creating and consuming the South. While each volume stands alone as a valuable contribution to a particular aspect of southern studies, collectively they allow us to take stock of a rich and diverse field, to ponder the substantive disagreement and methodological tensions—as well as the common ground—among scholars of the South, and to think about new areas and techniques for future research. Each volume and many of the individual essays are marked by an interest in interdisciplinary and multidisciplinary approaches to the region. Indeed, one aim of the series is to juxtapose the work of historians with that of scholars associated with the New Southern Studies in the belief that historians and those working out of literary and cultural studies traditions have much to learn from each other in their quest to understand the American

South in a variety of overlapping temporal, geographic, symbolic, cultural, and material contexts.

The coeditors of the series wish to thank all those colleagues who participated in the four conferences. Special thanks are due to Tony Badger at the University of Cambridge for his generous financial support and for hosting the Cambridge conference; to James Broomall, Heather Bryson, Angela Diaz, and Angie Zombek at the University of Florida for their logistical help; and, at the University of Manchester, to David Brown for coediting the *Creating Citizenship* volume, to Michael Bibler for his consistently constructive engagement with all aspects of the network, and to Tom Strange and Jennie Chapman for their invaluable administrative assistance. We would also like to express our gratitude to the Arts and Humanities Research Council for its sponsorship of the network, to the British Academy and the United States Embassy's Cultural Affairs Office in London for important additional funding, and to Meredith Morris-Babb at the University Press of Florida for her enthusiastic support of the Understanding the South series of books.

*Brian Ward*
*Martyn Bone*
*William A. Link*

# Introduction

WILLIAM A. LINK AND DAVID BROWN

In societies struggling to make sense of the post–Cold War geopolitical world, the U.S. War on Terror has provoked a battle of values and ideals as real as the earlier conflict with the Soviet Union. The brave, new post-9/11 world requires that young people should be educated in their duties as citizens; fierce battles have raged over school and university curricula. Citizenship has also been the subject of a steady stream of academic inquiry, most notably by sociologists and political scientists and also historians. They do not necessarily agree with one another on a formal definition of citizenship, but point to many different types of experiences—something underlined by the essays in this volume. However they disagree, scholars from different disciplines concur that "citizenship is not just a matter of formal legal status; it is a matter of belonging and being recognized as belonging . . . by other members of the community." Members police formal boundaries established by legal statutes, but they also interpret those boundaries in their own, sometimes idiosyncratic, ways.[1]

Citizenship has a long and complex history. The classical civilizations of Greece and Rome form the starting point for discussions of civic republican citizenship, a wide-ranging concept that broadly conceives of citizenship as the preserve of a minority of independent, property-owning males. The onus lay with the individual to participate, as a matter of duty, wisely and enthusiastically in governing by cultivating a sense of civic virtue and devotion to the common good. In the early modern period, citizenship gradually, and usually incrementally, moved from civic republicanism toward a liberal conception of the individual's basic entitlement to justice from his or her government based on the idea of universal rights. This changing view of citizenship began with debates over individual entitlement to legal rights in the Atlantic world, which then shifted to citizenship as political rights in the late eighteenth and nineteenth centuries, underpinning the rise of liberal democracies in Western societies.[2]

The liberal notion of citizenship as rights has significant implications for individual and group identity. As Rogers M. Smith writes in the most comprehensive study of American citizenship: "Citizenship laws—laws designating the criteria for membership in a political community and the key prerogatives that constitute membership—are among the most fundamental of political creations. They distribute power, assign status and define political purposes." But citizenship can become even more than that. Rights and duties accorded to each citizen become an integral part of that individual's social makeup, potentially intertwining with and shaping identity. To quote Smith again: "Citizenship laws also literally constitute— they create with legal words—a collective civic identity. They proclaim the existence of a political 'people' and designate who those persons are as a people, in ways that often become integral to individuals' senses of personal identity as well." This suggests that, far from a given or a label assigned to individuals, citizenship is much better understood as an ongoing and ever-evolving process.[3]

Current scholarly understandings of citizenship, much like those of race, class, and gender, thus seek to interpret citizenship within specific historical contexts.[4] This position is heavily influenced by the work of T. H. Marshall, the post–World War II British theorist. His historicized interpretation identified three integral strands to the development of citizenship in the modern era: civil, political, and social. Civil rights were drawn up and guaranteed by the legal process. Political rights allowed the citizen inclusion in the process of government by providing the opportunity to hold office as well as by voting. A third strand was broadly defined as social citizenship. In a departure from orthodox views locating citizenship primarily in the legal sphere, Marshall interpreted social citizenship as the state's provision of welfare and education to all within its jurisdiction, guaranteeing inclusion regardless of individual circumstances. For him, the history of citizenship reflected a fundamental tension between the principles of equality and inclusion and the practice of inequality and exclusion.[5]

Modern scholars remain indebted to Marshall's insights. They have demonstrated how the process of citizenship—that is, deciding who is entitled to what—became tied to the growth of bureaucracy and to the rapid expansion of local and national government. From the great revolutions of the eighteenth century to the present, political struggles over the inclusion and exclusion of certain groups to the body politic—excluded on the grounds of race, class, gender, ethnicity, or sexuality—have intimately shaped and helped to define modern Western societies. They were certainly critical to the historical development of the United States precisely because the Constitution failed to provide a definition of citizenship. Indeed, the late George M. Fredrickson suggested that citizenship in the American context is fundamentally distinguished by "the coexistence of a universalistic affirmation of human rights and a seemingly contradictory set of exclusions based on race or color."[6] In the century or so after the adoption of the Constitution, citizenship lay at the core of the shifting meanings of the Republic, and its importance extended way beyond the basic legal clarification of resident status.

It was precisely because the founding fathers failed to establish a definition of national citizenship, leaving details to individual states, that there was considerable ambiguity over what it meant to be a citizen in the new republic. Persisting tensions between state and federal government ensured that defining and interpreting citizenship in the American context was a dynamic and contested process. Most states asserted their own version of state citizenship and assumed that primary loyalty lay with them. In a patchwork pattern, citizens were only those who could vote and hold political office. Citizenship also guaranteed rights and status under the law, the ability to sue and be sued, and to own and sell property independently. The states varied considerably in how they defined these rights of citizenship, but they mostly agreed to a notion of limited rights. Citizenship probably meant more in the nineteenth-century United States than in any other era because, as Judith Shklar emphasizes, the founders shaped a "republic that was overly committed to political equality, and whose citizens believed that theirs was a free and fair society."[7] Elites continued to wield immense power, but the expectations of ordinary men and women grew in a nation that consciously sought to fashion a political culture distinct from that of European countries. Two revolutions during the first half of the nineteenth century—in communications and in the market—expanded opportunities and possibilities in a way unimaginable to the revolutionary generation. The growing importance of citizenship in the nineteenth century for some, and the exclusion of others, constitutes another integral element of the history of the Republic, even though it is rarely recognized as such in mainstream accounts.[8]

William J. Novak cautions against the assumption that citizenship in the nineteenth century was solely concerned with legal rights and individual entitlements. He seeks "to challenge the straightforward applicability of the modern conception of citizenship to nineteenth-century American understandings of individual rights, public power, and democratic governance." Novak rightly warns of the dangers in pursuing a presentist approach focusing solely upon the expansion of liberal rights or the legal codification of citizenship. In a similar vein, Linda K. Kerber reminds us that "rights are implicitly paired with obligations" in the "liberal tradition."[9] Undeniably, however, on either side of the Mason-Dixon Line, states legally restricted political and civil rights, excluded women and non-whites, and generally privileged adult white males. Legal dictates fundamentally defined the parameters and possibilities of citizenship. The struggle of Native Americans to assert basic political rights in the 1820s, followed by their eventual removal in the 1830s, also focused attention on who was or was not included in the body politic. Citizenship in the North revolved around questions of race and ethnic identity, most notably with respect to the status of Irish immigrants arriving in the tens of thousands in the mid-nineteenth century, but also concerning free blacks. This led to what Christian Samito describes as the "crisis of American citizenship" by the 1850s. In the years before the Civil War, then, the rights of native-born Americans and the civic position of alien residents depended upon the conflicting interests of the various states and of the federal government.[10]

Citizenship has attracted little attention from scholars of the nineteenth-century American South. Perhaps this reflects the fluidity of the concept and the ways in which southern citizenship has varied over time. Citizenship is not central to antebellum southern history, even though Michael O'Brien has stressed the tension between state and national loyalties, as most southerners primarily identified with their states.[11] The centrality of slavery in the Old South has made it easy to assume a simple and rigid binary interpreting citizenship in terms of white and black. Moreover, a vibrant literature examining the development of southern and Confederate nationalism may have stymied consideration of southern citizenship as a subject matter in its own right.[12] During Reconstruction, by contrast, the struggle to define civil and political rights took center stage. After this brief reappearance, however, citizenship once again fades from view in historical interpretations of the New South. In some respects, it is surprising that citizenship has not played a more significant role in understanding the South across the long nineteenth century. Citizenship was very important to colonial and revolutionary historians such as Edmund S. Morgan and Kathleen M. Brown. Moreover, the vigorous 1980s debate over republicanism—a debate that explicitly addressed issues of citizenship and political inclusion—occupied American historians, not just southern scholars. Since the demise of the republican paradigm, however, and the marginalization of political history in general, scholarly interest in citizenship also declined. Since 1990, little attention has been paid to the meanings of citizenship in the South.[13]

The American South has been defined by the struggle over social, political, and civil rights. This contestation has been a central, consuming drama that has arguably shaped the region to an even greater extent than the rest of the United States.[14] Historically, women in the South achieved legal and political equality later than they did in the rest of the country, as the rights of white men were exalted (although poor white men have often had occasion to question the value of their gender and skin color as they too have struggled for inclusion). At the same time, the rights of black people remained severely restricted in the South. The exclusion of black people starkly defined the rights of southern whites. In this way, citizenship by the mid-nineteenth century was defined negatively, as a means to distinguish those who had from those who had not. "The value of citizenship," Shklar writes, "was derived primarily from its denial to slaves, to some white men, and to all women."[15]

The essays in this volume, divided into three parts, explore the evolving understanding of citizenship in the nineteenth-century South. We see citizenship as fluid in its implications and wide in its meanings, and we thus attempt to engage a range of scholars across disciplines. Our purpose is to expand the conceptualization beyond the realm of electoral politics by considering citizenship as a concept with implications in culture, social life, and literature. The scholars in this volume offer different assumptions, methods, and approaches, but they are guided by a common inquiry into the roles of marginalized people in the nineteenth-century South.

At the outbreak of the Civil War, many states regarded citizenship as something other than national in definition. The Constitution of 1787 established a built-in, constitutional ambiguity to what defined a citizen. The language of the Constitution employs "citizen" eleven times, yet it said very little specifically about what a citizen was. Article II, section 1, states that the citizens of each state were "entitled to all Privileges and

Immunities of Citizens in the several States," but this itself reveals the deliberate ambiguity of the 1787 system. On the one hand, this article recognized that citizenship was defined by the states, while on the other it insisted that state citizenship had a national, federal dimension in that an equality of citizenship should be respected across state lines. The Constitution left other questions unanswered. What were the obligations of citizenship, and how should Americans exercise them? What rights of citizenship existed under the federal system of the Republic? The debates over federal power, and how much or how little the federal government should intervene in matters such as the national debt, the national bank, the tariff, and internal improvements, reflected how and where Americans located their primary loyalties and responsibilities. They were related as well to slavery and the power of southern slaveholders who jealously guarded their rights against outside infringement.

Part 1 of *Creating Citizenship* considers the ambiguities of an enslaved society, which required a hierarchy of citizenry and rights—from the full citizenship of some white males to the "anti-citizen" of enslaved African Americans. Women, meanwhile, were only partly citizens, with no voting rights until the adoption of the suffrage in 1920. The dominance of chattel slavery in economic, social, legal, and constitutional life provided an essential distinctiveness to the Old South, a society exalting the political liberty of white males. The presence of enslaved people created obvious contradictions in southern society between slaves' status as human beings and non-citizens.

The status of black people in the antebellum South remained a fundamental contradiction in the political system. Yet emphasizing the political repression and exclusion of black people misses some of the subtlety of their position. As Daina Ramey Berry argues, there was an important connection between commodification and citizenship. She examines the relationship between property and power, and what she calls "the multifaceted meanings of the commodification of human beings who were outside the bounds of legal citizenship." Although slaves were denied citizenship, their value as chattel property demonstrated their significance to white society. African Americans became living, breathing examples of the contradictions of citizenship in the South—and in the United States generally. The significance of the commodification of black people lay beyond the boundaries of defining citizenship. There was a "duality of commodification and personhood," according to Berry, shaping enslaved African American identity and the position of slaves within wider society.

If the historical trajectory of citizenship was essentially one of expansion for the majority of white men in the antebellum era, it was a very different experience for other groups of southerners. The citizenship status of black people provides a case in point. In 1857, in the *Dred Scott* case, Chief Justice Roger Taney issued one of the most important and controversial rulings in the history of the U.S. Supreme Court. Scott had petitioned for his freedom when his master took him from a slave state, Missouri, to the free state of Illinois. Taney ruled against Scott, denying his right to standing in the Court because he was not a citizen. On the contrary, Taney declared, the founding fathers considered Scott and all black people in the United States to be "a subordinate and inferior class of beings who had been subjugated by the dominant race, and, whether emancipated or not, yet remained subject to their authority, and had no rights or privileges but such as those who held the power and the Government might choose to grant them." Citizenship, said Taney, was defined by the states. "Each State may still confer them upon an alien, or anyone it thinks proper, or upon any class or description of persons, yet he would not be a citizen in the sense in which that word is used in the Constitution of the United States, nor entitled to sue as such in one of its courts, nor to the privileges and immunities of a citizen in the other States." In apparent contradiction of Article IV, section 2, Taney asserted that rights of citizenship only pertained to individual states and that no state could make citizens of a race and expect that citizenship to be recognized beyond its borders. Basing this assertion on the constitutional authority of the federal government to determine naturalization requirements, Taney declared that no states possessed the power "to raise to the rank of a citizen anyone born in the United States who, from birth or parentage, by the laws of the country, belongs to an inferior and subordinate class." No laws enacted by a state could provide "any right of citizenship outside of its own territory." Taney thus made clear the constitutional understanding that the United States was composed of a "government of free white citizens" and that considering black people citizens would be "an abuse of terms, and not calculated to exalt the character of an American citizen in the eyes of other nations."[16]

Watson Jennison discusses the legal framework of citizenship at the state level. In Georgia, free people of color suffered increasing restrictions to their citizenship during the antebellum period. During the 1790s, slave societies were haunted and besieged by slave uprisings, the most famous in Saint-Domingue, which unsettled slave societies throughout the hemisphere and prompted authorities in several colonies to reconsider the boundaries of race and citizenship. In Georgia, white citizens considered greater flexibility in extending some rights to the freed populations, except voting and officeholding, in a graded status of citizenship. "Blackness," Jennison writes, "did not preclude free people of color from becoming an accepted part of society." But this changed radically during the 1850s, as demonstrated by the career of jurist Joseph Lumpkin. Like other white Georgians, Lumpkin articulated a new, intensified form of racism that categorized all people as either white citizens or black slaves. This new racial environment decisively shaped the status of freedpeople, which deteriorated during the late-antebellum years. In the 1850s, southern state legislatures imposed new, and often harsher, restrictions limiting the economic, political, and civil rights of free blacks.

Perhaps the clearest indicators of the decline in the status of free blacks—and the creation of a kind of "anti-citizen"—came in the rise of "voluntary" enslavement of free blacks. As Emily West shows, a new phenomenon of the 1850s was the adoption of laws permitting free blacks to petition their reenslavement. Like Jennison, West describes a declining environment for the 250,000 free blacks who lived in the South during the late-antebellum period as whites came to fear their influence. Not only imposing restrictions on blacks' legal, political, and civil rights, southern legislatures also contemplated mass expulsions or deportations to West Africa. Free blacks were far from citizens. Indeed, they were "anti-citizens," as West explains, whose position had so deteriorated that, for many of them, "voluntary" enslavement became a real option. During the 1850s, the "anti-citizen" status of black people became validated by the adoption of a legal structure that enabled their "voluntary" reenslavement.

Race and gender were primary elements within evolving notions of citizenship. The American republic, as Jennison confirms, was defined by the exclusion of some groups. Slaveholders created a system mandating full citizenship for white males and a form of sponsorship and patronage for everyone else. But whites generally regarded it right and proper that the constitutional and political system would exclude women and blacks. By law, neither could own property, vote, or serve on juries. Women were under the nearly absolute authority of their husbands; slaves were similarly expected to submit to the authority, including the physical discipline, of their masters.

David Brown explores the balance of power among southern whites, the nature of southern democracy, and how citizenship was defined in this particular sociopolitical environment. He further discusses the complicated implications of political democracy among yeoman whites. Although political rights became expanded and the force of voters grew, in some ways politics remained essentially unchanged. According to Brown, historians have overemphasized the degree to which the Jacksonian era witnessed an opening of the political system. Democratization, Brown writes, "was neither complete nor universal across the South by 1850, let alone at the beginning of the Jacksonian era." Despite widespread reforms, the pace of change varied considerably from state to state, and for the South as a whole, elites continued to dominate the political system despite the advent of mass politics. White male suffrage was not an established fact; limitations on voting persisted. The apportionment of legislative districts—a key indicator of political power—still tended to privilege slaveholders at the expense of non-slaveholding whites in many southern states.

Part 2 considers how southern citizenship evolved in the aftermath of the Civil War. Emancipation fundamentally shook traditional relationships between white and black people, and in its aftermath a turbulent, and often violent, restructuring of the racial order occurred. Freed slaves expected, indeed demanded, full citizenship. Most southern whites saw citizenship through the lens of antebellum political discourse, and they vehemently disagreed with the Republican Party's attempt to make citizenship inclusive. The war altered the role of the state by establishing a new, national definition of citizenship. The Thirteenth Amendment, ratified in December 1865, abolished slavery and involuntary servitude. The Fourteenth Amendment, ratified in July 1868, granted citizenship to "all persons born or naturalized in the United States, and prohibited states from denying any persons their property without due process of law." The amendment further stated that no state "shall make or enforce any law which shall abridge the privileges or immunities of citizens of the United States." The Fifteenth Amendment, ratified by the states in February 1870, mandated that the citizen's ability to vote "shall not be denied or abridged by the United States or by any State on account of race, color, or previous condition of servitude." Providing a national standard, these three amendments redefined the constitutional basis and definition of citizenship. They also enfranchised millions of ex-slaves as voters and provided the constitutional basis for their claim to equal civil rights. Yet there was substantial resistance to this new conception of citizenship. Most southern states refused to ratify the Fourteenth Amendment and finally did so only under the extraordinary compulsion of the Reconstruction Acts of 1867. Under "military" reconstruction the postwar southern governments were swept out of existence, and the military supervised new elections and new constitutions that involved African American voters. Hostility to the new conception of citizenship galvanized southern white opposition to Reconstruction, creating a dynamic intensity during the postwar years.[17]

James Broomall explores how the thousands of returning Confederate veterans altered the meaning of citizenship. He finds a connection between former soldiers' emotional condition and their reconstruction of citizenship. The war changed veterans' "mental and emotional landscapes," according to Broomall, and "destabilized white southern manliness as it was socially constructed and understood." Veterans underwent a process of redefining themselves and their position as citizens. The trauma of defeat, for them, raised questions about duties and responsibilities in the reconstructed South, and veterans—who constituted the majority of southern males—helped to define post–Civil War citizenship. Citizenship might have become primarily focused on political rights, but its implications continued to extend beyond the realm of politics.

The uncertainty of defeat and Reconstruction shaped the postwar status of freed slaves. William A. Link examines the period immediately after the Civil War in Atlanta and finds that labor, crime, and migration all were contested areas, as whites and blacks sought to define a new variety of post-emancipation citizenship. During Reconstruction, Atlanta became a center of northern intervention as well as a symbol of the new racial order. While whites operated under older assumptions about citizenship, the freed slaves began to assert themselves and sought ways to develop economic and political power. The major actors—southern whites, northern whites, and freedpeople—triangulated into radically different, though interrelated, points of view. The Freedmen's Bureau became an object of southern white resentment against federal intervention, while northern whites insisted on the end of slavery and bristled at any signs that it was being reintroduced by other means. Military detachments, in the months after Confederate surrender, scoured the South to liberate slaves. But at the center of the indeterminacy of the postwar era was the extent to which freedom meant citizenship for ex-slaves. For black people, the face of northern occupation became the Freedmen's Bureau, which was created by Congress in March 1865. Freedpeople recognized that the bureau, despite its limitations, offered their only hope for citizenship. Certainly, southern whites suspected that the bureau was seeking to undermine the racial order by promoting black equality.

Using the rich records of the Southern Claims Commission, Susanna Lee unpacks the layered meaning that southerners attached to concepts of loyalty, unionism, and citizenship during the 1870s. She finds citizenship still a nascent, undeveloped concept, defined in part by the process of national integration. A debate raged, through the Claims Commission, about wartime loyalties, with some arguing that Unionism constituted a basis for citizenship in the Reconstructed South, while others argued that former Confederates deserved full recognition as citizens. The debate about whether to compensate southerners related to the antebellum debate about citizens and "anti-citizens." Republicans during Reconstruction took a restrictive view, while Democrats tended to see loyalty in terms of the current process of reconciliation. What constituted "good citizenship"—which had distinct racial and gendered meaning—lay at the center of the process of claims compensation. The contest over the meaning of citizenship, as played out in deliberations of the Claims Commission, reflected a continuing tension that persisted until the end of the nineteenth century.

While the first two sections of this volume explore the changing forms and meanings of citizenship in the South and the tensions those changes wrought, the third section interrogates citizenship from global and interdisciplinary perspectives. Here the interaction between historians and literary scholars proves fruitful. There is little doubt that, as Peter Schmidt writes, there is a "counter-productive split between literary and social historians." But without question the imaginary can inform the historian and, as Schmidt writes, can "expose fictional histories that pass for true in the 'real' world so as to provide us with alternative testimony and counter-narratives." This section explores the divergent meanings and contradictory outcomes surrounding citizenship in the American South, and especially how it related to slavery, emancipation, and white supremacy.

Through its astounding popularity, argues Jennifer Rae Greeson, *Uncle Tom's Cabin* (1852) became "a collective imaginative inquiry into the civic, ethical, and emotional responsibilities of U.S. citizenship." Slavery created an ethos of an imaginary, and Harriet Beecher Stowe provides an image of slaveholding society with powerful resonance beyond the confines of the U.S. South. As Greeson show, images of slavery shaped the ways Americans regarded themselves. "Stowe's novel," writes Greeson, "converted abolitionism from a radical political stance into a popular sentimental imperative."

Stowe's appeal was rooted in the changing nature of American culture. The market revolution spurred a "transformative symbiosis" in which the nation industrialized in the Northeast and experienced "galloping expansion of its southern and western peripheries and their productive capacities." But the market revolution and its consequences radically altered the bases of republican citizenship, argues Greeson. During the early nineteenth century, citizenship was linked to individuals' status as free men, but by the late-antebellum period "citizenship had come to describe a situation that earlier generations would have considered servitude, guaranteeing only a 'hireling' existence, only the personal possession of a commoditized and alienable self." *Uncle Tom's Cabin* was thus part of a cultural process by which freedom, independence, and citizenship were reconsidered. Slavery in Stowe's view represented the antithesis of liberty and independence, but it also provided a variant on Charles Dickens's characterization of the adverse consequences of industrialization. *Uncle Tom's Cabin* became, according to Greeson, "Dickens with a distinctively American twist." Stowe's novel became, she says, the "most important novel of metropolitan modernity published in the United States before the Civil War."

Scott Romine considers a more fluid application of citizenship, especially with regard to white supremacy, in the writings of Albion W. Tourgée and Thomas Dixon. He argues that citizenship and Reconstruction became wrapped up in conceptions of race that appeared in fictional and nonfictional form. Reconstruction, he writes, had a "distinctively literary dimension." Focusing on the figure of the citizen in its relationship to race, Romine shows that an intersection between citizen and character involved the confluence of a "legal category of national belonging and literary representations of figures inhabiting that category." This relationship became a "central pivot around which the racial story of Reconstruction gained ascendancy over the sectional one."

Writers of the southern imaginary fused together with contemporary commentators and historians. Reconstruction became a kind of fable with fictive and nonfictive qualities. There thus existed a gap between the citizenship of blacks and the "traumatic denial of citizenship to white characters" who more properly deserved it. There was contestation in this narrative, most powerfully from the Reconstruction carpetbagger/novelist Albion Tourgée. Romine further shows how the literary world followed politics. He considers the work of the vitriolic racist Thomas Dixon, author of *The Leopard's Spots* and *The Clansman*. Dixon's fiction emphasized black incapacity for citizenship but offered radical solutions—expulsion, forced colonization, and complete separation of the races. For Dixon, the black citizen was a "contaminant of the body politic, an alien presence that must be eliminated if the nation is to realize its best future."

Daryl Scott also explores the implications of black citizenship in the aftermath of emancipation. By the 1890s, white supremacy swept through the South and provided a formal rationale for the reduction of black civil and political rights. For Scott, citizenship was connected to different versions of nationalism, which can best be understood in global terms. On the one hand, civic nationalism, Scott contends, was a novel concept for white southerners. Civic nationalism required a leap of faith in the idea that all people automatically possessed citizenship. But this proved unacceptable for many white southerners. Rather, white supremacy, a form of ethnoracial nationalism, became a unifying concept among white people. Like many European nationalists, writes Scott, southern ethnoracial nationalists defined nationality by race and ethnicity.

Ethnoracial nationalism thus becomes an analytical lens through which white supremacy can be understood. Defined as "making racial or ethnic identity the basis for belonging to the nation," ethnoracial nationalism assumed notions of citizenship that were exclusionary and predicated on a caste system and racial subordination. A belief in a homogeneous nation defined by race or ethnicity left little room for "aliens," who existed apart from the political community. Ethnoracial nationalism prevailed before the Civil War, according to Scott, but after the war a "full-bodied" articulation of civic nationalism appeared in the Fourteenth and Fifteenth Amendments. Civic nationalism became the official ideology of the American republic during Reconstruction, but only in tension with the more popular ethnoracial nationalism. Still, a "central myth of civic nationalism" persisted. In the South especially, "the river refused to bend toward civic nationalism." White supremacy, in its basic form, was "straightforward nationalist belief that southerners, along with other whites, should govern themselves and all non-white people in what they considered to be their homeland."

Peter Schmidt also examines the implications of white supremacy and an exclusionary citizenship on a global level. He argues that fictional texts and imaginary works can tell us much about historical processes and that there is a strong connection between novelists and playwrights and the social contexts in which they exist. He examines three authors—Aurelio Tolentino, George Washington Cable, and Albion Tourgée—to explore ways in which white supremacy existed in a global conversation about race and citizenship. For Schmidt, form informed content; speech described a larger social reality. When considering the imaginary, he writes, "we must attend to their form, not just their plots and overt claims they may make about empirical historical events."

The Philippines came under American control following the Spanish-American War (1898), and Americans immediately confronted questions of race in an international context. Filipino author Aurelio Tolentino's *Yesterday, Today, and Tomorrow* (1903) provided a "counter-narrative to American imperial discourse," while it also suggested something about the American colonizers' "contradictory perceptions of the Filipinos and textual evidence that challenges the colonizers' key self-justifying claims." Tolentino's play suggests something about a "tension between human and citizenship rights built into the wording of the Fourteenth Amendment." It explores the tension between civic nationalism's embrace of inclusive citizenship versus a more limited view of individual rights. Tolentino's overt criticism of race and U.S. globalism was matched by George Washington's Cable's later novel, *Lovers of Louisiana (To-Day)* (1918), which criticized white supremacy. Racial oppression at home related to global anticolonial movements. Cable saw white supremacy as connected to American entrance into World War I. European powers were self-destructing because of their colonial policies, he suggested. *Lovers of Louisiana* fits into a "context of both global history and the 'local' complexities of citizenship/civil rights debates and changing clan, class, and race dynamics."

Similarly, Albion Tourgée used fiction to make a case for racial democracy in the South. Tourgée, who had witnessed the collapse and failure of Reconstruction, followed the rise of white supremacy in his novel *Bricks without Straw* (1880). In Tourgée's prose, fiction provided a counterfactual version of history and imagined "what the known facts cannot tell us." "Fictional texts," writes Schmidt, "may even prove eccentric to their era but prophetic of the future, sketching revisionary truths that are validated by professional historians only decades later." Tourgée's purpose in terms of remembering a version of the past was thus "deeply revisionary and dialectical." *Bricks without Straw* charts the reasons for the demise of Reconstruction—internal weaknesses among Republicans, the weak response of the federal government to vigilante violence, and fears about black supremacy.

This volume represents a larger attempt to bring together historians and literary scholars in conversation. In particular, these essays test how effectively the kinds of literary and cultural scholarship often associated with New Southern Studies can inform a historical understanding of the American South. Michael O'Brien, in the epilogue, reviews the ways in which historians and literary scholars have engaged. The New Southern Studies, O'Brien explains, posits that the South, far from being exceptional, was centrally involved in globalism. O'Brien charts the rise of globalism as an entry point of analysis in southern studies. There is a convergence with a social-scientific insistence on understanding the South globally, but by accident rather than design, as their assumptions and concepts are entirely different. The South, according to this view, should be understood as part of larger, global culture. The New Southern Studies, according to O'Brien, shares the "postmodernist mistrust of essence and the postmodernist trust in constructive acts of imagination and will." There is nothing like John Crowe Ransom's "natural Southern community," only "imagined communities, plural and hybrid," in which place was "not a social premise, but a usable fiction, sometimes an unusable fiction." The essays in this volume explore citizenships both imagined and real in many different contexts in the nineteenth-century American South.

## Notes

1. Evelyn Nakano Glenn, *Unequal Freedom: How Race and Gender Shaped American Citizenship and Labor* (Cambridge: Harvard University Press, 2002), 52.

2. Paul Barry Clarke, ed., *Citizenship* (London: Pluto Press, 1994); Herman van Gunsteren, *Organising Plurality in Contemporary Democracies* (Boulder: Westview Press, 1998); Keith Faulks, *Citizenship* (London: Routledge, 2000); Paul Magnette, *Citizenship: The History of an Idea* (Colchester: ECPR Press, 2005).

3. Rogers M. Smith, *Civic Ideals: Conflicting Visions of Citizenship in U.S. History* (New Haven: Yale University Press, 1997), 30–31. Contrast Smith's interpretation of the struggle for American citizenship with the far less pessimistic account of Michael Schudson, *The Good Citizen: A History of American Civic Life* (Cambridge: Harvard University Press, 1998).

4. George M. Fredrickson, "The Historical Construction of Race and Citizenship in the United States," in his *Diverse Nations: Explorations in the History of Racial and Ethnic Pluralism* (Boulder: Paradigm, 2008), 21–38.

5. T. H. Marshall, *Citizenship and Social Class* (Cambridge: Cambridge University Press, 1950). See also the influential critique of Marshall; Michael Mann, "Ruling Strategies and Citizenship," *Sociology* 21, no. 3 (1987): 339–54.

6. Fredrickson, "Historical Construction," 35.

7. Judith N. Shklar, *American Citizenship: The Quest for Inclusion* (Cambridge: Harvard University Press, 1991), 17.

8. Daniel Walker Howe, *What Hath God Wrought: The Transformation of America, 1815–1848* (New York: Oxford University Press, 2007). Neither "citizenship" nor "citizen" is found in the index.

9. William J. Novak, "The Legal Transformation of Citizenship in Nineteenth-Century America," in *The Democratic Experiment: New Directions in American Political History*, ed. Meg Jacobs, William J. Novak, and Julian Zelizer (Princeton: Princeton University Press, 2003), 85–119 (quotation on 87); Linda K. Kerber, "The Meanings of Citizenship," *Journal of American History* 84, no. 3 (1997): 835.

10. Christian G. Samito, *Becoming American under Fire: Irish Americans, African Americans, and the Politics of Citizenship during the Civil War Era* (Ithaca: Cornell University Press, 2009), 13–25. James H. Kettner, *The Development of American Citizenship, 1608–1870* (Chapel Hill: University of North Carolina Press, 1978), provides an exhaustive guide to the legal development and conceptualization of citizenship in colonial North America and the United States. The problem of defining Native American racial and political status is discussed in Susan Scheckel, *The Insistence of the Indian: Race and Nationalism in Nineteenth-Century American Culture* (Princeton: Princeton University Press, 1998), and Lauren L. Basson, *White Enough to Be American? Race Mixing, Indigenous People, and the Boundaries of State and Nation* (Chapel Hill: University of North Carolina Press, 2008). Susan Zaeske, *Signatures of Citizenship: Petitioning, Antislavery, and Women's Political Identity* (Chapel Hill: University of North Carolina Press, 2003), explores the politicization of female abolitionists.

11. Michael O'Brien, *Conjectures of Order: Intellectual Life and the American South, 1810–1860*, vol. 1 (Chapel Hill: University of North Carolina Press. 2004), 333–63.

12. John McCardell, *The Idea of a Southern Nation* (New York: Norton, 1979); Paul Quigley, *Shifting Grounds: Nationalism and the American South* (New York: Oxford Uni-

versity Press, 2012); Anne Sarah Rubin, *A Shattered Nation: The Rise and Fall of the Con-federacy, 1861–1868* (Chapel Hill: University of North Carolina Press, 2005).

13. Edmund S. Morgan, *American Slavery, American Freedom: The Ordeal of Colonial Virginia* (New York: Norton, 1975); Kathleen M. Brown, *Good Wives, Nasty Wenches, and Anxious Patriarchs: Gender, Race and Power in Colonial Virginia* (Chapel Hill: University of North Carolina Press, 2003); Daniel T. Rodgers, "Republicanism: The Career of a Concept," *Journal of American History* 79, no. 1 (1992): 11–38.

14. The complex interplay between race, status, and identity in the southern context is broadly pursued in David Brown and Clive Webb, *Race in the American South: From Slavery to Civil Rights* (Gainesville: University Press of Florida, 2007).

15. Shklar, *American Citizenship*, 16. An important recent study of the Revolutionary era has stressed the anomaly of the claim of "free" blacks to inclusion as citizens; "The status of non-enslaved black Americans was strikingly distinct from that of white citizens" in legal terms. Arguably the place of free blacks might best be represented by drawing on the English legal concept of denizen, "which extended only *some* of the rights and privileges of citizens. A denizen was not considered to be part of the body politic and was not governed by the laws relating to aliens, but was allowed to have certain privileges by fiat." Douglas Bradburn, *The Citizenship Revolution: Politics and the Creation of the American Union, 1774–1804* (Charlottesville: University of Virginia Press, 2009), 236, 238. Nineteenth-century historians might fruitfully engage with this insight.

16. *Scott v. Sandford*, 60 U.S. 393. On the wider implications of this landmark decision, Don E. Fehrenbacher, *The Dred Scott Case: Its Significance in American Law and Politics* (New York: Oxford University Press, 1978), remains the key text. For more on the conceptualization of the alien citizen, see Mae M. Ngai, "Birthright Citizenship and the Alien Citizen," *Fordham Law Review* 83 (April 2007): 2521–30.

17. Hannah Rosen, *Terror in the Heart of Freedom: Citizenship, Sexual Violence, and the Meaning of Race in the Postemancipation South* (Chapel Hill: University of North Carolina Press, 2009), provides a fascinating insight into the complex entanglement of race, class, gender, identity, and citizenship in the Reconstruction South.

# I

CITIZENSHIP IN
AN ENSLAVED SOCIETY

# 1

.....................

# "Ter Show Yo' de Value of Slaves"

## The Pricing of Human Property

DAINA RAMEY BERRY

In an interview on June 6, 1937, former Alabama bondman Mingo White remarked that "slavery wouldn't a been so bad, but folks make it so by selling us for high prices, an' of co'se folks had to try to git dey money's worth out of 'em."[1] Slaveholders' need to get their "money's worth" from the enslaved served as a logical explanation for high prices, according to White. Like many others, he knew well that enslaved labor was scrutinized, labeled, and commodified. Bondpeople, understanding the parameters of their worth, realized that slave status prevented them from legal access to citizenship. They also knew that their labor specialization, reproductive ability, and good health commanded strong prices in a market that viewed them as commodities rather than people. Willis Cofer, formerly enslaved in Georgia, summarized things succinctly. For young and strong males, "de biddin would start 'round $150 and de highest bidder got" the slave. "A good young breedin' 'oman brung $2,000 easy," he added, "'cause all de Marsters wanted to see plenty of strong healthy chillun comin' on all de time." Similar to the importance of reproduction and health, Cofer understood that enslaved people with trades such as "carpenters and bricklayers and blacksmith brung fancy prices from $3,000 to $5,000."[2] But Analiza Foster of North Carolina put it best when she noted that one way to "show yo' de value of slaves" was through the story of her grandmother, who "wuz sold on de block four times" and "eber time she brung a thousand dollars." She "wuz valuable ca[u]se she wus strong an' could plow day by day." Foster boasted that she "could have twenty chillens an' wuck right on."[3]

Why study slave prices in a volume on citizenship, given that the enslaved were not legally citizens until after the Civil War? Population analyses, legal statutes, definitions of citizenship, and notions of commodification offer some explanations. A sample of 8,686 individual slave market values from eight states represents concrete data, specific monetary values for human chattel in the face of more ephemeral expressions of citizenship.[4] The historical bookends of this essay are the Declaration of Independence in 1776 and the ratification of the Fourteenth Amendment of the United States Constitution in 1868. Combining the quantitative data found in these market sales, which included bondpeople age 0–99,[5] the opinions of the enslaved bring forth rich testimony filled with ideas about the prices placed upon their bodies. This commentary will expand our understanding of the complex relationship between commodification and citizenship because slavery in general, and the market in particular, shaped every aspect of American life. We cannot explore one without the other.[6] Their numbers alone suggest that the presence of enslaved people composed an important part of the American landscape.[7] But population demographics incorporate only one aspect of this important relationship. How does one make sense of the commodification of human beings, especially because "[t]he entire economy of the antebellum South," according to one historian, "was constructed upon the idea that the bodies of enslaved people had a measurable monetary value, whether they were ever actually sold or not."[8]

This essay examines the pricing of enslaved people for sale in the market with a particular emphasis on their identity and claims of personhood. Even though they could not legally acquire citizenship rights, bondpeople influenced their valuations, sale transactions, and ultimately the institution of slavery.[9] Understanding the link between market values and citizenship provides a window into pricing patterns of one of the most significant commodities, human chattel. As a result, enslaved people such as Cofer, Foster, and White understood their role as products in a marketplace rather than citizens in a society. For some, like Frederick Douglass and Josiah Henson, escaping to the North or Canada marked the first time they truly felt like citizens who could enjoy the fruits of their labor.[10]

The central objective of this essay is to examine the commodification of human beings who were outside the bounds of legal citizenship yet influential in their fate at the local level. "Localized law," historian Laura F. Edwards explains, "depended on information conveyed orally by ordinary people—even subordinates without rights" such as slaves.[11] The voice of the enslaved offers a fresh perspective on *their* ideas about citizenship and personhood rather than those imposed upon them. Few scholars look to slave testimony in search of their perspective on questions of citizenship. Most instead rely upon documents from the white elite because they left more detailed records on the subject. However, bondpeople knew they were excluded from the political arena and were keenly aware of their enslaved status. These realities did not leave them without opinions about their commodification or strategies to claim rights as citizens. By establishing a link between citizenship and commodification, this essay foregrounds the experience of the enslaved and their sense of personhood through their testimonies and market values.

Citizenship and commodification merged at shipyards, plantations, and courthouses across the United States when members of the slave-holding class purchased enslaved laborers. In these settings American citizens exercised their right to buy and sell property by negotiating the market values of bondpeople. Commodifying human chattel was an expression of their citizenship but an act of victimization for the enslaved. The bondpeople for sale were outside the bounds of citizenship yet at the center of a system that secured the elite full participation in a burgeoning capitalist society. An examination of individual slave sales provides a window into market patterns and preferences of the citizens who relied upon slave labor. The surviving records of more than eight thousand slave sales, for example, suggest general patterns that shed light on the connection between commodification and citizenship. Men were valued more than women, while the elderly and the young commanded lower prices. There was a premium for those with skills; the disabled were worth less. In an earlier study that employed a much smaller sample from Chesapeake plantation records ($N = 1,854$), it was clear that bondpeople "depreciated" in terms of their value at different ages based on gender.[12] Women in that sample were valued higher than men. Female prices reached maximum levels at age twenty-three and tended to decline from age twenty-four until death. Enslaved males reached their maximum value slightly later, between twenty-five and twenty-nine.[13]

Using this much larger sample from eight states rather than two, it is clear that men and women reach their maximum values between the ages of twenty-one and twenty-five. Females' prices declined from age twenty-five on, while males' plateaued until age thirty-five, when their prices

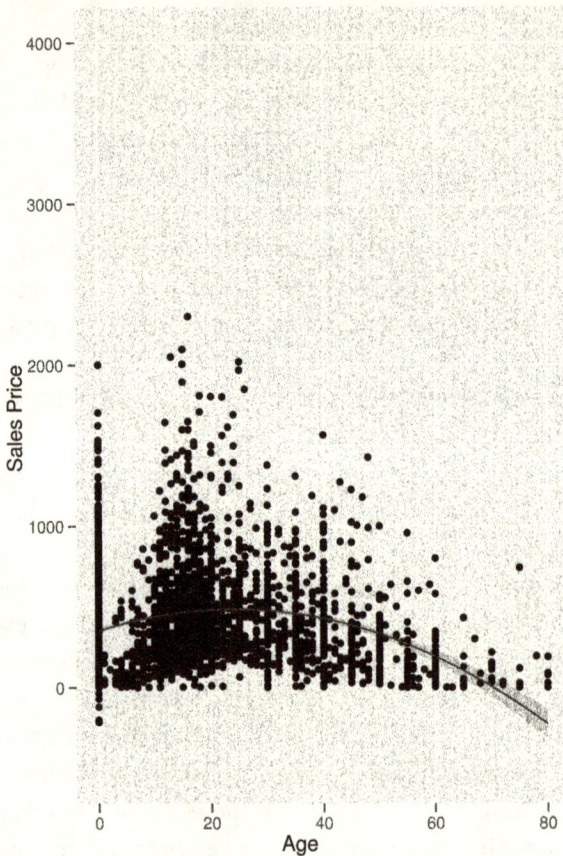

Figure 1.1. Enslaved female sale price by age. Figures compiled by Nate Marti based on gender and sale data in the *Berry Slave Value Database*.

begin a slow decline.[14] Age statistics such as these confirm that the value of enslaved labor changed over time based on gender and age. In addition to age and skill, location also affected the ways in which enslaved people experienced commodification while their access to citizenship remained off limits.

Aside from these general patterns, we have much to learn about citizenship and commodification from the enslaved. Georgia-born bondman Hardy Miller realized that his market value trumped any notion of citizenship. He recalled being separated from his mother, placed on a steamboat, and sold to a slaveholder in Arkansas. "In them days," he testified, "a doctor examined you and if your heart was sound and your

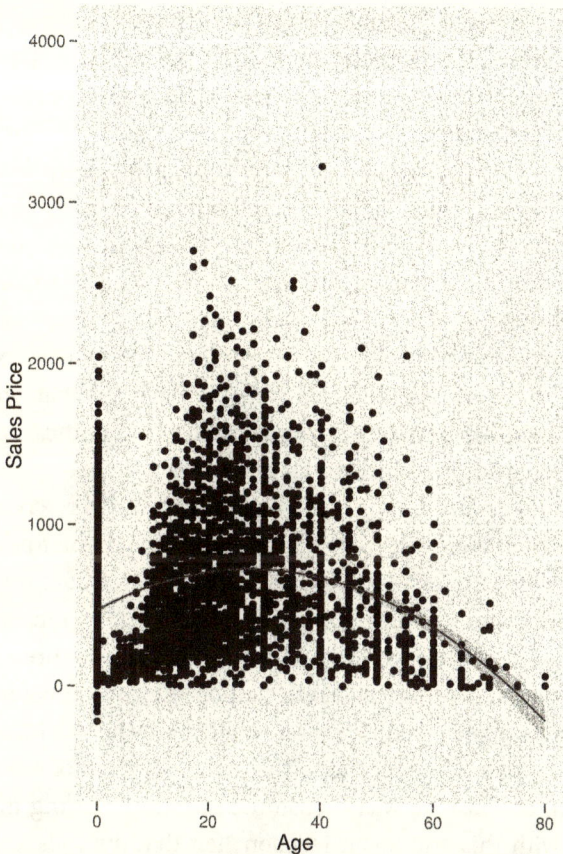

Figure 1.2. Enslaved male sale price by age. Figures compiled by Nate Marti based on gender and sale data in the *Berry Slave Value Database*.

lungs was sound and you didn't have no broken bones—[traders] have to pay one hundred dollars for every year you was old."[15] Although Miller and other bondmen were denied access to citizenship, their sense of "belonging to a civic body" was much more literal. Their healthy bodies and labor skills were more important than their right to vote, their ability to own property, or their right to testify in court. Enslaved men and women knew that a nation's economy hinged upon their commodification. For example, Perry McGee believed that "Abraham Lincoln offered $300 a head before de war for all de slaves but de people would not sell any more." Instead, he continued, "dey elected Jefferson Davis President . . . [and] dey would put slaves on de block and 'cry them off.'" McGee understood that slaveholders' objective was "to make profit on de deal" and that a "good strong man would sell for $300 and some for $100." A house slave, he added, was worth more than a field slave.[16] From McGee's perspective, auctions were about people being "cried off" rather than sold off. Slave sales represented places where families were separated at the expense of white citizens exercising their right to buy and sell human property. The findings presented here confirm that Miller's formula was incorrect and that McGee's thoughts on house and field hands were not always true. Barney Stone boasted that "my pappy was used much as a male cow is used on the stock farm and was hired out to other plantation owners for that purpose" because he "was regarded as a valuable slave."[17] What can we learn about the relationship between citizenship and commodification from slave testimony in addition to individual market valuations?

Across the antebellum South, bondpeople knew that they were commodities; some cared about their value, others did not. Through their narratives, one learns that they understood their sale prices, feared auctions, and often dreaded new owners. Other bondpeople recalled the transaction type and tender used in sales, while some made references to breeding, acknowledged physical prowess, and reflected on their value before and after freedom. For example, Josiah Henson recalled how he was hired out. "My employer soon found," he recalled, "that my labour was of more value to him than that of those he was accustomed to hire." During the three years he spent with this employer, Henson "felt that my toils and sacrifices for freedom had not been in vain."[18] He longed to have the same rights and access to his labor granted to white Americans. Citizenship rights, in his estimation, included paid labor, land, literacy, and family unity.

The connection between commodification and citizenship may not be entirely obvious to some readers, given that the majority of nineteenth-century African Americans were enslaved and therefore not considered part of the body politic. As noted throughout this volume, free people of color were also relegated to "slave status" through legal measures. Blacks were denied legal claims to citizenship, including the rights and prerogatives vested therein. But, as chattel property, the enslaved unwillingly enabled others to secure their social and political status as citizens and, in many cases, as extraordinarily wealthy and powerful citizens. The fact that slaves' prices reflected their market value represents a concrete expression of their non-citizenship, but this is not indicative of a binary wedge between citizenship and commodification. Free blacks were not commodities, yet they still had limited or little access to legal forms of citizenship. Many southern whites thought that those who were black and free should be deported outside of the United States. Southern slaveholders used enslaved labor to generate wealth, secure political power, and maintain an elite social caste as wealthy landowners.[19]

Despite these general patterns, legal definitions of citizenship remain too narrow and imperfect to understand the full lives of the enslaved and what they contributed to the nation, even in their state of diminished citizenship. Ironically, though bondpeople were outside the citizenry, they aided in its definition. Criticizing the celebration of American independence, Frederick Douglass told a predominantly white abolitionist audience in July 1852 that the "rich inheritance of justice, liberty, prosperity and independence, bequeathed by your fathers, is shared by you, not by me." He added: "The sunlight that brought life and healing to you, has brought stripes and death to me." In sum, he stated, "This Fourth [of] July is yours, not mine."[20] Slave ownership represented an added benefit for white citizens by elevating their status and distinguishing them from non-slaveholding whites. By contrast, it deprived the enslaved of their basic rights and fueled their desire to make a profit off of their own labor. Historian Edmund Morgan outlined this contradictory notion as a central paradox of American history. In 1972 he wrote that "the rise of liberty and equality in this country was accompanied by the rise in slavery" and that the two contradictory developments occurred simultaneously "over a long period of our history, from the seventeenth century to the nineteenth."[21] Then, what did this mean for bondpeople? How did they interpret and experience this paradox? For Douglass, living in the face of such contradictions angered him. "Your boasted liberty," he said, was "an unholy license; your national greatness, swelling vanity; your sounds of rejoicing are empty and heartless; your denunciations of tyrants, brass fronted impudence; your shouts of liberty and equality, hollow mockery . . . There is not a nation on the earth guilty of practices, more shocking and bloody, than are the people of these United States."[22]

Historians of slavery have also addressed the complexities of "a person with a price."[23] In many settings, slaveholders subjected slaves to harsh treatment, separated their families, and refused them even the most basic rights to humanity and personhood. On the other hand, bondmen and bondwomen fought against this mistreatment and found ways to carve out spaces for their own forms of dignity and respect. This struggle forced scholars to consider the human dimension of enslaved laborers in the face of their commodification.

In the 1970s, historian Leslie Owens argued that ignoring the humanity of the enslaved "distorts the historical record."[24] However, it was not until recently that historians such as Walter Johnson addressed the duality of commodification and personhood, underscoring that enslaved people disrupted market transactions by manipulating sale transactions. Middle Passage scholars offer a window into the human side of life at sea. Their work suggests that, no matter how much merchants, sailors, ship captains, and slaveholders tried to break human beings "into parts and recomposed [them] as commodities," captives did all they could to make their enslavers recognize them as people.[25] Upon their arrival into New World plantation communities, the struggle continued. Captives became enslaved laborers on plantations and farms, in factories and in urban areas. The micro-studies of the 1990s and first decade of the twenty-first century marked a watershed of scholarship that addressed the enslaved as human beings rather than marketable products. Scholars such as Ira Berlin, William Dusinberre, Anthony Kaye, Wilma King, Thavolia Glymph, Dylan Penningroth, and Brenda Stevenson explore various aspects of the intimate lives of the enslaved.[26] Bondpeople within the plantations, communities, families, and farms had a way of interacting with one another beyond their roles as commodities for sale. They courted, fell in love, "married," gave birth, and supported each other through loss, separation, and sale. In short, scholars recognized their humanity. As one historian argues, "The slaves did express and act according to their individual wills, fashion collective norms and aspirations, contest the authority of their owners on many fronts, build institutions to mobilize their resources and sensibilities, [and] produce leaders who wielded significant influence" in the face of complete disenfranchisement, degradation, and disrespect.[27] Despite residing on the margins of society, the enslaved influenced the system and left ample evidence, through their narratives, about "de value of slaves."

Bondpeople understood the impact of age and health on their value and commented on this during interviews during the 1930s. "Some few wasn't worth nothin' at all," H. B. Holloway remembered, "just about a hundred dollars." Childbearing women "cost a heap," and "fine" built women "bring a lot of money."[28] In fact, before George Womble was sold, three doctors examined him. One of the doctors said: "This is a thorough-bred boy. His teeth are good and he has good muscles and eyes. He'll live a long time." At the close of the transaction, the new owner remarked, "He looks intelligent too. I think I'll take him and make a blacksmith out of him." According to Womble, he was sold for $500 and his new owner was "meaner" than the former.[29] Tom Haskins, a bondman from South Carolina, recalled that his mistress trained her slaves: "She was always sellin' 'em for big prices atter she done trained 'em . . . to be cooks, housegals, houseboys, carriage drivers, and good wash 'omans."[30] Clearly, trained slaves meant higher profits at the market and citizenship rights through hiring out their time. Skilled bondpeople had greater access to political and economic rights because of their mobility, wages, and negotiation of labor contracts. Each of these acts granted them a taste of citizenship.

Male artisans were not the only skilled laborers in plantation and industrial settings. Bondwomen also had skills, as nurses, cooks, and in the fields, factories, and homes of their enslavers and employers.[31] "Lots of slaves bid off like stock and babies sold from their mammy's breast," according to Reeves Tucker of Texas. "Some brung 'bout $1,500, owing to how strong they is," he recalled.[32] "I also 'members de time I was put up on de block to be sold," George Taylor of Alabama said, "an' when de man only offered five hundred dollars, fer me, an' Ol' Marster tole me to git down, dat I was de mos' valuable nigger he had, 'ca'se I was so strong, an' could do so much work."[33] The records used in this essay support these definitions of skilled labor.[34]

Although bondpeople were excluded from citizenship rights, their labor skills elevated the monetary value assigned to them in the marketplace. There are nineteen occupational categories listed for 297 bondpeople in this sample, which represents a little more than 3 percent (table 1.1). Of the occupations identified, men and women tended to farm animals, work in the field, labor in gardens, and serve in the house. Other occupations were gender specific. For example, women served as nurses, market peddlers, and seamstresses (clothing work), while men served as blacksmiths, drivers, carpenters, engineers, and masons, to name a few. On average, male and female bondpeople with occupations specified commanded higher prices than those listed without such descriptors. Even though they were outside the bounds of citizenship, skilled bondpeople played an active role in the market. They represented the goods that slaveholders purchased and sold in order to secure their financial and social status. Fortunate

Table 1.1. Market Values for Enslaved Persons with Skills

| Trade Group | N | Mean | Std Dev | Minimum | Maximum |
|---|---|---|---|---|---|
| Artisan, general | 2 | $364.18 | $28.90 | $343.75 | $384.62 |
| Blacksmith | 20 | $1119.70 | $739.78 | $270.27 | $3225.81 |
| Boating/ship work | 6 | $847.47 | $403.06 | $325.88 | $1250.00 |
| Carpenter/sawyer | 72 | $731.72 | $422.07 | $132.45 | $1875.00 |
| Cook/food prep | 37 | $608.20 | $347.93 | $118.92 | $1641.41 |
| Driver (field work) | 5 | $439.60 | $312.68 | $140.85 | $781.25 |
| Driver (transportation) | 8 | $805.24 | $278.29 | $333.82 | $1170.21 |
| Fieldhand | 23 | $646.06 | $277.91 | $232.43 | $1138.39 |
| House servant | 35 | $639.79 | $286.93 | $213.27 | $1565.66 |
| Mason | 22 | $753.01 | $429.20 | $141.84 | $1666.67 |
| Farm equipment/mill | 8 | $287.42 | $139.38 | $108.11 | $500.00 |
| Clothing work | 16 | $472.42 | $265.49 | $154.41 | $1130.43 |
| Works with livestock | 5 | $866.73 | $165.77 | $666.67 | $1117.02 |
| Washer woman/man | 11 | $509.88 | $290.09 | $151.66 | $1010.64 |
| Cooper | 11 | $622.70 | $294.83 | $162.16 | $1089.11 |
| Timber | 1 | $450.00 | | $450.00 | $450.00 |
| Market | 2 | $631.60 | $69.40 | $582.52 | $680.67 |
| Nursing/attendant | 10 | $663.63 | $155.57 | $388.35 | $904.26 |
| Engineer | 3 | $803.52 | $662.01 | $163.04 | $1485.15 |

*Note*: Table compiled by Nate Marti based on skill and sale data in the *Berry Slave Value Database*.

ones could hire their time and work in urban and industrial settings for wages. The highest-priced female with an occupation was a forty-year-old "hairdresser" from Natchitoches County, Louisiana, appraised at $1,200 and sold for $1,500 in 1858. The highest-priced male with an occupation was also forty years old, but he was a skilled blacksmith worth $3,000 in 1853. Those without occupations and with elevated values include a female, age sixteen, also from Natchitoches County, Louisiana, valued at $2,300 in 1860, and a bondman with no age listed worth $3,201 in 1802.

As the place where people appeared as products, the marketplace also represented a convergence of citizenship and commodification. It marked an important locale where whites expressed their citizenship. Given that slave trading often occurred in public places such as town centers, on the steps of county courthouses, and at the docks of local shipyards, one cannot overlook the fact that these are the locations where citizens could sue or be sued, and buy or sell property. The court, as noted above, not only embodied formal citizenship but also represented the institutional home of enslavement. Notification prior to an actual slave auction began weeks before the event as evidenced in newspaper advertisements, broadsides posted in public spaces, and dinner-table conversations in pubs, hotels, and saloons.[35] If the market serves as the intersection of citizenship and commodification, then we need to examine what the market reveals about human commodities and how those traded understood their commodification.

The commodification of black bodies represented a common practice during slavery. Blacks and whites alike commented on this in their narratives and personal papers. As a result, one cannot ignore the human side of these equations.[36]

Considering the response to slave sales from various perspectives, this essay emphasizes enslaved prices among various age groups, health conditions, geographical locations, skill sets, and gender distinctions.[37] Even though the personhood of the enslaved was devalued, potential owners, agents, and traders assessed them as instruments of labor and spent countless hours and a great deal of money preparing bondpeople for the market. Yet, "slaveholders invested their money" and placed their "hopes in people whom they could never fully commodify."[38] How could such an important part of the economic and social landscape be humanized at times and dehumanized at others? Did enslaved people disrupt their commodification, separation, and sales when slaveholders and traders set specific prices on their bodies? Can we determine whether parties involved understood that enslavement elevated the social status of elite white citizens?[39] When given the opportunity, what did the enslaved do with their time and talents? Exploring these issues from the perspective of enslaved people *as* human property almost sounds like an oxymoron, but this essay offers innovative ways to think about the southern economy through the lens of domestic slave sales and the voice of the "goods" on the auction block. But first let us consider a cursory overview of the legal route to citizenship and the exclusion of enslaved people from the body politic.

Prior to the rise of domestic market slave sales, several key documents, proclamations, and amendments affected enslaved blacks in the United States at the local and national level. From federal slave codes to local city ordinances, as well as state regulation of the international and (later) domestic traffic in human commodities, the U.S. government eventually acknowledged African Americans as legal citizens. Still, it was a long road to legal recognition. At the birth of the new nation, the Declaration of Independence failed to address the status of the enslaved. Even though it stated that "all men are created equal, [and] that they are endowed by their Creator with certain unalienable Rights, that among these are Life, Liberty and the pursuit of Happiness," there were those who argued passionately that the "all men" in question did not include the enslaved. Using the language of the day, enslaved people were not created equal, and they did not have the freedom to pursue life, liberty, and happiness, primarily because they were considered property, which made human qualities unattainable. This was also true during the ratification of the U.S. Constitution. Like the Declaration of the Independence, there was no mention of enslaved African Americans. Instead, Article I, section 2, offered a sectional compromise. Three-fifths of the slave population counted for tax distribution and appointment of members of the U.S. House of Representatives. Notably, the word "slave" does not appear in the Constitution. Instead, bondpeople are referred to as "persons held to service or labor." The Constitution's language acknowledged the personhood of the enslaved—yet another example of Morgan's central American paradox at work.

The question of citizenship and personhood became even more salient when President Abraham Lincoln issued the Emancipation Proclamation. After permitting the Confederacy one hundred days to return to the Union, Lincoln issued the Emancipation Proclamation and, on January 1, 1863, freed bondpeople behind rebel lines. However, it took nearly two more years of war until emancipation took effect. When the Civil War ended in April 1865, nearly four million slaves finally became free. Ultimately, the Thirteenth Amendment, ratified on December 6, 1865, stated: "Neither slavery nor involuntary servitude . . . shall exist within the United States."[40] This marked the first time that all African Americans gained their liberty, but it was not earned without consequences. They fought for citizenship rights during every stage of their enslavement through grassroots activism as well as individual acts of resistance.[41] As a result of abolition, newly freed people had to find work and support their families. To hasten recovery, the War Department created the Bureau of Refugees, Freedmen and Abandoned Lands, referred to as the Freedmen's Bureau. With the commissioner's salary of $3,000 per year and nearly

$20,000 in U.S. Treasury bonds, the primary function of this organiza-
tion was to help emancipated slaves and other refugees in rebel states find
"immediate and temporary shelter."[42] Days before the official ratification
of the Thirteenth Amendment, a second Freedmen's Bureau Bill passed as
an amendment to the first. This new legislation extended aid to "refugees
and freedmen in *all* parts of the United States," not just the states in rebellion. The secretary of war had the authority to provide "clothing, fuel, and
other supplies" to suffering freedmen and refugees regardless of whose
side of the war they fought on. President Andrew Johnson vetoed this bill
on February 19, 1866, which led to the establishment of the Civil Rights
Act of 1866, one of the first official forms of legislation that addressed
African American citizenship.[43]

Just a few days shy of the one-year anniversary of the end of the Civil
War, the Civil Rights Act of 1866 acknowledged African American citizenship. It stated that "all persons born in the United States" were citizens
and that members of "every race and color, without regard to any previous
condition of slavery or involuntary servitude," had the authority to "make
and enforce contracts, to sue, be parties, and give evidence, to inherit,
purchase, lease, sell, hold, and convey real and personal property" in the
same manner that these measures were "enjoyed by white citizens."[44] The
Civil Rights Act of 1866 marked the legal acknowledgment of citizenship
for African Americans, and the Fourteenth Amendment (ratified July 9,
1868) confirmed these rights. Prior to this act, enslaved and in some states
free blacks were the goods exchanged, leased, sold, or held against their
will. They had real challenges to social issues as well as problems with
legal representations of citizenship. It would take a modern civil rights
movement in the following century to secure and protect these rights.[45]

The legal road to citizenship differed greatly from the grassroots efforts
of everyday bondpeople to break the chains of bondage. Enslaved people
had their own understanding of commodification and citizenship. Some
developed formulas on how values were determined while others relied
on physical characteristics. There is also strong evidence of bondpeople
who recalled the tender used to purchase them. They were well aware
of their limited rights and took pride in discussing their market experiences. James Davis of North Carolina noted that his slaveholder "paid
for me in old Jeff Davis' shin plasters." A shinplaster was a form of paper
money issued by the government between 1862 and 1878. These bills received their odd name because of the plaster-like material of which they

were produced. Oddly, it was the same material used to keep people's legs warm or to soothe leg injuries. A Jefferson Davis bill at that time was a $50 bill.[46] Another bondman remembered being paid with "cash down on the table,"[47] while an ex-slave from Georgia recalled that his "old mistress" sold one of his sisters and "took cotton for pay."[48] Walters McIntosh of Arkansas was sold for "$500 in gold" and his mother for "$1500 in gold." He noted that "the payment was made in fine gold. I was sold because my folk realized that freedom was coming and they wanted to obtain the cash value of their slaves."[49]

Considering the cash value of slaves represents one quantitative method to understand the domestic market. Reviewing the testimonies of the enslaved provides another way to understand the subject. Slavehold-ing whites controlled the market in people because they had the power to maintain family ties, set starting bids, and transfer human property from one state or owner to another. The enslaved influenced market transac-tions as well as a whole host of perceptions of them as commodities. View-ing the slave auction as a place where traders and slaveholders determined the fate of human chattels, then, also provides a way to analyze specific enslaved prices based on age, health, sex, and skill. Campbell Armstrong, a former slave from Georgia, shared the following thoughts about being auctioned: "They'd put you up on the block and sell you. That is just what they'd do—sell you. These white folks will do anything,—anything they want to do. They'd take your clothes off just like you was some kind a beast. You used to be worth a thousand dollars then, but you're not worth two bits now. You ain't worth nothin' when you're free."[50] Hearing from the very people who were commodified reminds us that the enslaved possessed opinions about their market value, their complicated sense of personhood, and indeed their eventual claims of citizenship. Some knew their value so well that in freedom they understood that their labor was now devalued because it was no longer free. In this regard, the right to one's own earning potential from one's labor—a hallmark of citizenship in a capitalist society—was, for formerly enslaved, commodified people an asset in their newfound freedom. Market values and debates over citizen-ship influenced slave prices—a process that many bondpeople expressed an interest in and used to assert their humanity.

# Notes

This essay would not have been possible without the generous donation of data compiled by Stanley Engerman and Robert Fogel and the ongoing support of Randy Fotiu, Peter Lindert, Alan Olmstead, Nate Marti, Marc Weidenmier, and Jewel Ward. I would also like to thank Jenifer L. Barclay, Terry Brock, Tiffany M. Gill, Meta DuEwa Jones, Nedra K. Lee, Bill Link, Jessica Millward, Nik Ribianszky, Cherise M. Smith, and Jermaine Thibodeaux for comments on earlier drafts of this essay.

1. *Born in Slavery: Slave Narratives from the Federal Writers' Project, 1936–1938*, Alabama Narratives, Volume 1, "Mingo White," pp. 413–22, quote on 422.

2. *Born in Slavery: Slave Narratives from the Federal Writers' Project, 1936–1938*, Georgia Narratives, "Willis Cofer," pp. 204–5.

3. *Born in Slavery: Slave Narratives from the Federal Writers' Project, 1936–1938*, North Carolina Narratives, Volume 11, Part 1, "Analiza Foster," p. 313.

4. This sample is extracted from a larger data set from a work-in-progress book on enslaved prices that contains appraisal and sale figures for more than 80,000 bondpeople (*Berry Slave Value Database*). The distribution of evidence here is as follows: Georgia (*N* = 160), Louisiana (*N* = 2,130), Maryland (*N* = 638), Mississippi (*N* = 7), North Carolina (*N* = 1,949), South Carolina (*N* = 2,462), Tennessee (*N* = 780), and Virginia (*N* = 560). See Daina Ramey Berry, *The Price for Their Pound of Flesh: The Value of Human Chattels, 1775–1865* (forthcoming); Robert W. Fogel and Stanley L. Engerman, *Time on the Cross: The Economics of American Negro Slavery* (1974; reprint, New York: Norton, 1989); and Trevor Burnard's forthcoming work on Jamaican slave prices.

5. Some of the age values are listed as 0 for unknown, elderly, and very young, essentially those whose age did not matter because they were no longer viable workers or *not* yet valuable workers on the plantation.

6. Using the lens of "generations," historian Ira Berlin concurs, noting that the institution of slavery affected most free persons whether they owned slaves or not. Ira Berlin, *Generations of Captivity: A History of African-American Slaves* (New York: Harvard University Press, 2003).

7. At the dawn of the nineteenth century the total slave population was approximately 887,612. By 1830 this number had more than doubled, to 2,009,043. On the eve of the Civil War, enslaved Americans numbered 4,037,735, reflecting a constant rate of population growth during the antebellum era. For the 1800 figure of 887,612, see *Historical Census Browser*, retrieved (December 17, 2010) from the University of Virginia, Geospatial and Statistical Data Center: http://fisher.lib.virginia.edu/collections/stats/histcensus/index.html. The 1830 and Civil War figures are derived from Richard Sutch, "Slave Population Table Bb214," in *Historical Statistics of the United Slaves, Millennial Edition On Line*, ed. Susan B. Carter et al. (Cambridge: Cambridge University Press, 2006).

8. Walter Johnson, *Soul by Soul: Life inside the Antebellum Slave Market* (New York: Harvard University Press, 1999), 25.

9. Johnson confirms this influence on market sales in his work as well. See also Edward Baptist's discussion of "bodies to rape and bodies to sell" in "Cuffy, Fancy Maids,

and One-Eyed Men: Rape, Commodification, and the Domestic Slave Trade in the United States," *American Historical Review* 106, no. 5 (2001): 1619–50.

10. Both Douglass and Henson hired their time and recognized the importance of their skills in the market. When they escaped and received help purchasing their freedom, they spent the remainder of their lives fighting to end slavery and live off of the fruits of their own labor. See Frederick Douglass, *My Bondage My Freedom* (New York: Miller, Orton & Mulligan, 1855), and Josiah Henson, *The Life of Josiah Henson, Formerly a Slave, Now an Inhabitant of Canada, as Narrated by Himself* (Boston: Arthur D. Phelps, 1849).

11. Laura F. Edwards, *The People and Their Peace: Legal Culture and the Transformation of Inequality in the Post-Revolutionary South* (Chapel Hill: University of North Carolina Press, 2009), 4.

12. See Berry, "'The Cargo Consisting of Negroes . . . was Easily Removed': Gender and Price Patterns among Human Chattels in the Domestic Market." Panelist, "'The Bloody Writing is for ever torn': Domestic and International Consequences of the First Governmental Efforts to Abolish the Atlantic Slave Trade," Conference hosted by UNESCO, the Omohundro Institute, the Gilder Lehrman Center, the W.E.B. Du Bois Institute, the Reed Foundation, and the Wilberforce Institute held in Ghana, August 12–15, 2007.

13. See *Berry Slave Value Database*. Calculations based on forty-four slaveholders listed in probate, orphan's court, and private papers housed at the Virginia Historical Society and at the National Archives in College Park, Maryland. This small sample contains data from eight counties in Maryland and one in Virginia for a total of 352 slaves. In computing the prices, the author used mean slave prices for male and female slaves between the ages of fifteen and thirty years. Jenny Wahl found similar patterns; see, for example, Wahl, "Slavery in the United States," http://eh.net/encyclopedia/article/wahl. slavery.us (accessed April 30, 2010).

The specific records include "Taxable Property of William Pollard, 31 May 1815," Pollard Family Papers, Virginia Historical Society, Mss1P7637b, 280–84; Joseph Miller, Orphan's Court Record, National Archives Records Administration RG 76, Box 5, Folder 35 [hereafter NARA]; and Probate Records for Robert Lloyd Nichols (Talbot County), James Lloyd (Talbot County), Samuel Mall (Dorchester County), Richard Liushicun (Dorchester County), William Thomas (Dorchester County), Philomon Geoghegan (Dorchester County), Charles Hodson (Dorchester County), Robert Armstrong (St. Mary's County), Mary Abell (St. Mary's County), Barnaby Greenwell (St. Mary's County), and Charles Bowling (St. Mary's County), Anna Jenkins (Prince George's County), Bladen Gragcroft (Prince George's County), Kidd Chasell (Prince George's County), Jonathan L. Lasper (Prince George's County), Alexander Read (Prince George's County), William Wall (Prince George's County), William H. Wilson (Prince George's County), Lucky Duckett (Prince George's County), Nicholas Norrian (Anne Arundel County), Joseph Hincks (Anne Arundel County), Edwin Kell (Anne Arundel County), Margaret Larrette (Anne Arundel County), Joseph Court (Anne Arundel County), Thomas Norris (Anne Arundel County), William Tillard (Anne Arundel County), Samuel Knighton (Anne Arundel County), Duvall Family (Anne Arundel County), John Phipley (Anne Arundel County), Stephen Beard (Anne Arundel County), Josias Crosby (Anne Arundel County), John

R. Brown (Anne Arundel County), Mary Watson (Anne Arundel County), John Warner (Baltimore County), Joseph Manus (Baltimore County), John Murphy (Baltimore County), Nicholas Grimes (Baltimore County), Thomas Parran (Calvert County), Elias Woolf (Calvert County), and John Beckett (Calvert County), NARA RG 76, Entry 185, Box 5, Folder 35, and "Maryland Slave Values," NARA RG 76 Entry 185, PI 177, Box 5, Folder 34.

14. These figures are of interest because my initial hypothesis suggested that women had higher values during their childbearing years. This earlier conclusion was derived from eight plantations in Glynn County, Georgia. Certainly such variations are often plantation specific and not representative of larger trends. See Berry, "'We'm Fus' Rate Bargain': Value, Labor, and Price in a Georgia Slave Community," in *The Chattel Principle: Internal Slave Trades in the Americas, 1808–1888*, ed. Walter Johnson (New Haven: Yale University Press, 2004), 55–71.

15. WPA Slave Narrative Project, Manuscript Division, Library of Congress *Arkansas Narratives*, Volume 2, Part 5, p. 74.

16. WPA, *Slave Narratives: A Folk History of Slavery in the United States from Interviews with Former Slaves*: Volume X, Missouri Narratives, http://www.gutenberg.org/license (accessed February 2011).

17. WPA, *Slave Narratives: A Folk History of Slavery in the United States from Interviews with Former Slaves*: Volume V, Indiana Narratives, http://www.gutenberg.org/license (accessed February 2011).

18. John Lobb, ed., *Uncle Tom's Story of His Life: From 1789–1876: An Autobiography of the Rev. Josiah Henson* (London: Christian Age, 1876), 97.

19. This is not only a southern phenomenon; northerners also carved out their citizenship on the backs of enslaved African Americans. Some of those who owned bondpeople in the North used them in their homes as a status symbol, while others participated in an international market of goods produced by enslaved laborers. Likewise, one cannot ignore the role northerners played in the transatlantic slave trade. A lengthy discussion of these regional variations is beyond the scope of this volume, although a handful of scholars write about slavery and emancipation in the North. See, for example, Ira Berlin, *Many Thousands Gone: The First Two Centuries of Slavery in North America* (New York: Harvard University Press, 1998); Leslie M. Harris, *In the Shadow of Slavery: African Americans in New York City, 1626–1863* (Chicago: University of Chicago Press, 2003); Graham Russell Hodges, *Root and Branch: African Americans in New York and East Jersey, 1613–1863* (Chapel Hill: University of North Carolina Press, 1999); Wilma King, *The Essence of Liberty: Free Black Women during the Slave Era* (Columbia: University of Missouri Press, 2006); Leon Litwack, *North of Slavery: The Negro in the Free States, 1790–1860* (Chicago: University of Chicago Press, 1961); Joan Pope Melish, *Disowning Slavery: Gradual Emancipation and "Race" in New England, 1780–1860* (Ithaca: Cornell University Press, 1998); Richard Wade, *Slavery in the Cities* (New York: Oxford University Press, 1964); and Shane White, *Somewhat More Independent: The End of Slavery in New York City, 1770–1810* (Athens: University of Georgia Press, 1991).

20. Frederick Douglass, "What to the Slave Is the Fourth of July," July 5, 1852, full text available online at http://teachingamericanhistory.org (accessed February 21, 2012).

21. Edmund S. Morgan, "Slavery and Freedom: The American Paradox," *Journal of American History* 59, no. 1 (1972): 5–29, quote on 5–6. See also his book, published a few years later, *American Slavery, American Freedom* (New York: Norton, 1975).

22. Douglass, "What to the Slave Is the Fourth of July?"

23. Johnson, *Soul by Soul*.

24. Leslie Howard Owens, *This Species of Property: Slave Life and Culture in the Old South* (New York: Oxford University Press, 1976), 215.

25. See Sowande' Mustakeem, "'She Must Go Overboard & Shall Go Overboard': Diseased Bodies and the Spectacle of Murder at Sea," *Atlantic Studies* 8, no. 3 (2011): 301–16 and 'I Never Have Such A Sickly Ship Before': Diet, Disease, and Mortality in 18th-Century Atlantic Slaving Voyages," *Journal of African American History* 93 (Fall 2008): 474–96; Marcus Rediker, *The Slave Ship: A Human History* (New York: Viking, 2007); and Stephanie Smallwood, *Saltwater Slavery: A Middle Passage from Africa to American Diaspora* (New York: Harvard University Press, 2007). Quote found in Johnson, *Soul by Soul*, 3.

26. See Berlin, *Generations of Captivity*; William Dusinberre, *Them Dark Days: Slavery in the American Rice Swamps* (Athens: University of Georgia Press, 1996); Anthony E. Kaye, *Joining Places: Slave Neighborhoods in the Old South* (Chapel Hill: University of North Carolina Press, 2007); Wilma King, *Stolen Childhood: Slave Youth in Nineteenth-Century America*, 2nd ed. (Bloomington: Indiana University Press, 2011); Thavolia Glymph, *Out of the House of Bondage: The Transformation of the Plantation Household* (New York: Cambridge University Press, 2008); Dylan C. Penningroth, *The Claims of Kinfolk: African American Property and Community in the Nineteenth-Century South* (Chapel Hill: University of North Carolina Press, 2003); and Brenda E. Stevenson, *Life in Black and White: Family and Community in the Slave South* (New York: Oxford University Press, 1996).

27. Steven Hahn, *A Nation under Our Feet: Black Political Struggles in the Rural South from Slavery to the Great Migration* (New York: Belkap Press of Harvard University Press, 2003), 16.

28. *Born in Slavery: Slave Narratives from the Federal Writers' Project, 1936–1938*, Arkansas Narratives, p. 289.

29. *Born in Slavery: Slave Narratives from the Federal Writers' Project, 1936–1938*, Georgia Narratives, p. 180.

30. *Born in Slavery: Slave Narratives from the Federal Writers' Project, 1936–1938*, South Carolina Narratives, p. 130.

31. See Daina Ramey Berry, *Swing the Sickle for the Harvest Is Ripe: Gender and Slavery in Antebellum Georgia* (Urbana: University of Illinois Press, 2007).

32. WPA, *Slave Narratives: A Folk History of Slavery in the United States from Interviews with Former Slaves*: Volume XVI, Texas Narratives, Part 4, http://www.gutenberg.org/files/35381/35381-h/35381-h.html (accessed February 2011).

33. WPA, *Slave Narratives: A Folk History of Slavery in the United States from Interviews with Former Slaves*: Volume I, Alabama Narratives, http://www.gutenberg.org/files/36020/36020-0.txt (accessed May 2011).

34. For a lengthy discussion of citizenship, gender, labor, and race, see Evelyn Nakano

Glenn, *Unequal Freedom: How Race and Gender Shaped American Citizenship and Labor* (Cambridge: Harvard University Press, 2002).

35. For a detailed discussion of court sales, see Steven Deyle, *Carry Me Back*; Ariela Gross, *Double Character: Slavery and Mastery in the Antebellum Southern Courtroom* (Princeton: Princeton University Press, 2000); Christopher Morris, *Southern Slavery and the Law, 1619–1860* (Chapel Hill: University of North Carolina Press, 1996); Thomas D. Russell, "Sale Day in Antebellum South Carolina: Slavery, Law, Economy and Court-Supervised Sales" (Ph.D. diss., Stanford University, 1993); Michael Tadman, *Speculators and Slaves: Masters, Traders, and Slaves in the Old South* (1989; reprint, Madison: University of Wisconsin Press, 1996); and Jenny Wahl, *The Bondsman's Burden: An Economic Analysis of the Common Law of Southern Slavery* (New York: Cambridge University Press, 1998).

36. Publications in the last decade reflect a slight increase in scholars' interest in enslaved people rather than the institution of slavery. See, for example, Berlin, *Generations of Captivity*; Johnson, *Soul by Soul*; Sowande' Mustakeem, "'I've Never Seen Such a Sickly Ship Before': Diet, Disease, and Mortality in 18th Century Atlantic Slaving Voyages," *Journal of African American History* 93, no. 4 (2008): 474–96; Marcus Rediker, *The Slave Ship: A Human History* (New York: Viking, 2007); and Stephanie Smallwood, *Saltwater Slavery: A Middle Passage from Africa to American Diaspora* (New York: Harvard University Press, 2007).

37. Several scholars have published work on slave prices; see, for example, Robert W. Fogel and Stanley L. Engerman, *New Orleans Slave Sale Sample, 1804–1862* (Ann Arbor: Inter-university Consortium for Political and Social Research, 2000); Gwendolyn Midlo Hall, *The Louisiana Slave Database, 1719–1820* (Baton Rouge: Louisiana State University Press, 2000); Herman Freudenberger and Jonathan B. Pritchett, "The Domestic United States Slave Trade: New Evidence," *Journal of Interdisciplinary History* 21, no. 3 (1991): 447–77; Herman Freudenberger and Jonathan B. Pritchett, "A Peculiar Sample: The Selection of Slaves for the New Orleans Market," *Journal of Economic History* 52, no. 1 (1992): 109–27; Laurence J. Kotlikoff, "The Structure of Slave Prices in New Orleans, 1804–1862," *Economic Inquiry* 17 (1979): 496–518; B. Greenwald and R. Glasspiegel, "Adverse Selection in the Market for Slaves: New Orleans, 1830–1860," *Quarterly Journal of Economics* 98, no. 3 (1989); and Johnson, *Soul by Soul*.

38. Johnson, *Soul by Soul*, 16. See also Daina Ramey Berry, "'Broad is da Road dat Leads ter Death': Enslaved Mortality and Human Chattel," in *Slavery's Capitalism: A New History of American Economic Development*, ed. Sven Beckart and Seth Rockman (Philadelphia: University of Pennsylvania Press, 2013).

39. I would argue that wealthy black slaveholders also benefited from slave ownership but at the same time wonder how race influenced their social status.

40. Thirteenth Amendment to the U.S. Constitution, full text found at http://www.usconstitution.net/const.tml#Am13 (accessed December 15, 2010).

41. For a lengthy discussion of political activism see Hahn, *A Nation under Our Feet*.

42. Freedmen's Bureau Bill, March 3, 1865, available online from Bruce Frohnen, ed., *The American Nation: Primary Sources* (Indianapolis: Liberty Fund, 2008) Accessed from http://oll.libertyfund.org/title/2282/216253 on October 23, 2010.

43. Ibid., Second Freedmen's Bureau Bill, December 4, 1865, and the Civil Rights Act, April 9, 1866.

44. Ibid. White and black women were excluded from expressing their rights as citizens.

45. For a discussion of the challenges African Americans faced in this transitional period, see Amy Dru Stanley, *From Bondage to Contract: Wage Labor, Marriage, and the Market in the Era of Slave Emancipation* (Cambridge: Cambridge University Press, 1998).

46. December 2, 1862, 5th currency issue see: http://www.csacurrency.com/csacur/cs209215.htm (accessed November 20, 2008).

47. Norman R. Yetman, ed., *Voices from Slavery: 100 Authentic Slave Narratives*, "Peter Clifton" (New York: Dover, 2000), 57–59.

48. *Born in Slavery: Slave Narratives from the Federal Writers' Project, 1936–1938: Arkansas Narratives*, Volume 2, Part 1, pp. 53–56.

49. Federal Writer's Project, *A Folk History of Slavery in the United States, Arkansas Narratives*, vol. 2, pt. 5 (Washington, D.C.: Library of Congress, 1941).

50. *Born in Slavery: Slave Narratives from the Federal Writers' Project, 1936–1938: Arkansas Narratives*, Volume 2, Part 1, p. 37.

# 2

..........................

# Rewriting the Free Negro Past

## Joseph Lumpkin, Proslavery Ideology, and Citizenship in Antebellum Georgia

WATSON JENNISON

By the 1850s the debate over slavery had reached its peak. In the midst of growing sectionalism and political conflict, slavery's defenders and its opponents engaged in a heated battle over the true nature of bondage in the U.S. South and its impact on those enslaved. Though both sides looked to similar sources, such as the Bible and science, to legitimate their respective positions, they came to radically different conclusions. These debates concerned not only the fate of the slave population in the South but also the place of the free black population.

Free blacks were a focal point in the ideological struggle over slavery. Their collective condition figured prominently in the discussions over the institution. At issue was their ability or inability to survive without white oversight. Slavery's proponents presented all people of African descent as incapable of caring for themselves, regardless of their legal status, and defended the institution by portraying it as a "civilizing school" that rid slaves of their supposed savagery and taught them basic life skills. They characterized free black life as an inescapable and endless cycle of poverty, ignorance, and vice that produced individuals who were a drain on society as well as a potential threat to the social order. As such, they contended, emancipating slaves was not only wrong but inhumane.

Although white northerners were similarly hostile to the notion that blacks were equal to whites, most were less inclined to cast free blacks in such unequivocally negative terms or to deprive them of basic rights. Indeed, free blacks retained privileges of citizenship, including the right to vote, in New York and most of New England throughout the antebellum era. By extending these privileges to free blacks, the legislatures in these northern states undermined one of the key pillars of the proslavery argument—that blacks were so racially inferior that they could never be capable of enjoying the rights and responsibilities of citizenship. In response to this challenge, legislatures and courts across the South rewrote their laws pertaining to free blacks and authorized the enactment of increasingly harsh restrictions in an effort to make their legal status in southern society adhere more closely to proslavery doctrine.

One of the leading figures in the assault on free black rights was Justice Joseph Lumpkin of Georgia. He was the legal architect of the state's antebellum slave regime. He arguably possessed the most influence of any man in Georgia in official matters relating to race and slavery, having authored the opinions in more than half of the sixty most important cases related to those issues during his twenty-one years on the bench. Through these decisions, Lumpkin molded Georgia's antebellum legal code to conform to his vision of a properly ordered slave society, one that had no place for free blacks. He ruled that free blacks were not and never had been and never would be citizens in Georgia. Indeed, he defined the free black population as the antipodes to Georgia's white citizenry. In his characterization of free blacks and his reshaping of Georgia's slave law, Lumpkin stood at the vanguard of a southern movement promoting proslavery ideology in the legal realm.[1]

In his opinions, Lumpkin erased free blacks from Georgia's early history and reduced their diversity in status to a simple stereotype. Lumpkin cast white Georgians' perceptions of free blacks in monolithic terms that defied historical reality. Some free blacks had acted as and been recognized as citizens of the state. In rewriting this past, Lumpkin ignored earlier white sentiments that provided space for free blacks as citizens in Georgia. Indeed, even in the 1850s, such sentiments still existed in pockets of the state. Yet, despite his errors, Lumpkin had a profound impact on southern law and national law. Moreover, it was his vision that served as the basis for future scholarship on race and the place of free blacks in society by legal scholars and historians. Thus the legacy of his decisions long outlasted his life.

* * *

That Lumpkin would emerge as the key defender of slavery in Georgia was far from clear during his early years. Lumpkin was born in 1799 in

Oglethorpe County. His family migrated to Georgia from Virginia and settled on the Broad River in the late 1700s. As a young man, Lumpkin attended the University of Georgia and later Princeton University. Soon after his return from the North, Lumpkin took up the study of law. During this time, he met and married his wife and, following her lead, became an evangelical Christian. Lumpkin's conversion shaped his worldview. Influenced by his newfound religious convictions and the perfectionist impulse, Lumpkin was drawn to national reform movements in the 1820s and 1830s. Like most evangelicals, Lumpkin embraced the temperance movement. In time, however, he gravitated toward abolitionism, going so far as to join the American Colonization Society (ACS). The depth of Lumpkin's commitment to the movement became clear in 1833 when he delivered a speech in Boston in which he tacitly endorsed emancipation. That Lumpkin chose to name his son after William Wilberforce, the famed English abolitionist, provided further proof of his convictions.[2]

And then all at once, Lumpkin completely changed course. After flirting with the abolitionist movement, Lumpkin backed away in the late 1830s as the sectional conflict over slavery escalated.[3] This reversal pushed him in the other direction; he embraced the proslavery ideology with the zeal of a reformer. His earlier ambivalence dissipated. In the mid-1840s he broke formally with the ACS over the group's direction and objectives. "I was once, in common with the great body of my fellow citizens of the South, the friend and patron of this enterprise. I now regard it as a failure, if not something worse; as I do every effort that has been made, for the abolition of negro slavery, at home or abroad."[4] All blacks, he believed, should be enslaved. With this change in his convictions, he adhered to a rigid application of these principles in forming his legal opinions.

Lumpkin's embrace of slavery came at a particularly auspicious moment. Having jettisoned his reservations about bondage, Lumpkin rose to prominence in Georgia at a time when the state's legal system was undergoing a radical transformation. Unlike other states in the union, Georgia had resisted the creation of a state supreme court in the years after independence, preferring instead to rely on a series of superior courts to mete out justice. By the second half of the 1830s, opposition to the state supreme court began to wane, culminating in the establishment of the tribunal in 1846.[5] Recognized by most Georgians as one of the state's leading attorneys, Lumpkin was the natural choice to lead the court. He served from 1846 until his death in 1867, and although he was not made the official chief justice until 1863, he was widely regarded as the court's leading jurist from the outset. From his position on the bench, Lumpkin led the effort to standardize the state's slave and racial laws.[6]

Lumpkin's shifts about slavery paralleled a broader transformation in proslavery thought in Georgia, and the South as a whole. In the revolutionary and early national periods, apologists defended slavery as a necessary evil when countering critics' condemnations of the institution. They acknowledged that slavery posed some ethical and moral quandaries in a nation founded upon freedom and equality, but, they reasoned, whites were ill-suited to the rigors of rice cultivation, which meant that African slavery provided the only solution to develop the area commercially. By the second decade of the nineteenth century, however, a transition was well under way. No longer willing to concede the principled high ground to their foes, slavery's defenders portrayed bondage as a positive good. Slave ownership was framed as a republican virtue that required no apology. Governor George Troup's words reflected the changed mind-set: "If this matter be an evil, it is our own—if it be a sin, we can implore the forgiveness of it; to remove it, we ask neither their sympathy or assistance—it may be our physical weakness—it is our moral strength. If, like the Greeks and Romans, the moment we cease to be masters, we are slaves."[7] In the 1830s and 1840s, as the abolition movement grew in force in the North and the sectional divide deepened, proslavery advocates increasingly looked to history, natural science, and religion to legitimate their position.[8]

Like other proslavery advocates, Lumpkin based his views of bondage on white supremacy and Christianity. As a deeply committed evangelical, Lumpkin relied upon the Bible for moral and ethical guidance as well as historical evidence to support his opinions on slavery. Lumpkin idealized slavery as an essential component of the South's perfect society. Invoking Christianity to sustain his position, he asserted that slavery "—like government itself—is of God. That being recognized and regulated by the Decalogue, it will, we have every reason to believe, be of perpetual duration. That it subserves the best interests of both races, and that we will persevere and defend it any and all hazards."[9] Central to the biblical justification of racial slavery was the identification of Africans as the descendants of the "tribe of Ham." According to the Book of Genesis, Lumpkin claimed, blacks were "cursed" and "judicially condemned to perpetual bondage."[10] Lumpkin viewed this decree as "unreversible. It will run on parallel with time itself. And heaven and earth shall sooner pass away, than one jot or title of it shall abate."[11] By the grace of God, they could not escape their fate, destined to remain enslaved forever.

In addition to the biblical explanations, Lumpkin relied upon the slaves' supposed racial inferiority to justify their condition. Without the direct aid and supervision of whites, he claimed, slaves were incapable of taking care of themselves. As proof, Lumpkin pointed to Liberia, which freed American slaves had founded in the early 1820s with the aid of the American Colonization Society.

> Liberia was formed of emancipated slaves, many of them partially trained and prepared for the change, and sent thousands of miles from all contact with the superior race; and given a home in a country where their ancestors were natives, and supposed to be suited to their physical condition. Arrived there, they have been for a number of years in a state of pupilage to the Colonization Society, in order that they might learn "to walk alone and by themselves." And at the end of a half century what do we see? A few thousand thriftless, lazy semi-savages, dying of famine, because they will not work!

He repudiated all emancipation and repatriation efforts as futile. "Under the superior race and nowhere else," Lumpkin concluded, "do they attain to the highest degree of civilization."[12]

According to Lumpkin, the failed Liberian experiment demonstrated that blacks could not possibly exercise the duties and responsibilities of citizenship. Even those freed from bondage could not overcome the taint associated with African heritage. That the settlers in Liberia, despite receiving some white guidance through the ACS, proved unable to create a functioning society was not surprising. Only whites possessed the traits necessary to achieve such lofty heights. Consequently, he insisted, subjugation and enslavement offered people of African descent the only options for progress.

*   *   *

Like his larger worldview, Lumpkin's attitude toward race was bifurcated with no gradations. Influenced by his religious convictions to see the world in Manichaean terms, all issues became black or white, good or evil, right or wrong. And unfortunately for free people of color, they contradicted his perfectionist vision of the slave South, a world where African descent and slavery were increasingly synonymous. All citizens were white men.

And all blacks were slaves. Consequently, Lumpkin decried the very existence of a free black class that could be composed of both blacks and citizens: "To him there is but little in prospect but a life of poverty, of depression, of ignorance, and of decay. He lives amongst us without motive and without hope. His fancied freedom is all a delusion. All practical men must admit, that the slave who receives the care and protection of a tolerable master, is superior in comfort to the free negro."[13] Indeed, Lumpkin considered the mere suggestion that any person of African descent should enjoy his or her liberty as an abomination. Free blacks offered proof of the falsity of his portrait of slavery. Free blacks, then, had to disappear. To that end, Lumpkin issued a series of opinions designed to halt the growth of the state's free black population and to reduce their legal status roughly equal to that of a slave. In justifying his position, Lumpkin relied upon two central arguments: that free blacks were not citizens and were roughly equivalent to slaves, and that it had always been that way. These principles shaped his legal interpretation, which, by virtue of his position on the court, became in effect the state's official position. In the process, Lumpkin ignored the ambiguity that had characterized the state's stand toward free people of color in the first decades after the Revolution, substituting a more contemporary and rigid view of race.

Georgia's supreme court dealt with a number of important cases pertaining to free blacks, but it was Lumpkin's decisions in the *Bryan v. Walton* case that established their legal standing in the state. The case made it to the supreme court three times before coming to a conclusion.[14] Ostensibly the case pitted two white men, Hugh Walton and Seaborn C. Bryan, against one another over the ownership of a group of slaves, but at its core it answered a fundamental legal question concerning the status of free people of African descent in Georgian society. The man who sold the slaves in question was Joseph Nunez, a free person of color from Burke County. The case turned on whether Nunez had the right to do so. In his ruling, Lumpkin declared the importance of the issue at hand. "This is a grave question," one that "involves a great principle" and "establishes an important precedent."[15] The opinion in the *Bryan* case defined the legal status of free people of African descent in Georgia both in the present and, as importantly, in the past.

According to Lumpkin, free people of African descent were virtually identical to slaves before the law. Indicative of his effort to draw as clear cut a divide between black and white Georgians while simultaneously lumping all free people of color and free blacks with slaves, Lumpkin referred to them all as "Africans," a curious decision since the Atlantic slave trade had ended more than four decades earlier. In doing so, Lumpkin erased differences of wealth, birth, and caste among free people of color and emphasized their foreignness. The "*status* of the African in Georgia," he remarked, "whether bond or free, is such that he has no civil, social or political rights or capacity." Blacks, regardless of their status as free or enslaved, could "never enjoy" civil freedom among whites.[16] "Like the *slave*," Lumpkin declared, "the *free* person of color" was associated "with the slave in this State in some of the most humiliating incidents in his degradation." As proof, he pointed to a list of laws that reduced free people of color to the status of the slave, including prohibitions against voting or holding office, testifying in court against whites, carrying firearms, preaching without a special license, selling or making drugs and medicines, learning to read or write, or working in any occupation that required those skills.[17]

Believing free blacks to be indistinguishable from slaves, Lumpkin declared that they could never be citizens of Georgia. The free black man, he proclaimed, "resides among us, and yet is a stranger. A *native* even, and yet not a citizen. Though not a *slave*, yet he is not free. Protected by law, yet enjoying none of the immunities of freedom. Though not in a condition of chattelhood, yet constantly exposed to it." To "be civilly and politically free, to be the peer and equal of the white man—to enjoy the offices, trusts and privileges our institutions confer on the white man, is not now, never has been, and never will be, the condition of this degraded race." Lumpkin concluded that "He is not and cannot become a *citizen* under our Constitution and Laws."[18]

Not only did Lumpkin contend free blacks and slaves were synonymous, but he also insisted that it had always been that way. He depicted a static vision of Georgia's racial order, relying upon biological and biblical justifications to support his position. He rooted free blacks' "social and civil degradation" in "the taint of blood, [which] adheres to the descendants of Ham in this country, like the poisoned tunic of Nessus." He asserted that "The blacks were introduced into [Georgia], as a race of Pagan slaves. The prejudice, if it can be called so, of caste, is unconquerable. It was so at the beginning. It has come down to our day."[19] His explanation was religiously inspired and eternal.

Lumpkin's efforts to deny the existence of a free black past as distinct from the slave past were essential to legitimate the ideology of slavery that emerged in the antebellum era. Lumpkin recognized that Georgia and the South as a whole were entering a new era. With slavery abolished almost everywhere else and abolitionism growing, it was time that Georgians charted their own path. In this context, Lumpkin and other white southerners faced the prospect of forging a new proslavery ideology alone. To do so, they rewrote history to justify their actions. The true history of free blacks in Georgia, indeed in the South, contradicted the rationale underlying white southerners' claims that slavery was necessary. By collapsing the broad range of distinctions among the state's free people of African descent, ruling repeatedly that their status in Georgia was the equivalent of slaves, and asserting that it had always been this way, Lumpkin erased the free black past in order to preserve the future of slavery.

\* \* \*

Despite the confidence of Lumpkin's declarations, his views of free people of color in Georgia and their past were ahistorical and inaccurate. While it was true that by the antebellum era most whites in Georgia shared Lumpkin's views of free blacks, this attitude was not monolithic, nor had whites always felt this way. There had always been white Georgians who viewed race in absolute terms, those who believed blacks had no rights, but by the middle third of the nineteenth century their numbers had grown substantially. Numerous interrelated factors contributed to this transformation, including the spread of slavery to the interior of the state, the rise of cotton cultivation, the removal of the Cherokee Indians, the subsequent increase in the white population, particularly the number of non-slaveholding whites, and the growth of abolitionist sentiment in the North. Black resistance also played a role. The rising fear of insurrection and the discovery of multiple plots in the 1830s and 1840s convinced whites that a large-scale insurrection was inevitable, and many assumed that free blacks would join slaves to destroy the institution. In this context, the flexibility that had characterized the state's earlier treatment of free people of African descent dissipated. Reflective of the growing antipathy toward free blacks, Georgia legislators passed a host of laws that imposed new scrutiny on free blacks' behavior and restrictions on their economic activities. Yet, as late as the 1850s, there continued to be pockets in Georgia where whites tolerated mobility and status for certain free people of color, places where an earlier racial sensibility persevered despite the rise of the cotton kingdom.[20]

Although Lumpkin collapsed the distinctions among all people of African descent, some of his predecessors in the state's judiciary had not endorsed this interpretation. Even as the legislature took an increasingly harsh stand toward free blacks in the antebellum era, the courts continued to recognize rights for free people of African descent as late as 1831. That year Judge William Crawford ruled in *State v. Philpot* that there was a "very broad and obvious distinction between the rights and conditions of slaves and free persons of color." The case centered upon the rights of free people of color, specifically the right to writ of habeas corpus. Crawford noted that "with but a single exception known to the court, the decisions and practice throughout the State are now and have been uniform, to extend to this class of persons the benefit of the writ of *habeas* corpus." The judge declared that, like a "Frenchman, Englishman, or other foreigner who might come among us," free blacks deserved such protections. Quoting from the 1798 state constitution, Crawford noted that the document stipulated that "all persons shall be entitled" to this right regardless of the "particular complexion of the individual." While acknowledging that slaves did not have the right to habeas corpus, he stressed the difference between the two: "Let it be remembered, while these positions are examined, with a view to ascertain their bearing on the present question, that it is not whether a slave may have the writ, but whether it may be legally awarded to a free person of color." Clearly, slaves and free blacks were not the same. For those who conflated the two because of "the general presumption against the liberty of the slave race," he wrote, "this is carrying the presumption of law too far." It would be "very hard and unreasonable," Crawford noted, to "reduce a whole class of free people to a level with slaves" and "deprive them of the most effectual means of protecting their personal liberty, and subvert a constitutional provision."[21] In this instance, Crawford regarded free people of African descent as little different from white foreign nationals. Whether free blacks had rights, therefore, had more to do with their status than their skin color. Race clearly was an important marker in Georgia, but in the first decades of the nineteenth century it was only one of several key identifiers.

Invoking the 1798 state constitution as a source of legitimacy was not simply a rhetorical device designed to support an opinion. Rather, it pointed to an era when free people of color were able to access a range of the rights and privileges associated with citizenship. In contrast to Lumpkin, who stated it was unnecessary for the court to go beyond 1818 to ascertain the condition of free people of African descent,[22] Crawford knew that in early decades of the nation the situation had been different. He understood that, in that time of racial and legislative flux, the place of free people of African descent had not yet been fully determined.

Not only were free people of color considered distinct from slaves, but there is considerable evidence that Georgia's authorities experimented with giving some people of African descent citizenship rights in the late eighteenth century. In 1802, Crawford coedited a digest of the state's laws, which included a section on emancipation. Though not comprehensive, the various laws appearing in the digest offer an interesting sample of the manumissions approved by the legislature and the status that the newly freed blacks and people of color received. There were some clear categories. Some were enslaved men whose meritorious service brought them freedom with the proviso that they were not entitled to "any privileges more than other people of color are allowed by the laws of this state." Other manumissions, those involving women and children, included language with more expansive provisions. In 1796, for example, an enslaved woman named Chany and her nine children gained their freedom and considerable land and property through the will of Anthony Haynes, who was most likely father of the children. In addition to authorizing the manumission, the legislature enabled the members of the family "to take, hold, and enjoy property of every kind, in like manner as if they were free citizens of this state." In the case of Sylvia Posner and her son David, the legislature went so far as to grant some privileges of whiteness. Responding to a petition from her husband, the legislature "declared [them] to be manumitted and made free, and be thereafter utterly, clearly and fully discharged from slavery, as if the said Sylvia and David, had been born free." Furthermore, the law declared that they would enjoy the status of "free white persons" if they ever found themselves charged and accused of a crime. That meant they would be "tried for such offence in the same manner, and be entitled to the same defence in the courts of this state, as allowed to free white persons in like cases." In juxtaposing these examples, Crawford drew attention both to the vast social and economic differences among free people of African descent and to the fact that the state authorities appeared to recognize these distinctions and to grant various gradations of citizenship accordingly.[23]

Thomas Going, James Stewart, and Judy Elliot received the most extensive grant of citizenship. In 1799 these three free people of color petitioned the state authorities to become citizens. These individuals had achieved high status within their communities and sought official recognition to reflect their place. The general assembly acquiesced, passing legislation that explicitly stated the petitioners were "entitled to all the rights, privileges and immunities belonging to a free citizen of this State."[24] Rather than singling out certain privileges and rights at their disposal as in the Posner case, the legislature provided a broad grant of citizenship and stipulated specific limitations. They could not testify against whites, nor could they vote or hold office. Beyond these exceptions, these "citizens of the state" were entitled to the benefits of freedom. The language contained in the legislation made clear that their status was different from the rest of the state's free black and free people of color population. The law shielded them against indignities that other free people of color faced. The citizens of color would have enjoyed property rights and protections from laws that prohibited blacks from working in certain occupations, required them to have guardians, and limited the kinds of punishments they faced. In a society in which the rights of individuals were still being determined, these three people of color sought to codify the privileges that they enjoyed, despite the fact that they did not amount to full political rights. Exemption from whipping would have likely meant more in their everyday lives than the right to vote on election days. Status as "citizens of the state" was meaningful to these men and women even with the accompanying restrictions.

The decision to grant rights and privileges of citizenship to certain free people of color was not so unique when compared to events elsewhere in the Americas. The period in question, the 1790s, was a time of considerable tumult in the Atlantic world. The insurrection in Saint-Domingue unsettled slave societies throughout the hemisphere, prompting the authorities in several colonies to reconsider the boundaries of race and citizenship. The French implemented policies that ended slavery in their colonies and bestowed citizenship upon the former bondsmen in a radical experiment.[25] In Jamaica, the authorities elevated the status of free men of color in the militia, who helped to quell a maroon uprising on that island in 1795.[26] Even Georgia's own history suggested there was an earlier time when the authorities demonstrated greater flexibility when considering whether to grant certain privileges and rights to free people of African descent. In 1765 the colonial authorities included a provision in the slave code that offered special status to free people of color who immigrated to the colony. "All Persons male and Female of what Nation or colour soever being born of free parents . . . may be intituled to an Act of Assembly for Naturalizing them . . . whereby they, their Wives and Children may have, Use and enjoy, all the Rights, Privileges, Powers and Immunities" enjoyed by "any Person born of British parents . . . except to vote for or be Elected a Member to serve in the general Assembly."[27] In effect, the authorities promised to grant them the same status that whites enjoyed except voting and officeholding. Though the Crown ultimately rejected the slave code, the provision demonstrated that Georgian authorities were not averse to extending privileges to people of African descent.[28] Blackness did not preclude free people of color from becoming an accepted part of society.

The graded notion of citizenship secured by free people of color in the 1790s contrasted with Lumpkin's absolute notion of citizenship in the 1850s. According to Lumpkin, Georgians fell into one of two categories: citizen or slave. Free blacks, in Lumpkin's reasoning, could be justifiably equated with slaves because of their racial inferiority but also because they had not been granted the right to vote. In focusing on suffrage, Lumpkin offered a masculine definition that ignored the citizenship status of white women. When speaking of free blacks, Lumpkin envisioned them as men, specifying "he" and never "she" in his decisions. This allowed him to use free white men as a foil, positioning all white men as equal citizens while simultaneously placing all free people of African descent into the same category—black men completely devoid of the rights and privileges of citizenship that all white men enjoyed. Lumpkin projected a black-white bifurcation back in time, imagining racial rigidity where there had been racial flexibility and equating blackness with bondage and whiteness with citizenship.

Lumpkin used the *Bryan v. Walton* case to argue that free blacks in Georgian society had always been equivalent to slaves, but ironically the facts in the case demonstrate that Lumpkin's portrait of the racial order in the past was wrong. Evidence from the Nunez family proved his error. Testimony revealed that Joseph Nunez's father, James Nunez, was a free man of color, who, in spite of his racial background, had become an accepted part of white elite society in Burke County in the late eighteenth and early nineteenth centuries. James's wealth and the standing of his father, Moses Nunez, who was part of a well-known Sephardic family who immigrated to Georgia in the 1730s, provided status in the community. James was particularly accomplished and well known. He was educated and met regularly with white men in the neighborhood. One white woman claimed James "was received by them as on a footing with whites." He was admitted to society functions and held a respectable position in the community. He attended social events with whites, including dances. James "lived together as husband and wife" with a white woman named Lucy Anderson. As evidence of James's status among his white neighbors, Lucy did not lose her standing in the community for having a nonwhite husband. She met regularly with other white women in the neighborhood. James's neighbors knew "he was of color" but were unsure as to what his mixture was. Some whites believed he was a "respectable Indian and white blooded man," while others were convinced he was a "free mulatto." His appearance offered few clues. He had "black and tolerably straight hair" and "a nose like a white man—not flat." His lips "were not very thick." As for his skin color, he "was a dark complected man" though there were "some white men darker than he was."[29] Regardless of his exact racial mixture, however, one fact was clear: he was a wealthy planter. And for most whites in his community that was enough.

When Lumpkin reached his opinion in the *Bryan* case, effectively defining the place of free people of African descent in Georgia, he dismissed most of the testimony regarding James's place in society. In reaching his decision, Lumpkin ignored this evidence because it contradicted his rigid and simplistic worldview. Instead, he simply projected his understanding of race back in time. In assessing the rights of free blacks in Georgia, Lumpkin fixated on the political component of citizenship, specifically voting; thus he ignored evidence that pointed to a past that contradicted his static vision of racial divisions in Georgia's past. Despite Lumpkin's failure to acknowledge as much, Georgia's policy toward free people of color and free blacks had changed over the course of the nineteenth century. In the first twenty-five years after independence, authorities displayed a flexible approach toward free people of color. Some free people of African descent gained citizenship status during the revolutionary era. Although the push to expand the rights of some elite free people of color dissipated in the first decade of the nineteenth century, most whites in

Georgia had not viewed free people of African descent as the same as slaves. The history of the Nunez family, as presented in *Bryan v. Walton*, shows that white attitudes and state government policies toward free people of African descent underwent a significant transformation between the turn of the century and the midpoint.

\*   \*   \*

By the time the *Bryan* case reached the supreme court, the world of James Nunez had long since passed. For Joseph, James's son, his choices in life were much narrower than his father's. Though phenotypically lighter than his father, he lived life as though he were much darker. He married, instead of a white woman, one of the slaves he inherited. His social circle was not composed of white planters, but other free blacks and slaves. Unlike his father, he faced a host of restrictions based upon his racial status, including a requirement that he register with the state officially as a "negro." Gone was the racial ambiguity that had characterized earlier times.

Just as Lumpkin's understanding of his state's past was clearly faulty in failing to convey the complexity of the racial order, so too was his understanding of his state's present. His assessment of race and the status of free blacks may have reflected life in large pockets of the state, especially in the upcountry. But white attitudes in Georgia were not monolithic, nor were the experiences of free people of African descent. The result was a patchwork of areas where free people of color found sanctuary from the imposition of state and local restrictions against them. In these areas, some prospered under the protection of whites who held views on race that deviated sharply from those of Lumpkin and those who agreed with his racial perspectives.

The status of free people changed over time along with the size of their population and their geographic distribution. After a rapid and substantial increase between 1790 and 1800, the number of free people of color in Georgia grew at a much slower and uneven rate in the decades that followed. By 1860 the population reached thirty-five hundred.[30]

In the first decades of the nation, the free black population concentrated on the state's periphery, a trend that continued until 1830. In the wake of the state's annexation of the Cherokee territory, however, free blacks abandoned the "frontier" counties. By the late antebellum era, free blacks were few and far between in the Georgia interior, scattered across the black belt and Cherokee territory in singles or in dozens. By contrast, the largest concentrations of free people of color were in the oldest counties in the state, areas along the Atlantic coast and the Savannah River. Beginning in 1810, for example, Chatham County emerged as the center of the population of free people of color in Georgia, and it remained so until the Civil War. Urban areas reflected this geographical imbalance, and the difference was striking. In 1860, Savannah and Augusta alone accounted for more than a quarter of the state's total free black population, with 705 and 386, respectively. Pushing toward the interior, to the newer areas of the state, cities such as Macon and Atlanta contained significantly smaller numbers of free blacks, with 22 and 25, respectively. Columbus, in the state's southwest, was somewhat of an exception to the rule in that it had 141 free blacks, yet this number was still far below that of the older cities.[31]

That the demographic patterns emerged the way they did was not by accident. White attitudes toward free blacks had an impact on the population distribution. How free blacks were treated and assessed by whites differed depending on region. In certain parts of the state, whites made it difficult, if not impossible, for free blacks to live among them. Through taxes and economic restrictions, local and county officials effectively made their towns off limits to free blacks. Two cities, Atlanta in the upcountry and Savannah in the lowcountry, provide excellent examples.

Atlanta was a center of white worker militancy, and local authorities went to great lengths to appease their constituents. White workers feared competition with free blacks for employment, believing it would degrade their labor and drive down their wages. Responding to local residents' wishes, city officials enacted ordinances to dissuade free blacks from relocating there, including a $200 tax on free blacks who moved to the town. Those who failed to pay the tax were subject to arrest and forced labor.[32] This was not an idle threat. City authorities arrested Robert Harden, a free black man, in 1855 for failing to pay the tax and auctioned him to the highest bidder.[33] In 1859 the city authorities increased the penalties in a further effort to deter the undesirables from moving there. In addition to the possibility of being sold off, free people of color who violated the ordinance could face a daily whipping of thirty-nine lashes for every day they remained in the city limits.[34] Those free people of color who could come up with the money also needed to have a local guardian to vouch for them before the city council, and even then permission was not always granted.[35] The *Atlanta Daily Intelligencer* expressed the sentiment of most white residents of the city when it noted, "We are opposed to giving free negroes a residence in any and every Slaveholding state, believing as we do, that their presence in slave communities is hurtful to the good order of society, and fraught with great danger to our 'peculiar institution.'"[36]

Those free blacks permitted to settle in Atlanta faced a host of restrictions on their economic activities, including prohibitions from engaging in even the most basic forms of petty commerce. In June 1856, for example, the city council even refused a petition on behalf of a free person of color, Jo Miller, who sought a license to sell ice cream, not the most sought-after occupation. Council members opposed the endeavor on principle alone, defending their actions on the premise that it "would be unwise, unjust, and impolitic." They explained that "it is not our policy to train negroes, whether bond or free, to become tradesmen, merchants, or speculators and to make exceptions . . . would be, not only highly prejudicial to the well being and contentment of those classes, but a source of envy and dissatisfaction to others."[37] In this way they denied economic mobility to free people of color in order to limit class and race tensions. The authorities suggested that allowing blacks entry into white occupations would make whites angry and blacks dissatisfied. As the examples indicate, it is little wonder that the free black population only grew from nineteen in 1850 to twenty-five in 1860. In Atlanta, then, free people of color faced significant restrictions on their economic opportunities and enjoyed little autonomy. The upcountry in general proved hostile to free people of color. Their status as "free" seemed merely nominal, and in the words of one historian, they existed as little more than "slaves without masters."[38]

In contrast to their counterparts in Atlanta, Savannah's free people of color benefited from significantly fewer restrictions and relatively greater acceptance by whites. Free blacks in Savannah enjoyed relatively diverse economic opportunities in both skilled and unskilled occupations, even dominating certain fields.[39] Some free people of color capitalized upon Savannah's economic opportunities and accumulated significant wealth. For example, the city's wealthiest and most influential free person of color, Andrew Marshall, possessed assets worth an estimated $25,000 to $30,000 by the 1850s.[40] In aggregate, the city's women of color fared even better financially than the men, prospering throughout the antebellum era. Susan Jackson embodied this success. As the owner of a bakery, six slaves, and twenty-three buildings, she owned property valued at $15,000.[41] As in Charleston and New Orleans, slave ownership among the free people of color was not uncommon, though the practice peaked in the 1820s when twenty free people of color owned a total of fifty-eight slaves. Many of these slaveholders were artisans who used their bondsmen in their workshops. In other instances, owners appear to have lived off of the income generated by their slaves, whom they hired out or allowed to work for themselves. Unlike the pattern in the Upper South, it seems these slaves were not related to their owners and were used to create wealth. The conditions in Savannah, and the Georgia lowcountry in general, facilitated the rise of an elite class of free people of color whose economic status, if not political or legal status, exceeded that of most white Georgians.[42]

Elite white toleration and acceptance of free people of color contributed to greater economic opportunities for them in Savannah than in Atlanta. These elite whites maintained deep connections with elite free people of color, who used these long-standing relationships to weather the increasingly frequent attempts to restrict their lives.[43] These relationships often took the form of sexual relationships, as the number of "mulattoes" in the city indicates.[44] Indeed, some elite whites in Savannah recognized "mulatto" free people of color as racially superior to black slaves. For example, Richard Arnold questioned the prevailing ideas about race, namely that any African blood "tainted" a free person of color. In countering this perspective, he remarked that "a mulatto is not a negro any more than he is a white man."[45] Arnold believed that a "mulatto" was different from both a "negro" and a "white," amounting essentially to a third race. In fact, in some respects he considered "mulattoes" closer to "whites" than "negroes." Like whites, he contended, mulattoes were incapable of laboring in the rice fields. Speaking for himself and other lowcountry planters, he claimed that "With us no man would buy a mulatto for field work."[46] Arnold, in contrast to Lumpkin, recognized degrees of racial mixture, not absolutes. Arnold was not a fringe character in antebellum Savannah; he was one of the city's most influential men, a prominent planter and doctor, and heavily involved in city politics, eventually serving as mayor in the 1850s and 1860s. Many elite whites in Savannah shared Arnold's beliefs about race in general and free people of color in particular.

In Savannah, free people of color formed an important and integral part of the city. They were not only tolerated by many elite whites, but were accepted as worthy, if not completely equal, members of the community. As such, many elite whites opposed attempts to place onerous restrictions on free people of color. Evidence of this sentiment emerged in the late 1850s when the legislature debated whether to enact a law that would have eliminated the free black population altogether by forcing free blacks to leave the state or face reenslavement. In the discussions over the proposed legislation, the delegation from Chatham County fought to amend the bill to exempt Savannah's free people of color from the terms of the bill, which would have enabled them to remain untouched. As for their reasoning, the representatives made quite clear that they hoped to protect free people of color not only for their contributions to the city's coffers through taxes but also for their services through firefighting.[47] In opposing the proposed bill, the representatives demonstrated that they valued the contributions of free blacks to society.

But these views were not represented on the state supreme court, which, before 1865, was solely composed of upcountry justices.[48] The timing of the court's creation coincided with the rising power of the cotton kingdom in the interior of Georgia. The composition of the court reflected the altered balance of power in the state. Thus the attitudes of the upcountry whites were well represented on the court while those of lowcountry whites, such as Arnold, were largely excluded. Lumpkin's opinions on free people of color, which were largely shared by his fellow justices, may have reflected the views of most whites in Georgia, but not all, in spite of Lumpkin's assertions to the contrary.

*   *   *

As the foregoing indicates, the attempt to relegate free blacks and free people of color in Georgia to the status of slaves reflected a growing reality, especially in the upcountry, but not a full reality, especially in the lowcountry. More significantly, the state's incorporation of proslavery interpretations ignored a complicated history under which free blacks and free people of color had enjoyed some rights and privileges of citizenship, if not full equality. Lumpkin's flat portrait of free black life failed utterly to convey the historical or actual experiences of free black life. Real life was more complex. Yet it was Lumpkin's perspective that emerged as the official voice of the state. When Georgia's authorities approved the state's first comprehensive code of laws in 1860, the section on free people of color bore Lumpkin's imprint. That portion of *The Code of the State of Georgia* was written by Thomas R. R. Cobb, who compiled and codified recently enacted laws and judicial decisions, particularly those of his chief mentor and father-in-law, Lumpkin. Based largely upon the justice's opinion in the *Bryan* case, the code stated that the "free person of color is entitled to no right of citizenship."[49] The unconditional nature of this assertion stood in stark contrast to citizenship laws in the North as well as those from the early national period in Georgia. Though adopted by Georgia's authorities on the eve of the Civil War, the code would serve as the legal foundation for the state following secession from the Union. With all traces of the ambiguity that characterized prior state laws removed, the code reflected the racial ideology at the core of the new Confederate nation, a rigid and absolute notion of white supremacy. Georgia's rebirth under the Confederacy allowed the state authorities to expunge completely the original sin that had failed to impose a clear and concrete status on the free people of color. As a result, Georgia became a white man's republic.

## Notes

1. For more studies on Joseph Lumpkin and his role in slave law in Georgia, see Mason W. Stephenson and D. Grier Stephenson Jr., "'To Protect and Defend': Joseph Henry Lumpkin, the Supreme Court of Georgia, and Slavery," *Emory Law Journal* 25 (Summer 1976): 579–608; John Philip Reid, "Lessons of Lumpkin: Review of Recent Literature on Law, Comity, and the Impending Crisis," *William and Mary Law Review* 23 (Summer 1982): 571–624; Timothy S. Huebner, *The Southern Judicial Tradition: State Judges and Sectional Distinctiveness, 1790–1890* (Athens: University of Georgia Press, 1999); Paul DeForest Hicks, *Joseph Henry Lumpkin: Georgia's First Chief Justice* (Athens: University of Georgia Press, 2002).

2. Huebner, *The South Judicial Tradition*, 71–77.

3. Hicks, *Joseph Henry Lumpkin*, 56.

4. *American Colonization Society* v. *Gartrell*, 23 Ga. 464 (1857).

5. For more on the creation of the state supreme court in Georgia, see Watson W. Jennison, *Cultivating Race: The Expansion of Slavery in Georgia, 1750–1860* (Lexington: University Press of Kentucky, 2012), 295–98; Hicks, *Joseph Henry Lumpkin*, 86–97.

6. Stephenson and Stephenson, "'To Protect and Defend,'" 581–82; Hicks, *Joseph Henry Lumpkin*, 125.

7. *Niles Register*, 28:238–40. Troup continued to reiterate his views in subsequent messages. In one instance he warned of the dangers posed by the growing antislavery sentiments in the country and its potential impact on Georgia should residents fail to act to protect their property and way of life.

8. The literature on proslavery thought is vast and continues to grow. For a recent interpretation, see Lacy K. Ford, *Deliver Us from Evil: The Slavery Question in the Old South* (New York: Oxford University Press, 2009). For an informative and illuminating overview, see Drew Gilpin Faust, *The Ideology of Slavery: Proslavery Thought in the Antebellum South, 1830–1860* (Baton Rouge: Louisiana State University Press, 1981), 1–20.

9. "Judge Lumpkin's Report on Law Reform," *Milledgeville Recorder*, December 4, 1849.

10. Joseph Henry Lumpkin to daughter Callie, October 13, 1853, as quoted in Hicks, *Joseph Henry Lumpkin*, 131–32. See also Huebner, *The Southern Judicial Tradition*, 87.

11. *American Colonization Society v. Gartrell*, 23 Ga. 464 (1857). On the biblical curse see Stephen R. Haynes, *Noah's Curse: The Biblical Justification of American Slavery* (New York: Oxford University Press, 2002).

12. *American Colonization Society v. Gartrell*, 23 Ga. 464 (1857).

13. *Seaborn C. Bryan v. Hugh [sic] Walton*, 14 Ga. 185 (1853), 205–6.

14. The state supreme court issued rulings on the case in 1853, 1856, and 1864. Several recent studies have examined this fascinating case. For alternative interpretations of the *Bryan* case see Martha Hodes, *White Women, Black Men: Illicit Sex in the 19th-Century South* (New Haven: Yale University Press, 1997), and Ariela Gross, *What Blood Won't Tell: A History of Race on Trial in America* (Cambridge: Harvard University Press, 2008).

15. *Seaborn C. Bryan v. Hugh [sic] Walton*, 14 Ga. 185 (1853), 197.

16. Ibid., 198. Lumpkin invoked a series of laws that restricted the rights of free people of color to support his larger argument about the place of free people of color in Georgia society, but he did not mention that most of the laws had only been enacted in the past three decades. Rather, Lumpkin portrayed the prohibitions against blacks as having been on the books forever. Many of the restrictions against free people of color that Lumpkin identified were created in 1829, after David Walker's *Appeal to the Coloured Citizens of the World* surfaced in Georgia, and in 1833 and 1835, when the legislature revised the state penal code. *Acts of the General Assembly, of the State of Georgia, Passed in Milledgeville, at Annual Session in November and December, 1829* (Milledgeville: Camak & Ragland, 1830), 168–75; *Acts of the General Assembly, of the State of Georgia, Passed in Milledgeville, at Annual Session in November and December, 1833* (Milledgeville: Polhill & Fort, 1834), 143–217, 226–29; *Acts of the General Assembly, of the State of Georgia, Passed in Milledgeville, at Annual Session in November and December, 1835* (Milledgeville: John A. Cuthbert, 1836), 264–69.

17. *Seaborn C. Bryan v. Hugh [sic] Walton*, 14 Ga. 185 (1853), 202.

18. Ibid.

19. Ibid., 198.

20. For a broader discussion of the structural and demographic changes that occurred in Georgia in the first half of the nineteenth century and their consequences on the political system in the state, see Jennison, *Cultivating Race*.

21. *The State v. Philpot* (1831), in G. M. Dudley, ed., *Reports of the Decisions Made by the Judges of the Superior Courts of Law and Chancery of the State of Georgia* (Charlottesville: Michie Company, 1903), 375–85, quote on 377.

22. *Seaborn C. Bryan v. Hugh [sic] Walton*, 14 Ga. 185 (1853), 204.

23. Horatio Marbury and William H. Crawford, eds., *Digest of the laws of the state of Georgia, from its settlement as a British province, in 1775, to the session of the General Assembly in 1800, inclusive. Comprehending all the laws passed within the above periods, and now in force, alphabetically arranged under their respective titles also the state constitutions of 1777 and 1789, with the additions and amendments in 1795, and the constitution of 1798 . . .* (Savannah: Seymour, Woolhoster & Stebbins, 1802), 203–7.

24. *Acts of the General Assembly of the State of Georgia: Passed at Louisville, in January*

*and February, 1799* (Louisville: Alexander McMillen, 1799), 118–19; *Acts of the General Assembly of the State of Georgia: Passed at Louisville, in November and December, 1799* (Augusta: John E. Smith, 1800), 5–6.

25. Laurent Dubois, *A Colony of Citizens: Revolution and Slave Emancipation in the French Caribbean, 1787–1804* (Chapel Hill: University of North Carolina Press, 2004).

26. For more on the history of free people of color in Jamaica and their position in society over time, see Gad J. Heuman, *Between Black and White: Race, Politics, and the Free Coloreds in Jamaica, 1792–1865* (Westport, Conn.: Greenwood Press, 1981). For contemporary white accounts of distinctions among free people of color in Jamaica, see Bryan Edwards, *The History, Civil and Commercial, of the British West Indies* (London, 1819), 2:18–38; Edward Long, *The History of Jamaica: Reflections on its Situation, Settlements, Inhabitants, Climate, Products, Commerce, Laws, and Government* (London, 1774), 2:320–37. See also Edward Brathwaite, *The Development of Creole Society in Jamaica, 1770–1820* (Oxford: Clarendon Press, 1971), 166–75, 188–92; Mavis Christine Campbell, *The Dynamics of Change in a Slave Society: A Sociopolitical History of the Free Coloreds of Jamaica, 1800–1865* (Rutherford, N.J.: Fairleigh Dickinson University Press, 1976), 39–117; Gad Heuman, "The Free Coloreds in Jamaican Slave Society," in *The Slavery Reader*, ed. Gad Heuman and James Walvin (New York: Routledge, 2003), 654–67.

27. "AN ACT For the better Ordering and Governing Negroes and other Slaves in this Province and to prevent the inveigling or carrying away Slaves from their Masters or Employers, 1765," *Colonial Records of the State of Georgia*, 18:659–60.

28. The provision pertaining to free mulattoes and mestizos has proven to be a difficult historical problem to solve, though several historians have made note of the measure in recent decades. Recently, Ben Marsh labeled the provision "an exceptional piece of legislation" reflecting the "interracial idiosyncrasy" that marked the racial order in Georgia prior to the 1750s and 1760s. His analysis and use of the term "begrudgingly" to describe whites' support for the measure illustrate his dismissal of its relevance. Ben Marsh, *Georgia's Frontier Women: Female Fortunes in a Southern Colony* (Athens: University of Georgia Press, 2007), 145. For a different interpretation of the importance of the 1765 provision, see Carl N. Degler, *Neither Black Nor White: Slavery and Race Relations in Brazil and the United States* (New York: Macmillan, 1971), 240–41. Degler referred to the measure as part of his analysis of the development of racial attitudes among the English, asserting that it indicated that "the idea of defining a Negro by ancestry was not a foregone conclusion among Englishmen." Despite the fact that it failed to become law, Degler states, "in this instance a mainland English colony came close to legalizing the mulatto escape hatch just as was done in Jamaica."

29. *Bryan v. Walton*, 20 Ga. 480 (1856), 492, 491, 495, 496, 501, 494. During the testimony in the trial, one of the witnesses, Joseph Bush, described James Nunez as "an American" whose "father was a Portuguese." He "passed as a white man." The witnesses in the trial gave strikingly different interpretations of James. Some suggested he was white or part Indian, while others depicted him as clearly a person of African descent. Of course, the testimony was based on recollections that were more than forty years old. James Nunez died between 1809 and 1813.

30. *U.S. Census, 1790, 1800, 1810, 1820, 1830, 1840, 1850, and 1860.* For earlier studies of

free people of color in Georgia, see Ralph B. Flanders, "The Free Negro in Ante-Bellum Georgia," *North Carolina Historical Review* 9 (July 1932): 250–72; W. McDowell Rogers, "Free Negro Legislation in Georgia before 1865," *Georgia Historical Quarterly* 16 (March 1932): 27–37; Edward F. Sweat, "Social Status of the Free Negro in Antebellum Georgia," *Negro History Bulletin* 21 (March 1958): 129–31; Edward F. Sweat, "Free Negroes in Ante-Bellum Georgia" (Ph.D. diss., Indiana University, 1957); Edward Sweat, *Free Blacks and the Law in Antebellum Georgia* (Atlanta: Southern Center for Studies in Public Policy, Clark College, 1976).

31. *U.S. Census, 1790, 1800, 1810, 1820, 1830, 1840, 1850, and 1860.*

32. Atlanta City Ordinance Book, May 20, 1853, Atlanta History Center. Those free people of color who were arrested under the ordinance were to be "hired out at public outcry" to a person who would pay their fine.

33. *Atlanta Weekly Intelligencer*, April 26, 1855.

34. Atlanta Ordinance Book, May 20, 1859. See also Atlanta City Council Minutes, vol. 3, May 6, 10, 13, 1859.

35. For examples of petitions, see Atlanta City Council Minutes, vol. 2, January 26, March 6, 1855.

36. *Atlanta Daily Intelligencer*, January 9, 1860.

37. Atlanta City Council Minutes, vol. 2, June 6, 1855.

38. Ira Berlin, *Slaves without Masters: The Free Negro in the Antebellum South* (New York: Pantheon, 1974).

39. For example, the number of free men of color in Savannah identified as craftsmen grew steadily over the antebellum era, reaching sixty-two in 1848 and sixty-eight in 1860. According to the English traveler James Silk Buckingham, "coloured persons" dominated "the laborious trades" while slaves performed "nearly all the severe and menial labor." James Silk Buckingham, *The Slave States of America*, vol. 1 (London: Fisher, Son, & Co., 1842), 122; Joseph Bancroft, *Census of the City of Savannah, 1848* (Savannah: Edward J. Purse, 1848), 16; *U.S. Census, 1860*; Michele Gillespie, *Free Labor in an Unfree World: White Artisans in Slaveholding Georgia, 1789–1860* (Athens: University of Georgia Press, 2000), 165.

40. J. P. Tustin, "Andrew C. Marshall, 1786–1856," in *Annals of the American Pulpit*, ed. William B. Sprague (Charleston, 1859), 257–58. See also Charles Lyell, *A Second Visit to the United States of North America* (London: John Murray, 1849), 2:2–3. For more on Marshall see Whittington B. Johnson, "Andrew C. Marshall: A Black Religious Leader of Antebellum Savannah," *Georgia Historical Quarterly* 69 (Summer 1985): 173–92.

41. Whittington B. Johnson, "Free African American Women in Savannah, 1800–1860: Affluence and Autonomy amid Adversity," *Georgia Historical Quarterly* 76 (Summer 1992): 273–75. See also Loren Schweninger, "Property-Owning Free African-American Women in the South, 1800–1870," *Journal of Women's History* 1 (Winter 1990): 13–44.

42. Loren Schweninger, *Black Property Owners in the South, 1790–1915* (Urbana: University of Illinois Press, 1990), 70; Whittington B. Johnson, *Black Savannah, 1788–1864* (Fayetteville: University of Arkansas Press, 1996), 62; Julia Floyd Smith, *Slavery and Rice Culture in Low Country Georgia, 1750–1860* (Knoxville: University of Tennessee Press, 1985), 196.

43. Richard Arnold, for example, exerted great efforts to protect those free people of color under his guardianship, including Georgiana Kelly, Hannah Cohen, and Maria Cohen. Other prominent elite whites in Savannah served as guardians, including Richard Richardson for Andrew Marshall, Richard Stites for Simon Jackson, and Mordecai Myers for Jack Gibbons. Johnson, *Black Savannah*, 147–49.

44. For example, Sarah Ann Black, who became nominally free when her mother purchased her freedom at the age of fifteen, considered herself "married" to John Washington, a white man. Black relied upon another white man to serve as a guardian and hold her property. Sarah Ann Black Deposition, April 14, 1874, Sarah Ann Black Allowed Claim, Chatham County, Georgia, RG 217, National Archives, College Park, Maryland. See also Johnson, *Black Savannah*, 77–78. By 1860 mulattoes accounted for roughly 70 percent of Savannah's population of free people of color.

45. Richard D. Arnold to A. P. Merrill, May 23, 1854, in Richard H. Shyrock, ed., *Letters of Richard D. Arnold, M.D., 1808–1876, Mayor of Savannah, Georgia, First Secretary of the American Medical Association* (Durham: Duke University Press, 1929), 66; Richard D. Arnold to Sol Cohen, September 29, 1854, ibid., 71.

46. Richard D. Arnold to Joe H. Gressoin, November 15, 1847, ibid., 32.

47. *Milledgeville Southern Recorder*, December 18, 1860.

48. Hicks, *Joseph Henry Lumpkin*, 89–90.

49. R. H. Clark, T. R. R. Cobb, and D. Irwin, codifiers, *The Code of the State of Georgia* (Atlanta: John H. Seals, 1861), 320–21. For biographical information on Cobb, see William B. McCash, *Thomas R. R. Cobb: The Making of a Southern Nationalist* (Macon, Ga.: Mercer University Press, 1982).

# 3

Free People of Color, Expulsion, and Enslavement in the Antebellum South

EMILY WEST

Free people of color in the antebellum United States were excluded from legal citizenship as defined in the 1790 Naturalization Act because they were not "free white persons." Like their enslaved counterparts, then, southern free blacks were excluded from legal marriage, although most black people, whether enslaved or free, strove to choose their own life partners and live as couples regardless of their status before the law. Southern free people of color were also unable to vote, and many faced considerable hardships in their attempts to earn a living. Moreover, during the antebellum era white concerns about the very existence of free people of color within southern states, both old and new, increased, and historian Evelyn Nakano Glenn has argued they were increasingly perceived to be "anti-citizens."[1] As notions of citizenship in the eyes of whites grew ever more exclusionary, then, the declining status of free people of color was formalized before law. On a national level, in the 1857 *Dred Scott* decision the Supreme Court declared that free people of color never had been and therefore never could be citizens.[2] But even before this time, at a local and state level, southern legislatures had been moving from the 1830s onward to restrict the freedoms afforded free people of color, and by the 1850s their aim was the removal of what they perceived to be an anomaly in the slave South: a free black person. During the 1850s, then, southern states moved toward the expulsion or enslavement of all free people of color, who were ultimately saved from either fate only by the Civil War.

So by the eve of war, the ideas of free people of color about concepts such as "liberty," "citizenship," and "equality" were superseded by the practicalities—the difficulties—of coping with everyday life. The majority of free blacks increasingly prioritized their intimate ties of affection within their affective communities and the ability economically to provide for their families before all else. Thinking of citizenship in terms of liberal entitlements to legal and political rights was generally the preserve of white members of society, and an investigation into citizenship's meanings at this uncertain time can expose some of the other white paradigms within which the lives of mid-nineteenth-century men and women have been framed. For example, most free black southern men were not able sufficiently to provide for their families, so women could not rely on them for economic well-being. Free black women, therefore, tended not only to work more outside the home than many of their white counterparts but also to encompass broader definitions of maternity and motherhood, in which providing for one's family in an economic sense was as important as the more "white" ideal of motherhood as the embodiment of "care and nurture."[3] Antebellum southern blacks therefore conceptualized citizenship not only in practical terms of providing but also as more of a process of belonging—and being recognized as belonging—to a family, group, or community.

This meant that notions of romantic love for southern blacks stood in stark contrast to those of whites. Citizenship granted the right to legal marriage, and it is often assumed that in the early nineteenth century wedlock was entered for reasons of property and pragmatism, but this was common only within white society. The enslaved were early pioneers in setting up life partnerships for romantic reasons notwithstanding their wedlock's lack of legal status.[4] And the same was true for many free black families. Devoid of wealth, they were able to marry for romantic love, and they placed their families before all else, including a legal citizenship that bore no relevance to their everyday lives. More specifically, exploring the lives of late-antebellum free people of color through the prism of enslavement petitions they submitted to state legislatures and county courts also reveals the extent to which marital ties of affection crossed the line from slavery to freedom. Historian Jeff Forret has recently stressed that relations between the enslaved and poor whites were often more complex and less hostile than has hitherto been recognized, and free people of color can be built into this analysis as well.[5] Many free people of color had enslaved spouses and lived in families that existed "somewhere in between" slavery and freedom. Historian John Wess Grant has labeled these as "stranded" families in his recent research into their lives in antebellum

Richmond.[6] But this was not just an urban phenomenon, and research into petitions for "voluntary slavery" suggests that such families existed across the South. As levels of racial hostility escalated in the 1850s, these people turned inward toward their families for support, in keeping with what "citizenship" meant to them, and across the South some free people of color sought recourse to the law in requesting enslavement.

Exploring the relationship of free people of color to "voluntary enslavement" legislation can, therefore, provide a framework for understanding their position in society and their attitudes toward legal citizenship on the eve of war. The idea of "voluntary slavery" is, of course, inherently problematic, and philosophers have grappled with the concept. Traditional liberal ideologies of slavery had supported the notion that "choosing" enslavement was conceptually impossible. Since slavery is regarded as a condition based upon compulsion and coercion, "voluntary enslavement" therefore involved a contradiction in the notion of liberty.[7] However, historians have shown that "voluntary slavery" existed in some ancient societies and in Africa, Asia, premodern Europe, and South America.[8] This type of bondage was often seen as a way of escaping financial difficulties, and sometimes it involved the sale of children as well as adults. In this sense, then, some parallels can be drawn with the petitioners in the antebellum South.[9] Notably, too, in premodern societies such as these, it has been argued, the antithesis of enslavement was not "'freedom' qua autonomy but rather 'belonging.'"[10] This resonates with free black southerners' notions of citizenship as a process of belonging. Freedom itself could be isolating for antebellum free people of color, especially when the threat of expulsion threatened familial separations across the free-slave divide.

Moreover, by opposing traditional liberal ideologies of enslavement, the very notion of "voluntary slavery" was not regarded as a conceptual impossibility by white slaveholders. They did not accept the view that "liberty" was, by definition, a positive good, and were thus able to convince themselves that the institution provided the enslaved with masters who protected them. They saw slavery as "a justifiable feature of well-ordered societies from ancient times to the present."[11] Therefore if the enslavement of blacks was "right" it could also be argued that white southerners had a moral duty to ensure that all remained in this condition.

During the 1850s and early 1860s, then, southern states debated compulsory enslavement, voluntary enslavement, and the expulsion of free people of color from their states of residence with an increasing degree of momentum, and all southern states were moving in the same direction. In seeking to expel or enslave free people of color, southern legislatures were taking them yet further away from any sense of citizenship and legal rights. While counterfactual history can be extremely problematic, it does seem as though free blacks were ultimately saved from bondage only through the Civil War and emancipation. And this was true even for states such as Louisiana, where a "mulatto elite" was traditionally deemed to have held a "middling" position between black and white.[12] Yet, various restrictions were imposed upon free blacks in this state (just as they were elsewhere) as concerns about their presence rose. For example, restrictions on free blacks' entry were passed from the 1840s onward.[13] The state also prohibited any future emancipation of slaves in 1857.[14]

Robert Reinders criticized historians' preoccupation with an overly romantic portrayal of "free negroes" in antebellum New Orleans as early as 1962, noting how their status steadily eroded over the 1850s.[15] Moreover, Louisiana legislated on voluntary enslavement in a similar way to other states, and free people of color likewise also petitioned for enslavement there. For example, Judith Kelleher Schafer devotes considerable time and attention to the complex motivations behind several enslavement requests in New Orleans.[16] Schafer quite rightly regards voluntary enslavement as the "culmination of the 'positive good' theory of slavery—that people of African descent lived happily as slaves and found freedom inconvenient or miserable."[17]

Throughout the South, hostility toward the quarter of a million free people of color—the majority of whom were poor agricultural laborers—had been growing since the early 1830s as they were increasingly regarded as anachronistic and threatening in a race-based society where slaves were black and whites were free.[18] John Boles has argued that growing sectional tensions caused paranoia among white southerners and that debates over enslavement or exclusion were a logical extension of this, despite the important economic contribution of free people of color through their labor.[19] Yet in a context where a proslavery writer such as George Fitzhugh could proclaim "A free negro! Why, the very term seems an absurdity," the momentum for change in the decade before war was placed behind proslavery forces.[20]

Demands to enslave free people of color were put forward on various grounds. One argument claimed that since slavery was morally a good thing, a failure to impose bondage would be wrong in the eyes of God.[21]

Enslavement would also have practical benefits. There would be no free blacks to assist runaways, the supply of labor would be enlarged, and new slaves could be sold to poor whites, helpfully defusing potential class conflict. The opportunities for race-based insurrection and rebellion would therefore also be diminished. The mooting of ideas about enslavement and expulsion within state legislatures was therefore linked, and while debates over the *enforced* expulsion and enslavement of free people of color were covered fairly extensively in the work of Ira Berlin in the 1970s, he does not address in any depth the linked but ideologically separate issue of permitting free people of color to choose bondage voluntarily. But for many states, permitting voluntary enslavement was the lesser—and easier—option. Shifting the onus onto the freedpeople themselves, it quelled the humanitarian doubts some held about enforced bondage.[22]

So in the 1850s the idea of "permitting" free people of color to "select" bondage for themselves grew in popularity. Several states passed laws that facilitated it, and others explored it in their legislative debates. Legal provision was made for voluntary enslavement in Alabama, Florida, Louisiana, Maryland, Tennessee, Texas, and Virginia, while South Carolina and Georgia approved of it by means of special acts of the legislature in individual cases.[23] As a whole, then, southern states can be characterized in terms of the similarities, rather than the differences, in how they approached the issue. Michael Johnson and James Roark have also stressed the confidence granted to southern lawmakers after the *Dred Scott* decision, when southern states moved to deliberate, not just on voluntary bondage, but also on the enforced enslavement and expulsion of free people of color with new vigor.[24] However, Arkansas was the only state to legislate on the enforced expulsion of free people of color before the war, when it harshly decreed that all free blacks living in the state had to leave by the beginning of January 1860.[25] Contrary to existing historiography, after this date I have found three people of color who were captured by local sheriffs in Pulaski County and forced into slavery (suggesting that, at least in some areas, the law was enforced), and three more in the state who petitioned county courts for enslavement.[26] In a broader context, legislation such as that passed in Arkansas seems to have related primarily to matters of timing: throughout the South there was a hardening of racial attitudes as a sense of insecurity about the future of slavery rose, taking free people of color yet further away from legal inclusion in society through citizenship.

Surviving cases of free people of color seeking recourse to the law—both before and after states' enslavement legislation—in an attempt to enter bondage or, occasionally, to return to bondage are extremely scant. Moreover, attempting to evaluate some of their motivations for doing so is also problematic. Motivations were often unclear, and petitions for enslavement could be made both to state legislatures and to local county courts. Yet some states have no surviving petitions about any issue at all, and many county courthouses were destroyed, along with their records, during the Civil War.[27] Collating all surviving enslavement requests may not, therefore, be representative of how many petitions were actually made. It is also mostly unknown who wrote the petitions. In some cases the documents are marked with an "X," and while the majority of those seeking enslavement were illiterate, the "real" writers of the petitions do not give their names. Sometimes, however, petitions had attached affidavits or supporting documents by community members or justices of the peace vouching for the petitioners' claims.[28]

There were only six instances where a petition was explicitly written by someone other than the petitioner. One of these concerned three men returning from Liberia. The other five were written by prospective owners.[29] In these cases, as well as others, of course, suspicions are aroused as to the true motives of those who were "choosing" bondage. Frustratingly, the outcomes of the vast majority of cases are either unknown or the decision was "postponed." Sometimes cases were referred to a committee; at other times, "approved" or "rejected" is written across the bottom of the petition. Yet it seems that the committees either never met or failed to report and record their findings. Only thirty-nine enslavement requests were granted, and ten were rejected or "dismissed."[30]

Enslavement petitions are also extremely atypical. I found only 143 enslavement petitions—of whom just ten had previously been enslaved—and there were a quarter of a million free people of color in the South in 1860.[31] These findings are presented in table 3.1.

Enslavement petitions are not therefore representative of the aspirations of the majority of southern free blacks, and their clustering around the time of legislative debates on the issue shows that during "normal" times, free people of color did not want enslavement. But their atypicality does not mean the petitions are insignificant for historians. On the contrary, Peter Parish argued some time ago for a more detailed and nuanced consideration of the "edges" of slavery in order to shed light on the

Table 3.1. Enslavement Requests by State

| State | Enslavement Petitions |
| --- | --- |
| Alabama | 16 |
| Arkansas | 8 |
| Delaware | 3 |
| Florida | 5 |
| Georgia | 3 |
| Louisiana | 13 |
| Mississippi | 14 |
| North Carolina | 27 |
| South Carolina | 8 |
| Tennessee | 4 |
| Texas | 7 |
| Virginia | 35 |
| **Totals** | **143** |

institution as a whole.[32] From the enslavement and expulsion debates and the discourses within the petitions, then, historians can explore a whole range of issues, including notions of citizenship and legal status, the economic conditions and the impact of legislation upon free people of color, the gendered roles of free blacks, marital and other familial ties across the slave-free divide, relationships across the color line, and the broader proslavery defense in the Old South. All these issues have relevance to how free blacks viewed their own sense of belonging in society, regardless of their citizenship before the law. Finally, enslavement petitions show that a lack of legal citizenship rendered the line between slavery and freedom blurred on the eve of the Civil War and that, especially in terms of economic situation, the two groups on either side of this line had much in common.

Of the 143 enslavement requests, 53 percent were from men, 39 percent were from women, and 8 percent were from family groups. Gender profiles were thus fairly equal. Moreover, nine women had children whom they included in their petitions. This is significant, as it suggests that men and women perceived the entering of bondage in rather different ways. For free black men, a request for enslavement was mostly an individualistic pursuit. Many who were attached to enslaved women would have had children already living in bondage. However, for some of the women seeking slavery a decision had to be made about whether bondage was desirable for their offspring as well as themselves, especially in states such as Florida, Louisiana, and Texas where the law permitted the bondage of free black children under fourteen. In contrast, both Virginia and Tennessee forbade the enslavement of children in this manner.[33] Moreover, while Ira Berlin wrote some time ago that most of those who sought enslavement were "paupers decrepit with age," the reality is actually much more complex. The majority of petitioners were adults of childbearing age, and a majority of the women were in their twenties.[34]

Explanations for enslavement requests for bondage fall into four distinct but sometimes overlapping areas, and in quantifying motivations (as explained later) some petitioners hence needed to be included twice. First, it is important to note that enslavement petitions were motivated not just through any "initiative" on the part of free people of color but also through oppressive measures designed by southern states to force free blacks in this direction. Some were tricked or cajoled by potential masters into submitting petitions, and a search of relevant census schedules indicated that the majority of potential owners were not from the ranks of the wealthy. They tended to own only a few slaves or none at all, and they saw their acquisition of free people of color as a way of consolidating their position in the slaveholding class. For example, in Wilkinson County, Mississippi, the legislature permitted Jim Wall to become the slave of Daniel Williams in 1860. Wall was a laborer, married to Susannah, who had four children under the age of nine. Williams does not appear in the 1860 census as a slaveowner, and Wall was married to a free black woman rather than one who was enslaved. Williams may have cajoled Wall into petitioning for enslavement for his own financial gain, perhaps because Wall was struggling to support his wife and children.[35]

More broadly, using the 1860 census it was possible to calculate the number of slaves belonging to sixty-seven of the total number of potential owners cited in enslavement requests, representing just under half the total number of petitions. Of these, fifty-four individuals (80.6 percent) held fewer than twenty slaves, the great majority. This information is presented in table 3.2. Historian Peter Kolchin places the median holdings of slaves, for the total South, at twenty-three for 1860.[36] The significant point, then, is that more than three-quarters of potential owners found here owned

Table 3.2. Slave Ownership by Potential Owners

| | |
|---|---|
| Fewer than five slaves | 20 (29.9%) |
| Fewer than ten slaves | 37 (55.2%) |
| Fewer than twenty slaves | 54 (80.6%) |
| More than twenty slaves | 13 (19.4%) |

fewer than twenty enslaved people. They did not come from the ranks of the super-wealthy and were seeking either to consolidate their position as slaveholders or to buy their way into the peculiar institution.[37]

Enslavement was also a way in which individuals could seek a way out of a specific debt or legal problems, or impoverishment, all of which could be a consequence of lack of legal citizenship. For example, in Mississippi, Billard Filmore requested enslavement from the state legislature in 1859. He had been charged with the attempted murder of a slave and wanted to belong to James J. Lindsey of Fulton. Lindsey was a lawyer, and Filmore wrote that he was "desirous of procuring counsel in his defense."[38] Filmore seems to have regarded enslavement as a way in which to "buy" Lindsey's services, which most likely he was unable to afford. His petition appears to have been successful, as James J. Lindsey of Itawamba County appears in 1860 slave schedules as owning one twenty-four-year-old mulatto man, his only slave.[39]

Unsurprisingly, poverty underscored many of the enslavement requests, and poverty could also be a consequence of non-citizenship. As Judith Shklar has noted, American citizenship includes the ability not just to vote but also to earn.[40] But an 1858 petition to the South Carolina Assembly highlighted the inability of free people of color to earn. Lucy Andrews claimed she was isolated from both white and slave communities and that she wanted to belong to her husband's master, Henry Duncan. She argued that she wanted to raise a family yet was unable to support them as a free black woman. Undoubtedly playing on white sentiments, she professed to believe that "Slaves are far more happy, and enjoy themselves far better than she does in her present, isolated condition of freedom." She therefore "prays that your honorable body would enact a law authorising and permitting her to go voluntarily into slavery, and select her own master."[41] Any motivation Andrews may have had for enslavement related not only to poverty and discrimination but also to the love she had for her husband, Robbin. She wanted to be with him and to live with him rather than be anywhere else, regardless of her status. Poverty therefore provides a backdrop—an undercurrent—in explaining the motivations for enslavement, yet it was not the only causal factor, and Lucy Andrews prioritized her family relationships above her legal status and any desire for "citizenship." Furthermore, in flattering the decision makers in their desire for their petitions to be passed, free people of color were actually placing primary importance on their own survival, be it economic or related to their emotional attachments. It is no accident that many of the petitioners appealed to the perceived benevolent worldview of the white slaveholding class through the language employed in their requests.

More tentatively, the enslavement petitions of women (some with children included) who appear to be single and of childbearing age are revealing of interracial sexual liaisons. Evidence here is scant, and the petitions often raise more questions than they answer. Following Stephanie Camp's notion that, when written evidence is limited, historians need to employ their imaginations and to speculate about meanings, it can be suggested that some enslavement requests may have come from free women of color who were involved in intimate relationships with white men with whom they wanted to remain.[42] One rather positive perspective is therefore that voluntary enslavement played a distinctive role in the political strategies of free women of color, who did not shy away from recourse to legal action when they were seeking to improve their quality of life. Did these women envisage that life as a slave would be better than being free? Laura Edwards has written extensively about the use of the legal system by antebellum enslaved and white women.[43] Might free women of color have done the same?

Alternatively, these women could have been victims of sexual abuse, and their requests merely a manipulative ploy by potential owners to increase the value of their chattel. Frustratingly, the petitions often refuse to divulge the "real" intent of petitioners or potential owners, yet if white men used their sexual relationships with black women as a tool to increase their property and their control, this is a realm of exploitation that has been somewhat overlooked. Furthermore, while census evidence can be used to trace the ages, marital profiles, and occupations of white men, neither age nor marital status served as a barrier to white men seeking sexual satisfaction from black females.[44] Some examples here include

Ann Archie of Marshall County, Mississippi, who wanted enslavement for herself, age twenty-two, and her daughter, Julia, to Andrew Caldwell, "with whom your petitioner has long been acquainted and whom she would prefer to live together with her offspring as slaves."[45] In 1861, Ellen Ransom petitioned for enslavement to Leon Perry of Franklin County, North Carolina. Records show that Ellen was "about" twenty-six in 1860. She appears to have lived with her mother, a washerwoman, and three siblings. Perry would have been thirty-one in 1860, and a farmer. Seemingly unmarried in 1860, he does not appear on the slave schedules as a slaveowner.[46] If Perry was a "poor white" he would most likely have come into contact with free blacks and the enslaved. Might he have been having an intimate relationship with Ellen Ransom?

A more difficult case is that of Celia Lynch, who requested to become the slave of Dr. J. T. Watson of Martin County, North Carolina, in 1861. She wrote that she desired a "legal protector in health, in sickness, and old age," and it is, initially at least, perhaps rather ironic that her wording is similar to that of many marriage vows. Yet, in reproducing the discourse of marriage and in the desire to appear "respectable," notions of liberty and obligation are explained in a language that straddles both issues.[47] Moreover, in making choices about what "citizenship" meant to them, love and marriage carried much resonance for free people of color seeking a sense of "belonging." J. T. Watson was a married physician, and in the 1860 census a twenty-three-year-old "mulatto" woman named Celia appears within his household. He also owned sixteen slaves in 1860, so perhaps she was married to one of his enslaved men and did not want to be parted from him.[48] This also raises the question of whether Celia knew that forced expulsion was being debated within the North Carolina legislature and was trying to make a preemptive strike. While the answers to these questions are unknown, cases such as these shed much light on ties between the enslaved and free and between blacks and whites, and the political awareness of free black women.

Finally, the petitions reveal much about the immediate, everyday concerns of free people of color under threat. In these harsh economic and social circumstances, free blacks turned inward to focus upon more intimate ties, namely, their attachments to their families, homes, and communities. A necessarily adaptable sense of belonging was more important to free people of color than citizenship under the law in a society where slavery and racial discrimination meant systematic exclusion.[49] The motivations behind enslavement requests are thus more complex than has hitherto been recognized, as were the affective ties that bound free people of color to the enslaved. Indeed, quantifying the motivations behind enslavement revealed that love for family members was the important explanatory factor behind these often desperate requests.[50] The affection felt for an enslaved spouse, and sometimes for children, too, was considered more important, to some, than the benefits of liberty or "citizenship," and people's families assumed priority, especially where people were afraid of being separated from their loved ones in the future. While it was not uncommon for free people of color to buy, or to attempt to buy, their enslaved loved ones—what Larry Koger has referred to as "nominal slavery"—to submit oneself to bondage for the love of another was surely the ultimate sacrifice.[51]

A related issue here concerns the desire to maintain broader familial and community ties. For example, there were a couple of petitions from those who had experienced failed migrations to Liberia and were desirous of returning to their previous homes and kin networks, even if that meant reentering slavery. Homesickness and the desire to be reunited with beloved kin appear to be the primary motivations in these cases, with some individuals struggling to adjust to life in Africa.[52] An 1850 petition on behalf of Mark, Claiborne, and Eppes Collier described how they had been sent to Liberia through the will of Nancy Cain but that the three men apparently preferred "American slavery to Liberian freedom."[53]

The often poignant testimony of the petitioners—both men and women—reveals the extent of this romantic attachment to spouses, as well as for wider familial networks. As early as 1813 in Virginia, a former slave named Lucinda, recently emancipated by the will of Mary Matthews, explained that she was unwilling to leave the state, as required by law. Her husband was enslaved in King George County, and "nothing could make her leave him, not even her freedom." She therefore requested a return to bondage as the slave of her husband's owner.[54] The significant point is that Lucinda wanted to belong to her husband's owner, not the family of her previous one. Likewise, Peggy Ann Martin of Davidson County, North Carolina, wanted to become the slave of her husband's owner, Henderson Adams. She had been married for the last five years, and described in her enslavement request of 1860 how "she is attached to her husband and does not wish to be separated from him."[55] Indeed, of the ten individuals found who were seeking reenslavement, only one asked that she belong to her former owner.[56]

Walker Fitch of Staunton, Augusta County, petitioned the Virginia legislature claiming he was "weary of freedom" and requesting enslavement to Michael G. Harman, the owner of his wife and children. Fitch was twenty-one in 1860 and lived with his mother, Margaret, and his sister, Elvira, both of whom were washerwomen. Michael Harman, master of Fitch's wife and enslaved children, owned twenty-four slaves. Despite impoverishment—Fitch was a laborer and unlikely to have made much money—the desire to live on a permanent basis with his beloved wife and offspring seems to have taken priority. He was also intrinsically bound up with Harman's family. The latter confirmed that he owned Fitch's wife and children and also that he "has had him in his employment for several years, and is willing to accept said Walker as his slave upon equitable terms."[57] Harman probably believed that owning Fitch's wife and offspring made it more likely the request would be granted. Also notable is Harman's prose in indicating that he would be "willing to accept" Fitch as a slave. The wording selected is typical slaveholder "benevolence," as though the responsibility of owning Fitch would outweigh the benefits he would bring as an enslaved worker.

In a tender and touching manner, enslavement petitions reveal the strength of marital and familial ties across the slave-free divide among the black population of the South, as well as some of the fears about enforced expulsion and its impact upon affective communities. Facing relentless hardships and discrimination, these free people of color did not think of slavery and freedom as two polar opposites, or in terms of fighting for legal citizenship and status. Instead they were motivated by more practical concerns about their everyday behavior: to live with families, within communities, in their homes, and to "belong."

The severity with which free blacks were treated increased sharply in the few years preceding the Civil War. During this anxious time southern states attempted to create an idealized biracial system where all whites were free and all blacks enslaved, and there was a flurry of debate and legislation over excluding or enslaving free people of color. Callous slaveholders or would-be slaveholders—anxious about their own future—also cajoled or pressured desperate and impoverished free blacks into petitioning for enslavement. In particular they exploited free people of color's emotional ties within a changing legal climate in a bid to increase their chattel. Some other white men may also have pressured free black women with whom they were having intimate relationships, whether consensual or not, into petitioning for enslavement. These admittedly rare examples remind us that American slavery had a harsh market at its heart, despite the public language of benevolence.

Because of all that enslavement petitions reveal, their relative absence in discussions of antebellum historiography is surprising. Moreover, as noted by Ira Berlin, the origins of post-emancipation racial institutions such as the black codes, sharecropping, and segregation can be found not in slavery but in antebellum legislation about free people of color.[58] But maybe the relative absence of discussion is not only a result of the petitions' scarcity: the very notion that individuals could "want" slavery can cause unease simply because of the implicit notion that to be a slave could be "better" than to be free. A minority of free people of color employed individualistic strategies of survival in placing their family ties and kin networks above their status before the law, yet these notions of individualism provide a useful, less celebratory way of considering issues of race, enslavement, and exclusion in the U.S. South. The actions of the petitioners are also illustrative of "agency," used here with caution in the light of Walter Johnson's call for a more nuanced use of the term, and a separation of "activity" from "resistance." Indeed, enslavement petitioners provide a prime case in point of individuals enacting the former but not the latter.[59]

At the margins of the regime, the blurry line between slavery and freedom on the eve of war, there were personal and economic ties that bound people together whether slave or free, black or white. Despite efforts by many white southerners to create a biracial society of free whites and enslaved blacks, there were significant interactions between the enslaved, free blacks, and poorer whites, and for the first two groups the relevance of legal citizenship was minimal. Instead, they constructed pragmatic and adaptable conceptualizations of "belonging" that prioritized their affective ties in their everyday struggle for economic survival. For every rare enslavement petition there were probably many more southern households where free people of color worked under a more ad hoc system of informal bondage or servitude without recourse to the law. In the American South there were slaveries rather than slavery, and a complex relationship between race and class. The regime can best be conceptualized as a range of unequal relationships with various permutations.

## Notes

1. Evelyn Nakano Glenn, *Unequal Freedom: How Race and Gender Shaped American Citizenship and Labor* (Cambridge: Harvard University Press, 2002), 33.

2. See Michael P. Johnson and James L. Roark, *Black Masters: A Free Family of Color in the Old South* (New York: Norton, 1984), 165.

3. See Camellia Cowling, "Defining Freedom: Women of Color and the Ending of Slavery in Havana and Rio de Janeiro, 1870–1888" (unpublished paper presented at the International Federation for Research in Women's History conference in Amsterdam, August 2010). See also Cowling, "Negotiating Freedom: Women of Colour and the Transition to Free Labour in Cuba, 1870–1886," *Slavery and Abolition* 26, no. 3 (2005): 377–91.

4. See Emily West, *Chains of Love: Slave Couples in Antebellum South Carolina* (Urbana: University of Illinois Press, 2004), chapter 3.

5. Jeff Forret, *Race Relations at the Margins: Slaves and Poor Whites in the Antebellum Southern Countryside* (Baton Rouge: Louisiana State University Press, 2006), 3–5.

6. See John Wess Grant, "Stranded Families: Free Colored Responses to Liberian Colonization and the Formation of Black Families in Nineteenth-Century Richmond, Virginia," in *The United States and West Africa: Interactions and Relations*, ed. Alusine Jalloh and Toyin Falola (New York: University of Rochester Press, 2008), 61–74.

7. I acknowledge the controversial nature of the term "voluntary slavery" here through placing it in quotation marks. John Locke argued against the notion of voluntary slavery, writing that a man cannot by own consent enslave himself to anyone. See Gary D. Glenn, "Inalienable Rights and Locke's Argument for Limited Government: Political Implications of a Right to Suicide," *Journal of Politics* 46, no. 1 (1984): 90–91. John Stuart Mill also opposed voluntary slavery contracts, writing, "The Principle of freedom cannot require that he should be free not to be free. It is not freedom to be allowed to alienate his freedom." John Stuart Mill, *On Liberty*, ed. and intro. Gertrude Himmelfarb (Harmondsworth: Penguin, 1974), 173. See also David Archard, "Freedom Not to Be Free: The Case of the Slavery Contract in J. S. Mill's *On Liberty*," *Philosophical Quarterly* 40 (1990): 453–65; John Kleinig, "John Stuart Mill and Voluntary Slavery Contracts," *Politics* 18, no. 2 (1983): 76–83; and Thomas D. Morris, *Southern Slavery and the Law, 1619–1860* (Chapel Hill: University of North Carolina Press, 1996), 32–34.

8. Historically, "voluntary" slavery has reflected different types of indentured servitude rather than the involuntary enslavement of Africans and their descendants. See Randy E. Barnett, *The Structure of Liberty: Justice and the Rule of Law* (Oxford: Oxford University Press, 1998), 78. For a summary of voluntary slavery in the ancient world, see Stefano Fenoaltea, "Slavery and Supervision in Comparative Perspective: A Model," *Journal of Economic History* 44, no. 3 (1984): 659. Information about the types of slavery, including "voluntary," existing in medieval and early modern Russia is included in Richard Hellie, "Recent Soviet Historiography on Medieval and Early Modern Russian Slavery," *Russian Review* 35, no. 1 (1976): 11, 17–18. See also Morris, *Southern Slavery*, 33 n. 82. A. E. M. Gibson writes of men who would submit themselves to bondage in West Africa as a means of avoiding fines in "Slavery in Western Africa," *Journal of the Royal African Society* 3, no. 9 (1903): 20–21, 40. "Voluntary" enslavement among sixteenth-century native

Brazilians is considered in Jose Eisenberg, "Cultural Encounters, Theoretical Adventures: The Jesuit Missions to the New World and the Justification of Voluntary Slavery," *History of Political Thought* 24, no. 3 (2003): 375–96.

9. See Stanley Engerman, "Slavery, Freedom and Sen," *Feminist Economics* 9 (2003): 193, and "Some Considerations Relating to Property Rights in Man," *Journal of Economic History* 33, no. 1 (1973): 44 n. 2.

10. See Frederick Cooper, Thomas C. Holt, and Rebecca J. Scott, *Beyond Slavery: Explorations of Race, Labor and Citizenship in Postemancipation Societies* (Chapel Hill: University of North Carolina Press, 2000), 5. The authors do acknowledge that both concepts were contested across time and space For more on the importance of "belonging" to a "local" place, see Jon-Christian Suggs, *Whispered Consolations: Law and Narrative in African American Life* (Ann Arbor: University of Michigan Press, 2000), 64–65.

11. For example, being a free person of color was, to many white southerners, a much "worse fate" than being enslaved to a white master. For more on proslavery thought in the Old South, see Elizabeth Fox-Genovese and Eugene Genovese, *The Mind of the Master Class: History and Faith in the Southern Slaveholders' Worldview* (New York: Cambridge University Press, 2005), 70 and 159.

12. See Peter J. Parish, *Slavery: History and Historians* (New York: Harper & Row, 1989), 108, for more on this historiography.

13. Annie Lee West Stahl, "The Free Negro in Ante-Bellum Louisiana," *Louisiana Historical Quarterly* 25 (1942): 330–33.

14. Robert C. Reinders, "The Decline of the New Orleans Free Negro in the Decade before the Civil War," *Journal of Mississippi History* 24 (1962): 97.

15. Ibid., 88–91.

16. Judith Kelleher Schafer, *Becoming Free, Remaining Free: Manumission and Enslavement in New Orleans, 1846–1862* (Baton Rouge: Louisiana State University Press, 2003), especially 153–55.

17. Ibid., 150.

18. Parish, in *Slavery*, 107–9, summarizes well the research on free people of color that has distinguished between the majority, who were poor, and the "mulatto elite" of the cities of the Deep South.

19. John Boles, *Black Southerners, 1619–1869* (Lexington: University Press of Kentucky, 1983), 138. See also Michael P. Johnson and James L. Roark, "Strategies of Survival: Free Negro Families and the Problems of Slavery," in *In Joy and in Sorrow: Women, Family, and Marriage in the Victorian South, 1830–1900*, ed. Carol Bleser (New York: Oxford University Press, 1991), 90.

20. George Fitzhugh, *Sociology for the South: Or, The Failure of Free Society* (Richmond: A. Morris, 1854), 264, quoted in Morris, *Southern Slavery*, 31.

21. See Ira Berlin, *Slaves without Masters: The Free Negro in the Antebellum South* (New York: Pantheon, 1974), 368–70.

22. Berlin briefly considers "voluntary" enslavement in *Slaves without Masters*, 367. For more on humanitarian arguments against "voluntary" enslavement, see John Hope Franklin, *The Free Negro in North Carolina, 1790–1860*, 3rd ed. (Chapel Hill: University of North Carolina Press, 1995), 214–16.

23. Records of "voluntary" enslavement debates also exist for North Carolina and Mississippi, though neither legislated on the issue. See Morris, *Southern Slavery*, 32. See also Wilbert E. Moore, "Slave Law and the Social Structure," *Journal of Negro History* 26, no. 2 (1941): 194 n. 53; John Codman Hurd, *The Law of Freedom and Bondage in the United States*, vol. 2 (Boston: Little, Brown, 1858–62), 12, 24, 94, 166, 174, 195, 199; Engerman, "Some Considerations Relating to Property Rights," 44 n. 2; Lewis Cecil Gray, *A History of Agriculture in the Southern United States to 1860*, vol. 1 (Washington, D.C.: Carnegie Institution of Washington, 1933), 527 n. 125.

24. See Johnson and Roark, *Black Masters*, 165.

25. See Hurd, *The Law of Freedom and Bondage*, 174; Berlin, *Slaves without Masters*, 373–74; and Morris, *Southern Slavery*, 30–31.

26. Thomas Morris claimed that, apparently, no one chose bondage, and in 1860 only 144 mostly elderly free people of color remained in the state. The three individuals forced into enslavement in Pulaski County were Robert Deam, Mary Brock, and Elizabeth Keatts. See the entries for May 17, 1860, and May 6, 1861, Microfilm Roll Misc.39. Circuit Court Record Book "Z" (Civil) pages 1–639, May 1859–July 1863, Pulaski County, Arkansas, 281, 443–44, Arkansas History Commission and State Archives (AHCSA). I also suspect there are more surviving enslavement cases lurking within local courthouses, and this is a topic in need of further exploration. The three individuals who petitioned for enslavement were Mark Dodd, Lewis Green, and James Truman. See the minutes for May 1860, Phillips County Circuit Court Records, 388–89, and 392–93; and the entry for November 13, 1862, Lafayette County Circuit Court Minutes, 1852–1869, Book 5, 111, AHCSA.

27. For example, Arkansas, the District of Columbia, Kentucky, and Maryland have no surviving legislative petitions. See Loren Schweninger, Robert Shelton, and Charles Edward Smith, eds., *Race, Slavery and Free Blacks: Series One: Petitions to Southern Legislatures, 1777–1867* (Bethesda: University Publications of America, 1999); and Loren Schweninger, ed., *The Southern Debate over Slavery*, vol. 1, *Petitions to Southern Legislatures, 1778–1864* (Urbana: University of Illinois Press, 2001). Many of the petitions cited here were traced via the *Race and Slavery Petitions Project* at the University of North Carolina at Greensboro. Each petition holds a unique Petition Analysis Record Number (PAR), and hereafter each petition will be referenced by its PAR. Information on the project can be found at http://library.uncg.edu/slavery.

28. See, for example, Percy Ann Martin (PAR 11286301), Emmarilla Jeffries (PAR 11086010), and Ann Archie (PAR 11086007), all of whom signed with an "X." See also John Hope Franklin, "The Enslavement of Free Negroes in North Carolina," *Journal of Negro History* 29, no. 4 (1944): 424.

29. Twenty-six residents of Sussex County, Virginia, petitioned the county court requesting that three free people of color returning from Liberia would prefer "American slavery to Liberian freedom" (PAR 21685020). In 1861, W. G. Gore of Laurens District requested from the South Carolina Legislature in 1861 that William Jackson be enslaved to him. Series S165005, item 00079, Legislative Petitions, South Carolina Department of Archives and History (SCDAH). The previous year, Charles Lamotte of the same county requested the enslavement of Lizzie Jones (PAR 11386005). See also Series S165015, item

00055, Legislative Petitions, SCDAH. In 1859, W. P. Hill of Greenwood, South Carolina, requested that Elizabeth Bug and her eleven-month-old child belong to him (PAR 11385902). See also Series S165016, item 00054, Legislative Petitions, SCDAH. In North Carolina, C. A. Featherston of Gaston County requested the enslavement of a "negro boy" named Wyat, "about 35 years of age" (PAR 11286203). John Hope Franklin is skeptical about the motives of Featherston. Quite rightly he concludes that Wyat seems to have been virtually a slave prior to the petition, and that Featherston, in requesting a "bona fide deed," seems to be concerned with Wyat becoming his "legal property." Action was never taken in this case. See Franklin, "The Enslavement of Free Negroes," 424–25, and *The Free Negro*, 220. Finally, Wilson Melton and John W. Sproles petitioned the Mississippi legislature in 1859 requesting that Wesley Moore, a "free man of yellow complexion," be exempted from the bill designed to drive free people of color from the state. He was married to a slave belonging to one of the petitioners (PAR 11085915).

30. Where the outcome of a petition is known, this has been indicated either in the text or endnote.

31. Boles writes that, in 1860, the free black population in the South stood at 261,918. This made up 6.2 percent of all blacks, "with the proportion in the upper South (12.8) eight times greater than in the Deep South" (*Black Southerners*, 135).

32. Parish, *Slavery*, 111. See also Parish, "The Edges of Slavery in the Old South: Or, Do Exceptions Prove Rules?" *Slavery and Abolition* 4, no. 1 (1983): 106–25.

33. See Berlin, *Slaves without Masters*, 375, 379; and Hurd, *The Law of Freedom and Bondage*, 166, 195, 199. It is hard to think of a reason why the enslavement of children should be forbidden other than for humanitarian concerns.

34. Berlin, *Slaves without Masters*, 367. Other historians have also drawn attention to the complexity, and sometimes the elusiveness, of motivations for enslavement. See, for example, Morris, *Southern Slavery*, 35; William A. Link, *Roots of Secession: Slavery and Politics in Antebellum Virginia* (Chapel Hill: University of North Carolina Press, 2003), 157–58; Schafer, *Becoming Free, Remaining Free*, 162.

35. "An Act for the relief of James Wall, a free man of color," approved February 11, 1860. "Laws of the State of Mississippi passed at a regular session of the Mississippi legislature held in the city of Jackson, 1860" (Jackson: E. Barksdale, State Printer, 1860), 243–44, Mississippi Department of Archives and History (MDAH). See also the 1860 census for Wilkinson, Mississippi; Roll M653_594; 573; image 55. Family History Library Film 803594. Accessed via www.ancestry.com.

36. Peter Kolchin, *American Slavery* (New York: Penguin, 1993), 244.

37. I was reluctant to include here potential owners who did not appear as slaveholders as "non-slaveholders," because they could simply have been missed off the census by enumerators. Out of caution I assumed that their ownership of slaves was unknown. However, that some of these people were indeed "poor whites" who possessed no enslaved people serves only to strengthen my arguments about the aspirations of less wealthy whites to buy slaves.

38. PAR 11085919.

39. "Slave inhabitants in the County of Itawamba, State of Mississippi, enumerated on the 29th June 1860," 475. Accessed via www.ancestry.com.

40. Judith N. Shklar, *American Citizenship: The Quest for Inclusion* (Cambridge: Harvard University Press, 1991), 3.

41. See Lucy Andrews, petitions to be allowed to return to slavery and to choose her own master. Series S165005, item 02534; series S165015, item 00026; series S165015, item 00011. Legislative Petitions, SCDAH. See also PAR 11385806 (1858 petition), 11386101 (1861 petition), and 11386302 (1863 petition).

42. Stephanie M. H. Camp, *Closer to Freedom: Enslaved Women and Everyday Resistance in the Plantation South* (Chapel Hill: University of North Carolina Press, 2004), 95.

43. See Laura Edwards, "Enslaved Women and the Law: Paradoxes of Subordination in the Post-Revolutionary Carolinas," *Slavery and Abolition* 26, no. 2 (2005): 307, 317–18. See also Edwards, "Law, Domestic Violence and the Limits of Patriarchal Authority in the Antebellum South," *Journal of Southern History* 65, no. 4 (1999): 733–70; and Edwards, *The People and Their Peace: Legal Culture and the Transformation of Inequality in the Post-Revolutionary South* (Chapel Hill: University of North Carolina Press, 2009).

44. For more on the sexual assault of black women by white men in the antebellum era see Susan Brownmiller, *Against Our Will: Men, Women and Rape* (Harmondsworth: Penguin, 1975), 160; Angela Davis, "Reflections on the Black Woman's Role in the Community of Slaves," *Black Scholar* 3, no. 4 (1971): 2–15; Darlene Clark Hine, "Rape and the Inner Lives of Black Women in the Middle West: Preliminary Thoughts on the Culture of Dissemblance," *Signs* 14 (1989): 912–20; West, *Chains of Love*, 126–31.

45. PAR 11086007.

46. See Franklin, *The Free Negro*, 219, and the 1860 census for Franklinton, Franklin County, North Carolina; Roll M653_897, 432, image 297. Family History Library Film 803897. Accessed via www.ancestry.com.

47. See Franklin, *The Free Negro*, 219, and "The Enslavement of Free Negroes," 415.

48. See the 1860 census, District 9, Martin, North Carolina; Roll M653_905, 446, image 297. Family History Library Film 803905; and "Slave inhabitants in District number nine, County of Martin, State of North Carolina, enumerated on the 26th day of September 1860," 48. Both accessed via www.ancestry.com.

49. See Shklar, *American Citizenship*, 16.

50. I was able to assess the motivations for enslavement in ninety-eight cases. These were categorized into seven themes, as follows, with the percentage of comments made in parentheses: "love of family" (39 percent), possible interracial relationship (28 percent), the notion that slavery was "better" (11 percent), fear of expulsion (9 percent), court costs (5 percent), being aged or in ill health (4 percent), and poverty or debt (4 percent). Some of my earlier arguments about the motivations behind "voluntary" slavery requests can be found in Emily West, "'She Is Dissatisfied with Her Present Condition': Requests for Voluntary Enslavement in the Antebellum American South," *Slavery and Abolition* 28, no. 3 (2007): 329–50. See also West, *Family or Freedom: People of Color in the Antebellum South* (Lexington: University Press of Kentucky, 2012).

51. See Larry Koger, *Black Slaveowners: Free Black Masters in South Carolina, 1790–1860* (London: McFarland, 1985), 69.

52. The colonization movement gathered momentum over the antebellum era, and petitions from white residents to various state assemblies illustrate growing enthusiasm

for it. For example, in Virginia more than twenty petitions to the state legislature urging support for colonization exist, the majority of which were written in the early 1830s, when anxiousness about the Nat Turner rebellion was still fresh in white minds. Enforced colonization grew in popularity again in the 1850s, especially in the Upper South, where the free population was growing relatively quickly. Berlin, *Slaves without Masters*, 355. See also Link, *Roots of Secession*, 155–57; Marie Tyler-McGraw, *An African Republic: Black and White Virginians in the Making of Liberia* (Chapel Hill: University of North Carolina Press, 2007). On the Liberian disease environment, see Tom W. Shick, *Behold the Promised Land: A History of Afro-American Settler Society in Nineteenth-Century Liberia*, 2nd ed. (Baltimore: Johns Hopkins University Press, 1980), 27–28. Letters from emigrants to Liberia are contained within Bell I. Wiley, ed., *Slaves No More: Letters from Liberia, 1833–1869* (Lexington: University Press of Kentucky, 1980).

53. PAR 21685020.

54. PAR 11681303.

55. PAR 11286301. I am grateful to Christopher Meekins, Correspondence Archivist at the Office of Archives and History, Raleigh, North Carolina, for providing me with a copy of the original document: "Request of Percy Ann Martin," Legislative Petitions, 1863. This seems to be the "Peggy Ann Morton" of Davidson County who sought enslavement to Henderson Adams, as cited in Franklin, *The Free Negro*, 220.

56. This was Emily Hooper. See Franklin, *The Free Negro*, 219, and Morris, *Southern Slavery*, 35 n. 92.

57. See PAR 11686102; the 1860 census for Staunton, Augusta, Virginia; Roll M653_1333, 786, image 266. Family History Library Film 805333; and "Slave inhabitants in Staunton District Number 1, County of Augusta, State of Virginia, enumerated on the 20th June 1860," 11. Both accessed via www.ancestry.com.

58. Ira Berlin, "Southern Free People of Color in the Age of William Johnson," *Southern Quarterly* 43, no. 2 (2006): 10.

59. See Walter Johnson, "On Agency," *Journal of Social History* 37, no. 1 (2003): 113–24, especially 116. Other works that have questioned the extent and the use of the term "agency" among enslaved communities include Orlando Patterson, *Rituals of Blood: Consequences of Slavery in Two American Centuries* (New York: Basic Civitas, 1998), chapter 1; Kolchin, *American Slavery*, 148–49; Wilma Dunaway, *The African-American Family in Slavery and Emancipation* (Cambridge: Cambridge University Press, 2003), especially the introduction; William Dusinberre, *Strategies for Survival: Recollections of Bondage in Antebellum Virginia* (Charlottesville: University of Virginia Press, 2009), especially chapter 12; and Ben Schiller, "Selling Themselves: Slavery Survival and the Path of Least Resistance," *49th Parallel* 23 (Summer 2009): 1–23.

# 4

# Citizenship, Democracy, and the Structure of Politics in the Old South

## John Calhoun's Conundrum

DAVID BROWN

In the South, John C. Calhoun asserted in 1848, "the two great divisions of society are not the rich and poor, but white and black; and all the former, the poor as well as the rich, belong to the upper class, and are respected and treated as equals, if honest and industrious, and hence have a position and pride of character of which neither poverty nor misfortune can deprive them." In isolation, this passage suggested not only the unity of southern white men but the egalitarianism between them as well. Yet Calhoun was actually attacking the idea that "all men are born free and equal" in this speech, something that he was concerned "has become an axiom in the minds of a vast majority on both sides of the Atlantic." There is "not a word of truth in it," he countered. "They are not born free. . . . They grow to all the freedom of which the condition in which they were born permits." Far from endorsing white male equality on the basis of skin color, Calhoun's conceptualization of the "divisions of society" retained distinctly hierarchical overtones of liberty as something attained rather than granted by birthright. In the context of the times, however—Calhoun was speaking in the middle of the tumultuous year of European revolutions—this position was decidedly at odds with the rising clamor for democratic citizenship in which rights resided with the individual.[1]

Calhoun spoke to the central dilemma of democratic citizenship in his age: should the political sphere, for so long the preserve of the privileged few, be opened to the masses? "All men," Calhoun asserted, did not have "the same right to liberty and equality" but were entitled to particularistic rights according to their station. The Greeks and the Romans, among others, shared this view: citizenship was suitable only for those capable of responsibly exercising civic duties. As Aristotle put it, "that some should rule and others be ruled is a thing not only necessary, but expedient." Classic republican theory of government distrusted the masses and sought to keep political control in the hands of propertied gentlemen. Inalienable and universal political rights, the cornerstone of modern liberal citizenship, were deeply worrying to elites whose control of government had hitherto been assured by restricting the franchise to property holders, effectively a minority of wealthy men.[2]

By the mid-nineteenth century, contrary to Calhoun, the proslavery argument loudly proclaimed the equality of white men, secured on the bedrock of universal suffrage. James D. B. De Bow insisted that non-slave-holding sons were "among the leading and ruling spirits of the South; in industry as well as in politics" in his 1860 appeal.[3] The notion of political democracy bridging class differences was projected forcefully by southerners in the 1850s. This model of democratic citizenship subsequently became the dominant historiographical interpretation. Fletcher M. Green set the tone in his seminal 1946 article depicting the clash "between the forces of aristocracy and democracy" from the Revolution to the Civil War, in which democracy emerged triumphant. "The establishment of white manhood suffrage, the abolition of property qualifications for office holders, the election of all officers by popular vote, and the apportionment of representation on population rather than wealth, with periodic reapportionment, dealt a death blow to the political power of the landed, slaveholding aristocracy of the Old South." Charles Sydnor's contemporaneous, and equally influential, work agreed that "a broader and more equitable distribution of political power . . . was in large measure gained." William J. Cooper was typical of later historians who depicted a vibrant political system paying "equal homage to the same sovereign—the people or the voters." [4]

Structural changes in the Jacksonian period, facilitated by the writing of new state constitutions, nurtured the transition from republican to democratic politics. As J. William Harris puts it, "a wave of political democratization swept the South . . . after 1820." The Jacksonian period, Lacy K. Ford suggests, was a major political watershed "that enshrined

whiteness as the standard measure of citizenship and racial entitlement"
in which "the slaveholding elite had to accept white equality, the spirit
of herrenvolk democracy, in the public realm to ensure white solidarity."
This compromise resulted in a redistribution of political power. "Lacking
wealth but boasting numbers," Ford argues, "white egalitarians used the
ideological imperative of whiteness to wrest meaningful political concessions, if not outright control, from wealthy elites at key moments." Citizenship became bound up in whiteness, "leaving race rather than class
the key social divide in the public realm." Sean Wilentz underscores the
links among slavery, the writing of new state constitutions, and political
egalitarianism in creating "a democratic slavery that, as enshrined in their
state constitutions, secured equality among white men."[5]

It is an opportune moment to reconsider this dominant interpretation.
In their revision of the "democratizing" paradigm, Andrew W. Robertson,
Jeffrey L. Pasley, and other historians of the early national and antebellum
North point toward the ebb and flow of democratic politics across the late
eighteenth and nineteenth centuries, questioning whether developments
of the Jacksonian era were quite so far-reaching. The traditional narrative
"does not seem very accurate," contends Pasley. At the same time, detailed
studies of southern state politics also complicate the orthodox picture.
The metanarrative of consensual democracy has been chipped away, in
many respects, state by state.[6] This chapter builds on these insights in
surveying citizenship in the antebellum South from the perspective of
ordinary southerners. It provides a new assessment of southern antebellum state constitutions in which the focus concerns the legal structures
of democracy, rather than democratic processes, and the extent to which
political power was formally transferred to other groups. What, specifically, were yeomen and poor whites enabled to do by political reforms?

Answers reveal that while suffrage was broadened considerably, the
timing, depth, and significance of political reform differed widely state by
state. Politicians might rhetorically claim that all were equal, but revised
constitutions of the Jacksonian era and beyond did not always deliver
on that promise. Geography is crucial here: proponents of democratization find their best evidence in the trans-Appalachian and Gulf states
(excepting Louisiana), although there are important caveats and counter-
currents to the notion of political egalitarianism even there. Their case is
far less convincing in older southern states where elites resisted political

reform tenaciously. It is also apparent that two distinct spheres of civic engagement existed in the Old South, and each must be considered separately. At the state level, suffrage allowed for the popular election of candidates to legislative, executive, and, more rarely, judicial positions (as well as participating in federal elections, of course). At the county level, the central unit of local government in the Upper South was the county court. Its equivalent in the Lower South had various names—the inferior court in Georgia; the board of commissioners in Florida; the board of police in Mississippi; the police jury in Louisiana—but essentially performed the same functions as the legislative, executive, judicial, and administrative hub of the county (or parish in Louisiana and South Carolina).[7] Local government, downplayed in studies privileging party politics in a national context, was of far more immediate importance to yeomen and poor whites than state politics, but its reform was long, drawn out, and often incomplete.

## Democracy Rising: Glass Half Full

The trans-Appalachian states were at the forefront of southern democratization. Kentucky was the second state in the nation whose constitution (1792) contained no property restrictions on holding office or voting, save that of a residency requirement of two years (or one year in "the county in which they offered to vote"). Tennessee's 1796 constitution had a residency requirement of only six months but stipulated that voters must also possess "a freehold in the county wherein he may vote"—a more discriminatory property requirement. Property and voting were inseparable to classical republican conceptions of citizenship—a "linchpin of both colonial [American] and British suffrage regulations," observes historian Alexander Keysaar—in two respects. First, property owners were considered to have a vested interest, a stake, in shaping the government of their community. Second, property owners were by definition independent and beholden to no one else, and thus not in a position to be manipulated or corrupted. Not until the revised constitution of 1834 was the freehold requirement abolished in Tennessee along with property qualifications for holding office. Missouri's 1820 constitution followed Alabama's in mandating universal suffrage, with residency in state for one year, and in county for three months. Residency requirements were even shorter in Arkansas, whose 1836 constitution stipulated just six months in state. Neither Missouri nor Arkansas had property requirements for holding office or voting.[8]

Political representation was also equitable in these states. In Missouri and Arkansas, apportionment was decided by the total number of free whites, and in Kentucky by the total number of voters. In 1834, Tennessee followed suit—"according to the number of qualified voters"—reforming a system based previously on taxation favoring the wealthy. Non-elite concerns often focused on the problem of the enslaved being included with the white population in calculating legislative seats, giving planters greater political influence. Advantages (and inequalities) on this basis were only really significant in states with large concentrations of planters, however, which was not the case west of Appalachia. Less than 2 percent of Tennesseans in 1850, for example, met the threshold of twenty or more slaves qualifying them for planter status. Indeed, the 1834 reform succeeded precisely because Tennessee "lacked a black-belt region comparable to those that sustained determined conservative opposition to egalitarian reform" elsewhere, argues Lacy K. Ford. This important observation serves Missouri, Arkansas, and Kentucky equally well, where white-belt counties were also the norm. Southern states with smaller and less concentrated numbers of slaveholders were far more likely to include ordinary whites in the political process.[9]

And yet restrictions on popular participation in politics remained. Voters in Missouri, Arkansas, Tennessee, and Kentucky were not trusted with the responsibility to choose judicial and executive positions of state, save that of governor, for most of the antebellum period. The attorney general, secretary of state, state judges, auditor of public accounts, and other offices were centrally appointed rather than elected, exposing rarely recognized *limitations* of "universal" white male suffrage. The governor made these appointments in Missouri and Kentucky, where he also maintained a veto over the legislature. Not until 1850–51 were these appointive powers, and the veto, lost. It was the same in Arkansas and Tennessee, except the governor's (elected) position was essentially ceremonial and the legislature made appointments. Not until 1848 in Arkansas and 1853 in Tennessee were state offices popularly elected. Jonathan M. Atkins's observation that the governor was "the only office in the state for which Tennessee's entire electorate could cast a ballot" until midcentury is true of Missouri, Arkansas, and Kentucky as well. Historians should not be too hasty in automatically associating suffrage with full civic inclusion in all aspects of the political process.[10]

Voters had more input into the selection of officials at the local level. In Missouri, sheriffs and coroners were popularly elected from 1820 and county clerks and justices of the peace a decade later. Most county-level positions in Arkansas were placed in the hands of the electorate by the original 1836 constitution. Tennessee's constitutional amendments in 1834 opened up all county positions for election, although justices of the peace appointed the county coroner and ranger. The major exception to this trend was Kentucky. Overturning the original constitution of 1792, which provided for popular election of the sheriff, Kentucky's 1799 constitution required county courts to "recommend to the governor two proper persons to fill" local positions, "one of whom he shall appoint." In practice the governor usually endorsed the preferred candidate, effectively allowing the county court to select whom it wanted. As in North Carolina, these appointments could last for life. The oligarchic nature of "the court's power of self-perpetuation," argues Robert M. Ireland, "immunized them in many ways from democratic pressures." It was not until May 1851 that Kentucky held elections for local officials.[11]

The Gulf states, with the exception of Louisiana, enjoy a reputation for having the most democratic political structures in the nation. Alabama's state constitution of 1819 granted universal white male suffrage without restrictions based on tax, property, or militia requirements (with a state residency requirement of one year). Political representation within Alabama was based on the total white population, excluding slaves. Moreover, a provision for periodic reapportionment also advantaged yeomen and poor whites, who resided in the greatest numbers in newer, expanding, counties, while slaveholders resided in the older, settled parts. County positions were popularly elected, although at the state level the treasurer, secretary of state, comptroller of public accounts, judges, and militia officers were appointed by the legislature, as were judges at the county level. It was not until 1850 that county and circuit judges were popularly elected. Why did Alabama, a state with a significant concentration of slaveholders, implement these democratic reforms? According to historian Mark W. Kruman, the key lies in the sociopolitical realities and precise timing of the constitutional convention. Contrasting the situation in Alabama with

North Carolina's persistent reluctance to democratize, Kruman explains that "it was much easier to establish the white basis . . . when that state was formed in 1819, since no constitution had to be changed and no particular group would *lose* power because of the alteration of the constitution."[12]

Thirteen years later, Mississippi's reforms surpassed those of its neighbor to become "the most democratic state in the entire South," according to Ralph Wooster. The revised constitution of 1832 abolished tax, property, and militia qualifications for suffrage and apportioned representation according to the total white population. The only voting requirement was residency of one year in state and four months in county. All state positions were popularly elected, even the judiciary, which was uncommon at the time. Local offices were also placed in the hands of the electorate for the first time from 1832, as the county court was replaced by the five-man board of police. Justices of the peace, constables, tax collectors, and surveyors, all formally appointed by the legislature, were now popularly elected. As Christopher J. Olsen puts it, "voters had nearly unprecedented power in Mississippi."[13]

Texas and Florida entered the Union in 1845, and their political structures reflected the heightened democratic expectations of the times. Neither placed restrictions on adult white male suffrage save that of one year's residency in state and six months in county. The governor, legislature, and most offices of state were popularly elected, as were most judicial positions by the 1850s. County officials were also elected, having been appointed by the assembly prior to joining the Union. Political representation was democratically decided in Texas. Apportionment to the lower house was based on the total white population, and in the upper on total number of voters (a concession to the sparsely populated frontier counties).[14]

Democratic reform was not complete, however. The major blemish on Florida's record was the apportionment of the state legislature by federal ratio (thereby counting the enslaved population as three-fifths), favoring slaveholding counties. But both states had long political histories before 1845, complicating easy assumptions that their politics were organized to serve the interests of the non-elite as much as any other group. In Florida especially, but also in Texas to an extent, power and political dynamics were indelibly shaped by Spanish and British colonial heritages as powerful landholders wielded influence outside of formal political networks. Planters were deeply involved in the highly lucrative ventures of land speculation and commandeering the rewards of political office, which "were more important to Florida politicians than were their own constituents," according to Edward E. Baptist. Democratic restructuring could be put in place, then, but this did not prevent vested interests and long-standing cliques from continuing to exert a disproportionate influence.[15]

What was true of Florida and Texas applies to other states as well. Reforming the system was only the first step in the implementation of democratic citizenship. The granting of suffrage allowed more white men to participate in politics, but it did not of itself allow yeomen and poor whites significantly greater influence, much less control, of the political process, especially in states where there were significant numbers of planters. Long-standing inequities of wealth, experience, status, and influence existed, critical commodities in any political system. As William L. Barney reminds us, voting "cannot automatically be equated with political power, particularly when the voter represents a class with next to no influence in the decision-making process." With the exception of Mississippi, each was wary of opening up *all* offices for popular election at both the state and the local level, although by the 1850s the majority of political appointments were made by voters. Undeniably, though, white men voted in unprecedented numbers and, with the exception of Florida, their vote counted in equal measure. It was a different situation in other southern states.[16]

## Republicanism Resilient: Glass Half Empty

The least democratic political structure below the Mason-Dixon Line was found in South Carolina. This might seem surprising given that suffrage was effectively granted without qualification in 1810 (voters were required to hold fifty acres or a town lot, but failing that only needed to be resident within their election district for six months). It was a measure, however, "changing next to nothing," notes William W. Freehling. The enfranchised voted only for representatives to the legislature, representatives who had to meet property requirements of £150. The legislature remained all-powerful in the Palmetto State throughout the antebellum period. It appointed all significant political positions, from governor to senator—and even presidential electors, unlike anywhere else in the United States—as well as all state offices. All judicial positions were also appointed by the legislature. "Before the Civil War," J. William Harris reminds us, "no South Carolinian was able to cast a ballot in an election for a statewide office," not even governor.[17]

Local offices were selected by the respective legislative delegation of each county or parish, subject to the approval of the state legislature. The legislature effectively allowed local delegations to appoint whom they wanted, creating what Lacy K. Ford terms "an informal two-way patronage network which could be nicely manipulated by local politicians and their cliques of followers." Apportionment within South Carolina was complex but favored planter interests. The Compromise of 1808 made some concessions to the upcountry (and hence to the yeomanry), such as periodic reapportionment, but fundamentally maintained the power of the lowcountry parishes. Political representation was calculated on the basis of both the total white population and tax returns paid by each parish/district. The lowcountry thus retained control of the senate, but the upcountry held "a nominal majority" in the lower house. Even so, black-majority parishes continued to exert greater "influence in the legislature" than white-majority districts, according to Ford. By midcentury, Beaufort and Georgetown in the lowcountry had ten seats in the house representing eleven thousand whites, while Greenville and Spartanburg in the upcountry had nine seats representing thirty-two thousand whites. It would be difficult to dispute Freehling's characterization of South Carolina having "as aristocratic a government as ever took a democratic form."[18]

In Georgia, adult white males meeting a county residency of six months enjoyed a long history of voting, being enfranchised by the 1789 constitution. Significantly, however, this privilege was restricted to taxpayers, a qualification reaffirmed in 1798. Voters must "have paid all taxes which may have been required of them, and which they may have had an opportunity of paying, agreeably to law, for the year preceding the election." This was typical of early southern state constitutions but remained in force in Georgia throughout the antebellum period, distinguishing the state from all others except North Carolina. The Georgia governor was popularly elected from 1824, and property qualifications for the legislature were removed in 1835. However, the general assembly continued to appoint key state offices, such as attorney general, treasurer, secretary of state, and supreme and superior court judges.[19]

Scholars concur that reform of county politics in Georgia fell way short in actually redistributing power to the electorate. Justices of the peace were popularly elected from as early as 1812, and at various times other positions were placed in the hands of the electorate. However, Steven Hahn suggests that the inferior court was "technically subject to the authority of the General Assembly" for most of the antebellum period, only achieving "virtual autonomy by the 1850s." J. William Harris finds that county government may have had "a democratic cast" but that "the power of a relatively small elite guided and limited local democracy." And Anthony Gene Carey agrees that "dense kinship networks among leading families played a crucial role in structuring county politics."[20] Georgia also maintained use of the federal ratio, including the enslaved population, in calculating representation to the lower house, while each county held one seat in the senate. Provisions for periodic reapportionment served non-elite interests, but when the maximum number of legislative seats per county was limited to two in 1843, "the differences in legislative power" between black- and white-belt counties narrowed. This measure, Peter Wallenstein continues, "enhanced the power of planters at the expense of yeomen farmers and poor whites." In 1840, coastal, black-belt Glynn County, representing 891 whites, had two seats in the legislature, the same as upcountry, white-belt Campbell County, representing 4,526 whites.[21]

Reform came slowly in Virginia and was marked by chronic tensions over suffrage qualifications and political representation between the planter-dominated east and white-belt counties of the rapidly developing west. Those seeking change were severely disappointed by the reform convention of 1829–30. Characterized by Lacy K. Ford as a clash of western "egalitarian republicans" and eastern "conservative republicans," it brought "contentious questions regarding the relationship of slavery, republican values, and raw political power into sharp relief." Amended suffrage rules remained fundamentally at odds with democratic measures taken elsewhere. The property requirement for voting was reduced from a land holding of fifty dollars (disfranchising about half of white men) to twenty-five dollars, or twenty for those leasing land for at least five years at an annual cost of twenty dollars. At least a third of white Virginians, and possibly as many as 40 percent, remained disfranchised. Key political offices remained in the hands of the assembly, including the governor, judges, and other executive state officers. Reformers prevented planters from including the enslaved in calculating legislative seats, but their success was tempered by an apportionment formula based on the total white population of 1820, not 1830. The west remained proportionately underrepresented because its population had expanded most rapidly in the 1820s. A further convention was almost inevitable given the intense levels of dissatisfaction over this outcome.[22]

Tidewater planters continued to oppose democratic reform in fierce and lengthy debates at the subsequent 1850 constitutional convention. Their biggest compromise was finally accepting universal suffrage, ending property restrictions (albeit with a lengthy residency requirement of two years in state and one year in town or county). The governor was to be popularly elected, as were judges in the higher courts. The offices of secretary of state, state treasurer, and auditors of public accounts remained in the hands of the assembly, however. The 1850 constitution also opened up the county system to the electorate; previously, justices of the peace had appointed local officials in conjunction with the governor (as in Kentucky, the governor selected justices of the peace from recommendations made by the county court). Apportionment was a far more difficult problem. The convention debated a variety of systems—the white population, the total population, the federal ratio, or a combination of taxation and population—but none was acceptable. Legislative representation was eventually bluntly recalibrated to give the west more seats than the east in the lower house (83–69) but the east a majority in the upper house (30–20), with reapportionment to be considered again in 1865. As Freehling wryly observes, "elitist republicans restrained egalitarians from confiscating rich folks' fortunes" because the east maintained its veto over any new policy initiatives that might emerge from the new constituency of the house. Moreover, tax laws were rewritten to the planters' advantage, abolishing taxation on slaves under twelve and setting the maximum taxable figure per slave at just three hundred dollars, far below rising market valuations.[23]

Although much had changed in Virginia by 1851, it is difficult to agree with William G. Shade that "the liberal, democratic political culture of the Commonwealth contrasted sharply with the aristocratic republicanism" of the eighteenth century. William A. Link provides a better characterization in stating that "Virginians adopted mass politics but still operated at least partially under the old rules." It is undoubtedly true that the newly enfranchised participated enthusiastically in Virginia politics in the 1850s. They began to mobilize and sought further change within the political system. Merchants and lawyers in particular played an increasingly prominent role in state politics, and many were elected to office.

However, the Tidewater elite's power, in conjunction with allies from the rapidly expanding piedmont, was far from moribund. The terms of the 1850 constitution, it should not be forgotten, retained the possibility that apportionment might be based on slaves or other property in the future.[24]

Universal suffrage was established much earlier in Virginia's neighbor Maryland. Property requirements for voting and officeholding were abolished in Maryland in 1810, with a residency requirement of one year in state and six months in county. Not until amendments effective in 1837, however, was the governor popularly elected. Executive and judicial officials at the state level were appointed by the governor until becoming popularly elected in 1851, although the secretary of state continued to be selected. County politics were opened up to the electorate at the same time, the governor having appointed all local officials until 1851 save that of sheriff, elected from as early as 1776. In comparison to other states, yeomen and poor whites in Maryland were not as well catered to as they were in the Lower South, but were seemingly much better off than peers in the Upper South.[25]

It was the problem of legislative representation, however, that tarnished Maryland's democratic credentials. Tensions between the rapidly growing population of the northern counties, in which the major city of Baltimore was situated, with the much smaller slave counties in eastern and southern sections reflected the development of "two Marylands," one thriving on the basis of free labor and commerce, the other stagnating due to the long-term decline of tobacco. Despite the widening gap in numbers between the sections, however, it was the more sparsely populated, older counties that held the balance of power to "dominate the government," according to historian Barbara Jeanne Fields. Regardless of population, each county held four seats in the house, with Baltimore and Annapolis restricted to just two seats. Constitutional reform in 1851 made some concessions to underrepresented parts of the state, although it did not go nearly as far as reforms in Virginia. A complex apportionment formula "preserved a grossly inequitable apportionment" in favor of the status quo, Fields contends. Most glaringly, the 1851 constitution calculated representation in the house "according to the population of each" county, that is, counting slaves fully for the purposes of political apportionment—not just three-fifths—making each slave as valuable as any white person in terms of political currency. Louisiana was the only other southern state to do likewise. As a result, seats in the house were evenly split at thirty-seven each, even though northern Maryland had twice the white population of the south and east. "Despite the superiority of northern Maryland in population and in economic strength and vitality," Fields concludes, "the landed and slaveholding upperclass of southern Maryland and the Eastern Shore retained the political advantage."[26]

Arguably, North Carolina elites resisted political change more successfully than any of their southern peers. Planters in the east endured a steady stream of criticism from the piedmont and the mountains for failing to implement democratic reform. Just one reform convention was held in North Carolina, in 1835; however, its results "continued to offer special protection for property and gave disproportionate influence to the wealthier east," Kruman finds. Qualifications remained in place for holding state office (one hundred acres of land for the house of commons, three hundred for the senate, and one thousand for governor) after the 1835 convention. There were no changes to the suffrage laws of 1776. All free men meeting a residency requirement of twelve months in county and paying taxes voted for the lower house (with suffrage taken away from free blacks in 1835, this effectively meant all *white* men). However, only those possessing fifty acres of land were qualified to vote for the upper house. Approximately half the white male population was barred from voting for the senate until the abolition of the fifty-acre rule was ratified in December 1856 (effective 1857), the result of many years of hard campaigning. Even then, only those who had "paid public taxes" for twelve months were enfranchised—a qualification to this reform that is easily overlooked and continued to exclude white men from voting.[27]

Moreover, the 1835 constitution did not apportion seats in the legislature on a democratic basis, but advantaged counties with the wealthiest property holders paying the most in taxes. Representation in the upper house was calculated on the basis of total taxation within fifty newly formulated political districts within the state. Seats in the lower house remained apportioned on the basis of the federal ratio including slaves as well as whites. Both methods gave eastern plantation counties more seats in the legislature. A single county in the east with 560 voters (Hertford) enjoyed the same representation in the senate as did four western counties with a combined total of 3,873 voters (Burke, Caldwell, McDowell, Wilkes). This hardly seemed like democracy to citizens in the piedmont and the mountains, who complained regularly and vociferously. While not taking their objections as far as Hinton Rowan Helper—a piedmont native who claimed the only remedy was abolition—they understood the system to be inequitable.[28]

From the perspective of yeomen and poor whites, the situation was even worse at the local level. The county system in North Carolina was unchanged throughout the antebellum period. Justices of the peace were appointed by the governor based on recommendations from the general assembly and the relevant county court. They held those positions for life. In turn, justices of the peace selected all local officials, with the exception of constables (from 1838) and sheriff (from 1848), and thus controlled tax rates and public spending. Paul D. Escott characterizes county government in the Tar Heel State as a "squirarchy." Wealthy families monopolized local positions of prominence, in some cases for decades, with little or no check on their power. Their decisions had an immense bearing on the lives of county residents. "Justices of the peace laid down county policies, elected various county offices, and made important decisions on tax rates, the location of roads, provisions for education of the poor, and many other social and economic matters." Moreover, squires enjoyed a symbiotic relationship with their representative in the legislature. Charles C. Bolton's study of counties in the central piedmont demonstrates that "the concentration of political power . . . at times gave political office the appearance of hereditary right." Even Robert C. Kenzer's analysis of Orange County, a classic account stressing democratization, accepts that the county court "had a near monopoly over the control of county affairs."[29]

While most Gulf states made discernible, if not unequivocal, strides toward egalitarian politics, it was a very different story in the oldest Gulf state. Suffrage in Louisiana was limited by the 1812 constitution to those paying taxes or purchasing land. The consequence, calculates historian Roger Shugg, was to exclude two-thirds of white men from participating in the political process. This problem was not addressed until 1845, when a new constitution ended property qualifications for voting and officeholding, as well as opening up many more political positions to the voters—the governor became popularly elected, for example. Residency requirements in Louisiana were set at two years, in large part because of sizable numbers of immigrants in New Orleans. Provisions for reapportionment in the 1845 constitution were conservative. In a compromise between the mercantile leaders of New Orleans and the vested interests of planters in the slave parishes that were approximately 50 percent black, the elite actually increased its control of the upper house. While the lower house was elected on the basis of the total numbers of voters, the upper house was apportioned on the basis of total numbers including slaves. Moreover, the constitution did nothing to change the earlier division of Louisiana into "fourteen senatorial districts, which shall forever remain indivisible," decisively favoring older parishes. Slave parishes, with about a third of the white population, held two-thirds of seats in the senate.[30]

This unsatisfactory situation invited pressure for further reform. The planter elite, worried by the potentially destabilizing effects of widened suffrage, had its own agenda to pursue in the subsequent 1852 convention, however. Some concessions were granted: judges became popularly elected for the first time, and the residency requirement for voting was reduced to just one year. More state and inferior court positions were placed in the hands of the electorate. Indeed, the majority of local offices—including constables, justices of the peace, surveyors, and tax collectors—that had been formerly appointed by the legislature were opened to popular election as a result of the 1845 and 1852 reforms. Remarkably, though, in a move diametrically at odds with Jacksonian reform culture, the 1852 constitution proposed the same principle of apportionment for the upper house as it did for the lower: "Representation in the house of representatives shall be equal and uniform, and shall be regulated and ascertained by the total population of each of the several parishes of the State." The enslaved were to count fully for the purposes of apportionment, not just three-fifths. This serious affront to yeomen interests illustrated the ability of planters to maintain political control despite widened suffrage. Despite considerable unease over the measure, the new constitution was narrowly ratified by planter delegates from the slave parishes in conjunction with allies from the piney woods. The slave parishes actually strengthened their position further in 1854 and 1859, ensuring that "with slightly less than one third of the white population" they "elected over one half of the state's lawmakers."[31]

As elsewhere, universal suffrage did not bring the rewards that yeomen and poor whites hoped for. Critics in the house of representatives even complained that "the discrepancy in representation between the heavy slaveholding parishes and those . . . more congenial to the laboring white man will not perpetuate the liberty of the yeoman and the people will not stand for it." It was to no avail. Samuel C. Hyde shows that measures favored by whites in non-plantation areas—to protect property from seizure, control rates of interest, promote public schooling and welfare, and build communication routes, such as a railroad from New Orleans to the interior—were ignored in the legislature. Down to the Civil War, the political system in Louisiana was elitist, not democratic.[32]

## The Boundaries of Southern Citizenship

Democratization was neither complete nor universal across the South by 1850, let alone at the beginning of the Jacksonian era. In considering citizenship from the non-elite perspective, first and foremost, much greater attention must be paid to the precise timing of reform. Progressive measures were not in place as early as is often assumed, and white men continued to be excluded from the political process in a number of ways across the antebellum period. A generalization such as "the diffusion of political rights in America was such that by 1820 adult white males were uniformly eligible to vote" conceals as much as it reveals about southern politics.[33]

Rather than one gigantic democratic "wave" sweeping all before it, it is more accurate to state that a piecemeal process of democratization was in motion rather than being complete by midcentury. The structural transition from classical republicanism—and particularistic rights—to liberal democracy—and universal rights for white males—in each state's legal culture proceeded at varying speeds and reached variable depths. Where elite power had been entrenched for the longest duration, namely, Louisiana and the eastern seaboard, the political system continued to underpin planter control. Apportionment, contrary to Fletcher Green's assertion, worked to the advantage of plantation districts in seven of fourteen southern states discussed here. It was the new Gulf states, settled in the first half of the nineteenth century, and the trans-Appalachian states, where slavery was not as economically critical nor planters as numerous, that held out better prospects for yeomen and poor whites.

The assumption that *all* political restrictions and inequalities were removed in the Jacksonian era also does not hold up to close scrutiny. For white men the franchise was considerably expanded across the southern states, but not until the 1850s were the majority of political offices popularly elected, and some remained centrally appointed. Even so, reforms generally placed white men in an advantageous—indeed, highly enviable—situation. Lacy K. Ford rightly emphasizes the significance of the "whitening" of southern state constitutions and the exclusion of African Americans from southern politics. The promise of southern citizenship, at least in the formal sense of political participation, became restricted to white men only; other essays in this volume document the struggles of slaves and free blacks and the creative ways in which they interpreted "citizenship." The southern boast that all were equal in political terms was not without substance, especially in an age when British and European working classes were struggling to secure basic political rights. If the sine qua non of modern liberal citizenship is the right to vote, it was becoming that way in the American South as suffrage replaced property as the key marker of civic status. Nonetheless, class politics and elite privilege did not disappear. To characterize citizenship as solely a matter of whiteness is to ignore ways in which elites remained influential in southern politics after universal suffrage was implemented. Despite the rhetoric of herrenvolk democracy, classical republicanism sat uneasily alongside nineteenth-century liberal democratic claims of white male equality. There was not a wholesale and decisive transition from one to the other by the eve of the Civil War.[34]

Most fundamentally, basic impediments to voting remained and some white men were denied citizenship. Property and taxpaying requirements were mostly eliminated by the 1850s, but Georgia and North Carolina remained major exceptions. We do not know how many whites were disfranchised as a consequence, but if a sizable number were excluded, claims of white egalitarianism are placed in a somewhat different light. Elites might have conceded ground in the struggle over suffrage and property, but they continued to police the boundaries of civic inclusion. Southern states, like their northern counterparts, passed legislation restricting the voting rights of criminals and of paupers. Although we know next to nothing about their implementation and effects, Alabama (1819), Florida (1838), Kentucky (1792 and 1850), Louisiana (1812 and 1845), Maryland (1851), Missouri (1820), Mississippi (1817), Tennessee (1834), Texas (1845), and Virginia (1830 and 1850) drew up legislation disfranchising criminals convicted of a range of offenses, but especially "felonies or so-called infamous crimes," which Alexander Keysaar states "were crimes that made a person ineligible to serve as a witness in a legal proceeding." At the same time, Louisiana (1845), South Carolina (1810), and Virginia (1830) barred paupers from voting. Defining "pauper" with any level of precision is difficult, but the legislation was most likely directed at those receiving public relief from the state or county or from charitable organizations. These measures remind us of John Calhoun's stipulation that honesty and industriousness were vital qualities for prospective citizens. They suggest that yeomen, but not poor whites, were the chief beneficiaries of antebellum reforms, which demanded a measure of wealth and respectability.[35]

Residency requirements also remained. Treated as technicalities in most accounts of antebellum southern politics, they are easily overlooked. However, residency requirements were an extension of classic republican thinking tying suffrage to property and civic suitability rather than to manhood. As Keysaar explains, "in the absence of property or taxpaying qualifications, it seemed sensible to restrict the franchise to those who were familiar with local conditions and likely to have a stake in the outcome of elections."[36] Immigrants most obviously were affected by these rules. Louisiana set longer residency requirements, for instance, because politicians feared the effects of immigration. But Virginia also set high residency requirements (two years) precisely because elites were wary of universal suffrage. Residency qualifications applied to all potential voters and cut out internal as well as external migrants. They penalized yeomen, and even more frequently poor whites, to a much greater extent than planters. The cost of moving was simply too prohibitive for repeated relocation of planters who were economically successful and almost always important figures in their local communities anyway. Migrant yeomen and poor whites were looking for better opportunities elsewhere and, having moved once, were highly likely to do so again. More than seventy years since Roger W. Shugg asserted that "numerous farmers who had migrated from the southeastern states would suffer temporary disfranchisement," we still do not have an idea of how many were excluded by residency qualifications.[37]

This is unfortunate, because rules and regulations for voting were rigorously enforced, as Richard Franklin Bensel's *The American Ballot Box in the Mid-Nineteenth Century* demonstrates. Any prospective voter could be challenged by election officials, and by others (most often members of political parties), and if they could not present the required documentation their ballots were refused. While the electoral process followed certain universal rules, Bensel shows that their application depended heavily on local contexts as officials at polling booths held considerable power in determining outcomes: "laws compelled election officials to exercise broad discretion in the determination of voter eligibility and other aspects of the election process." Their control was rooted "in the social understandings of the community in which the voting took place and influenced by the partisan interests of the officials themselves" and could determine "whether and how individual men participated in elections."[38]

In this respect, though, yeomen again held the advantage over poor whites, tending to follow friends and relatives already established in new communities. "When yeomen farmers moved they did so as communities rather than as individuals," James Oakes stresses.[39] The localized nature of southern rural life prized familiarity and operated on a face-to-face basis. Upstanding, property-owning heads of households, then, were immediately recognizable as the kind of middle-class citizens suggested in Calhoun's 1848 speech. Poor whites had always been seen as suspicious by those higher up the social scale because they lacked qualities of honesty and industry. That had turned into mounting distrust by the 1850s as the sectional conflict heated up. During this decade there were more southern voters than ever before, and, not inconsequentially, newcomers were scrutinized intensely. Electoral commissioners skilled in the art of recognizing "respectable" voters were unlikely to interrogate yeomen for very long, however, and perhaps in some cases were willing to overlook residency rules. Given the importance of the setting, it is easy to imagine local officials being lenient for the "right" sort but far less willing to accommodate the less respectable.

This emphasis on the local is critical to understanding the continuities of elite political power across the antebellum period. Democratization at the county rather than the state level places the limitations of reform in sharp relief, and not just because it was usually opened up to the electorate long after suffrage was obtained. Quite simply, local politics were dominated by vested interests. Counties were composed of neighborhoods in which prominent families, their status defined by the age-old elitist criteria of property and wealth, exerted political control and influenced the distribution of resources. When county politics finally opened to voters in all but three states by the 1850s, decades of tussles and spats between local political rivals had typically become an integral part of each county's history and folklore. Wherever historians have examined county politics in the South, cliques of leading families, or in some places individual patrons, retained control of local government.[40]

Even in Mississippi, "the most democratic state" in Wooster's view, planters continued to oversee county politics regardless of reform. "The distribution of election-day duties," Christopher J. Olsen writes, "suggests

Mississippians' faith in an organic, deferential society and reveals the gentry's influence in a supposedly democratic, free process." Christopher Morris's study of Warren County, Mississippi, concurs: "Power, that is, the ability to make and execute decisions that affect others, rested first and foremost in the hands of Warren County's leading property holders. Public office, elected or otherwise, did not on its own provide officials with the authority to overrule decisions already hammered out in big-house parlors of ruling patriarchs scattered around the county." The daily reality of county-level politics across the South in the mid-nineteenth century was its control by a small number of powerful, networked individuals or families.[41]

Moreover, in Mississippi as well as at least three other states—Georgia, Louisiana, and South Carolina—political candidates at the county level were required to post a sum of money before *being allowed* to take office. Many southerners, not just those from humble backgrounds, would have struggled to meet these bonds. Local patriarchs could secure these payments, however, and it is probable that they expected to do so for their chosen candidates. The posting of bonds urgently requires further investigation, for it seemingly allowed planters continued control of political appointments long after suffrage was broadened. Perhaps this is why Mississippi was able to implement far-reaching democratic reforms at such an early date, or more likely a response to democratization. Southern politics might no longer be the sole preserve of the wealthy, but elite power was wielded in other, more subtle ways.[42]

While acknowledging important continuities in southern politics, it must not be overlooked that the expanded electorate had a measure of influence over local and state politics (calculating precisely *how much* is the tricky matter). No aspiring politician could ignore their whims. "Forging an identity with the voters," notes Cooper, "occupied the thoughts and energies of politicians," and something of a dialectic was established.[43] Revised state constitutions opened up new possibilities for rank-and-file citizens that were unavailable in colonial governments tied to property rights. As partisanship extended to the local level, moreover, the oligarchic nature of county government was potentially challenged. Only one study considers this issue in depth. Daniel W. Crofts's superb analysis of Southampton County shows that by 1856, five years after county politics was opened up to the Virginia electorate, the candidate's party affiliation could be a significant factor in local elections. There is no evidence to suggest, however, that this necessarily compromised the power of leading families or patriarchs, who naturally aligned themselves to party.[44]

Inequalities were retained in revised southern constitutions at the same time as they reserved the privileges of citizenship for (the majority of) white males, sharpening civic boundaries between white men and other groups. The historical focus on popular participation in party politics in the late antebellum era has minimized, even neglected, ways in which southern politics continued to privilege and be overseen by a powerful minority. As Laura F. Edwards has recently emphasized, the various legal cultures of democracy in the southern states—and the translation of laws into reality at the county level—demand careful examination if we are to understand the political culture(s) of the Old South. Steven Hahn writes that in Georgia the "process of democratization grew out of extended agitation, much of which originated in the upcountry, but in many ways it bolstered instead of challenged the influence of the well-to-do." This essay suggests that Hahn's verdict applies to all southern states, but especially those with a significant concentration of planters.[45]

## Notes

1. John C. Calhoun, "Speech on the Oregon Bill" (June 27, 1848), in Clyde N. Wilson and Shirley Bright Cook, eds., *The Papers of John C. Calhoun*, vol. 25, *1847–1848* (Columbia: University of South Carolina Press, 1999), 533–34. Thanks to Robert Cook, Martin Crawford, David Gleeson, Bill Link, Erik Mathisen, Chris Olsen, Daniel Peart, Frank Towers, and Brian Ward for their help and wise counsel in my completion of this essay.

2. Ibid., 537; Aristotle, *Politics* (New York: Cosimo, 2008), 32; Keith Faulks, *Citizenship* (London: Routledge, 2000), 14–28. On Calhoun's elitism see William W. Freehling, "Beyond Racial Limits: Paternalism over Whites in the Thought of Calhoun and Fitzhugh," in his *The Reintegration of American History: Slavery and the Civil War* (New York: Oxford University Press, 2004), 82–104. The persistence of republican elitism as an anti-democratic ideology in the South is the subject of Manisha Sinha, *The Counterrevolution of Slavery: Politics and Ideology in Antebellum South Carolina* (Chapel Hill: University of North Carolina Press, 2000).

3. James D. B. De Bow, *The Interest in Slavery of the Southern Non-Slaveholder* (Charleston: Evans & Cogswell, 1860), 10.

4. Fletcher M. Green, "Democracy in the Old South," *Journal of Southern History* 12, no. 1 (1946): 4, 17–18; Charles S. Sydnor, *The Development of Southern Nationalism, 1819–1848* (Baton Rouge: Louisiana State University Press, 1948), 275; William J. Cooper

Jr., *The South and the Politics of Slavery, 1828–1856* (Baton Rouge: Louisiana State University Press, 1978), 29.

5. J. William Harris, *The Making of the American South: A Short History, 1500–1877* (Oxford: Blackwell, 2006), 144; Lacy K. Ford, "Making the 'White Man's Country' White: Race, Slavery, and State-Building in the Jacksonian South," *Journal of the Early Republic* 9, no. 4 (1999): 736–37; Sean Wilentz, "Why Did Southerners Secede?" in *In the Cause of Liberty: How the Civil War Redefined American Ideals*, ed. William J. Cooper Jr. and John M. McCardell Jr. (Baton Rouge: Louisiana State University Press, 2009), 33.

6. Jeffrey L. Pasley, "Party Politics, Citizenship, and Collective Action in Nineteenth-Century America: A Response to Stuart Blumin and Michael Schudson," *Communication Review* 4, no. 1 (2000): 45; Jeffrey L. Pasley, Andrew W. Robertson, and David Waldstreicher, eds., *Beyond the Founders: New Approaches to the Political History of the Early American Republic* (Chapel Hill: University of North Carolina Press, 2004). Glenn C. Altschuler and Stuart Blumin, *Rude Republic: Americans and Their Politics in the Nineteenth Century* (Princeton: Princeton University Press, 2000), also vigorously contest the democracy thesis. Key studies of southern state politics appear in the notes below. For a judicious overview of major works, see Daniel W. Crofts, "Politics in the Antebellum South," in *A Companion to the American South*, ed. John B. Boles (Oxford: Blackwell, 2002), 176–90.

7. Ralph A. Wooster, *The People in Power: Courthouse and Statehouse in the Lower South, 1850–1860* (Knoxville: University of Tennessee Press, 1969), 81–84.

8. Francis N. Thorpe, comp., *The Federal and State Constitutions, Colonial Charters, and Other Organic Laws*, 7 vols. (Washington, D.C.: GPO, 1909), vol. 3 (Kentucky), 1269, and vol. 6 (Tennessee), 3418; Alexander Keyssar, *The Right to Vote: The Contested History of Democracy in the United States* (New York: Basic Books, 2000), 5. Thorpe's compilation is essential to evaluating structural reforms in U.S. politics, as is Wooster, *People in Power*, and Ralph A. Wooster, *Politicians, Planters, and Plain Folk: Courthouse and Statehouse in the Upper South, 1850–1860* (Knoxville: University of Tennessee Press, 1975).

9. Thorpe, *Federal and State Constitutions*, vol. 6 (Tennessee), 3430; Jonathan M. Atkins, *Parties, Politics, and the Sectional Conflict in Tennessee, 1832 to 1861* (Knoxville: University of Tennessee Press, 1997), 7; Lacy K. Ford, "Popular Ideology of the Old South's Plain Folk: The Limits of Egalitarianism in a Slaveholding Society," in *Plain Folk of the South Revisited*, ed. Samuel C. Hyde (Baton Rouge: Louisiana State University Press, 1997), 222. Freehling defines black-belt counties as "communities with populations 25 per cent or more enslaved." William W. Freehling, *The Road to Disunion*, vol. 2, *Secessionists Triumphant, 1854–1861* (New York: Oxford University Press, 2007), 15.

10. Wooster, *Politicians, Planters, and Plain Folk*, 58–60; Atkins, *Parties, Politics, and the Sectional Conflict*, 5.

11. Wooster, *Politicians, Planters, and Plain Folk*, 105–8; Thorpe, *Federal and State Constitutions*, vol. 3 (Kentucky), 1285; Robert M. Ireland, *The County Courts in Antebellum Kentucky* (Lexington: University Press of Kentucky, 1972), 65.

12. Thorpe, *Federal and State Constitutions*, vol. 1 (Alabama), 103–7, 116; Mark W. Kruman, *Parties and Politics in North Carolina, 1836–1865* (Baton Rouge: Louisiana State University Press, 1983), 94.

13. Wooster, *People in Power*, 21; Christopher J. Olsen, *Political Culture and Secession in Mississippi: Masculinity, Honor, and the Antiparty Tradition, 1830–1860* (New York: Oxford University Press, 2000), 30.

14. Wooster, *People in Power*, 14–15, 24–25.

15. Thorpe, *Federal and State Constitutions*, vol. 2 (Florida), 676; Edward E. Baptist, *Creating an Old South: Middle Florida's Plantation Frontier before the Civil War* (Chapel Hill: University of North Carolina Press, 2002), 98; Andrés Reséndez, *Changing National Identities at the Frontier: Texas and New Mexico, 1800–1850* (Cambridge: Cambridge University Press, 2004).

16. William L. Barney, *The Secessionist Impulse: Alabama and Mississippi in 1860* (Princeton: Princeton University Press, 1974), 91.

17. Thorpe, *Federal and State Constitutions*, vol. 6 (South Carolina), 3267; William W. Freehling, *The Road to Disunion*, vol. 1, *Secessionists at Bay, 1776–1854* (New York: Oxford University Press, 1990), 222; J. William Harris, *Plain Folk and Gentry in a Slave Society: White Liberty and Black Slavery in Augusta's Hinterlands* (Middletown, Conn.: Wesleyan University Press, 1985), 107.

18. Lacy K. Ford, *The Origins of Southern Radicalism: The South Carolina Upcountry 1800–1860* (New York: Oxford University Press, 1988), quotations from 305, 107, 281–82; Freehling, *Road to Disunion*, 1:223.

19. Thorpe, *Federal and State Constitutions*, vol. 2 (Georgia), 789, 800. Wooster, *People in Power*, 12, unintentionally confuses the wording of these tax requirements; this is the accurate citation of the 1798 text.

20. Wooster, *People in Power*, 10–13; Steven Hahn, *The Roots of Southern Populism: Yeoman Farmers and the Transformation of the Georgia Upcountry, 1850–1880* (Oxford: Oxford University Press, 1983), 92; Harris, *Plain Folk and Gentry*, 117; Anthony Gene Carey, *Parties, Slavery, and the Union in Antebellum Georgia* (Athens: University of Georgia Press, 1997), 11.

21. Peter Wallenstein, *From Slave South to New South: Public Policy in Nineteenth-Century Georgia* (Chapel Hill: University of North Carolina Press, 1987), 20.

22. Lacy K. Ford, *Deliver Us from Evil: The Slavery Question in the Old South* (New York: Oxford University Press, 2009), 363–64; Freehling, *Road to Disunion*, 1:169, 176–77. The figure of approximately 40 percent disfranchisement after 1830 is given in Ronald L. Heinemann, John G. Kolp, Anthony S. Parent Jr., and William G. Shade, *Old Dominion, New Commonwealth: A History of Virginia, 1607–2007* (Charlottesville: University of Virginia Press, 2007), 182. Ford and Freehling suggest a slightly lower total of around one-third.

23. Wooster, *Politicians, Planters, and Plain Folk*, 5; Fletcher M. Green, *Constitutional Development in the South Atlantic States, 1776–1860: A Study in the Evolution of Democracy* (Chapel Hill: University of North Carolina Press, 1930), 290–96; Freehling, *Road to Disunion*, 1:515. On apportionment in 1850 see Thorpe, *Federal and State Constitutions*, vol. 7 (Virginia), 3833–36.

24. William G. Shade, *Democratizing the Old Dominion: Virginia and the Second Party System, 1824–1861* (Charlottesville: University of Virginia Press, 1996), 262; William A. Link, *Roots of Secession: Slavery and Politics in Antebellum Virginia* (Chapel Hill:

University of North Carolina Press, 2003), 76; Thorpe, *Federal and State Constitutions*, vol. 7 (Virginia), 3837.

25. Thorpe, *Federal and State Constitutions*, vol. 3 (Maryland), 1698; Wooster, *Politicians, Planters, and Plain Folk*, 57.

26. Wooster, *Politicians, Planters, and Plain Folk*, 7; Barbara Jeanne Fields, *Slavery and Freedom on the Middle Ground: Maryland during the Nineteenth Century* (New Haven: Yale University Press, 1985), 21, 20; Thorpe, *Federal and State Constitutions*, vol. 3 (Maryland), 1721. Fields entitles the first chapter of her book "Two Marylands: 1850."

27. Kruman, *Parties and Politics*, 12; Thorpe, *Federal and State Constitutions*, vol. 5 (North Carolina), 2799.

28. John C. Inscoe, *Mountain Masters, Slavery, and the Sectional Crisis in Western North Carolina* (Knoxville: University of Tennessee Press, 1989), 142; David Brown, *Southern Outcast: Hinton Rowan Helper and the Impending Crisis of the South* (Baton Rouge: Louisiana State University Press, 2006).

29. Paul D. Escott, *Many Excellent People: Power and Privilege in North Carolina, 1850–1890* (Chapel Hill: University of North Carolina Press, 1985), 15–16; Charles C. Bolton, *Poor Whites of the Antebellum South: Tenants and Laborers in Central North Carolina and Northeast Mississippi* (Durham: Duke University Press, 1994), 115; Robert C. Kenzer, *Kinship and Neighborhood in a Southern Community: Orange County, North Carolina, 1849–1881* (Knoxville: University of Tennessee Press, 1987), 53.

30. Roger W. Shugg, *Origins of Class Struggle in Louisiana* (Baton Rouge: Louisiana State University Press, 1939), 122; Thorpe, *Federal and State Constitutions*, vol. 3 (Louisiana), 1382; Wooster, *People in Power*, 18.

31. Thorpe, *Federal and State Constitutions*, vol. 3 (Louisiana), 1412; Wooster, *People in Power*, 19.

32. "Report of the Committee on Amendments to the Constitution," cited in Samuel C. Hyde Jr., *Pistols and Politics: The Dilemma of Democracy in Louisiana's Florida Parishes, 1810–1899* (Baton Rouge: Louisiana State University Press, 1996), 46–91. A different interpretation is given by John M. Sacher, *A Perfect War of Politics: Parties, Politicians, and Democracy in Louisiana, 1824–1861* (Baton Rouge: Louisiana State University Press, 2003).

33. Paul F. Bourke and Donald A. DeBats, "Identifiable Voting in Nineteenth-Century America: Toward a Comparison of Britain and the United States before the Secret Ballot," *Perspectives in American History* 11 (1978): 262. Curiously, the authors recognize Virginia "as the major exception" to this generalization, although, as shown, universal suffrage was not in place in other southern states in 1820.

34. A point reinforced by Ford recently: democratic pressures "along the emerging lines of 'one white man, one vote' sentiment, were resisted by potent elites almost everywhere. The conservative opposition was effective in limiting democratic reform in some states and forcing it to compromise in others, but in other states conservatives failed." Lacy K. Ford, "Democracy and Its Consequences in Antebellum America: A Review Essay," *Journal of Southern History* 74 (February 2008): 136–37.

35. Keysaar, *Right to Vote*, 62, 355–57, 358–61.

36. Ibid., 63.

37. Olsen, *Political Culture and Secession*, 124; Shugg, *Origins of Class Struggle*, 129. The timing of migration is also important: Joan E. Cashin, *A Family Venture: Men and Women on the Southern Frontier* (Baltimore: Johns Hopkins University Press, 1991), 51–52, suggests that the rate of planter emigration slowed in the 1840s and 1850s (at precisely the time electoral politics were opened to more and more ordinary southerners).

38. Richard Franklin Bensel, *The American Ballot Box in the Mid-Nineteenth Century* (Cambridge: Cambridge University Press, 2004), 8–9.

39. James Oakes, *Slavery and Freedom: An Interpretation of the Old South* (New York: Knopf, 1990), 114–15.

40. Wooster, *People in Power*, 105, offers a different interpretation that has been overturned by recent works.

41. Olsen, *Political Culture and Secession*, 125; Christopher Morris, *Becoming Southern: The Evolution of a Way of Life, Warren County and Vicksburg, Mississippi, 1770–1860* (New York: Oxford University Press, 1995), 91, 96.

42. Hahn, *Roots of Southern Populism*, 95; Hyde, *Pistols and Politics*, 67; Stephanie McCurry, *Masters of Small Worlds: Yeoman Households, Gender Relations, and the Political Culture of the Antebellum South Carolina Low Country* (New York: Oxford University Press, 1995), 246. My understanding of bonds is informed by Erik Mathisen, "'Know All Men by These Presents': Bonds, Politics and Localism in the Antebellum South" (Commonwealth Fund Conference, University College London, June 2011). Mathisen's work in progress provides the most extensive analysis to date.

43. Cooper, *South and the Politics of Slavery*, 30.

44. Daniel W. Crofts, *Old Southampton: Politics and Society in a Virginia County, 1834–1869* (Charlottesville: University of Virginia Press: 1992), 164–69.

45. Laura F. Edwards, *The People and Their Peace: Legal Culture and the Transformation of Inequality in the Post-Revolutionary South* (Chapel Hill: University of North Carolina Press, 2009); Hahn, *Roots of Southern Populism*, 91.

# II

## Reconstructing Citizenship

# 5

........................

# Personal Reconstructions

## Confederates as Citizens in the Post–Civil War South

JAMES J. BROOMALL

On May 2, 1865, the tired remnants of the Army of Tennessee, encamped in Greensboro, North Carolina, gathered to hear Confederate general Joseph E. Johnston's final orders.[1] He asked his men to return home and discharge the "obligations of good and peaceful citizens" as effectively as they had "performed the duties of thorough soldiers in the field."[2] Johnston's decree represented a hopeful augur for Confederates' transition from war to peace by delineating the respective roles of citizens and soldiers. The hand of war, however, did not discriminate between field and home, and many white southern men could not separate the trauma of battle from the tranquillity of the hearth. Subsequently the southern landscape was rife with private and public disorder, often provoked by Confederate veterans suspended between the spheres of soldier and citizen.

Defeated in war and uncertain of their future, many southerners struggled to define their place and their role in society. White men who had once largely defined their lives around an ancient code of honor and mobilized into armies believing in the righteousness of their cause were now exposed to self-doubt, shame, and submission.[3] How these traumas shaped men's understanding of and transition into southern society directed their personal transformations from Confederate soldiers to United States citizens. The Civil War and its events had altered veterans' mental and emotional landscapes and had destabilized white southern manliness as it was socially constructed and understood.[4] The surrender of Confederate armies did not mark an end to men's martial lives or bring closure to their wartime experiences. The aggressive manliness of a warrior and the emotional upheaval brought by war clashed with a more controlled civilian masculinity.[5] The internal contest manifested itself in personal and social turmoil. The majority of men, pressed by the necessity of want and exhausted by prolonged military service, peacefully returned home, started working, and parsed out their emotions quietly. Other battle-hardened veterans, undeterred by defeat, desperately sought to continue fighting or fled the country entirely.[6] For both groups, the shock of battle lingered well past military conflict and became an essential part of how veterans comprehended the postwar South. Only after a period of intense disorder could white southerners begin to reconstitute themselves as a people and look toward reconstruction.[7]

In locating their place as citizens, former soldiers had first to evaluate their understanding of defeat, which generated, especially among those of prewar economic and social prominence, feelings of uselessness. The Confederacy's political collapse and the economic ruin of an antebellum aristocracy unmasked white southern men.[8] In the antebellum era public masks ensured absolute mastery—relationships with women, children, and slaves defined manhood. Patriarchy and paternalism depended upon personal conduct, and power was realized only through the successful governance of family and the continued maintenance of independent households.[9] Once unmasked, men felt unmanned. Responses to this emotional tumult directed veterans' relationships to the South, to the collapsing Confederacy, and to the United States, and therefore deeply informed their conceptions of postwar citizenship. Veterans' responses varied, but many, desperate to restore a semblance of order, reasserted their masculinity in the protection of their families, which lent personal meaning to postwar life and citizenship.[10]

Rather than viewing citizenship strictly through its political connotations, this essay understands the term expansively. Charles Tilly writes that citizenship "is *relational* in the sense that it locates identities in connections among individuals and groups rather than in the minds of particular persons." Further, it is *cultural* "in insisting that social identities rest on shared understandings," and *historical* "in calling attention to the path-dependent accretion of memories, understandings and means of action."[11] Wartime memories, Confederate identity, and cultural heritage formed the fabric of southern men and shaped postwar citizenship. This essay seeks to understand how some of these men closed their civil wars and on what terms they reestablished themselves in postwar society. Using a select group of veterans—educated whites who created extended and introspective records during a period in which few southerners were writing extensively—this essay considers the interplay between men's private lives and their public actions between 1865 and 1867, and in doing so offers a new way of understanding veterans' inner responses to war and the tumultuous, prolonged transition to peace.[12] Conjoining the typically bifurcated areas of men's personal and public lives exposes how intimate feelings and cultural expressions reshaped the problems of civic strife and social reconstruction.

Scholars almost uniformly recognize the Civil War's transformative effects upon southern society, but they have reached no consensus as to the degree or extent of change. On the one hand, historians have charged that the war was remembered but its pains and its consequences were eventually forgotten. By extension, the conflict did not decisively change whites' intellectual frameworks, excepting the monumental readjustment to emancipation.[13] On the other hand, cultural and intellectual historians, in particular, have stressed that the forces of Civil War and emancipation forever shifted white mind-sets. Former Confederates' war of defiance continued into the years of Reconstruction and beyond.[14] The latter camp is foundational to this consideration of some white southerners' feelings, thoughts, and behavior. Men grappled with a sense of self at the same time they were struggling to reimpose a public self, especially vis-à-vis freedpeople. Responses to these internal crises ranged from bewilderment to depression to numbness to rage. Military surrender temporarily paralyzed veterans, creating feelings of uselessness and emasculation. These emotional reactions to civil war and military defeat shaped Reconstruction as much as political commitments and ideological expressions.

The Civil War was too momentous and the events afterward too injurious for Confederate veterans to reconstruct quickly, indeed to sometimes even comprehend their worlds during the war's conclusion. The prewar foundations of white citizenship—independence, individual autonomy, and belief in states' rights—had once sustained the honor and liberty of social elites, especially, but were now undermined by the consequences of war.[15] As Laura F. Edwards charges, the "changes unleashed by war and emancipation shattered the center around which elite white men and women organized their identities, their roles within households, and their place in the social order."[16] Indeed, war and emancipation recast antebellum white manhood, and southerners confronted a world controlled, for a period, by Union soldiers and shaped by the federal government.

Veterans' concerns about postwar citizenship, social and political, had as much to do with the effects of emancipation as Confederate defeat. Some men, rather than returning home immediately, began extended journeys that served to clarify their personal needs and public place. In the first days of April 1865, scores of southern soldiers from the Army of Northern Virginia determined to strike south from Virginia and reach either Joseph E. Johnston's army in North Carolina or Edmund Kirby Smith's men in the Trans-Mississippi. The resolve of many parties quickly faded in the final weeks of April, however, as they learned first of Robert E. Lee's and then Johnston's surrenders. Moreover, belief in the Confederate cause faltered after many veterans witnessed crowds of civilians and soldiers in South Carolina and Georgia seizing Confederate government property, confiscating large stores of powder, and gathering in large and sometimes violent crowds.[17] Visions of a prolonged military struggle were replaced instead with scenes of violence, disheartening news of military defeat, and personal despair. As faith in the Confederate cause faltered, veterans had to confront their potential place as a United States citizen.

Exogenous forces and internal dynamics created an ontological shift among many southern whites. Grappling with a profound series of changes, men responded to these internal crises in a variety of ways but most often expressed either bewilderment or depression. On May 4, 1865, Brigadier General Josiah Gorgas—a Pennsylvania-born high-ranking Confederate ordinance officer stationed in Richmond during the war— reflected on what had transpired. "The calamity which has fallen upon us in the total destruction of our government is of a character so overwhelming that I am as yet unable to comprehend it. I am as one walking in a dream, and expecting to awake. I cannot see its consequences."[18] George Anderson Mercer, a prominent Savannah lawyer and former Confederate officer, expressed a similar sense of bewilderment and confusion. He recorded in his diary that he was unable to recover from "the stunning effect of mingled surprise and grief caused by the sudden prostration of our cause. The noble structure we had reared was leveled like a house of cards."[19] The Confederacy's spectacular collapse left William Alexander penniless and stranded in Texas, yearning for his North Carolina home. In a July 9 letter to his mother, he apologized for its having been some time since he last wrote: "I could not write," he explained, "in fact could not for some time open my mouth to any one [as I] felt so badly about our national affairs[.] The result of the hard contest left such a heavy weight upon my heart." He only now felt better because he was more resigned, no less satisfied with the war's results.[20] Thus, in the spring and summer of 1865 soldiers were confronted by the specter of defeat in the form of a disintegrating country. Shocked by the sudden fall of their nation, these men were left reeling, unable to assume allegiance to the Union and unwilling to believe that the Confederate project was now lost. The emotional void created by these political developments shaped conceptions of citizenship as men occupied a liminal space between the former Confederacy and the reunited Union. The cultural bedrock on which Confederate citizens' self-identities were founded had now collapsed.

Veterans' recorded words, taut with emotion, give voice to how military service and the Confederate cause forever altered their self-perceptions and reshaped their understanding of civilian life. For the white South, civil war destabilized the control and communication of emotions, and a heightened sense of melancholy pervaded southern culture deep into the postbellum era. For Confederate veterans, in particular, the humiliation of defeat, the lingering terror of combat, and the postwar South's economic and political uncertainties powerfully reshaped men's emotional lives. Men who had fallen on the battlefield facing the enemy had died a "good death," thereby allowing their friends and families to justify and make sense of the loss.[21] But unlike death on the battlefield, the grief of defeat brought humiliation and alienation—a psychic pain not easily remedied. This emptiness proved a formidable challenge to white southern men facing both Reconstruction and citizenship.

As Confederates endeavored to make sense of military surrender they also confronted the realities of defeat, most prominently in the form of federal soldiers. Josiah Gorgas's encounter came quickly. Confused and deeply unsettled, he decided to travel to Alabama after abandoning his plans to continue fighting for the Confederacy in another theater of war. Here, in his adopted state, he would wait "before again coming under the control of the authority of the U.S. Govt."[22] Though he remained silent on the subject, Gorgas was perhaps drawn to a familiar place to anchor himself during a period of momentous change. By late May he was traveling and trying to adjust to a new life station. On the twenty-sixth he stopped in Montgomery and "[t]ook tea with Yankee officers at [the] same table." A novel sensation, he wrote, but one to which he had to adjust, as white southerners' "late enemies" were now their new "masters."[23] The word *master* evoked an antebellum social order inverted by civil war in which northern rule undermined white southerners' independence. Such relationships—real or imagined—shaped some veterans' strides toward citizenship as they considered the possibilities of their own inequalities.

Veterans had to face how their submission affected personal and social understandings of manhood and citizenship. Many in the northern press emasculated defeated Confederates, most famously in the lampoons and cartoons of Jefferson Davis during his capture—the Confederate president was accused of fleeing disguised as a woman.[24] While northern stories used hyperbole they also contained core truths, for the war's results provoked some southerners to look inward and question themselves and their changing station. The political and economic foundations that defined the upper echelons of antebellum southern society had been shaken by war. Men altered their self-concept, LeeAnn Whites charges, "by attaching themselves more firmly to the domestic arena, as *the* location of self-realization."[25] Intimate ties of affection bonded individuals together and, as Emily West has argued in this volume, could supplant other forms of self-identity, thereby providing a foundation for the construction of public standing. While George Mercer struggled to reestablish his prewar economic standing he found immediate solace in his family, reflecting, "some of the happiest moments of my life were spent here . . . in the companionship of my little family, my books and my thoughts, when I had no money, was thankful that I could even live, and, putting aside the spirit of discontent, made a virtue of necessity."[26] For men who had lost everything, family became a sustaining source of pride and support. Former Confederates had to now refashion their culture, reconstruct their "civilization," while contending with psychological ruin.[27]

In adapting to postwar life, white southerners struggled to understand the meaning and consequences of their wartime experiences. For many, the significance of the war's events was too great not to reshape the bridge between the antebellum and postbellum eras. Prewar expectations could never be fully reconciled with the war and its traumas. South Carolinian E. B. Richardson captured these tensions when he pronounced that they "who go forth to the wars, with high hopes and bounding hearts—who picture of their minds the glorious rewards of great achievements—should blind their eyes to the horrors and injustice of the cause they bleed for."[28] The shock and terror of the battlefield were too severe for soldiers' ideas and belief systems to remain unchanged. Divergent outlooks between soldiers and civilians created, in a sense, two wars, which after 1865 had to be recombined and made whole in the public's understanding.[29] Although wounded and demobilized soldiers had been returning to southern communities since 1861, the sustained influx of defeated veterans in the spring and summer of 1865 proved shocking. Historian Jeffrey W. McClurken demonstrates that the war's survivors returned home as changed men, only to be greeted by women and children also profoundly affected by the conflict and its consequences.[30] White southerners' emotional outpourings pointedly communicated their hardships. Virginian Catherine Barbara Broun recorded in May 1865—too "*distressed*" to have written in her diary throughout April—that the young men of Winchester were in tears. "It is *very very* sad," she noted, "to see our soldiers at home or riding about without arms. It is a *terrible disappointment* so unlooked for."[31] Pained by the loss of men, horrified by the physical reminders of war, and distraught over military surrender, southern civilians confronted infinite difficulties in the conflict's aftermath. Men, women, and children together reshaped the white South as they responded to the crisis of civil war.

For some Confederate veterans the personal emotions of anger, pain, and confusion shaped civilian life and the contours of citizenship just as much as ideological commitment to either the Confederacy or the United States. Personal feelings were grounded in broader tensions between public and private lives. Surrendered soldiers had a public obligation to the reunited country and its governing systems. But privately white men's structure of feelings remained founded in family, the fallen Confederacy, and their military lives. These conflicting loyalties induced feelings of uselessness and depletion. Such ideas and sentiments swirled together as veterans confronted reconstruction. Rather than adhering to an overarching ethos, white southerners gradually reordered new and old cultural materials that both reacted to the new order and reinforced older values.[32] Though their military service was over, veterans' inner wars continued—many became consumed by depression.[33] Veterans struggled in the postwar South, often unable to reach any real sense of settlement or finality. For these veterans the past and present mixed together as they grappled with self-definition. Negotiating these private landscapes, whites tried to comprehend what the Civil War meant and how it changed them as men.

The vast majority of men looked forward to getting back home and beginning life again, though few envisioned what personal struggles awaited them. Stripped of the traditional trappings of antebellum authority, white men became unmasked. And as Nancy D. Bercaw has remarked, they discovered that their self-identities were "not fixed but fluid, susceptible to the ignominy of defeat."[34] Certainly despair continued to conflict with a regenerative drive as military service had altered self-perception and re-shaped veterans' roles in civil society. By attempting to reestablish them-selves in civilian life, however, men such as Josiah Gorgas and George Mercer decided on moderation, representative of a common impulse to restore order. These men slowly yielded to federal rule and started the process of personally embracing United States citizenship. Others, wary of federal prosecution or determined to continue the war, left the country. These actions were an explicit rejection of citizenship under an American flag and within a reunited country. Ironically, on the very day that Gor-gas took tea with federal soldiers, May 26, the Trans-Mississippi Depart-ment under the command of General Edmund Kirby Smith, a West Point graduate who served with distinction in the Mexican-American War and the man whom Gorgas initially hoped to join to continue fighting, was formally surrendered.[35] The Confederate cause, as manifest in combat it-self, was all but lost.

Throughout the nineteenth century, violence and self-restraint marked two distinct faces of southern men. Power and authority were derived through the balance and display of these two masks.[36] At the Civil War's close, Confederate veterans struggled with the inherent tension between these systems of behavior and determined courses of action that pro-pounded either violence or restraint. Kirby Smith's dedication to the Con-federate cause and fear of federal reprisal compelled him to look beyond southern borders. In the beginning of May, he had asked one of leading private citizens of Shreveport, Louisiana, Robert Rose, to convey his re-gards to the emperor of Mexico and to make certain that the emperor understood that the services of Confederate troops could be invaluable to him.[37] Whatever preparations were made for this plan collapsed in mid- to late May as the armies of the Trans-Mississippi evaporated and Kirby Smith became a commanding general in name only. Unable to se-cure "terms honorable alike to . . . soldiers & citizens," Kirby Smith did not participate in the formal surrender and pledged instead to "struggle to the last." He admonished his men in a public proclamation issued in late May: "Soldiers! I am left a command without an army—a General without troops. You have made yr. choice. It was unwise & unpatriotic. But it is final. I pray you may not live to reject it."[38] The speech's strident tone suggested a man who had been pained to watch his armies dissolve and was now unsure of his future. Especially striking is how the speech's sentiments contrast with those offered by Joseph E. Johnston to his men at the war's close (recorded in the essay's beginning). Johnston called for his men to embrace citizenship and peace, whereas Kirby Smith rejected any station not connected with the Confederacy and expressed concern over his men's choices. Susanna M. Lee has observed in this volume that postwar contests over definitions of citizenship rested on wartime loyalties. The oppositional words and behavior of Kirby Smith and Johnston demonstrate substantial differences in understandings of wartime and postwar loyalties and how ties of allegiance shaped models of citizenship.

On June 26, 1865, a beleaguered band of Confederate soldiers buried their frayed battle flags under the sands of the Rio Grande's north bank, forded the river's murky waters, and then crossed into Mexico. Kirby Smith led the party. In shirtsleeves with a silk handkerchief around his neck, a revolver at his side, and a shotgun across his lap, Kirby Smith fled the South mounted on a mule having left behind everything except, he later explained to his wife, Cassie, "a clear conscience and a sense of having done my duty."[39] Though he was assured of his personal honor, his future remained unclear. But even the "darkness and uncertainty" that awaited him could not "entirely check the feeling of lightness and joy experienced" when he felt himself to be "plain Kirby Smith," relieved from all cares and responsible only for his own actions.[40] These actions and words unmoored Kirby Smith, disrupting any connections to the United States and freeing him as a man. The bold actions of Kirby Smith—among a set of "diehard rebels"—marked an overt rejection of both the postwar social order and the prospects of American citizenship.[41] An odd mixture of fear and hubris directed their journeys into Mexico and beyond. But they were also driven by the requirements of masculinity, for the men's sense of honor and duty required that they continued the cause despite the momentous disasters witnessed in the spring of 1865. For these men the Confederacy remained the only nation to which they swore allegiance.

Scores of soldiers from the Confederacy's eastern and western armies eventually joined Mexico's fight for independence, while others established the short-lived Confederate colony of Carlota.[42] Even those white southerners who had traveled beyond the South's borders, however, never let home drift far from their minds but instead incorporated these experiences into their southern identity.[43] Charles G. Talcott, writing to a friend in Virginia, described large numbers of Confederates in Mexico. Yet, while Talcott and his associates were well, they longed "for dear old Virginia as it was, & our kind friends as they are."[44] The heavy presence of exiled Confederates on the Texas border and Mexico's volatile government was enough for Union general Ulysses S. Grant to dispatch Phil Sheridan and an entire army corps to the Rio Grande to patrol the border—a command that eventually reached fifty-two thousand men.[45] Defiant under defeat but still desperately yearning for home while exiled, these southerners maintained a liminal position—balanced between two lands, they had lost their sense of self.[46] Such men were resting their claims of citizenship on a defeated nation in a foreign country.

Kirby Smith decided to cast his fortunes elsewhere once in Mexico and opted to travel to Cuba, compelled by prudence and "duty" to escape the "excited feelings" of the northern people and the federal government.[47] In truth, then, Kirby Smith's bold public posture betrayed a deeper reality of personal conflict that formed his inner experiences and outer identity. His reaction to the Confederacy's collapse and his rejection of United States citizenship formed the fabric of his political identity but also underpinned his personal life. Only once the public and the personal are entwined together, then, do Kirby Smith's actions, his understandings of citizenship, gain clarity. Deeply troubled, Kirby Smith's otherwise strong facade quickly dissolved as he penned loving words to his wife. Once settled in Cuba in the late summer of 1865, Edmund anxiously related: "I do not know rightly how to determine upon my future course, whether I shall adopt a new country, see a new home . . . or return to my own people, share their fate and recommence the battle of life amongst those we have long known and loved and who will sympathize with and cheer us in our trials and difficulties."[48] Conflicted, he continued his public stand against the federal government, though in his private correspondence this decision weighed heavily. Kirby Smith wanted both to return to his wife and to maintain his public honor. The diehard Confederate may have come to recognize, or at least explicitly confront, the reality that by fleeing the country he had abandoned his duties as a man to protect and care for his family. By considering a return to the United States, Kirby Smith was also rethinking the familial obligations and duties that he had heretofore eschewed.

White southerners worried that military defeat had repudiated their manliness.[49] Many women reassured weary veterans that the values underpinning antebellum southern manhood—honor, virtue, and sacrifice—had been preserved. These beliefs would now serve as the building blocks for the reconstruction of manliness and facilitate the veterans' shift from soldier to citizen.[50] Yet, civil war had altered the personal relationships between men and women, and power dynamics were renegotiated accordingly.[51] War had afforded women the opportunity to expand their control over the domestic sphere and beyond, thus empowering elite whites especially.[52] These new critical positions underpinned domestic reconstructions as southern women demonstrated heroism and resilience in the face of innumerable hardships.[53]

Throughout the late summer of 1865, Edmund and Cassie exchanged letters that attempted to resolve the tangled web of Kirby Smith's exile—a resolution that could bring them together while maintaining honor. At least for Kirby Smith, then, the prospects of United States citizenship became more palatable if he could rejoin his wife. With increased distance from the Confederate cause, Kirby Smith began a new battle to rejoin his wife. Edmund surrendered himself to Cassie lovingly, writing, "Your wishes darling will govern me fully; let me know how you feel; what you desire and what you believe to be best."[54] Cassie wanted her husband back, having been long separated because of war. "I cannot nor, *will not*, live much longer" apart, she wrote, and pledged to do "anything *in honor*" to have him with her.[55] For Edmund, he preferred to return to the United States if it could be done "without degradation and humiliation." But, he refused to sacrifice his personal respect or his monetary interests, and most importantly, did not want to lose face. To Cassie, though, he also finally admitted defeat. "The war is over & our cause irretrievably lost." He questioned his earlier actions as unwise but refused to acknowledge his course as wrong.[56] In Cassie, Edmund found a confidant, someone with whom he could share his innermost fears and humiliations. Moreover, in Cassie, Edmund found a cause more worthy than war.

Kirby Smith's words both reveal and obscure. Self-doubt and internal turmoil wind through his letters, but a strong demeanor and a determined course counterbalanced those sentiments. By late summer the couple determined a strategy. Cassie would petition President Andrew Johnson, in person, for her husband's return, while Edmund would write General U. S. Grant, his friend from the Mexican-American War, about his status.[57] Cassie's bold resolve and direct action reflect a broader change in the politicalization of white southern women. During the Civil War women had entered the public sphere by maintaining plantations and farms, participating in the war effort, and voicing political opinions. In the war's aftermath men actively attempted to reassert their authority, though under different terms.[58] Cassie and Edmund could only resolve their separation through joint effort. Once assured that he could return to the United States without penalty or imprisonment, Kirby Smith set sail.[59] Now, steeled by his family and assured of his honor, Edmund cast his lot with the southern people within the borders of his native land. He wrote, "our people should not leave, instead of seeking asylums abroad, their own destinies and the triumph of the principles for which they fought are in their own hands, let them seek by every possible means the reestablishment of the state government in the natural course of events the military must then give way to the civil rule."[60] With these words Kirby Smith resurrected his earlier defiance, perhaps more vested in the South after his experiences abroad and more assured of his manliness by rejoining his family. And so, on November 14, 1865, Edmund Kirby Smith took his amnesty oath in Lynchburg, Virginia, thereby joining the Union once more.[61] Kirby Smith's return to the South and his declaration of loyalty illustrate a model of citizenship rebuilt from both public and private self-identities and allegiances.

By swearing allegiance to the United States, southerners publicly repudiated the Confederacy and declared a new political identity. Nothing about this transition was seamless, and public declarations barely masked private discomfort. The oath of allegiance and the contours of citizenship, as historian Anne Rubin argues, were understood by white southern men through gendered terms, for honor and manliness were linked to loyalty.[62] Southerners had to parse out these conflicts as they looked forward to United States citizenship and backward to a Confederate past. By swearing an oath, former Confederates obligated themselves to maintain a strict promise of loyalty. How they emotionally dealt with the repercussions of this decision largely directed southerners' perceptions of their place and role in the reunited Union. While many scholars have emphasized how defiance subsumed depression, white southerners' militancy during Reconstruction should not overshadow their continued misery and despair.[63] Collectively, white soldiers and civilians suffered from a culture of defeat—trauma and mourning that produced doubt and confusion.[64] Southern whites could not easily address or reverse these processes, as many were left paralyzed and reeling. George Mercer described the oath as "a painful but necessary procedure" while also contending that southerners' "hearts cannot change."[65] Veterans were honor-bound to recognize the war's victors, but honor also directed continued fidelity to the fallen Confederacy. Torn between two worlds, veterans attempted to strike a painful balance.[66]

Confederate veterans dealt with and suffered from despondency and depression to varying degrees, but their emotional lives deeply influenced the atmosphere and shape of southern society. Whereas "diehard rebels" determined a path of resistance, at least for a period, other veterans became utterly despondent, not knowing what to do. Men's personal and emotional landscapes—their desires and their inclinations—influenced responses to and understandings of citizenship in particular and postwar life more broadly. Former Confederates watched as unbounded possibilities and bright prospects corroded into dark horizons clouded by uncertainty. The emotional consequences proved devastating. White men, especially those of prewar prominence, took solace in the present but only reluctantly planned for the future. War disrupted their public and private lives; the disaster of defeat only heightened this interruption. Southerners' readjustment to postwar life was filtered by an overwhelming sense of apprehension that deeply affected mental states and social standings. The private responses of southerners often ran counter to public accounts, which typically emphasized the importance of rebuilding region.[67] Destruction and reconstruction coexisted in their worldviews, for these men did not think in simple dichotomies. Rather, men who were internally plagued managed also to maintain a strong facade and emphasized the importance of regrowth.

The forbidding veneer of a closed southern culture had been partially shattered, and southern men, changed by war, sought out ways to express and examine their new emotions. In considering postwar citizenship and its many facets, the dilemmas these men faced, the feelings they expressed, and the depression they experienced serve as guides in understanding their relationships to region and country. As Stephen Berry and Bertram Wyatt-Brown have ably demonstrated, whites grappled with despondency and doubt throughout the antebellum era.[68] But the sheer scale of military defeat and its accompanying effects were unparalleled. Men who had used work, pride, and honor as foundations for manhood faced uselessness, pain, and melancholy. James B. Mitchell of Glenville, Alabama, returned to the University of North Carolina in 1866 after having discontinued his studies in 1861 to join the Confederate army. In a revealing letter to his friend Ruffin H. Thomson—also a student from North Carolina who left in 1861 for military service—Mitchell laid bare his feelings. He was much pained to see his friend "so much disposed to melancholy," but remained helpless for he, too, found himself "in the same condition" and unable to offer consolation. This dark depression cast a long shadow over Mitchell's future. Not able to see "any light ahead," he lost all faith in a once promised bright future. During the war, he recalled, "old wiseacres" had cried out, "Never mind Boys, keep a good heart. You know the darkest hour is just before day." These sentiments now disgusted Mitchell, who believed that happiness could only be found in those who contented themselves with "the old aphorism that 'whatever is, is right' and endeavor to make the best of it."[69]

Steering between life's extremes, wary of fanatical doctrines, Mitchell embraced a few simple truths. Among them was the enjoyment of life's basic comforts. Deprived of basic necessities while in the army, southern men enjoyed niceties but were now constantly reminded of just how fleeting such luxuries could be. By instilling deeper meaning into what was once meaningless, life appeared more enjoyable. Mitchell composed his letter comfortably seated by a warm fire while the ground outside was covered in sleet and snow. He could remember only a short time ago when it was different: "I had nought but the ground for a bed and rocks for a pillow, and in this I perceive a blessing." Taking Alexander Pope's words to heart ("One truth is clear, whatever is, is right"), Mitchell stopped here.[70] For now, his "limited vision" was "incompetent to pierce the thick darkness further. The future of the South is to me a mysterious horror and I decline to contemplate it. My imagination has not even yet shaped my own future but awaits the development of events."[71] And with these words Mitchell embodied Confederate veterans' unsure future as they faced Reconstruction.

The emotional lives of southern men held great sway over their understandings of the reunited country and citizenship. George Mercer reflected on his place as an American and a southerner after having read an excerpt of William Makepeace Thackeray's *Vanity Fair* in which an English traveler to foreign lands rejoiced after hearing "God Save the King." Mercer was moved to tears as he "reflected that now there was no national song capable of producing similar emotions in me—that I could enjoy none of those grand public feelings that the citizens of a noble and free

Government . . . so constantly experience. Alas, I must confess, all my national feeling is buried with the overthrown Confederacy, and there is nothing in the attitude of the U.S. . . . calculated to arouse similar emotions."[72] Mercer maintained a diary of the "workings and feelings of the mind"—his attempt to rationalize and dissect the abstract and ambiguous.[73] While Mercer eventually reestablished his prewar social standing and managed to accumulate some wealth, feelings of despondency continued to plague him. His bouts of melancholy were directly connected to his new role as a United States citizen in the reunited country. The station, although an outward reflection of legal status, in no way reflected personal commitments or attachments. Rather, he felt a void created by the Confederacy's collapse but never filled by the country's reunification.

Geographic place, in particular, provoked considerable self-reflection and consternation. Beginning in the fall of 1866, Mercer renewed annual trips that he had taken before the war to New York City and Saratoga Springs. Once in these cities his "excited temperament was carried away by the noise and busy life—the crowded streets—the gay equipage and handsome buildings—and the beauty of the women one sees in the moving throng." "After reaching home," however, "everything . . . seemed dull and listless." Mercer justified his northern excursions with his wartime experiences, reinforcing the proposition that both war and peace now formed equal parts of his identity. During military service, he noted, he had "seen no gaiety and had necessarily submitted to many privations." Now he sought to fully embrace that of which he had been deprived. Moreover, he wanted to escape the "stern requirements" of his profession. Mercer's emotions ebbed and flowed after each visit north: neither completely resigned to his new station in Savannah nor willing to resettle in the North, he constructed an uncomfortable middle ground during the Reconstruction era. Mercer would never fully escape the South that he both loved and loathed or his former travails as a soldier, for these mixed emotions were foundational to his new sense of self.

Whatever monetary gains Mercer enjoyed proved unattainable to Josiah Gorgas, who drifted from job to job in Alabama—his destination in the spring of 1865. In the final months of 1866 and into the winter of 1867 Gorgas complained of severe depression caused, he perversely hoped, by poor health, though "mental anxiety" seemed the only real explanation.[74] On January 6, 1867, Gorgas entered a troubled passage into his diary. For the last four months he had lived "in a state of profound depression," which had made life a burden. He desperately wrote: "I am certain that for no imaginable recompense would I live this life over again . . . annihilation must be the only thing left. Nothing is so terrible as despair."[75] Nearly paralyzed by depression, Gorgas struggled in the years after the war to resettle, to reestablish himself, in an increasingly foreign South.

Ultimately, then, Gorgas, Mercer, and Kirby Smith each sought different paths toward their personal reconstructions: journeys that attempted to mend the wounds of war and reaffirm their position as southern men and citizens. Rather than tidy conclusions, however, the stories of these men remained unsettled as they tried to reconstitute themselves, their society, during the years before congressional Reconstruction. More than simply personal trials, veterans' passages between war and peace were central to the broader project of national reconstruction, for the actions and emotions of Confederates not only determined on what terms the Civil War closed but also shaped the contours of white southern culture during the postbellum era.[76] Stripped of the traditional trappings of antebellum authority, white men were unmasked. And they discovered that their self-identities were fluid and shaped by the experience of defeat.[77] The recognition of such ruptures created consternation, confusion, and emotional outpourings. Capturing the forms in which these thoughts were expressed offers deeper understandings into how white men negotiated the transition between civil war and civic peace. Despondency and depression, while familiar emotions, are rooted in specific historical experiences.[78] The emotional landscape of southern men was fraught by inadequacy and depression, which compelled these men to actively strive to reorder a world undone by war. Most turned within, talking only to family or other veterans about their experiences. But emotions of depression also generated anger, for many southerners connected their despondency to the advancement of African Americans.[79]

The disconnect between public order and private disorder suggests a more complicated narrative of Reconstruction and citizenship. Strides toward peace, stability, and reunion, while deeply significant to the political and economic processes of Reconstruction, only partially explain Confederate veterans' personal reconstructions. Sharp divisions between war and peace do not accurately reflect the personal ambiguities of this period or the experiences of its participants. Scores of veterans experienced a sense of aimlessness and profound confusion, suggesting that the wounds of war were not easily healed. These men employed an array of means to grapple with both their inner struggles and outer turmoil, resulting in fractured landscapes. For these men the transition into civilian life proved halting and difficult, but pivotal to the South's changing character. Veterans' actions and experiences dictated the atmosphere and direction of postwar life in many southern communities—their memories of the war and their struggles to find peace contributed to the tumult of the Reconstruction era. Though these pains, indeed, lessened over time, the consequences of this period echoed for decades.[80] These men simply could not return to prewar society, for the war's consequences were too varied, the sting of defeat too strong, and the forces of emancipation too monumental. In the end, the war's traumas, pains, and conclusions proved too decisive in white southerners' personal reconstructions.

## Notes

1. The writer would like to acknowledge the thoughtful comments offered by the conference's participants, especially those of Catherine Clinton, Michael Bibler, Scott Romine, Aaron Sheehan-Dean, and Brian Ward, and the formal comments of David Brown, Joseph Forte, Chris Graham, Bill Link, Brian Luskey, and the two anonymous readers.

2. J. E. Johnston, General Orders, No. 22, in U.S. War Department, *The War of the Rebellion: A Compilation of the Official Records of the Union and Confederate Armies*, series 1, vol. 47, part 1 (Washington, D.C.: Government Printing Office, 1895), 1061.

3. The classic statement on southern honor remains Bertram Wyatt-Brown, *Southern Honor: Ethics and Behavior in the Old South* (New York: Oxford University Press, 1982). See also Kenneth S. Greenberg, *Honor and Slavery: Lies, Duels, Noses, Masks, Dressing as a Woman, Gifts, Strangers, Humanitarianism, Death, Slave Rebellions, the Proslavery Argument, Baseball, Hunting, and Gambling in the Old South* (Princeton: Princeton University Press, 1996); Edward E. Baptist, *Creating an Old South: Middle Florida's Plantation Frontier before the Civil War* (Chapel Hill: University of North Carolina Press, 2002); and Edward E. Baptist, Stephen Berry, Orville Vernon Burton, Kenneth S. Greenberg, and Mark M. Smith, "Looking Back on Bertram Wyatt-Brown's *Southern Honor*: A Roundtable," *Historically Speaking: The Bulletin of the Historical Society* 9 (July/August 2008): 13–18.

4. Whites' responses to these forces form what C. Vann Woodward famously deemed "the burden of southern history." C. Vann Woodward, *The Burden of Southern History*, rev. ed. (1960; reprint, Baton Rouge: Louisiana State University Press, 1991), 189–91. For the emotional consequences of defeat among white southerners see Bertram Wyatt-Brown, "Death of a Nation" and "Honor Chastened," in his *The Shaping of Southern Culture: Honor, Grace, and War, 1760s–1880s* (Chapel Hill: University of North Carolina Press, 2001); and Jeffrey W. McClurken, *Take Care of the Living: Reconstructing*

*Confederate Veteran Families in Virginia* (Charlottesville: University of Virginia Press, 2009), esp. 44–52 and 120–28. Jackson Lears isolates a pervasive sense of doubt that shaped postwar life despite a public optimism, which he partially roots in the presence of Civil War veterans. T. J. Jackson Lears, *No Place of Grace: Antimodernism and the Transformation of American Culture, 1880–1920* (New York: Pantheon, 1981). In a later work Lears describes this as the "long shadow of Appomattox." Lears, *Rebirth of a Nation: The Making of Modern America, 1877–1920* (New York: HarperCollins, 2009). On the shifting terrain of gender identity and gender hierarchy, see LeeAnn Whites, *The Civil War as a Crisis in Gender: Augusta, Georgia, 1860–1890* (Athens: University of Georgia Press, 1995), 3–14 and 132–59, and Craig Thompson Friend, "From Southern Manhood to Southern Masculinities: An Introduction," in *Southern Masculinity: Perspectives on Manhood in the South Since Reconstruction*, ed. Friend (Athens: University of Georgia Press, 2009). My understanding of manhood relies heavily upon the notion that gender is a historical, ideological process. Gail Bederman, *Manliness and Civilization: A Cultural History of Gender and Race in the United States, 1880–1917* (Chicago: University of Chicago Press, 1995), especially 5–10. See also Michael Kimmel, *Manhood in America: A Cultural History* (New York: The Free Press, 1996).

5. Robert A. Nye, "Western Masculinities in War and Peace," *American Historical Review* 112 (April 2007): 417–22.

6. On the process of mustering out and the meaning of defeat for Confederate soldiers, see James Marten, *Sing Not War: The Lives of Union and Confederate Veterans in Gilded Age America* (Chapel Hill: University of North Carolina Press, 2011), 38–49.

7. By using the term reconstruction, small "r," I am avoiding a strictly political interpretation of Reconstruction. Moreover, I concur with Heather Cox Richardson's recent observation that "Reconstruction is a process, not a time period." Heather Cox Richardson, "North and West of Reconstruction: Studies in Political Economy," in *Reconstructions: New Perspectives on the Postbellum United States*, ed. Thomas J. Brown (New York: Oxford University Press, 2006), 90. For insights on the intellectual dimensions of the shift from civil war to civic peace see Leslie Butler, "Reconstructions in Intellectual and Cultural Life," in Brown, *Reconstructions*, 172–205.

8. On the construction and function of "masks" among white southerners, see Greenberg, *Honor and Slavery*. On the broad constellation of reactions to defeat and emancipation among the planter class, see James L. Roark, *Masters without Slaves: Southern Planters in the Civil War and Reconstruction* (New York: Norton, 1977), 120–34.

9. The relations of power and dependency, shaped within the household, directed white independence and its public meanings. Stephanie McCurry, *Masters of Small Worlds: Yeoman Households, Gender Relations, and the Political Culture of the Antebellum South Carolina Low Country* (New York: Oxford University Press, 1995), 37–43 and 81–85.

10. Aaron Sheehan-Dean, *Why Confederates Fought: Family and Nation in Civil War Virginia* (Chapel Hill: University of North Carolina Press, 2007), 192–95; and Marten, *Sing Not War*, 64–72.

11. Charles Tilly, "Citizenship, Identity and Social History," in *Citizenship, Identity and Social History*, ed. Tilly (Cambridge: Cambridge University Press, 1996), 5.

12. Rather than a broad survey, this account draws from men of the upper classes who left extended records during a period in which there is a great paucity in evidence. On source issues during 1865, see Jason Phillips, *Diehard Rebels: The Confederate Culture of Invincibility* (Athens: University of Georgia Press, 2007), 5.

13. See especially Paul M. Gaston, *The New South Creed: A Study of Southern Mythmaking* (1970; reprint, Montgomery: NewSouth Books, 2002), prologue and chapter 1; and Gaines M. Foster, *Ghosts of the Confederacy: Defeat, the Lost Cause, and the Emergence of the New South, 1865 to 1913* (New York: Oxford University Press, 1987), 15–35, specifically. Roark, *Masters without Slaves*, chapter 4; and Peter S. Carmichael, *The Last Generation: Young Virginia in Peace, War, and Reunion* (Chapel Hill: University of North Carolina Press, 2005), chapter 8.

14. See especially Jack P. Maddex, *The Reconstruction of Edward A. Pollard: A Rebel's Conversion to Postbellum Unionism* (Chapel Hill: University of North Carolina Press, 1974); Anne C. Rose, *Victorian America and the Civil War* (New York: Cambridge University Press, 1992); Stephen Kantrowitz, *Ben Tillman and the Reconstruction of White Supremacy* (Chapel Hill: University of North Carolina Press, 2000); W. Scott Poole, *Never Surrender: Confederate Memory and Conservatism in the South Carolina Upcountry* (Athens: University of Georgia Press, 2004); and McClurken, *Take Care of the Living*.

15. On these forces in southern society, see Wyatt-Brown, *The Shaping of Southern Culture*, 65–66.

16. Laura F. Edwards, *Gendered Strife and Confusion: The Political Culture of Reconstruction* (Urbana: University of Illinois Press, 1997), 107.

17. Josiah Gorgas, May 3 and 4, 1865, in Sarah Woolfolk Wiggins, ed., *The Journals of Josiah Gorgas, 1857–1878* (Tuscaloosa: University of Alabama Press, 1995), 162–67.

18. Josiah Gorgas, May 4, 1865, [typed copy of journal], Josiah Gorgas Papers, Louis R. Wilson Library, Southern Historical Collection, University of North Carolina at Chapel Hill [hereinafter SHC].

19. George Anderson Mercer, June 11, 1865, Personal Diary, George Anderson Mercer Papers, SHC.

20. W. L. Alexander to Mother, July 9, 1865, William Alexander Hoke Papers, Series 1.2, Box 2, Folder 12, SHC. For similar reactions see McClurken, *Take Care of the Living*, 66.

21. On the "good death" see Drew Gilpin Faust, *This Republic of Suffering: Death and the American Civil War* (New York: Knopf, 2008), 6–31.

22. Gorgas, May 4, 1865, *Journals of Josiah Gorgas*, 167.

23. Gorgas, May 26, 1865, Gorgas Papers, SHC.

24. Whites, *The Civil War as a Crisis in Gender*, 135–36, and Anne Sarah Rubin, *A Shattered Nation: The Rise and Fall of the Confederacy, 1861–1868* (Chapel Hill: University of North Carolina Press, 2005), 136–37. See also John Taylor Wood Journal, May 10, 1865, Volume 3, John Taylor Wood Papers, SHC.

25. Whites, *The Civil War as a Crisis in Gender*, 135.

26. Mercer Diary, June 10, 1866, Box 1, Volume 5, Mercer Papers, SHC.

27. Wyatt-Brown, *The Shaping of Southern Culture*, 256.

28. E. B. Richardson to Ben, July 10, 1867, Box 1, Folder 1860–1869, Benjamin

S. Williams Papers, David M. Rubenstein Rare Books & Manuscript Library, Duke University.

29. Gerald F. Linderman, *Embattled Courage: The Experience of Combat in the American Civil War* (New York: The Free Press, 1987), 1–3.

30. McClurken, *Take Care of the Living*, 44–45. See also Whites, *The Civil War as a Crisis in Gender*, 114–15.

31. Catherine Barbara Broun, May 2, 1865, Personal Diary [typed copy], Catherine Barbara Hopkins Broun Papers, SHC. Emphasis in the original.

32. How southerners reacted to the war is a long-standing historiographical debate. For brevity I will discuss only two of the most relevant works. Gaines Foster suggests that white southerners used the Lost Cause as a mechanism to overcome the anxieties brought with military defeat and New South social and economic change. White southerners remembered the battle but had forgotten the war's pain, its cost, and its issues, and instead formed an understanding of the past forged by ceremonial activities and rituals. Foster, *Ghosts of the Confederacy*, introduction. More recently, W. Scott Poole has argued that upcountry South Carolinians fashioned an "aesthetic of the Lost Cause," which they used to publicly articulate a vision for an ordered and organic society. "Devotion to the Confederacy," he writes, "became a religious value for South Carolinians who sought to shape a southern scared world." Poole, *Never Surrender*, 3.

33. See especially Gorgas, June 2, 1865, and August 31, 1865, *Journals of Josiah Gorgas*, 175 and 186. For the scholarly perspective see McClurken, *Take Care of the Living*, and Diane Miller Sommerville, "'Will They Ever Be Able to Forget?': Confederate Soldiers and Mental Illness in the Defeated South," in *Weirding the War: Stories from the Civil War's Ragged Edges*, ed. Stephen Berry (Athens: University of Georgia Press, 2011), 321–39.

34. Nancy Bercaw, *Gendered Freedoms: Race, Rights, and the Politics of Household in the Delta, 1861–1875* (Gainesville: University Press of Florida, 2003), 80.

35. Andrew F. Rolle, *The Lost Cause: The Confederate Exodus to Mexico* (1965; reprint, Norman: University of Oklahoma Press, 1992), 50; and Robert L. Kerby, *Kirby Smith's Confederacy: The Trans-Mississippi South, 1863–1865* (New York: Columbia University Press, 1972), 424.

36. Stephen Kantrowitz, "The Two Faces of Domination in North Carolina, 1800–1898," in *Democracy Betrayed: The Wilmington Race Riot of 1898 and Its Legacy*, ed. David S. Cecelski and Timothy B. Tyson (Chapel Hill: University of North Carolina Press, 1998), 96. Ted Ownby offers a broader reading of tensions within southern culture by exploring the competition between southern male culture and evangelical culture, which resulted in emotionally charged behavior among men. Ted Ownby, *Subduing Satan: Religion, Recreation, and Manhood in the Rural South, 1865–1920* (Chapel Hill: University of North Carolina Press, 1990).

37. Kerby, *Kirby Smith's Confederacy*, 415.

38. Proclamation Draft [May 26, 1865], Edmund Kirby-Smith to the Trans-Mississippi Department, Edmund Kirby-Smith Papers, SHC.

39. [Edmund Kirby Smith to Cassie Selden Kirby Smith], N/D Papers [June–July 1865], Kirby-Smith Papers, SHC. See also Kerby, *Kirby Smith's Confederacy*, 428–29.

40. [Edmund Kirby Smith to Cassie Selden Kirby Smith], N/D Papers [June–July 1865], Kirby-Smith Papers, SHC.

41. Historian Jason Phillips argues that recalcitrant Confederates were "diehard rebels" who constructed an ethos of Confederate invincibility that outlasted the Civil War. Phillips, *Diehard Rebels*.

42. Carl Coke Rister, "Carlota: A Confederate Colony in Mexico," *Journal of Southern History* 11 (February 1945): 33–50.

43. Rister, in his article on Carlota, held that despite good fortune most "former Confederates felt bitter about being exiles from the land of their birth." Ibid., 45.

44. [Charles G.] Talcott to [Robert G. H.] Kean, February 9, 1866, Robert Garlick Hill Kean Papers, Box 1, Folder 1, University of Virginia, Small Special Collections, Charlottesville.

45. Rolle, *The Lost Cause*, 54–55.

46. Anne Sarah Rubin nicely captures the broader sense of ambiguity experienced by white southerners who "were no longer Confederates but were not yet Americans either." Rubin, *A Shattered Nation*, 145–46.

47. [Edmund Kirby Smith], N/D Papers [June–July 1865], Kirby-Smith Papers, SHC. Emigration, notes Gaines Foster, "offered a means of psychological as well as physical escape from the consequences of the war." Southerners accepted the outcome of the war, he continues, "but still feared its implications." Ultimately, though, Foster concludes that that emigrants represented so small a minority of the white population that most whites must not have feared the war's aftermath. Foster, *Ghosts of the Confederacy*, 17.

48. [Edmund Kirby Smith to Cassie Selden Kirby Smith], August 21, 1865, Kirby-Smith Papers, SHC.

49. Carmichael, *The Last Generation*, 216.

50. See, for instance, Cornelia Phillips Spencer, May 4, 1865, Box 14, Volume 3, Cornelia Phillips Spencer Papers, SHC.

51. LeeAnn Whites, *Gender Matters: Civil War, Reconstruction, and the Making of the New South* (New York: Palgrave Macmillan, 2005), chapter 5; and Drew Gilpin Faust, *Mothers of Invention: Women of the Slaveholding South in the American Civil War* (1996; reprint, New York, Vintage Books, 1997), 51–52.

52. Faust, *Mothers of Invention*, 27–35.

53. Whites, *The Civil War as a Crisis in Gender*, 145–50.

54. [Edmund Kirby Smith to Cassie Selden Kirby Smith], August 21, 1865, Kirby-Smith Papers, SHC.

55. [Cassie Selden Kirby Smith to Edmund Kirby Smith], August 15, 1865, Kirby-Smith Papers, SHC.

56. [Edmund Kirby Smith to Cassie Selden Kirby Smith], August 21, 1865.

57. [Cassie Selden Kirby Smith to Edmund Kirby Smith], August 15, 1865, and [Edmund Kirby Smith to Cassie Selden Kirby Smith, October 2, 1865], Kirby-Smith Papers, SHC.

58. Faust, *Mothers of Invention*, 248–54; Whites, *The Civil War as a Crisis in Gender*, 132–59; Rubin, *A Shattered Nation*, 208–39.

59. U. S. Grant to E. Kirby Smith, October 16, 1865, Kirby-Smith Papers, SHC.

60. [Edmund Kirby Smith to Cassie Selden Kirby Smith, October 2, 1865].

61. Edmund Kirby Smith, "Amnesty Oath," November 14, 1865, Lynchburg, Virginia, Kirby-Smith Papers, SHC.

62. Rubin, *A Shattered Nation*, 164–71.

63. For counterpoints positing the primacy of anger and defiance over the effects of depression and despair, see Rubin, *A Shattered Nation*, 146–47; and Poole, *Never Surrender*, 57–58. On the lingering effects of emotional tumult, see McClurken, *Take Care of the Living*, 51–52 and 132–33; and Eric T. Dean Jr., *Shook over Hell: Post-Traumatic Stress, Vietnam, and the Civil War* (Cambridge: Harvard University Press, 1997).

64. Wolfgang Schivelbusch, in Jefferson Chase, trans., *The Culture of Defeat: On National Trauma, Mourning, and Recovery* (New York: Metropolitan, 2003), 10–19.

65. George Anderson Mercer, June 24, 1865, Diary, Box 1, volume 5, Mercer Papers, SHC.

66. Sidney Andrews, *The South since the War, as Shown by Fourteen Weeks of Travel and Observation in Georgia and the Carolinas* (1866; reprint, Boston: Houghton Mifflin, 1971), 319.

67. For the public face of white southerners' efforts at rebuilding, see Rubin, *A Shattered Nation*, especially 172–90.

68. Stephen Berry, *All That Makes a Man: Love and Ambition in the Civil War South* (New York: Oxford University Press, 2003); Bertram Wyatt-Brown, *Hearts of Darkness: Wellsprings of a Southern Literary Tradition* (Baton Rouge: Louisiana State University Press, 2003).

69. J[ames] B. Mitchell to Ruffin H. Thomson, December 20, 1866, Box 1, Folder 10, Ruffin Thomson Papers, SHC. Mitchell's quote comes from Alexander Pope's *Essay on Man I*, x (1733).

70. Alexander Pope's *Essay on Man I*, x (1733).

71. Mitchell to Thomson, December 20, 1866.

72. Mercer, June 22, 1866, Diary, Box 1, Volume 5, Mercer Papers, SHC.

73. Mercer, June 10, 1866, Diary, Box 1, Volume 5, Mercer Papers, SHC.

74. Gorgas, October 15, 1866, *Journals of Josiah Gorgas*, 201.

75. Gorgas, January 6, 1867, ibid., 203.

76. For the historical importance of this transformation among Western cultures see Nye, "Western Masculinities in War and Peace," especially 417–22.

77. Bercaw, *Gendered Freedoms*, 80.

78. On the historicization of emotions see Peter N. Stearns and Jan Lewis, eds., *An Emotional History of the United States* (New York: New York University Press, 1998), 1–12.

79. Dolores Janiewski, "The Reign of Passion: White Supremacy and the Clash between Passionate and Progressive Emotional Styles in the New South," in Stearns and Lewis, *An Emotional History of the United States*, 126–54.

80. In his provocative 1981 essay, "A Generation of Defeat," David H. Donald posited that "segregation and disfranchisement should be viewed as the final public acts, the last bequests, of the Southern Civil War generation." Donald holds that white southerners' simultaneous traumas of defeat and emancipation eventually facilitated racial segregation

and disfranchisement. His conclusions, while more far-reaching than what I hope to argue, suggest how deeply the war affected white southerners' ideas and identities. David H. Donald, "A Generation of Defeat," reprinted in *The Civil War Veteran: A Historical Reader*, ed. Larry M. Logue and Michael Barton (New York: New York University Press, 2007), 334; see also 334–40.

# 6

.......................

## Citizenship and Racial Order
## in Post–Civil War Atlanta

WILLIAM A. LINK

In 1866, residents of Atlanta celebrated the Fourth of July in a way that suggested basic tensions about the meaning of citizenship and freedom in the post–Civil War South. Few places in the Confederacy had experienced defeat with more devastating results than Atlanta, which was besieged and destroyed by William T. Sherman's large army during the summer and fall of 1864. After capturing the city, Sherman expelled civilians and then left, burning much of the downtown district. During Reconstruction, Atlanta became a center of northern intervention but also a symbol of the new racial order.

Before the Civil War, Atlantans, like other white southerners, had celebrated the Fourth with what an observer described as "a respect almost amounting to idolatry." Only a year after the war ended in the spring of 1865, many whites expressed little interest in the holiday. "How changed things are!" one white exclaimed. Another Atlantan commented that if "a Southern gentleman gets drunk [on the Fourth], friends might think he is celebrating the day, and I wish to be *above suspicion*." Freed slaves exhibited no such reluctance. They enthusiastically embraced the holiday, flaunting their love of Union with a festive parade in the city's downtown district. The procession, dominated by black people, offered a statement about how the world was turned upside down. The parade was led by an "African, mounted on a magnificent white charger," wrote a white reporter, and was followed by a marching band, the parade's grand marshal, and members of local African American voluntary groups. The marchers clashed with a group of white firemen, also parading, and with a local group of celebrating northern troops. The public presence of Atlanta blacks dismayed the editor of the *Daily Intelligencer*, who commented how painfully the celebration contrasted with past Fourths and how a "deep sense of regret" was "keenly felt in witnessing the retrograde movements being made by civilization in our midst."[1]

Atlanta's Fourth of July celebration indicated the conflicting feelings surrounding the meaning of citizenship in the aftermath of the Civil War. Confederate defeat, for whites, meant emasculation. A few miles east of Atlanta, white diarist Thomas Maguire recorded in May 1865 that "the times are out of joint. . . . I fear we will have bad times, but we must take them as they come." "What a country we have at the present time! We have nothing that we can call our own. The vile Yankees take everything they please and go where they please. We are a powerless people, but by no means a conquered people. I have lost hope of yet gaining our independence."[2]

In Atlanta and in the counties surrounding it, whites operated under older, untenable assumptions about citizenship. When Atlanta residents met weeks after Confederate surrender, in June 1865, they urged a "speedy restoration of all political and national relations, the restoration of mutual confidence and friendship, the uninterrupted intercourse of trade and commerce with every section." White Atlantans wanted to restore "our old position in the list of states, the sovereign and sole conservators of an unbroken and imperishable Union." But restoration meant, for them, the reconstruction of white supremacy. Whites did not intend to "deprive the freedman of the results of his labor," the group explained, noting that "the late slaves of the South had the sympathy of all intelligent, Christian, moral Southern men." They unequivocally opposed enfranchising freedmen, repudiating "every effort to stir up strife among those who had differed upon questions which had produced the late war." They instead recommended "a forgetfulness of the past."[3]

During the months after the end of the war, the pages of the *Daily Intelligencer*—the city's leading newspaper—were filled with characterizations of the racial qualities of black people that supposedly made them unsuited for citizenship. The newspaper described freedpeople as living in "idleness, vice and profligacy"—a self-inflicted condition, it believed, as former slaves had deserted the happy homes and kindness their masters offered. The freedpeople's "persistent idleness," the *Intelligencer* concluded, meant that "a life of freedom" was a "curse." "Nothing short of the strong arm of the law," it concluded, could "ameliorate their condition."[4]

"Freedman he may be," the *Intelligencer* later observed, "but he will still retain the characteristics of the African race. What God has implanted in his *nature*, man may not, cannot remove."[5] The transition to freedom was fraught with difficulties, the *Intelligencer* maintained. "Those who have labored so strenuously to free the slave," wrote a correspondent, "seem to have thought that the change from proprietory to compensated labor would be of easy transition." Southern whites knew otherwise. They realized that "compensated labor will not do for the negro, as a freedman, what compensated labor has done for the white man." By nature "indolent and careless," black people would "only work under compulsion and to gratify temporary wants." Ex-slaves, claimed the *Intelligencer*, spent all they earned "in extravagant dress, trinkets, and for the temporary gratification of any and every caprice which may enter his fickle brain." Black people were "proverbially improvident—never taking heed for to-morrow, so long as he can gratify the wants of to-day." Emancipated slaves were currently in a "state of anarchy, apparently conscious of nothing but the fact of their liberty to go where and do what they please." They infested streets and alleys, "straggle over the suburbs, intrude upon private premises, and with characteristic aimlessness of purpose, lounge hither and thither, heedless of the time coming when they must either become a useful member of, or a burthen to society."[6] Governed by these clashing perspectives, former masters and ex-slaves sized each other up warily during the months after the war ended. Whites were usually convinced that former slaves could only work under the old regime, under strict regimentation and brutality.

The months immediately after the war were chaotic for both whites and blacks. "No man in the North can realize the condition of affairs in this region," wrote a northern African American minister visiting Atlanta in August 1865. In some areas, ex-slaves did not know they were free, and if they did "their surroundings are such that they would fear to speak of it, as they would have done in the palmy days of rebellion." But wherever the Freedmen's Bureau was a presence "this state of affairs vanishes." Although emancipated slaves generally remained with former masters "at least until they can find profitable employment elsewhere," they were increasingly empowered to "demand that their former masters pay due wages, or share the crop."[7]

The instance of Atlanta offers fertile ground for examining how the crucial years following the end of the Civil War played out, how the transition from slavery to freedom occurred, and how the process of Reconstruction involved both successes and failures. The major actors—southern whites, northern whites, and freedpeople—triangulated into radically different, though interrelated, points of view. Northern whites insisted on the end of visible signs of slavery, and military detachments scoured the South to liberate slaves in the months after Confederate surrender. But at the center of the indeterminacy of the postwar era was the extent to which freedom meant citizenship for ex-slaves.[8]

For black people, the face of northern occupation became the Freedmen's Bureau. Against a background of acute postwar economic and social distress, a political vacuum, and uncertain racial interactions, the bureau remained the most important advocate of African American citizenship. In its brief existence it would attempt something unprecedented: to introduce federal power over labor, governance, and law at the community level. Created by Congress in March 1865 and remaining in existence only four short years, the Freedmen's Bureau was charged with the daunting task of providing for the transition from slavery to freedom, what W.E.B. Du Bois described as a "tremendous undertaking" that gave the federal government responsibility for freedpeople as the "ward of the nation." With ex-slaves "emasculated by a peculiarly complete system of slavery, centuries old," Du Bois wrote, emancipation had brought them "suddenly, violently . . . into a new birthright, at a time of war and passion, in the midst of the stricken, embittered population of their former masters."[9]

First arriving in Atlanta in October 1865, the bureau functioned with local agents. Four different army officers ran the bureau's Atlanta office between 1865 and 1868, though it was not until 1867 that sufficient resources were made available through the creation of a larger sub-district office. The most energetic federal official, Fred Mosebach, was a New York army veteran who, by the time he arrived in Atlanta in 1867, had achieved the rank of brevet major and was serving in the reserve army corps of officers who tended to dominate among bureau officials. Mosebach also had bureau experience, having headed field offices in Albany and Columbus, Georgia.[10]

Although the Freedmen's Bureau was run by soldiers, a sizable portion of the white troops were unsympathetic toward freedpeople. During the early weeks of northern occupation, the army issued orders requiring all black people to register with the provost marshal and to receive passes to live in the city. The orders threatened arrest for transients who could not document their whereabouts. The occupying authorities only sporadically enforced the order, however, despite urgings from local whites.[11] On Christmas Day 1865, John Richard Dennett, visiting Atlanta and reporting for *The Nation*, described an encounter with a Union soldier officer in Atlanta. He was going to "punch every d——d nigger I see," the officer told Dennett. He then randomly assaulted two blacks walking on the street; the men "seemed too much astonished to retaliate." That same day, a fracas occurred in which two freedmen were shot by soldiers. No arrests were made.[12] After 1867 the military government of the Third Military District located itself in Atlanta, with General George G. Meade in charge. He remained in command until July 30, 1868, when civil authority was restored. The military unit was posted in a new fifty-three-acre base completed in southwest Atlanta in late 1867, the McPherson Barracks, and remained into late 1868, after Meade had relinquished control to a new civilian government.

Clashes between freedpeople and troops were not unusual. In September 1867, soldiers from a New Jersey regiment robbed and beat some freedmen, some of whom were reported to be severely injured. Despite an investigation, there were no prosecutions.[13] In October 1868, in what became known as the Fourth Ward Riot, troops housed at the McPherson Barracks knocked down chicken coops and pulled down the fences of the freedpeople. According to the *Atlanta Constitution*, the troops "came to the very natural conclusion that the city belonged to them, and that they had a right to do just what they pleased, the prerogatives of municipal authority to the contrary notwithstanding." The riot ended when local police opened fire, wounding some of the troops. Mockingly, the *Atlanta Constitution* concluded its account with Ulysses S. Grant's presidential campaign slogan, "Let Us Have Peace."[14]

Freedpeople recognized that the Freedmen's Bureau, despite its limitations, offered their only hope for citizenship. Certainly, southern whites suspected that the bureau was undermining the social order by promoting racial equality. Their critique of the bureau folded into their critique of black freedom: that ex-slaves were "unprepared" for emancipation, that they had left the guiding hand of slavery too quickly, and that northern outsiders upset the racial equilibrium. In most respects the bureau was a "miserable failure," wrote the *Intelligencer* in June 1866, by fostering "idleness and vagrancy" and by alienating the "affections of the freed population from their former owners, and from their natural protectors."

The bureau, according to this interpretation, had "sown seeds of discord where breaches should have been healed, and had done an incalculable amount of injury to the very people for whose good it was intended."[15]

During 1865 and 1866 the bureau and the army provost marshal remained the only police force in Atlanta, with their main targets black people. As early as August 1865, the army indicated that it would police the transient population, and it required that temporary huts and tents be moved to outside the city limits.[16] The provost marshal's record included a regular number of freedpeople jailed for petty crime, and they occupied a growing share of the space in the military guardhouse.[17] Despite the transition to civilian policing, local whites continued to complain about disorder and even a reign of terror evident in rising black crime.[18] The bureau's concern for crime also affected their attitudes toward work; vagrancy became criminalized. George Waldridge, in charge of the Atlanta bureau, complained about a "worthless set" who were jailed and then obtained a "few days rest rations & quarters, and then are turned loose to again violate the laws and commit further depredations." He sought to contract them forcibly to employers as far away as Mississippi.[19] The bureau took other measures. In March 1866, Waldridge collaborated with local Atlanta city government to crack down on vagrancy. He ordered daily military details to arrest and put to work "all the idle, loafing and vagrant negroes, who now infest the public thoroughfare; until they signify a willingness to enter into a permanent contract for their future support."[20]

The bureau also wanted to move freedpeople off rations and out of the camps as quickly as possible. In October 1865, Assistant Commissioner Davis Tillson prohibited the distribution of rations to freedmen who were able-bodied and unwilling to work. He further ordered that only working freedpeople could remain in cities, with the unemployed compelled, if necessary, to work in labor arranged by contract. Tillson's policies reduced rations substantially by 1866. At the same time, rations were no longer made available to destitute whites.

Increasingly, local whites called on the Freedmen's Bureau to adopt compulsory labor measures to deal with the transient poor black population. The cotton crop, warned the *Intelligencer*, was imperiled if ex-slaves refused to work in the fields. "Shall either a mistaken philanthropy, or misdirected judgment," it asked, "prevent what is so absolutely necessary to the maintenance of the nation's credit?" It would be necessary to sponsor a new, revised labor system in which freedpeople would be "induced, and where he cannot be induced, by his being compelled, to labor, in his cultivation of the cotton fields of the South." The *Intelligencer* proposed an intersectional convergence of interests: "Let the Southern States be received in the Union, and let them regulate the labor of the freedman, as they would do in a manner both liberal and just to those of them who will labor."[21]

During 1865 and 1866 the bureau at least partly accepted these Atlanta whites' views about black "idleness."[22] The bureau also exercised what can best described as spasmodic influence in northern Georgia, exhibiting indifference toward the plight of freedpeople. During the six months after Appomattox, the bureau operated in Atlanta with one sub-assistant commissioner, Lieutenant Colonel George Curkendall, who arrived in October 1865 and remained only two months. He was succeeded by three other sub-assistant commissioners during the next year. They supervised nineteen counties, relying on local agents who were paid by fees charged to freedpeople and former masters. Only after early 1867 did the bureau actually pay its agents. The bureau's activities were "crippled by the want of cavalry," observed Dennett in late 1865, and outside of Atlanta federal authority often went unenforced. Instances of white fraud and cruelty, according to Dennett, "occurring at a distance from the town and from railroads necessarily go unpunished."[23]

In 1866, Atlanta's first sub-assistant commissioners, D. C. Poole, George Waldridge, and John Leonard, occupied the office. None of these officials had much sympathy with freedpeople; they bought into the white version of emancipation. Nonetheless, for freedpeople, Atlanta became a refuge that represented the possibilities of freedom. With the end of slavery, freedpeople flocked to urban areas, and the city became, according to one historian, a "mecca" for black migrants. They lived in huts, tents, lean-tos, and dilapidated housing.[24] Freedpeople, Tera Hunter notes, "eagerly rushed into Atlanta in even greater numbers than before," as their population grew from 1,900 to 10,000 out of a total population of nearly 22,000.[25] The presence of the northern army, which made Atlanta headquarters of the northwestern district of the Department of Georgia—one of four divisions in the state—acted as a protective umbrella for the black community.[26]

The Atlanta black enclave was bolstered in May 1867 with the arrival of Fred Mosebach as Atlanta's sub-assistant commissioner. Under Mosebach, the bureau's approach changed radically. His arrival suggested a regime change: Davis Tillson departed in January as head of the state bureau, succeeded by Caleb C. Sibley, described by historian Paul A. Cimbala as "foremost a soldier who followed orders." The spring of 1867 also brought military government and the imposition of theoretically equal civil rights for freedpeople and enfranchisement.[27] Unlike his predecessors, Mose bach was sympathetic with the freedmen and was consequently more likely to suspect systemic problems of white oppression than to blame the inadequacies of freedpeople. The local Atlanta police, previously allied with the bureau, now came under scrutiny, as did local government in the counties surrounding the city. Mosebach was more interventionist in working with field agents, more supportive of those willing to take chances with local whites and to champion the freedpeople's cause. Unlike his predecessors, he spent less time with issues related to labor contracts and more time focused on providing some minimum of justice for freedpeople.

The differences between Mosebach's and Waldridge's dealings with the Atlanta authorities can be seen in two events a year apart, in May 1866 and May 1867. In May 1866 police arrested Sally Ann Donohoe, a freedwoman, at the railroad depot on a charge of "indecency & vulgar conversation & abuse to passengers." It is difficult to evaluate the charges, but it is likely that the arrest reflected a perception of insubordinate, arrogant public behavior on the part of Donohoe, a serious transgression of the racial code. Donohoe was arrested, released, and then arrested again. Waldridge reported that Donohoe had now become so "uncontrollable and unmaneagable that she has to be kept in close confinement to prevent her from injuring herself and those in the camp." A year later, Atlanta police arrested another black woman, Mary Price, charging her with using "profane language." Mosebach questioned the arrest. "It is evident to me," he wrote to the mayor of the city, "that there was no necessity whatsoever for making the arrest, if the woman had violated any city ordinance a summons to appear before the proper court and answer to the charge would have been sufficient." The policeman had revealed by his behavior, Mosebach said, "that he has no respect for the rights of the free people, that instead of protecting them in their rights he uses his position to impose upon them, and therefore he is in my opinion not fit for the position."[28]

Bureau agents confronted a legal vacuum after the U.S. Supreme Court prohibited military authority over civilian courts in 1866 in *Ex parte Milligan*.[29] Mosebach nonetheless remained convinced that Atlanta's justice system worked to oppress freedpeople. In August 1867 he complained that a city policeman exercised "wanton cruelty towards the colored people of this city" and that black citizens were treated "very roughly."[30] The problem went beyond the Atlanta police, as local magistrates worked against black citizens. In January 1868, Mosebach wrote to Assistant Commissioner Caleb Sibley describing A. G. Gaulding and William M. Butts as magistrates who handled African Americans in a way that was "arbitrary unjust and partial." Gaulding was an "unprincipled, corrupt, and worthless man," Mosebach said, who used his office "for the sole purpose of obtaining the fees thereof, without much regard for justice, law or duty."[31] In August 1868, Mosebach urged the newly elected civilian governor of Georgia, Rufus Bullock, to remove the Atlanta magistrates and replace them with more competent, and even-handed, officers.[32]

Mosebach frequently intervened in local justice. After John Blake, a freedman, complained to Mosebach that an Atlanta magistrate had unlawfully seized his cow, he ordered the magistrate to return the property "immediately, or appear at this office and exhibit legal grounds and authority for the above mentioned seizure."[33] In early 1868, freedman Richmond Nutting was convicted of simple larceny in Atlanta Superior Court. The case probably involved a small amount of property, but Nutting was nonetheless sentenced to nine months in the penitentiary. Stating that Nutting had a wife and five children "who need his support and pray that you may pardon him and remit the remainder of the sentence," Mosebach endorsed a petition to Georgia's military governor, Thomas H. Ruger.[34] Mosebach took the same aggressive approach with local officials outside of Atlanta under his jurisdiction. After a white man refused to pay a black worker with whom he had contracted in Carroll County, Mosebach encouraged a bureau agent, Edwin Belcher, to seize his wagon and oxen.[35]

Freedpeople were unquestionably committing crimes; not all accusations of law-breaking reflected racial oppression, and untangling white supremacy from criminal conduct remains difficult. The maze of disrupted family relations among slaves that existed by virtue of slavery's very nature—with the constant family separation occasioned by the slave trade—meant that reconstituting black families often proved difficult, a thicket of conflicting claims. There were plenty of instances of blacks exploiting each other in the chaotic postwar years and after, and there were complications in determining lines of familial authority. An Atlanta freedwoman, Mahaley Wright, apprenticed her son to learn plastering and painting from a black artisan in Ringold, north of Atlanta, only to learn that the artisan had unlawfully subcontracted him.[36] In February 1868, Mosebach investigated a case of ex-slave children separated from their family and indentured to a white family. But he discovered that the children's mother was dead, and the person making the claim was unrelated, with uncertain motives, and the children were reportedly well treated. The matter had assumed a "different aspect," Mosebach wrote, and he found it difficult to advise a local agent with "definite instructions in regard to cases of similar character." If the law was observed, he was cautious about interfering in family matters. Although parents were entitled to their children, other relatives had more uncertain claims, unless demonstrable instances of "cruel treatment or neglect of the apprentice can be established, or the law gives the right." "In all these cases we must proceed with caution and carefully examine the claims of the applicant," Mosebach advised, and ordered the agent "not to make any decision yourself, but collect all facts connected with a case and submit them with your own opinion thereon to the Asst. Comr and let him cancel the indenture or reject the application."[37]

In the postwar chaos, many former slaveholders, especially in the first two years of emancipation, continued to treat black people as slaves. Earlier, in the summer of 1865, German revolutionary and Union general Carl Schurz toured the South to report to Congress on postwar conditions. Although most Georgians might be reconciled to the end of chattel slavery "in the old form," he discovered, "many attempts were made to introduce into that new system the element of physical compulsion, which, as above stated, is so generally considered indispensable." Slavery's brutalization prevailed, and the practice of whipping continued "to a great extent, although, perhaps, not in so regular a manner as it was practiced in times gone by." The habit of violence remained "so inveterate with a great many persons as to render, on the least provocation, the impulse to whip a negro almost irresistible."[38]

The brutalization of ex-slaves that Schurz described was even more apparent—and increasing—in the counties surrounding Atlanta during the late 1860s.[39] As these accounts suggest, many African American refugees from white violence in surrounding counties ended up in Atlanta. White violence was rarer in the city because of the federal presence, and it provided sanctuary from the rising tide of Ku Klux Klan violence sweeping through Georgia during the late 1860s. "How many republicans have fled from their homes to this city to save their lives or avoid other personal injuries I am unable to say," wrote an Atlanta resident in 1869.[40] Abraham Colby, an African American elected to the Georgia legislature in 1868 from Greene County, fled to Atlanta after the Klan ordered him to leave.[41] In April 1870, Klansmen raided the home of ex-slave Jeter Columbus in Douglas County, about twenty miles west of Atlanta. Jeter escaped with a buckshot wound in his shoulder, and when he complained to a local magistrate the official refused to provide him with any protection. Columbus declined to swear out a warrant, "for it will do no good to do it, because, after the trial is over they will kill me." Columbus asked the magistrate a pointed question "between you and me and God": "Can you give me justice here?" The magistrate admitted that he could not, "for if I do my house will be burnt up before four-and-twenty hours." The magistrate urged Columbus to "go right through the woods to Atlanta, from here." As Columbus started out for Atlanta, his dog, which he thought the Klan had killed, joined him, and he arrived in the city about sunrise. After he recovered from his wounds, Columbus testified about his experiences a year later to a congressional committee investigating the Klan.[42]

The bureau became an object of southern white resentment against federal intervention. According to one account, the idea of a "strong Federal agency placed in the midst is naturally repulsive to the [white] masses."[43] Confined to urban areas and encircled by hostile rural whites, the bureau required its sub-assistant commissioners and their agents to document "outrages" against freedpeople. They reported dutifully about a rising level of terror and intimidation against freedpeople in the counties surrounding Atlanta. John Leonard, in September 1866, wrote of the "bushwhackers and Regulators" in Heard and Coweta Counties who were engaged in recent murders and assaults against freedpeople.[44] Such violence became commonplace. Those associated with newly established black schools also became targets. White teachers were accused of "sowing ill feeling and hatred among the colored people" and convening "secret meetings" to mobilize African Americans politically, and many were run out by local vigilantes.[45] Federal officials, a northern white observed in 1868, had a limited ability to control this violence, as a majority of Georgians "seldom come into contact" with federal officials.[46]

The American Missionary Association (AMA) founded an important outpost of northern educators in late 1865 in Atlanta. This group, which worked closely with the Freedmen's Bureau in education, was so ostracized that they constructed and maintained a teacher's home because locals would not house them. The AMA enclave would become an important outpost in Atlanta, but it was only grudgingly tolerated. Edmund Asa Ware, a native New Englander and leader of the AMA contingent in Atlanta, later served as the bureau's superintendent of education in 1868 and 1869. In October 1867 he was denounced by an Atlanta newspaper as one of a group of "Yankee interlopers" invading Georgia schools and "a signal illustration of Yankee impudence and officiousness," whose "sole mission is to stir up strife and sow the tares of hate and evil in the minds of their pupils."[47] In March 1868 the local Ku Klux Klan told Ware to retract his call for expanded education, or the "sun will shine on a new made grave." Ware brushed the threat aside, saying, "I shall not lie awake to-night and am quite sure I shall take nothing back I said."[48]

In 1868, violence against African Americans peaked in portions of the state, and outside Atlanta the Klan organized bands that beat, abducted, and murdered. Thus in May 1868, in Forsyth County, John Lambert, a black man, was attacked by a party of white men who broke into his home at night and shot up his house. No charges were filed. The following October, also in Forsyth County, freedman Adam Holbrook was shot and severely beaten by a party of white men. Local authorities refused to issue arrest warrants. In Henry County, Peter Turner was shot by "unknown parties, all disguised," and died two days later. The murderers went unpursued. In nearby Cherokee County in October 1868, a party of disguised white men burst into the home of Jerry Garrison, a black man, and shot him and his sons. In this wave of violence in 1868 in the Atlanta bureau district, nine freedmen were assaulted with intent to kill, while six more were assaulted and murdered.[49]

Near the end of the bureau's existence there were four cases of murder and four of assault in Fulton County—despite Atlanta's reputation as a refuge—though these cases were more likely the result of individualized conflict than part of an organized Klan campaign.[50] In one of these cases in October 1868 in nearby Campbell County, William Latham, a black man, was stabbed and killed by his white employer, Thomas Latham. After a coroner's inquest dismissed the case, the bureau agent intervened and arrested Latham. But, lacking any mechanism to try him in civilian courts, he went free.[51] Bureau agents found themselves overwhelmed outside Atlanta with too few resources and insufficient military force and police power. In all of the surviving records of murder or assault by whites of blacks, there is no record of prosecutions, let alone any convictions. Whites realized that attacking ex-slaves could occur with impunity because federal authorities lacked the wherewithal to act differently, even if they wanted to. In February 1868, Mosebach investigated a case in Heard County, near Franklin, of one Matthew A. Straighorn, accused of assaulting with intent to kill James Moore, a Coweta County freedman. Mosebach traveled to Newnan, Georgia, where he discovered Straighorn's address. After arriving at his house, he found it unoccupied. A local black farmer told him that Straighorn had sold his property and left for Alabama three weeks earlier. Using "due precaution" with local whites, Mosebach discovered Straighorn's new address, but without a way to travel there, he returned to Atlanta. Mosebach then requested that Assistant Commissioner Sibley dispatch a squad of cavalry to arrest Straighorn. There is no evidence that Sibley followed up on the request.[52]

In March 1866, while Mosebach ran the bureau in Augusta, he reported to his superiors that ill-treatment of freedpeople in rural areas grew "worse from day to day." African Americans were moving to urban areas because "here they are protected, but beyond 10 miles from town they must live in continual fear of their lives and property." He found it nearly impossible to provide much protection in rural areas without enough military force.[53] Mosebach expressed his frustrations two years later in Atlanta. Requesting additional staff in his district, he wrote Sibley that the "great number of complaints made by freedpeople" were impossible to address because of his inability to enforce the law. Cases involving ex-slaves required "regular judicial proceedings to investigate and determine, which takes time and patience, neither of which I have at the present time." Consulting "eight of the best colored citizens of this City," Mosebach recommended Bluford Smith, a judge of the Fulton County Court, as a "suitable and proper person for the office." Smith had a good reputation among ex-slaves as a judge who worked with "impartiality and justice, doing right without making any distinction of race or color." He would act "to your satisfaction and in Justice to the colored people." Because of the "inefficiency of the local Courts and the daily increase of duties," Mosebach was unable to work effectively as a bureau agent.[54]

Mosebach's frustrations suggest a mixed legacy for the Freedmen's Bureau in Atlanta—and for the meaning of African American citizenship at the ground level after the Civil War. The northern presence remained an invading, occupying force in the late 1860s, and that remained especially true in Reconstruction Georgia. For ex-slaves, the meaning of freedom remained ambiguous, as white violence reinstalled white supremacy throughout Georgia. But, as elsewhere, freedom and the end of the Civil War provided enclaves of difference and exceptionalism. Atlanta provided a distinctive locale for encounters between northern whites, ex-slaves, and native-born whites. White supremacy reigned supreme in the city, yet African Americans migrated there in large numbers, seeking jobs and refuge. In the antebellum period Atlanta had been a fortress of white solidarity. In the postwar period freedpeople gained a toehold for what would subsequently become a center of black cultural, economic, and political power. That toehold found its roots in postwar Atlanta, and the Freedmen's Bureau played a role, unwitting or not, in that evolution.

## Notes

1. *Atlanta Daily Intelligencer*, July 6, 1866.
2. Franklin M. Garrett, *Atlanta and Environs: A Chronicle of Its People and Events*, 3 vols. (Athens: University of Georgia Press, 1954–87), 1:676–81.
3. Thomas H. Martin, *Atlanta and Its Builders: A Comprehensive History of the Gate City of the South* (Atlanta: Century Memorial Publishing Company, 1902), 1–6.
4. Garrett, *Atlanta and Environs*, 1:689.
5. "'What Can Be Done for the South,'" *Atlanta Daily Intelligencer*, June 6, 1865.
6. "Legislation Necessary," *Atlanta Daily Intelligencer*, June 7, 1865.
7. Rev. E. Weaver, "Letter from Atlanta, Ga.," August 2, 1865, *Christian Recorder*, August 19, 1865.
8. For more on northern attitudes see Heather Cox Richardson, *The Death of Reconstruction: Race, Labor, and Politics in the Post–Civil War North, 1865–1901* (Cambridge: Harvard University Press, 2001).
9. W. E. B. Du Bois, "The Freedmen's Bureau," *Atlantic Monthly*, March 1901, 357.
10. Paul A. Cimbala, *Under the Guardianship of the Nation: The Freedmen's Bureau and the Reconstruction of Georgia, 1865–1870* (Athens: University of Georgia Press, 1997), 54.
11. "Papers Wanted," *Atlanta Daily Intelligencer*, June 7, 1865.
12. John Richard Dennett, "The South as It Is," *The Nation*, January 25, 1866.
13. Fred Mosebach to C. C. Sibley, September 10, 1867, Freedmen's Bureau, Sub-Assistant Records, Atlanta, Georgia, National Archives, Washington, D.C. [hereafter FB/SA], reel 43.
14. *Atlanta Constitution*, October 16, 1868, quoted in Garrett, *Atlanta and Environs*, 1:793.

15. "Generals Steadman and Fullerton," *Atlanta Daily Intelligencer*, June 7, 1866.

16. Special Orders no. 1, August 26, 1865, in *Atlanta Daily Intelligencer*, August 29, 1865.

17. In August 1865, twenty-five prisoners were black, fifty-three white; in September 1865, forty prisoners were black, fifty-seven white; and in October 1865, forty-one prisoners were black, thirty-seven white. Provost Marshal Records for Atlanta, Register of Prisoners at Atlanta, 1865–66, RG 393, National Archives, Washington, D.C.

18. Griggsby Hart Wooton Jr., "New City of the New South: Atlanta, 1843–1873 (Ph.D. diss., Johns Hopkins University, 1973), 137.

19. George R. Waldridge to Davis Tillson, April 29, 1866, FB/SA, reel 43.

20. George R. Waldridge to Louis Beckwith, March 15, 1866, FB/SA, reel 43.

21. *Atlanta Daily Intelligencer*, January 5, 1866. For a comparison with a rural region of Georgia, see Susan Eva O'Donovan, *Becoming Free in the Cotton South* (Cambridge: Harvard University Press, 2007).

22. Garrett, *Atlanta and Environs*, 1:792.

23. Dennett, "The South as It Is."

24. Garrett, *Atlanta and Environs*, 1:689–90.

25. Tera W. Hunter, *To 'Joy My Freedom: Southern Black Women's Lives and Labor after the Civil War* (Cambridge: Harvard University Press, 1997), 21.

26. Garrett, *Atlanta and Environs*, 1:676–81.

27. Cimbala, *Under the Guardianship of the Nation*, 10.

28. Fred Mosebach to James W. Williams, May 31, 1867, FB/SA, reel 43.

29. Eric Foner, *Reconstruction: America's Unfinished Revolution* (New York: Harper and Row, 1988), 272.

30. Fred Mosebach to C. C. Sibley, August 1, 1867, Freedmen's Bureau, Field Office, Georgia, National Archives [hereafter FBFOGA], reel 43.

31. Fred Mosebach to C. C. Sibley, January 24, 1868, FBFOGA, reel 43.

32. Fred Mosebach to C. C. Sibley, August 28, 1868, FBFOGA, reel 43.

33. Fred Mosebach to Adam Poole, November 23, 1867, FBFOGA, reel 43.

34. Fred Mosebach to Thomas H. Ruger, March 4, 1868, FBFOGA, reel 43. In H. A. G. Williams to Mosebach, March 5, 1868, FBFOGA, reel 43, Ruger informed Mosebach that he would consider the case if Mosebach sent the proceedings.

35. Case file, James Bloodgood, February 5, 1868, FBFOGA, reel 44. On the difficulty blacks had attaining justice see Steven Hahn, *A Nation under Our Feet: Black Political Struggles in the Rural South from Slavery to the Great Migration* (Cambridge: Harvard University Press, 2003), 236.

36. Fred Mosebach to J. R. Lewis, December 4, 1867, FBFOGA, reel 43; case file, January 9, 1868, FBFOGA, reel 43.

37. Fred Mosebach to George W. Nolan, February 20, 1868, FBFOGA, reel 43.

38. Carl Schurz, *Report on the Condition of the South*, 38th Congress, 1st session, Sen. Ex. Doc. no. 2.

39. Testimony of Abram Colby, October 27, 1871, *Report of the Joint Select Committee to Inquire into the Condition of Affairs in the Late Insurrectionary States*, 13 vols. (Washington, D.C.: Government Printing Office, 1872), 6:644–48.

40. John W. O'Neil, January 7, 1869, *The Condition of Affairs in Georgia* (1869; reprint, Freeport, N.Y.: Books for Libraries Press, 1971), 90.

41. *Report of the Joint Select Committee*, 6:249–64.

42. Ibid., 559–63.

43. T. B. Thorpe, "Affairs in the South," *New York Times*, June 18, 1866.

44. John Leonard to Tillson, September 4, 1866, FBFOGA, reel 43.

45. Fred Mosebach to C. C. Sibley, April 9, 1868, FBFOGA, reel 43.

46. Testimony of Amos T. Ackerman, December 19, 1868, in *Condition of Affairs in Georgia*, 22. Ackerman subsequently served as attorney general and prosecuted Klan depredations in the South.

47. *American Missionary* 11 (October 1867): 225.

48. "The Life of Edmund Asa Ware," TS, undated, Presidential Papers, Archives and Special Collections, Robert W. Woodruff Library, Atlanta University Center.

49. Fred Mosebach to C. C. Sibley, November 6, 1868, FB/SA, reel 43.

50. Fred Mosebach to C. C. Sibley, April 9, 1868, FB/SA, reel 43.

51. Fred Mosebach to C. C. Sibley, November 6, 1868, FB/SA, reel 43.

52. Fred Mosebach to C. C. Sibley, February 15, 1868, FB/SA, reel 43.

53. Mosebach to Tillson, March 8, 1866, in Ira Berlin et al., *Freedom: A Documentary History of Emancipation, 1861–1867, Series II: The Black Military Experience* (New York: Cambridge University Press, 1982), 759–61.

54. Fred Mosebach to C. C. Sibley, January 28, 1868, FBFOGA, reel 43.

# 7

## The Antithesis of Union Men and Confederate Rebels

### Loyal Citizenship in the Post–Civil War South

SUSANNA MICHELE LEE

After the official closing of the Civil War, former enemies waged new battles over reunion, most pressingly over membership in the reunited nation. "Confederates" and "Unionists" were wartime categories that did not
necessarily carry postwar implications. To what extent would distinctions
according to loyalty limit or expand conceptualizations of citizenship?
Insisting upon the relevance of wartime loyalties, northern and southern
Republicans argued that Confederates had abandoned the Union, incur-
ring penalties, while Unionists had stood by the nation, earning rewards.
Emphasizing the significance of postwar loyalties, northern and southern
Democrats contended that former Confederates deserved equality with
former Unionists because they had sincerely returned to their loyalties
and had accordingly been pardoned and amnestied. Both sides agreed on
the centrality of loyalty to citizenship, but they disagreed over its definition, with one side fixing loyalty in the war years and the other side dis-
placing loyalty to the postwar years.

During Reconstruction, politicians debated the role of loyalty as a
qualification for access to the rights and privileges of citizenship, including property claims, land restoration, rations, pensions, jury service,
suffrage, and officeholding. Loyalty could potentially remake the power
structure of the South, disfranchising former Confederates and enfranchising former Unionists. This potential was not achieved, in part, because of the ways that federal officials defined loyalty and its relationship

to citizenship. In the battles over Reconstruction, former Confederates and their allies successfully decoupled most aspects of postwar citizenship from wartime loyalty. The federal government's extension of pardon and amnesty and failure to prosecute alleged traitors signaled an official policy of forgetting. During its ten-year operation, the Southern Claims Commission acted as a key bulwark against this trajectory by preserving wartime loyalty as the prerequisite for the payment of property claims. Congress created the commission in 1871 to compensate "loyal citizens" of the South for property appropriated by the Union army. President U. S. Grant appointed three commissioners, all white northern radical Republicans, who decided the cases until they closed their Washington, D.C., offices in 1880. But, even the commissioners defined loyal citizenship in ways that limited its potential to reconstruct the South.

The commissioners imagined the "loyal citizen" as an implicitly white masculine actor. They expected southerners to prove active citizenship, specifically the fulfillment of their political obligations through contributions to suppress secession.[1] The ideal loyal citizen in the South, according to the commissioners, voted against secession at the ballot box and fought against secession on the battlefield. This conceptualization of citizenship rested upon racial and gendered assumptions about the capabilities of white men and the incapabilities of all non-white men and all women. White men possessed the ability to think and act independently. Blacks and women, the antithesis of ideal citizens, did not. The commissioners held white male claimants to these standards of white masculinity in their determinations of loyal citizenship.

Historians often use the commission's records in accordance with its original goal to uncover the wartime motivations and experiences of loyal southerners.[2] This essay adopts a new approach by placing the records in their immediate context to examine the postwar contestation over loyal citizenship between southerners and the federal government. The records of the commission reveal southerners' understandings of the requirements for reconciliation with northerners and their acceptance or rejection of those terms. Claimants omitted relevant but damning facts, stretched the truth, and committed outright perjury in their testimony in order to appease representatives of the federal government. But some self-professed loyal citizens, generally those whom historians would identify as conditional Unionists and former Confederates, refused to conciliate the commissioners, often telling the truth, even when doing so damaged their prospects for compensation, because they believed that they possessed the right to claim membership in the Union on their own terms. The commissioners' decisions, then, do not simply reveal southerners as Unionists or Confederates in the war years. Instead, a decision of loyalty signaled a consensus and a decision of disloyalty indicated a disparity between the claimants' and the commissioners' ideas about who qualified as good citizens in the postwar years. These contestations reveal the conservatism embedded within even the most radical conceptualizations of citizenship.

Historians focus on the political struggles over disfranchisement and other restrictions on the rights and privileges of citizenship for white southern men, usually in the context of partisan struggles between Democrats and Republicans. They accept that a race and, less frequently explored, a class bias against former Unionists in the South ultimately facilitated the abandonment of Reconstruction. Some former Unionists in the North joined former Confederates in the South in rejecting "negro" and "scalawag" rule as incompetent and unscrupulous.[3] In exploring these issues, historians tend to neglect a shared conceptualization of citizenship between former enemies that presumed a particular brand of white masculinity. Partisans on both sides celebrated white men who had acted as patriots by fulfilling their obligations to their nation despite grave danger to themselves and their families. Some could meet the standards, but many could not. As they deemphasized the ideological divisions of the war, former Confederates and former Unionists could celebrate a shared conceptualization of citizenship that focused on manly bravery at the ballot box and on the battlefield. In this regard, devoted former Confederates and Unionists shared more than they differed, paving the way for reconciliation. The logic of the retreat from Reconstruction, then, was embedded in conceptualizations of citizenship, even those advocated by so-called radical Republicans.[4]

Examining the claims of white southern men before the Southern Claims Commission highlights disputes over the specific obligations that citizens owed their nation. White southern men advanced their claims within an official conceptualization of citizenship encumbered with racial and gendered assumptions. In this context, three sets of citizenship claims deserve analysis. "Notorious Union men" earned the commissioners' approbation by meeting their standards of active citizenship to the Union through their contributions to the cause. "Independent rebels and traitors" incurred the commissioners' anger by meeting standards of active citizenship, but to the Confederacy rather than the Union. "Timid and neutral men" suffered the commissioners' scorn by fulfilling their obligations neither to the Union nor to the Confederacy and instead advancing a form of subject citizenship that challenged the equation of loyal citizens with independent actors but that also ultimately linked them with household dependents, namely blacks and women. At stake in this contest lay control over the postwar South and, more broadly, the reunited nation.

## "A Notorious Union Man"

Robert Heflin of northern Alabama had earned a reputation as a "notorious Union man." Heflin had offended his Confederate neighbors because, according to one witness, "He is a very impulsive man and expressed his sentiments very earnestly and heartily." Heflin's outspoken support for the Union along with his services to Unionists and disaffected Confederates fleeing to Union lines had prompted Confederate authorities to arrest him on several occasions. Heflin swore that "My whole life from the beginning of the war until I was forced to flee to the Union army for safety, was one continual scene of molestation and injury of every kind short of death, which I only escaped by fleeing from the county." One witness speculated that "it was very fortunate for him that he did as his course would have brought trouble if not death upon him." Heflin had resisted Confederate orthodoxy and had upheld Union loyalties in so "notorious" a manner that he had rendered himself anathema to his Confederate relatives, friends, and neighbors.[5] "Notorious Union men" underscore the public nature of active citizenship. Their Unionism was evident not just as inwardly held devotion but as outwardly expressed action. These loyal citizens, then, proved their allegiances by providing evidence of, first, their anti-secessionist sympathies but, more importantly, their anti-secessionist conduct and reputation. "Notorious Union men" met the ideals of active citizenship performed in the public realm on behalf of the public good.

The white southern men who won the commissioners' praise as Union men evinced little ambivalence in their sympathies. Joseph E. Segar of southeastern Virginia declared in his testimony that "I never had a sentiment in my life time that was not Union, down to the bottom of my soul, and have not now." Keeping with the commissioners' focus, he insisted that he had rejected both "the policy and doctrine of secession." He further emphasized that he had sacrificed his private interest for the public good. After stressing the danger incurred as a result of his antisecessionist sympathies, he declared that "I had determined to sacrifice my life." And he had been so uncompromising that "I never put my foot on rebel soil until after the peace," even though such a vow meant that "I never saw my family." The commissioners accepted Segar as "a notoriously loyal man, devoted to the Union." Indeed, they considered his loyalty so "well known" that they suspended their standard practice of recounting the testimony in their report to Congress and "simply refer[red] to the evidence."[6]

True Union men demonstrated their Union sympathies through their Union actions. The commissioners' understanding of Union contributions, however, was severely restricted. Their interrogatories reveal their understanding that citizenship required the performance of a small set of implicitly white and masculine political obligations. A vote against secession constituted a Union man's first act of loyalty. The commissioners asked claimants "on which side did you exert your influence and cast your vote," particularly on the ratification of the various ordinances of secession.[7] Charles H. Wilson successfully established his credentials as a loyal citizen by stressing his vote against secession. He knew that, in his neighborhood in southside Virginia, "everybody was for secession nearly or if not kept quiet and did not talk politics." He had voted against the ratification of the ordinance, cognizant that his side would lose, simply so that "my sentiments be known publicly."[8] More than Union voters, Union soldiers stood as preeminent loyal citizens in postbellum official citizenship. The commissioners only included an interrogatory specifically addressing Union military service (along with civil service) in 1874.[9] Nevertheless, they focused upon Union military service from the outset of their tenure. In their first report, the commissioners informed Congress that "of the claimants found loyal, many . . . have actually served in the Union Army, many have aided our military operations as scouts and guides, and in other ways."[10] Melvin B. Carr testified that he had twice tried to escape from northern Alabama to Union lines in Georgia to enlist in Union service. He had evaded Confederate arrest and, with the assistance of a family slave, escaped to Union lines. Carr then went to Indiana where he enlisted in the Indiana Cavalry, serving from October 1864 to

July 1865.[11] According to the commissioners' counts, 10 percent of claimants had volunteered for Union service. The commissioners considered Union military service the only loyal act significant enough to count for reporting purposes to Congress. Though they maintained statistics on various contributions to the Confederate cause, they did not bother to tally any other contributions to the Union cause.

Public expressions of Union sympathy and public performance of Union actions earned white southern men notoriety as Union men. The commissioners considered evidence that white male claimants had been recognized as Union men as key in their determinations of loyal citizenship. In all three versions of their interrogatories, they queried witnesses on the "public reputation" of the claimant for loyalty or disloyalty.[12] The requirement for a Union reputation built upon wartime and postwar practices in which military and government officials relied upon certifications by known Unionists as evidence of loyalty. Witnesses before the commission knew the value of the label, over and over again identifying the "Union men" in their communities. William Mitchell knew that Thomas Nation, a former Alabama slaveholder, had been a "Union man" because Confederates had harassed him. Mitchell speculated that "I don't think there was another loyal man for miles, if there was they never showed their hands."[13] "Notorious Union men" had shown their hands and in the process had endangered their necks. These Union men had become "notorious" through their "outspoken" and "public" denunciations of the Confederacy and praise of the Union. Over and over again, the commissioners noted in their reports to Congress that witnesses "testify to his loyal conversation and reputation."[14] This emphasis on conversation and reputation as a Union man demonstrated the public nature of loyal citizenship.

White southern men in certain regions had greater opportunity to offer the kind of evidence the commissioners required. Areas of the Confederacy with significant Union presence throughout the war provided white southern men with more opportunities to assist the Union cause. In areas of long-standing Union occupation, white southern men also felt more emboldened to openly express and act upon their Union sympathies. Significant populations of Unionists in the mountainous and non-plantation districts of western Virginia, northwestern Arkansas, western North Carolina, and eastern Tennessee provided a community to nurture Union sympathies and foster Union actions. In areas of significant Confederate strength in the Confederate interior, in contrast, white southern men who dissented from the Confederate cause had fewer opportunities to assist the Union cause and, with fewer allies in the vicinity, faced greater peril if they chose to do so.[15]

The commissioners sympathized with the "peril, hardship, sacrifice, and suffering" experienced by Unionists and praised them for their "steadfast courage and patriotic devotion to the Union, which do them honor and entitle them to the grateful consideration of the Government."[16] In their efforts to compensate "notorious Union men" for their wartime losses, the commissioners recognized the importance of southern dissenters in Union victory. The Confederacy's manpower disadvantage necessitated the full mobilization of the southern population for Confederate victory. The Confederacy resorted to a draft a year before the Union faced the same necessity. Approximately 100,000 men joined the Union army from the Confederate states. Combined with the 200,000 Union soldiers from the border slave states, the 100,000 Union soldiers from the Confederacy represented a significant manpower gain for the Union. Indeed, these men replaced every Union casualty from the first year of the war.[17]

The federal government through the Southern Claims Commission rewarded "notorious Union men" who had served the public and not just private interest in a public and not just private manner. These men had regarded secession as reckless and had favored the preservation of the Union. Even more, they had translated their sympathies into actions. Through their voting and soldiering, these men had earned Confederate enmity and contributed to the Union cause. In doing so, they had placed themselves and their families at risk for their nation. The commissioners celebrated these white southern men as uncompromising heroes who, by virtue of their bravery in the face of Confederate repression, deserved the full benefits of postwar citizenship.

### "Independent Rebel and Traitor"

Reuben H. J. Garland, a Georgia farmer, petitioned the Southern Claims Commission as a loyal citizen of the United States, to which the commissioners responded "Bah!" In their report to Congress, the commissioners noted that Garland had contributed to the raising of a Confederate company, encouraged his relatives and neighbors to enlist, collected taxes for the Confederacy, held Confederate bonds, and received passes from

Confederate authorities. Moreover, Garland admitted that, though he had been opposed to secession, he had "went with his state," not wishing to see his state "overthrown." The commissioners marveled that "after swearing to all this, the independent rebel and traitor has the 'cheek' to ask the Government of the United States to treat him as a loyal adherent to the Union and the Government during the war."[18] To the commissioners, Garland embodied the "independent rebel and traitor" who claimed loyalty to the Union in order to fraudulently reap the benefits of postwar citizenship. To expose these rebels and traitors, the commissioners directed their interrogatories and investigations to uncover the numerous ways in which white southern men had assisted the Confederacy. In response, white male claimants offered a variety of excuses for their disloyal actions, which the commissioners summarily rejected.

To guard against disguised "independent rebels and traitors," the commissioners placed the burden of proof upon claimants. They regarded "voluntary residence in an insurrectionary State during the war" as "*prima facie* evidence of disloyalty." The secession of their states from the Union did not terminate southerners' obligations to the Union. In order to overcome the presumption of their disloyalty by virtue of their residence, "the party claiming to be loyal must *prove* his loyalty. It is a fact to be established by proof, and is not to be presumed."[19] The commissioners had little trouble imagining the various ways white southern men could assist the Confederacy. They packed their interrogatories with questions on disloyal deeds. Altogether, twenty-five of the thirty-four items in their first version covered claimants' participation in almost every aspect of Confederate services compared with the four items on Union services.[20] In the second and third versions of their interrogatories, the commissioners drastically increased the list by adding disloyal actions that they had neglected in the first. These interrogatories built upon a significant wartime and postwar inheritance of loyalty testing, encompassing many of the disloyal classes prohibited from amnesty, voting, and officeholding in state and federal policy.[21] The commissioners, then, began each case with the intention of uncovering the various ways claimants had contributed to the Confederate cause.

The commissioners rejected as many as 40 percent of all claimants on charges that they had offered aid and comfort to the enemy. They considered Confederate military or civil service, a vote for secession, and an oath of allegiance to the Confederacy as the most unequivocal indications of disloyalty. Altogether, 20 percent of rejected claimants fell in one or more of these categories.[22] Other justifications for denial included procuring a substitute, selling supplies to the Confederacy, purchasing Confederate bonds, receiving wages for Confederate service, and contributing to the outfitting of Confederate soldiers, including sons.[23] The commissioners also rejected claimants for more minor contributions to the Confederate cause. They disallowed one claim, in part, because a father had supplied his son, a Confederate soldier, with a blanket that he had used while in service.[24] From the commissioners' perspective, these claimants, in performing these services, had acted as Confederate citizens.

White male claimants had little success in their attempts to recast disloyal acts as loyal acts. Some argued that they had served the Union cause while Confederate soldiers by encouraging desertion. Asa Daniel of Mississippi boasted that he had convinced 150 soldiers to return home during his one month in a Confederate camp.[25] Other white male claimants insisted that they had accepted Confederate office in order to serve Union families in their communities. Thomas P. Lewis excused his term in the Alabama legislature in 1863 and 1864 because "the Union men of my county thought that I could be of more benefit to them in the Legislature, than out of it, and by so doing I could keep out of the rebel army and could support my family and help the Union men in my county."[26] Without additional evidence of loyalty, the commissioners viewed these claimants essentially as liars, dismissing stories of Union conspiracies to encourage desertion and "Union candidates" serving in Confederate office as "hardly credible" and "highly improbable."[27]

Former Confederates unsuccessfully insisted that discriminations as "rebels" and "traitors" were relics of the war. They rejected past loyalty in favor of future loyalty as the standard of citizenship and argued that their pardons and amnesty oaths restored their rights of citizenship, including their right to compensation for their wartime losses. John Hawk of Mississippi informed the commissioners that "I took the amnesty oath to the Union government in the year 1865 and claim that I am entitled to and received full pardon and amnesty for anything I might have done during the war."[28] Recipients presented their pardons and oaths as evidence of their status as loyal citizens of the reunited nation. In making these declarations, claimants could cite as authority the rulings of the U.S. Supreme Court, which declared that a pardon "releases the punishment and blots out of existence the guilt, so that in the eye of the law the offender is as innocent as if he had never committed the offence."[29] The commissioners disapproved of the doctrine that pardon and amnesty obliterated treason. Orange Ferriss, one of the three commissioners, had served in the House of Representatives during President Andrew Johnson's impeachment trial. During the debate over the articles of impeachment, Ferriss had charged that "instead of punishing traitors, he has pardoned thousands." In doing so, Johnson had wronged the loyal people who had sacrificed their lives on the battlefields of the South in order to turn "vanquished rebels and their sympathizers" into his most "ardent admirers and earnest supporters."[30] Ferriss and the other commissioners refused to allow "rebels" and "traitors" to claim compensation from their commission as loyal citizens of the United States. They rejected pardons as evidence of loyalty and, indeed, considered an application for a pardon as evidence of disloyalty, noting that "pardons were granted upon special application to persons who had given aid and comfort to the rebellion" and that "Union men had no occasion to ask for pardon."[31] They also dismissed oaths of future allegiance to the Union government as worthless in determining southerners' loyalty. "It was a current and standing joke of the Union troops," the commissioners observed, "that they administered the oath and turned confederates loose only to meet them in arms the next day."[32]

The federal government refused to compensate "independent rebels and traitors" for their wartime property losses, an action considered akin to paying for the Confederate war effort. The commissioners condemned these men for withdrawing their allegiances from the Union and bestowing them upon the Confederacy. "Independent rebels and traitors" and "notorious Union men" yielded opposite outcomes in the claims process, but their conceptualization of citizenship shared many similarities. "Independent rebels and traitors," like "notorious Union men," had fulfilled their political obligations to their nations, the former to the Confederacy and the latter to the Union. These white southern men could not meet the commissioners' standards of active citizenship in opposition to secession but could have met standards of active citizenship in defense of secession. Both good Union men and good Confederate men had voted in elections, served in the military, accepted public office, and outfitted and equipped soldiers. They had supported opposing causes, but they had shared their independence.

## "A Timid and Neutral Man"

From the commissioners' perspective, John N. Gatewood, a former Virginia slaveholder, offered little evidence of his loyal citizenship. Gatewood insisted that "I was a Union man all the time," but in support of his contention he could only offer that "I never did anything to injure the Union cause." He also had done little to support the Union cause or harm the Confederate cause. Though "willing to help [the Union] as far as I could," Gatewood had not voted against secession, had not enlisted in the Union army, had not served in the Union civil service, and had not rendered services to Union soldiers or civilians. In sum, Gatewood had fulfilled none of the obligations of loyal citizenship that the commissioners set forth in their interrogatories. Gatewood had not performed his political obligations to the Union, a characteristic of the "notorious Union man," or to the Confederacy, an attribute of the "independent rebel and traitor." White southern men who identified themselves as "Union men" despite their inability to meet the commissioners' standards of active citizenship proposed an alternate conceptualization of subject citizenship that emphasized their obligations to their families and deemphasized their obligations to the Union. The commissioners did not share this conceptualization of loyal citizenship, condemning Gatewood as "a timid and neutral man."[33] In doing so, they guarded the federal government against such cowardly shirkers who represented the antithesis of good citizens by denying the claims of white southern men who had committed few loyal actions and had not suffered for their allegiances.

Many white male claimants reported that they had performed no services for the Union. These claimants generally asserted Union sympathies and then denied involvement in the long list of disloyal actions and the short list of loyal actions. In rejecting active citizenship, some white male claimants swore that they had little opportunity to aid the Union cause. They argued that their personal circumstances had prevented their service to the Union. Adam Fix of Virginia explained that he "did not vote either for or against the ordinance of secession, would have voted against it but I was sick."[34] Other white male claimants explained that their isolation from the theaters of war had prevented them from offering their assistance to the Union war effort. In areas inside Confederate lines for much of the war, potential recruits had faced a dangerous journey to enlist in the Union army. Peter McArdle of Mississippi asserted that "I would have helped the United States if called on as far as I could. If I had to fight I would have helped the North if I had an opportunity."[35] These claimants challenged the commissioners' understanding of citizenship in practice though not in theory. They did not identify an inability to act as citizens according to the commissioners' requirements, just an opportunity.

More challenging to the commissioners' conceptualization of active citizenship, other claimants insisted that they had lacked not only the opportunity but the capability to assist the Union war effort. Historians of southern politics debate the extent of democracy in the prewar and wartime South. Some emphasize the hierarchical character of southern society, planters' attempts to exert dominance over slaves and non-slaveholders, or popular disinterest in political affairs. Most historians, however, emphasize the pervasiveness of a political ideology that stressed democracy for white men.[36] Regardless of this historiographical debate, many white male claimants before the commission eschewed democratic politics in favor of deferential politics. These southerners rejected conceptualizations of white male citizenship rooted in political participation and political obligation.

Over and over again, white male claimants repudiated public affairs. These claimants were often yeomen and poor whites, and generally resided in plantation or high slaveholding districts where planter dominance was most assured rather than the nonplantation or low slaveholding districts where white male egalitarianism was most prevalent. These elites refused culpability for the war and placed the responsibility for politics strictly on politicians, repeatedly uttering statements like "I was no politician" and so "I didn't take either side."[37] Some white southern men found themselves so unaccustomed to speaking about politics and other matters of public interest that they provided little evidence in their own defense. These men manifested a deferential attitude toward politics. Peter P. Perkins, formerly a Virginia overseer, discerned that "something"—probably the dissolution of the Whig Party—"was wrong" with the political process around the time of Franklin Pierce's election. In response, Perkins withdrew from politics. When the war commenced, he "took no part" in the war just as he had taken no part in politics before. Perkins had continued to defer to others during the war, explaining that he "wanted to see the North succeed and take charge of our affairs" because "I thought they would do better for us than had been done."[38] He suggested that the ruling class had done little for non-slaveholders and he expressed his hope that the North would better represent his interests. Tellingly, Perkins did not concede a role for himself in governance. Many nonelite white southern men positioned themselves as passive actors in the drama of the Civil War, refusing to assume responsibility for the war.

White men who disclaimed responsibility for the state or who subordinated themselves to the state explained their positions in various ways. Some nonelite white men claimed that their rudimentary educations had rendered them null in the politics of secession and war. John W. Edwards, a Virginia artisan, emphasized his inadequacies, explaining that "I was confused and didn't know which was right" because "I had very little education."[39] White male claimants also suggested that they had been effectively disfranchised in southern society. Henry Ambos, a Georgia nonslaveholding farmer and fisherman, removed himself from politics, not bothering to vote before or during the war. He explained that "when the State voted to secede I did not interfere one way or the other" as "it was-not-in-my-power to interfere against secession."[40] These white southern men completely rejected the commissioners' requirement for active citizenship as beyond their capabilities as a result of their positions within southern society.

With their assertions that they lacked opportunity and capability to oppose the Confederacy, these white male claimants advanced a form of subject citizenship and identified themselves as "citizen-subjects" as opposed to "citizen-soldiers" or "citizen-voters."[41] One attorney, C. W. Dudley, remarked that "they have been the victims of a heartless political conspiracy . . . which has overwhelmed them with ruin, and that they deserve the sympathy of all right minded men." Dudley further argued that "they were not leaders in this conspiracy, nor even followers, except where drawn into an apparent acquiescence at the point of the bayonet." For these citizen-subjects, Dudley declared that to prove loyalty "by outward acts, in open resistance to rebellion, is almost impossible, because the friends of the Union dared not avow their sentiments publicly, or do any act in that direction, for their lives would have been endangered thereby." As a result, Dudley noted that Unionists could do nothing to aid their cause and in fact had often been forced to assist the Confederacy. Dudley suggested that claimants' solemn oaths that they had stood by the Union should be considered "*prima facie* evidence" of their loyalty. Dudley insisted that loyalty was "a sentiment best felt by him who professes it" and not judged by distant northern commissioners.[42] According to this argument, citizen-subjects had not been leaders or followers or actors of any sort but had instead supported the Union in their hearts and minds.

As they denied accountability for governmental affairs, white male claimants embraced responsibility for familial affairs. John T. Mitchell of Virginia admitted that "my feelings were not very strongly enlisted as I was too much occupied with taking care of my farm and managing my business to give much attention to the matter."[43] These private-oriented men may have reflected wartime reassessments of courage. Many white male civilians and soldiers remained devoted to manly courage and its manifestation: acting on principle in defense of slavery, nation, and home. Others, in contrast, learned that the vaunted "courageous" men often suffered or died while more pragmatic men survived to provide for their families. Courage seemed to offer few rewards, as disease and devastation recognized no distinctions and conferred no immunities.[44] Many white male claimants regarded caution and lying low as the wiser course for themselves and their families. These white southern men protected the safety of themselves and their families and property rather than stand for their principles.

Self-professions of Union sympathies provided necessary but not sufficient evidence of loyal citizenship for the commissioners. In weighing the testimony, "we invariably place more confidence in the conduct and acts of claimants" than in "their present professions of loyalty."[45] Arguing that "it is easier and more profitable to be loyal now than during the war," the commissioners refused to rely upon stated sympathies alone in reaching their determinations.[46] This is reflected in the overwhelming attention in the interrogatories to actions over sympathies. Of the thirty-four interrogatories in the 1871 version, forty-three interrogatories in the 1872 version, and fifty-three interrogatories in the 1874 version, only two in each directly queried claimants on their sympathies and only in a vague manner.[47]

The commissioners rejected claimants' assertion of subject citizenship. Charges of timidity revealed the commissioners' standards of masculine citizenship. They rejected one claimant because "he sat still, accepted the situation, and at the most simply sympathized."[48] Loyal citizens did not merely "wish" for the preservation of the Union; "they were willing to aid in the preservation of the Union."[49] The commissioners condemned another claimant as "a timid man who could not stand by his principles" because he had refused to serve in the army, either in defense of the Union or the Confederacy.[50] They criticized these men for their "cowardice" and likely agreed with one claimant who admitted that he had "lost for the time my manhood."[51] The commissioners refused to recognize such unmanly men as loyal citizens. Accusations of neutrality emerged from the commissioners' expectation that loyal citizens defended public concerns, even when they conflicted with private interests. They also suspected that such claimants had not been conscientiously neutral out of conflicting sympathies but had been willing to sell their loyalties to the highest bidder.[52] They charged that such claimants had "court[ed] the favor of the power in the ascendant" and had been "ready to serve either side or anybody for a consideration."[53] The commissioners denounced them as "free and easy persons who without injury to their feelings or personal inconvenience can adapt themselves to any and all circumstances."[54] These men did not sacrifice self for nation but instead sacrificed nation for self. They did not stand for principles; indeed, they possessed no principles.

In the cases of "timidity" and "neutrality," white male claimants and the commissioners clashed over the necessity for white men to perform political obligations to their nation. White male claimants advanced a form of subject citizenship that emphasized private over public obligations. The commissioners refused to abandon their requirement for active citizenship by rewarding white southern men who had not fulfilled the obligations of patriotic citizenship. The gap between subject and active citizenship for white southern men contributed to the disempowerment of "timid" and "neutral" men and the reempowerment of "rebels" and "traitors." In terms of politics, "timid" and "neutral" men occupied the middle ground between "notorious Union men" and "rebels" and "traitors," but in terms of citizenship they represented the opposite of both. Both Unionists and Confederates had supported their cause armed with courage, principles, and patriotism. Neutral men had shirked their duties, revealing themselves as uncourageous, unprincipled, and unpatriotic, the antithesis of the good citizen.

\* \* \*

The commissioners' rulings on "notorious Union men," "independent rebels and traitors," and "timid and neutral men" took place amid a momentous discussion over political authority in the postwar South. By the early 1870s, a growing consensus among former Confederates, northern Democrats, and liberal Republicans complained that limitations on postwar political power in the South according to wartime loyalties disqualified those best able to rule and empowered those least able to rule. Acting on these conclusions, the federal government gradually withdrew from intervening in southern affairs. Historians have generally accepted this perspective, citing this issue as one of the intractable problems of Reconstruction. There is, however, some evidence which suggests that these fears reflected an elitist (and racist) bias rather than an insurmountable problem. Where the federal government required ironclad loyalty to the Union as a condition for employment, for example, federal officials found sufficient numbers of eligible candidates. In any case, the commissioners' rejection of "timid" and "neutral" men contributed to a conceptualization of citizenship that, with the abandonment of wartime loyalty as a key component, facilitated the retreat from Reconstruction.

Full citizenship in the postwar years presumed a particular brand of white masculinity. The federal government, through the Southern Claims Commission, rewarded loyal citizens who had actively defended the Union, especially as politicians, voters, and soldiers, all activities restricted to white men. The government dismissed the claims of white southern men who expressed ideological devotion to Union principles but could not prove that they had contributed to the Union cause in ways befitting their race and sex. And the government refused to compensate former Confederates who had contributed to the bid for southern independence. But once former Unionists forgave trespasses against the Union and forgot the divisions of the war, former Confederates could garner praise for manifesting the attributes of good citizenship of the Confederacy, if not Union. Former Unionists ignored the ideological divisions at the center of the war and, even, came to admire former Confederates' exploits of bravery and their devotion to their principles. Over time, attention to actions over ideology facilitated the federal government's move to forgive wartime disloyalty and celebrate postwar loyalty. By 1898, Congress removed most of the remaining restrictions on citizenship related to wartime loyalties. With their cause forgotten, former Confederates were forgiven as independent (though perhaps misguided) citizens.

## Notes

1. For use of the term "active citizenship" see Judith N. Shklar, *American Citizenship: The Quest for Inclusion* (Cambridge: Harvard University Press, 1991).

2. For examples see Frank W. Klingberg, *The Southern Claims Commission* (Berkeley: University of California Press, 1955); Sarah Larson, "Records of the Southern Claims Commission," *Prologue* 12, no. 4 (1980): 207–18; John Hammond Moore, "Getting Uncle Sam's Dollars: South Carolinians and the Southern Claims Commission, 1871–1880," *South Carolina Historical Magazine* 82, no. 3 (1981): 248–62; John Hammond Moore, "Richmond Area Residents and the Southern Claims Commission, 1871–1880," *Virginia Magazine of History & Biography* 91, no. 3 (1983): 285–95; John Hammond Moore, "Sherman's 'Fifth Column': A Guide to Unionist Activity in Georgia," *Georgia Historical Quarterly* 68, no. 3 (1984): 382–409; Eugene A. Hatfield, "Stephen Green Dorsey and the Southern Claims Commission: A Question of Loyalty," *Atlanta Historical Journal* 29, no. 2 (1985): 19–29; John Hammond Moore, "In Sherman's Wake: Atlanta and the Southern Claims Commission, 1871–1880," *Atlanta Historical Journal* 29, no. 2 (1985): 5–18; Michael K. Honey, "The War within the Confederacy: White Unionists of North Carolina," *Prologue* 18, no. 2 (1986): 75–93; Kenneth W. Noe, "Red String Scare: Civil War Southwest Virginia and the Heroes of America," *North Carolina Historical Review* 69, no. 3 (1992): 301–22; Reginald Washington, "The Southern Claims Commission: A Source for African-American Roots," *Prologue* 27, no. 4 (1995): 374–82; Rebecca M. Dresser, "Kate and John Minor: Confederate Unionists of Natchez," *Journal of Mississippi History* 64, no. 3 (2002): 188–216; Margaret M. Storey, "Civil War Unionists and the Political Culture of Loyalty in Alabama, 1860–1861," *Journal of Southern History* 69, no. 1 (2003): 71–106; Edna Greene Medford, "'I Was Always a Union Man': The Dilemma of Free Blacks in Confederate Virginia," *Slavery and Abolition* 15, no. 3 (1994): 1–16; Stephen S. Michot, "'War Is Still Raging in This Part of the Country': Oath-Taking, Conscription, and Guerrilla War in Louisiana's Lafourche Region," *Louisiana History* 38, no. 2 (1997): 157–84; Noel G. Harrison, "Atop an Anvil: The Civilians' War in Fairfax and Alexandria Counties, April 1861–April 1862," *Virginia Magazine of History and Biography* 106, no. 2 (1998): 133–64; Anthony E. Kaye, "Slaves, Emancipation, and the Powers of War: Views from the Natchez District of Mississippi," in *The War Was You and Me: Civilians in the American Civil War*, ed. Joan E Cashin (Princeton: Princeton University Press, 2002); Margaret M. Storey, *Loyalty and Loss: Alabama's Unionists in the Civil War and Reconstruction* (Baton Rouge: Louisiana State University Press, 2004).

3. Eric Foner, *Reconstruction: America's Unfinished Revolution, 1863–1877* (New York: Harper & Row, 1988); Heather Cox Richardson, *The Death of Reconstruction: Race, Labor, and Politics in the Post–Civil War North, 1865–1901* (Cambridge: Harvard University Press, 2001); Michael W. Fitzgerald, *Splendid Failure: Postwar Reconstruction in the American South* (Chicago: Ivan R. Dee, 2007); Terry L. Seip, *The South Returns to Congress: Men, Economic Measures, and Intersectional Relationships, 1868–1879* (Baton Rouge: Louisiana State University Press, 1983); Richard H. Abbott, *The Republican Party and the South, 1855–1877: The First Southern Strategy* (Chapel Hill: University of North Carolina Press, 1986).

4. This analysis does not disagree that white resistance in the former Confederacy, both nonviolent and violent, also played a primary role in the retreat from Reconstruction. See Allen W. Trelease, *White Terror: The Ku Klux Klan Conspiracy and Southern Reconstruction* (New York: Harper & Row, 1971); George C. Rable, *But There Was No*

*Peace: The Role of Violence in the Politics of Reconstruction* (Athens: University of Georgia Press, 1984); Michael Perman, *The Road to Redemption: Southern Politics, 1869–1879* (Chapel Hill: University of North Carolina Press, 1984); Steven Hahn, *A Nation under Our Feet: Black Political Struggles in the Rural South from Slavery to the Great Migration* (Cambridge: Harvard University Press, 2005).

5. Charles S. Cherry Deposition, April 18, 1871, Robert S. Heflin Allowed Claim, Randolph County, Alabama, Records of the United States General Accounting Office, Southern Claims Commission, Allowed Claims, 1871–1880, RG 217, National Archives, Washington, D.C. [hereafter "Allowed Claim"]; John G. Stokes Deposition, April 18, 1871, ibid.; Christopher G. Sheats Deposition, April 18, 1871, ibid.; Robert S. Heflin Deposition, March 30, 1872, ibid.; Summary Report, 1872, ibid.

6. Joseph E. Segar Deposition, February 26, 1874, Joseph E. Segar Allowed Claim, Elizabeth City County, Virginia.

7. See number 33 in "Standing Interrogatories," 1871, in United States Congress, House of Representatives, "First General Report of the Commissioners of Claims," 42nd Congress, 2nd session, 1871, H. Doc. 16 [hereafter "First General Report"]; number 40 in "Standing Interrogatories," 1872, in United States Congress, House of Representatives, "Second General Report of the Commissioners of Claims," 42nd Congress, 3rd session, 1872, H. Doc. 12 [hereafter "Second General Report"]; and number 44 in "Standing Interrogatories," 1874, in United States Congress, House of Representatives, "Fourth General Report of the Commissioners of Claims," 43rd Congress, 2nd session, 1874, H. Doc. 18 [hereafter "Fourth General Report"].

8. Charles H. Wilson Deposition, August 19, 1875, Charles H. Wilson Allowed Claim, Dinwiddie County, Virginia. For corroboration, see also W. L. Hobbs Deposition, August 19, 1875, ibid.

9. See numbers 8, 10, 11, 44, and 51 in "Standing Interrogatories," 1874, in "Fourth General Report."

10. "First General Report," 8.

11. Melvin B. Carr Testimony, May 21, 1874, Melvin B. Carr Allowed Claim, Cherokee County, Alabama. For corroboration, see also Willis Carr, Willis Carr Testimony, May 21, 1874, Melvin B. Carr Allowed Claim, Cherokee County, Alabama, and Elijah C. Carr Testimony, May 21, 1874, Melvin B. Carr Allowed Claim, Cherokee County, Alabama. Carr produced his discharge papers as evidence of his Union military service. He later applied for a pension for his service in the Indiana Cavalry, Regiment 8, Company M.

12. See questions for witnesses in "Standing Interrogatories," 1871, in "First General Report"; questions for witnesses in "Standing Interrogatories," 1872, in "Secondary General Report"; number 60 in "Standing Interrogatories," 1874, in "Fourth General Report."

13. William Mitchell, July 17, 1873, Thomas Nation Allowed Claim, Blount County, Alabama.

14. See, for example, Summary Report, John T. Bailey Allowed Claim, Cherokee County, Alabama.

15. For an analysis that divides the Confederacy into zones related to Union occupation, see Stephen V. Ash, *When the Yankees Came: Conflict and Chaos in the Occupied South, 1861–1865* (Chapel Hill: University of North Carolina Press, 1995).

16. "First General Report," 8.

17. For this argument, see William W. Freehling, *The South vs. the South: How Anti-Confederate Southerners Shaped the Course of the Civil War* (Oxford: Oxford University Press, 2001), 61.

18. Reuben H. J. Garland Deposition, October 4, 1871, Reuben H. J. Garland Disallowed Claim, Upson County, Georgia, Records of the Commissioner of Claims, Southern Claims Commission, 1871–1880, RG 56, Microfilm Publication M87, National Archives, Washington, D.C. [hereafter "Disallowed Claim"]; Summary Report, ibid.

19. "First General Report," 2–3.

20. See numbers 3–18, 23–31, and 33 in "Standing Interrogatories," 1871, in "First General Report." For questions on loyal deeds, see numbers 21–23 and 30 in "Standing Interrogatories," 1871.

21. Harold M. Hyman, *Era of the Oath: Northern Loyalty Tests during the Civil War and Reconstruction* (Philadelphia: University of Pennsylvania Press, 1954); Jonathan T. Dorris, *Pardon and Amnesty under Lincoln and Johnson: The Restoration of the Confederates to Their Rights and Privileges, 1861–1898* (Chapel Hill: University of North Carolina Press, 1953); Harold M. Hyman, *To Try Men's Souls: Loyalty Tests in American History* (Berkeley: University of California Press, 1959).

22. This estimate is based upon an extrapolation of Klingberg's analysis of large claims (over $10,000). Klingberg, *The Southern Claims Commission*, 162.

23. For an example of a claimant rejected because he had procured a substitute, see Summary Report, 1871, Noah Flory Disallowed Claim, Rockingham County, Virginia. For an example of a claimant rejected because he had supplied his son in the Confederate army, see Summary Report, 1873, John V. Nunnally Disallowed Claim, LaFayette County, Mississippi. For an example of a claimant who had purchased Confederate bonds, see Summary Report, 1871, Reuben H. J. Garland Disallowed Claim, Upson County, Georgia. For an example of a claimant rejected for services rendered to the Confederacy, see Summary Report, 1877, Thomas M. Mathews Disallowed Claim, Dallas County, Alabama.

24. For an example see Summary Report, 1873, James D. Scott Disallowed Claim, Clark County, Arkansas.

25. Summary Report, 1872, Asa Daniel Disallowed Claim, Monroe County, Mississippi.

26. Thomas P. Lewis Deposition, November 23, 1871, Thomas P. Lewis Disallowed Claim, Tuscaloosa County, Alabama.

27. Summary Report, 1873, Richard Appling Disallowed Claim, Tuscaloosa County, Alabama; Summary Report, 1872, Asa Daniel Disallowed Claim, Monroe County, Mississippi.

28. John Hawk Deposition, September 14, 1872, John Hawk Disallowed Claim, Marshall County, Mississippi. See also Summary Report, 1873, Robert Jamison Disallowed Claim, DeSoto County, Mississippi.

29. *Ex parte Garland*, 71 U.S. 333 (1866). Augustus Garland petitioned to practice law in federal courts without taking the prescribed ironclad oath. See also Dorris, *Pardon and Amnesty*, 397–98.

30. *Congressional Globe*, 40th Congress, 2nd session, March 2, 1868, p. 234.

31. Summary Report, 1873, Henry Ormsby Disallowed Claim, Marshall County, Mississippi.

32. Summary Report, 1878, John H. Gibbons Disallowed Claim, East Baton Rouge Parish, Louisiana.

33. John N. Gatewood Deposition, October 24, 1871, John N. Gatewood Claim, Caroline County, Virginia, in Docket No. 2,719, Court of Claims, RG 123, National Archives, Washington, D.C. [hereafter "Court of Claims"]; John H. Burruss Deposition, October 24, 1871, ibid.; F. S. Tukey Deposition, October 24, 1871, ibid.; Summary Report, ibid. Some rejected claimants later appealed their cases before the Court of Claims; these cases are filed in the records of that body.

34. Adam Fix Deposition, September 14, 1871, Adam Fix Disallowed Claim, Augusta County, Virginia.

35. Peter McArdle Deposition, May 3, 1872, Peter McArdle Disallowed Claim, Hinds County, Mississippi, in Court of Claims, Docket No. 1,013.

36. The scholarship on this question is extensive. For an excellent overview see Charles C. Bolton, "Planters, Plain Folk, and Poor Whites," in *A Companion to the Civil War and Reconstruction*, ed. Lacy K. Ford (Malden, Mass.: Blackwell, 2005), 75–93.

37. John W. Edwards Deposition, November 11, 1875, John W. Edwards Disallowed Claim, Prince George County, Virginia.

38. Peter P. Perkins Deposition, April 25, 1872, Peter P. Perkins Disallowed Claim, Halifax County, Virginia.

39. John W. Edwards Deposition, November 11, 1875.

40. Henry Ambos Deposition, July 11, 1872, Henry Ambos Disallowed Claim, Chatham County, Georgia.

41. For this terminology see Shklar, *American Citizenship*. Shklar has traced this "citizen-subject" back to Bodin and Hobbes's justification for monarchial absolutism.

42. C. W. Dudley, Brief for Claimant, filed in Wiley Tipton Allowed Claim, Fanin County, Georgia.

43. Joseph T. Mitchell Deposition, February 22, 1875, Joseph T. Mitchell Disallowed Claim, Augusta County, Virginia.

44. William Fletcher Thompson, *The Image of War: The Pictorial Reporting of the American Civil War* (New York: T. Yoseloff, 1960); Gerald F. Linderman, *Embattled Courage: The Experience of Combat in the American Civil War* (New York: Collier Macmillan, 1987).

45. Summary Report, 1879, Logan Osburn Disallowed Claim, Jefferson County, West Virginia.

46. "First General Report," 3.

47. This count only includes questions directed toward claimants in the loyalty section and excludes questions directed toward claimants in the property section and questions directed toward witnesses.

48. Summary Report, 1871, John Wampler Disallowed Claim, Augusta County, Virginia.

49. Summary Report, 1877, James C. Owen Disallowed Claim, Williamson County, Tennessee.

50. Summary Report, 1875, Winfield Scott Baugher Claim, Rockingham County, Virginia, in Docket No. 8736, Court of Claims.

51. Summary Report, 1876, Daniel Cullers Disallowed Claim, Shenandoah County, Virginia; Summary Report, 1876, W. J. Miller Disallowed Claim, Rockingham County, Virginia.

52. Number 64 in "Standing Interrogatories," 1874, in "Fourth General Report," question 64.

53. Summary Report, 1875, Daniel Lowry Disallowed Claim, Bartow County, Georgia, and Summary Report, 1878, Joel H. Dyar Disallowed Claim, Bartow County, Georgia.

54. Summary Report, 1878, Erasmus L. Houff Disallowed Claim, Augusta County, Virginia, in Docket No. 8,638, Court of Claims.

# III

## REIMAGINING CITIZENSHIP

# 8

........................

## Dark Satanic Fields

### Uncle Tom's Cabin, Industrialization, and the U.S. Imperial Imaginary

JENNIFER RAE GREESON

> "I say, Sambo, you go to spilin' the hands, I'll tell Mas'r o' you," said Quimbo, who was busy at the mill, from which he had viciously driven two or three tired women. . . .
>
> "And I'll tell him ye won't let the women come to the mills, yo old nigger!" said Sambo. . . .
>
> Tom waited till a late hour, to get a place at the mills. . . . for the mills were few in number compared with the grinders, and the weary and feeble ones were driven back by the strong.
>
> Harriet Beecher Stowe, *Uncle Tom's Cabin; or, Life among the Lowly*

Harriet Beecher Stowe's novel *Uncle Tom's Cabin* set the scene and organized the story of the antebellum South in U.S. national imagination, serving as the master narrative of southern slavery from the time of its publication in 1852 well into the twentieth century and holding sway still, incalculably, in the historical memory of our own time. In the United States of the 1850s, Stowe's novel converted abolitionism from a radical political stance into a popular sentimental imperative. So great was the influence of the book that Lincoln was reported to have said, on meeting Stowe in 1862, "So you're the little woman who wrote the book that started this great war."[1]

It is startling, then, to notice how much Simon Legree's plantation—Stowe's very archetype of the South—looks like Lowell, Massachusetts, or any of the other mill towns that had sprung up in the industrializing Northeast in the 1830s and 1840s.[2] Indeed, Stowe organizes the first chapter of her novel set on Legree's infernal territory around an apparently gratuitous bit of stage business—his enslaved workers are using a hand mill to grind individual portions of parched corn for their dinners—which is useful primarily for its telegraphic punch on the page, allowing her to locate their slave labor at, quite literally, "the mill," that icon of modern industry. As she introduces Legree's plantation in this way, Stowe figures enslaved people in the South as a modern mass of proletarians—denominated "hands," in the parlance of contemporary factory management—who are forced into a desperate competition with each other on the wage-labor playing field of work-or-starve: "[F]or the mills were few in number compared with the grinders, and the weary and feeble ones were driven back by the strong."[3] As she focuses with especial anxiety on the women workers whose presence drew most attention in the New England textile mills, and as she introduces as a guide to Legree's realm a classic urban prostitute figure—in the character of the "quadroon" Cassy, who has "walked the streets when it seemed as if I had misery enough in my one heart to sink the city"—Stowe fully realizes the South as the dark satanic field of U.S. industrial modernity.[4] In the decade before the Civil War, the novel most definitively about and definitional of the South actually obliterates it, as Stowe writes the dystopian visions of the modernizing national center over the imaginative terrain of its southern other.

This essay takes the massive popular reading of *Uncle Tom's Cabin* in the United States in the decade before the Civil War as a collective imaginative inquiry into the civic, ethical, and emotional responsibilities of U.S. citizenship. As such, the novel addresses not only the slavery question but also a broader (and related) transformation in the meaning of U.S. citizenship at a critical juncture in national life: the emergence of the United States into the modern industrial and imperial world order. In place of the American Revolution, Stowe's generation faced the "market revolution," a perhaps equally transformative symbiosis: rapid industrialization at the northeastern core of the nation spurred and was fed by galloping expansion of its southern and western peripheries and their productive capacities.[5] The epochal transformations of the market revolution, felt first and most acutely at the northeastern centers of U.S. literary production, radically undermined the most basic premises of republican citizenship.[6] In the first decades of the nineteenth century, a U.S. citizen had been understood to be a "freeman," his independence secured by his possession of both his means of production and an array of people dependent upon him (women, children, servants, slaves). By the eve of the Civil War, though, and under the pressures of industrialization, U.S. citizenship had come to describe a situation that earlier generations would have considered servitude, guaranteeing only a "hireling" existence, only the personal possession of a commoditized and alienable self.

To conserve the most basic terms of republican ideology—"freedom" and "independence"—under the market revolution, Stowe's generation had to remake those terms in the 1840s, uncoupling them from their former connotations of mastery and ownership and reinscribing them as accurate descriptors of a personal status recently considered "dependence" or "servitude." If we focus on the problem of freedom as the great challenge to national ideology and culture in the era of industrialization and expansion, then the reanimated relevance of the South at this time springs immediately into view.[7] From its beginnings, the South in U.S. culture had been the location of slavery within the slaveholding republic. Now, American slavery emerged as the antithetical baseline against which all permutations of and infringements on republican "freedom" had to be conceptualized. Newly centered in U.S. national imagination, American slavery now appeared not as an inherited sin, a provincial connection to past colonial origins, but as an impending condition of life at the industrializing northeastern core. The confusion surrounding the word itself in U.S. print in the 1840s—the extent to which enslavement had to be described as "chattel slavery" in order to distinguish it from the "wage slavery" of proletarianization—speaks both to the interpolation of southern slavery into every register of U.S. culture and to the reimagination of that term that went along with its new centrality.[8]

In the second part of this essay I propose that *Uncle Tom's Cabin* became the central story of Stowe's age not only because it allowed readers to relive and to mourn what they had lost through the market revolution, but also because Stowe's novel transmutes the fall into the market into a felix culpa. (We perhaps would expect no less of the daughter of a New England divine—to find redemption, for the regenerate at least, in a seeming reversal of fortune.) If the stature of U.S. citizenship had been reduced under industrialization, Stowe suggests in the second half of her novel that it could be expanded anew by the assuming imperial mastery of southern peoples and places.

\* \* \*

It was Stowe's reclamation of the South as a vehicle for the fantastic projections of the industrializing metropolis that made *Uncle Tom's Cabin* the book that put the United States on the map of Western literary culture. While U.S. critics and readers, from 1852 until quite recently, have tended to focus on the political efficacy and ramifications of the novel, from the perspective of Europe Stowe's aesthetic interventions have always mattered more.[9] British, French, German, and Russian critics found in *Uncle Tom's Cabin* at last a recognizably distinctive American literary production, a novel uniquely in conversation with, rather than merely imitative of, broader Western artistic innovations and concerns.[10] For European readers, Stowe was able to represent and to fathom the traumatic dislocations of the modern era in a novel way, precisely because of the anomalously simultaneous presence of domestic slavery with industrialization in the United States. British readers, for instance, who were by 1852 well schooled in the new social novels of the industrial era, received Stowe's novel more enthusiastically than their U.S. counterparts during its first year in print: the novel sold three times as many copies in Britain as in Stowe's native land. During a triumphal tour of Britain in 1853, Stowe found herself hailed not so much for having written an anti-slavery novel as for having written a Dickensian chronicle of "Life among the Lowly," as she had subtitled the book.[11] At a ceremonial dinner with the Lord Mayor of London she was even seated across from Dickens, and the two authors were toasted together "as having employed fiction as a means of awakening the attention of their respective countries to the condition of the oppressed and suffering classes."[12] Stowe's South captured the attention of European capitals, in other words, insofar as it could be understood to provide an analogue or metaphor for metropolitan proletarianization. It was her American access to this fertile field for metaphorizing the problems of metropolitan modernity that made Stowe's novel "a really healthy indigenous growth," in the opinion of British novelist Charles Kingsley, rather than a derivative entry into the Condition of England debates.[13]

This British identification of *Uncle Tom's Cabin*—as Dickens with a distinctively American twist—highlights Stowe's innovations in novel form. For though her subject was the South, the narrative structure she employed made *Uncle Tom's Cabin* perhaps the most important novel of metropolitan modernity published in the United States before the Civil War.[14] Stowe's novel attempts above all to encompass, contain, and order an overwhelmingly complex and variegated social field. As she presents a huge cast of minutely rendered characters, drawn from across lines of class, race, place, and religion, Stowe essays the imaginative scope commensurate with the urban reality of her native New England, where readers constantly encountered strangers of fortunes and origins alien to their own. As she causes this widely ranging cast of characters to interact with one another in constantly shifting configurations across an episodic plot, Stowe stresses a fundamental interconnectedness in what might otherwise seem the superhumanly scaled, anonymous world confronting her metropolitan readers. And as she binds together this broad range of disparate social "pictures," as she famously called the scenes of her novel, with a single, didactic, omniscient narrative voice, Stowe reveals explanatory relationships not perceivable in the lived experience of her readers. She instructs them in the relative places and values of her characters, and thereby models a coherent moral and social order in the place of their transformed modern world that felt random, arbitrary, and chaotic.

For all the structural similarity to Dickens's novels, though, *Uncle Tom's Cabin* achieved, as contemporary European critics recognized, a major innovation in Western portrayals of modernity precisely because of the imaginative geography provided to Stowe by the situation of the sectionalist United States circa 1850. With a generative collision of urban-industrial northern narrative form and ostensibly premodern South setting, Stowe created a powerful new chronotope in which temporal progress into modernity figured as geographical movement to the southward. In so doing, she put peripheral (colonial) production back into the picture of industrialization—Legree's realm is simultaneously cotton plantation *and* textile mill—rather than maintaining the classic city/country ideological binary that Dickens and his European peers continued to assume as natural. (Indeed, it is tempting to see the powerful affinity of nineteenth-century Russian novelists for *Uncle Tom's Cabin* as resonating with Stowe's setting of her inquiry into modernity on rural, provincial ground.)[15] If *Edinburgh Review* founder Sidney Smith had stoked the fires of literary nationalism in 1820 by impugning the utter derivativeness of U.S. fiction with his famously dismissive "Who reads an American book?" New England transcendentalist minister Theodore Parker had, in 1849, pointed out the path to national literary distinctiveness that Stowe trod just a few years later: "We have one series of literary productions that could be written by none but Americans, and only here; I mean the Lives of Fugitive Slaves."[16] While Parker intended this insight as a sardonic provocation, it provides a window onto what Stowe's distinctively American novel offered to mid-century Western literature: a sense that republican freedom—the sine qua non of U.S. citizenship—could exist under industrial modernity only fugitively, in flight and under siege.

## Stowe Retells the Market Revolution

Stowe's South is not a singular, static setting but rather a sequential progression through three markedly distinct plantations. The novel begins with Tom at the place of his birth, in his titular "cabin" on the harmonious, folksy Shelby plantation near the banks of the Ohio River. At the center of the novel, the reader follows Tom down the Mississippi to the paradisiacal but doomed St. Clare plantation in Louisiana. And as the nightmare nadir of Stowe's South, Tom lands at last in Legree's infernal realm, somewhere south of Louisiana (read: in Hell). Stowe organizes this sequence, from the uppermost border of the South to its unfathomable depth, around two unfortunate falls for Tom: first, when his lifelong master, Mr. Shelby, is forced to sell him to a slave trader named Haley, who mysteriously holds the Shelby plantation "in his power"; and then, when his new, benevolent master, Augustine St. Clare, suddenly is killed, leaving behind an insolvent estate that allows Tom to be sold to the perverse Legree. At each of these junctures between the three emblematic plantations, in other words, Stowe pushes the action of the novel southward by staging a conflict between an established, moral, patriarchal order and an encroaching, profit-driven, market economy. Each time, the market wins: the patriarchal planters Shelby and St. Clare, for all their seeming power and wealth, prove incapable of protecting their worthy dependent Tom; and the moral fortitude and Christian belief those masters have instilled and encouraged in Tom may lead to his spiritual "victory" over Legree, but cannot forestall his ultimate bodily destruction by the commodification, dehumanization, and profit motive that hold sway in Legree's weirdly industrial realm.

Rehearsing the geographic sequencing of Stowe's tripartite South sketches how geographical progression to the southward in the novel reads simultaneously as a temporal progression forward in time, from the paternalistic New England village world of Stowe's childhood in the 1820s to the urban-industrial modernity of the years during which she wrote.[17] The novel narrativizes, in other words, the radical shift in the definition of U.S. citizenship that Stowe's generation already had experienced in their own lifetimes. The illustrations commissioned by Stowe's U.S. publisher for the first edition of *Uncle Tom's Cabin* powerfully bear out this idea that the overarching thrust of the novel is to retell the market revolution, to relive the transformation of the idea of U.S. citizenship that had taken place during the lifetimes of Stowe and her readers. The artist, Hammatt Billings—a Bostonian best remembered for his 1859 design for the monument to the Pilgrim "Forefathers" at Plymouth, Massachusetts—drew upon a quite extensive array of Anglo-American visual styles for his illustrations, rather than establishing a cohesive visual vocabulary for the entire work. His swings between styles can become telling, as when he depicts each of Tom's falls to the southward as, effectively, falls into industrial modernity. Each fall operates for Billings on a country/city binary: for the benevolent, ostensibly premodern faces of Stowe's South—the Shelby plantation and St. Clare's refuge—Billings creates idealized rural scenes based on anachronistic painting styles, while for the malevolent, industrialized South—the trader Haley's enterprise, Legree's factory-plantation—he images urban scenes using contemporary engraving conventions.

Billings chooses to use attractive, lavish detail to render the heart-rending scene of the Shelby plantation on the night before Tom is to be taken away by the trader Haley. Tom, Chloe, Eliza, and Harry are clad in rather elegant rustic wear, rendered particularly romantic by Eliza's shawl and bonnet-ribbons streaming in the breeze; they stand on the threshold of Tom's eponymous and imperiled cabin, which appears to be nestled in a bower; the mother with child is attended by a faithful watchdog, showing harmony between the humans and their natural setting; and a pastoral landscape complete with protecting manor house forms the backdrop of the scene. Here Billings draws upon the early-nineteenth-century English genre paintings of rustic scenes that idealized the lives and surroundings of rural laborers, paintings usually seen in the British context as providing a nostalgic distraction from or a critical comment on the comparatively debased condition of urban workers.[18] While the characters all bear distressed expressions, their discomfiture clearly stems not from their enslavement on the Shelby plantation but rather from the impending collapse of this idealized village life Billings spreads before the gaze of the reader.

The second illustration, next in Billings's sequence for the novel, depicts a slave auction that Tom, now under Haley's control, observes immediately after leaving the Shelby plantation. In this image Billings jarringly introduces a visual vocabulary starkly opposed to that of the previous plate: the bucolic scene is replaced by a crowded urban streetscape in which rustic peasants cower on pavement before a menacing sea of top-hatted capitalists. Here, Billings channels the contemporary work of the famous illustrators of Dickens's novels, George Cruikshank and Hablot Browne ("Phiz"), who produced many such crowd-in-the-street scenes organized around a portrayal of some extreme power differential or moment of coercion.[19] To illustrate the first stage of Tom's progress through the stations of Stowe's South, Billings literally replaces the rural village with the industrial city in the turn of a page.

His envisioning of Tom's second fall to the southward poses an even starker country/city contrast. Billings images St. Clare's plantation with conventions of mid-eighteenth-century English romantic portraiture, in which aristocrats appear in the context of their extensive rural landholdings. Here Tom and Eva, dressed at an unusual height of fashion—Tom's lace cuffs and spats are particularly nice—sit in a pleasure garden and gaze out at a wide vista of unspoiled landscape, opening into a harbor and the sea beyond, toward which Eva gestures, signifying her ownership. But when Billings next depicts Tom, after his first whipping on Legree's plantation, he once again veers to the precedent of Dickens's illustrators, this time by using the set pieces they had developed to portray the hovels inhabited by London's wretched poor. With his use of a strong single light source to organize the scene, Billings emphasizes darkness, filth, and shadows, while also lending an air of interior claustrophobia to the plantation scene. He follows the lead of Cruikshank and Phiz in placing a woman or girl in the scene—here, Cassy—who is struggling to carry out offices of feminine compassion even as she appears physically crushed by her environment: pale, gaunt, bedraggled, on her knees.[20]

Again, Stowe's sequential progress from one incarnation of her South to the next suggested to Billings powerfully divergent visual modes separated by decades of modernization—and again, none of those visual styles had any customary association with the southern United States. The odd disjuncture between the avowed subject of *Uncle Tom's Cabin* and the images that it generated in the mind of its first U.S. illustrator seems to support the complaint of Stowe's critics from the southern states that she had no firsthand experience of their section and that the entire novel was the product of her fevered imagination, unmoored from an actual place. But to the vast majority of her readers, living as they did in modernizing metropolises, Stowe's knowledge or ignorance of the realities of southern slavery was quite beside the point; the verisimilitude of her novel inhered in its powerful description of the recent history of their own lives. *Uncle Tom's Cabin* narrativized the epochal transformation that Stowe's readers had lived through in the preceding decades and that they continued to struggle to assimilate in the 1850s. The novel provided these readers with an extended mourning of what they had lost in the fall from orderly, patriarchal village life into the anonymity and brutalization of the industrial city.

Sketching the contours of Stowe's novel, in which movement southward becomes progress into industrial modernity, helps to reconcile the undeniable emotional force of the novel with its admittedly garbled antislavery politics.[21] While Stowe's synthesis of sections was clarifying on some points—in particular, deflating the defense of southern slavery as autonomously patriarchal and premodern—it was obfuscating on many others, as the novel displaced its dystopic representations of the industrial center onto othered imaginative terrain. Consider, for instance, *New York Tribune* editor Horace Greeley's defense of Stowe against charges, from southern partisans, that northern cities held horrors as foul as those assigned by Stowe to her South.[22] Greeley argues that Stowe shares her authorial "spirit" with that of French socialist Eugène Sue, formative writer of city exposé fiction, and that she has in *Uncle Tom's Cabin* written a brief on behalf of *all* of the oppressed and "lowly" of the United States.

> Sue . . . is a humanitarian or socialistic writer whose avowed purpose is to hold up to reprobation and reform the evils of so-called "free labor" as at present existing in Europe. He shows how the working classes are driven to crime by oppression. . . . He does cite "the murders, adulteries, seductions, thefts, cheatings, lyings, false swearings, starvings," &c. &c. as "effects of free labor" as it prevails under the political and social system of his country. The *same* category of shames and crimes caused by the effects of slave labor in the South is set forth by Mrs. Stowe, who is of the *same* school of humanitarian

thinkers and writes in this country with precisely the *same* object as Sue and his colaborers abroad—the abolition of slavery and the elevation of the mechanical, manufacturing and laboring masses.[23]

Observe the neat work of displacement here: if U.S. proletarians are southern slaves, then the United States confesses to no proletarians outside of its already deviant and peculiar South. Greeley preserves an imaginative space of republican freedom for his *New York Tribune* readers: with Sue's *Mystères de Paris* in one hand and Stowe's *Uncle Tom's Cabin* in the other, they can better comprehend life in their metropolis in 1852—but they can at the same instant understand their status as U.S. citizens as existing in a sphere above either "the evils of so-called 'free labor' as at present existing in Europe," or the "crimes caused by the effects of slave labor in the South."

But what would it mean to see Stowe as the great "socialistic writer" of the first generation of U.S. industrialization? What analysis of modernity, what plan of action did *Uncle Tom's Cabin* engender for those readers who consumed it so eagerly and with such intensity? Following Tom through Stowe's sequential South chronotope reveals that she constructs each of her archetypal plantations in a distinct narrative register that allows for a specific sort of traction on her overarching inquiry into the conditions of U.S. modernity. The first third of *Uncle Tom's Cabin*, set on the Shelby plantation, exhibits a realistic texture unique in the novel; by comparison, the subsequent scenes set on the St. Clare and Legree plantations unfold in far more formulaic and allusive terms. In the Shelby chapters, Stowe's rich descriptions focus on the details of daily life, lingering on delicious food, comfortable clothes, and the amusements that occupy her characters during their plentiful hours of rural leisure; she also develops the action of the plot in dialogue rather than overbearing omniscient narration, and experiments with an array of dialects signifying the class and regional identities of her varied characters. Reminding us that Stowe primarily wrote New England local color fiction for most of her subsequent career, Steven Nissenbaum has suggested that the Shelby plantation section of the novel is so realistic because Stowe is portraying a world intimately known to her: "the village life she remembered as a child in Litchfield, Connecticut."[24] More explicitly, Stowe is remembering this village life as a child of its ruling class: the Shelby plantation is benevolently patriarchal and blissfully hierarchical, with relations between labor and capital governed by face-to-face exchanges of deference for protection. All parties in this village world know their places, and none resent or are demeaned by them.

The sentimental thrust of the rural utopia in this first section of the novel, though, inheres in Stowe's detail of its demise even before she unfolds its attractive scenes. She opens the novel with the exchange between Mr. Shelby and Haley, the slave trader, in which Mr. Shelby agrees to sell Tom, his "good, steady, sensible, pious" farm manager, and this intrusion of the market into the domain of reciprocal duties and loyalties utterly corrupts the moral contract upon which the Shelby society rests. By showing that the entire social order she will detail so lovingly in the following pages has already been undermined fatally, Stowe puts the Shelby plantation squarely into the register of sentimental narrative; as Philip Fisher has observed, "Uncle Tom's cabin" on the Shelby plantation becomes the powerful U.S. analogue to Goldsmith's "Deserted Village" and Wordsworth's "Ruined Cottage." Tom's cabin, which we know from the first page of the novel he must leave, and to which he never returns after the novel carries him southward beyond the Shelby plantation, becomes "the uninhabited place to which human reality can never be restored," a site for meditation on how the progression of time "has created ruins that cannot be repaired, nor can they be erased or forgotten."[25] Stowe's first instantiation of the South, in other words, becomes a site for registering the anguish of the fall into the market that has already happened for her metropolitan readers, an anguish she encapsulates in Mrs. Shelby's response to her husband's announcement of Tom's impending sale.

> O, Mr. Shelby, I have tried—tried most faithfully, as a Christian woman should—to do my duty to these poor, simple, dependent creatures. I have cared for them, instructed them, watched over them, and know[n] all their little cares and joys, for years; and how can I ever hold up my head again among them, if, for the sake of a little paltry gain, we sell such a faithful, excellent, confiding creature as poor Tom, and tear from him in a moment all we have taught him to love and value? . . . How can I bear to have this open acknowledgment that we care for no tie, no duty, no relation, however sacred, compared with money?

This original loss in many ways forms the emotional core of the book. Stowe uses her sentimental narration of the Shelby plantation to put before her readers what has irrevocably escaped them under industrialization: a stable, hierarchical order with a presumably natural and moral basis, in which the Shelbys of the world "do [their] duty" to secure the loyalty and deference of their "poor, simple, dependent creatures," an order that rejects commodification and capital accumulation for "higher principles," proclaiming with Mrs. Shelby that "one soul is worth more than all the money in the world."

If sentimental narrative is concerned only with moments when action is impossible, then the tears that the Shelby plantation section of *Uncle Tom's Cabin* is designed to evoke should be understood as a sign of powerlessness in the reader. Tom has been sold; the village order has been violated; there is nothing to be done but mourn. Stowe's concern in this section, in other words, is not to analyze what has happened, who is at fault, or how and why she and her readers have found themselves expelled from the garden of their pre-industrial childhoods. Indeed, she leaves remarkably vague the conditions of economic necessity impelling Mr. Shelby's acquiescence to the destruction of the village order over which he presides, relying upon a deus ex machina device never further explained. "Haley has come into possession of a mortgage," Mr. Shelby replies to his wife's emotional protest. "That man has had it in his power to ruin us all." And then Stowe goes on to personify Haley as the market incarnate, "a man alive to nothing but trade and profit—cool, and unhesitating, and unrelenting, as death and the grave." As Stowe engenders this primary sense of powerlessness before a loss as inevitable as death, she puts her readers in the place of the victims of her story.[26] Again, Mrs. Shelby serves as a guide for the reader in this identification, this collectivity of victimhood and mourning, as when she comes to Tom's eponymous cabin just before he is forever taken from it by Haley.

Here one of the boys called out, "Thar's Missis a-comin' in!"

"She can't do no good; what's she coming for?" said Aunt Chloe....

"Tom," [Mrs. Shelby] said, "I come to—" and stopping suddenly, and regarding the silent group, she sat down in the chair, and, covering her face with her handkerchief, began to sob.

"Lor, now, Missis, don't—don't!" said Aunt Chloe, bursting out in her turn; and for a few moments they all wept in company. And in those tears they all shed together, the high and the lowly, melted away all the heart-burnings and anger of the oppressed.

The "weeping in company" that Stowe calculates the first third of her novel to evoke does not necessitate a primary identification with Tom, his wife, Chloe, or the other enslaved characters on the Shelby plantation. Taking Stowe's central problematic to be modernization more broadly, rather than chattel slavery alone, illuminates the way that she employs Mrs. Shelby to model for her metropolitan U.S. readers an understanding of *themselves* as primary, rather than merely empathetic or transitive, victims of the demise of the old order. Their stake in what comes next, thus, is all the greater.

## The Imperial New Jerusalem in *Uncle Tom's Cabin*

By all accounts, the Shelby plantation section of the novel came quickly to Stowe, but when she left the imaginative environs of that setting, and her elegiac sentimental narrative mode, for Tom's first journey southward into modernity, her composition faltered. From July to December 1851 she missed a string of deadlines for the *National Era*, the magazine in which *Uncle Tom's Cabin* was serialized, and she submitted late each of the chapters (12 through 19) that immediately follow Tom's removal from the Shelby plantation.[27] During this time she was soliciting, in urgent tones, firsthand information on southern slavery from sources ranging from Frederick Douglass to a cousin who had worked as a financier in New Orleans.[28] She seems to have regained her writerly equilibrium only when she gave up on continuing the novel in the intimate, realistic register in which she had begun it, and instead created the second archetypal South setting of the novel in markedly distinct terms. Tom's new home, the St. Clare plantation, serves as a fantastic refuge from the market forces that swept Tom away from his cabin in the first place: Louisiana planter Augustine St. Clare, "indolent and careless of money," willfully has refused to operate his plantation in a productive capacity, creating an isolated, utopic dominion engaged in an orgy of consumption. St. Clare's plantation thus introduces a relationship between capital and labor, between "the high and the lowly," divergent from that represented either by Shelby's preindustrial village or Haley's modern trade in workers. "To hold [slaves] as tools for money-making, I could not," St. Clare explains to his visiting cousin from Vermont, Miss Ophelia. "[To] have them to help spend money, you know, didn't look quite so ugly to me." In the same vein, Little

Eva pleads with her father, "Papa, do buy [Tom]! it's no matter what you pay. . . . I want to make him happy."

This truly prelapsarian incarnation of the South, where no one need work, can exist only in escapist fantasy, and Stowe indicates as much when she eschews the realistic dialogism of the first third of the novel, veering instead into the lengthy objective descriptions, typed characters, and soliloquies of romance as she introduces St. Clare, the tragic victim of a thwarted youthful love, and his daughter Evangeline, the Wordsworthian angelic child. This Edenic incarnation of the South, further, makes sense in Stowe's typological imagination only with the anticipation of its coming fall; and she makes clear from her first introduction of St. Clare's environs that although Tom perceives the new plantation "with an air of calm, still enjoyment. . . . his beaming black face perfectly radiant with admiration," it nonetheless will provide him only a temporary respite from his forced march into the market. Just as she identifies Little Eva as perfect, and therefore marked for death ("Has there ever been a child like Eva? Yes, there have been; but their names are always on grave-stones"), Stowe brands the paradisiacal St. Clare environs "perishable" from the outset. St. Clare's bizarre, reactionary social experiment at the center of the novel is a last stand against modernity, and, as such, it is doomed.

The fundamental "perishability" of her second incarnation of the South is mandated, in Stowe's imagination, not only by the biblical typology of Eden but also by the imperialist ideology that holds temperate places and peoples to be inevitably ascendant over tropical ones.[29] With her initial description of the St. Clare plantation, and the relationship of its inhabitants to it, Stowe's relentless invocation of tropicality prescribes the ultimate disposition of this entire central section of the novel.

> The carriage stopped in front of an ancient mansion, built in that odd mixture of Spanish and French style, of which there are specimens in some parts of New Orleans. It was built in the Moorish fashion. . . . The court, in the inside, had evidently been arranged to gratify a picturesque and voluptuous ideality. Wide galleries ran all around the four sides, whose Moorish arches, slender pillars, and arabesque ornaments, carried the mind back, as in a dream, to the reign of oriental romance in Spain. . . . On the whole, the appearance of the place was luxurious and romantic. . . .

"O, isn't it beautiful, lovely! my own dear, darling home!" [Eva] said to Miss Ophelia. "Isn't it beautiful?"

"'Tis a pretty place," said Miss Ophelia, as she alighted; "though it looks rather old and heathenish to me."

Tom got down from the carriage, and looked about with an air of calm, still enjoyment. The negro, it must be remembered, is an exotic of the most gorgeous and superb countries of the world, and he has, deep in his heart, a passion for all that is splendid, rich, and fanciful. . . .

St. Clare, who was at heart a poetical voluptuary, smiled as Miss Ophelia made her remark on his premises, and, turning to Tom . . . he said,

"Tom, my boy, this seems to suit you."

"Yes, Mas'r, it looks about the right thing," said Tom.

Stowe modulates here between figures of the deep colonial past of tropical America and modern imperatives of Anglo-Saxonist empire. As "French and Spanish style" morphs into "the Moorish fashion" in her opening two sentences, Stowe reveals that her interest in the heterogeneous colonial background of the South hinges fundamentally on what she understands to be its "ancient" and "odd mixture" of races. Under the sign of racial intermixture, we see that all of the native southerners here, black and white—"exotic[s]," as they are, "of the most gorgeous and superb countries in the world"—share the same relationship to this plantation "arranged to gratify a tropical and voluptuous ideality." Equally at home in this environment, Eva, Tom, and St. Clare (the "voluptuary"-in-chief) reveal themselves to be equally children of the tropics—and thus equally doomed to extinction by the progressive modernity of Stowe's plot. Nativity, not race—or, perhaps, nativity *as* race—is destiny here: Vermonter Miss Ophelia alone, with her correct, Anglo-Saxonist, temperate perspective on the tropical plantation—for "old and heathenish" read "marked for righteous subjugation"—will be able to negotiate, survive, and indeed benefit from the predestined demise of the St. Clare realm.

Perhaps because the St. Clare plantation section of the book is so formulaically focused upon the ephemerality of its setting, Stowe uses the pause in plot action—we are, after all, only waiting for the predestined fall to come to pass—to direct the attention of her readers toward the question of what sort of (inevitably northern) social order will replace this attractive-but-doomed incarnation of the South. And perhaps because the mode of romance frees Stowe from the specificities of sentimental realism and leads her instead toward abstraction and typology, this central section of the novel becomes her site for testing "theories," airing ideological approaches to interpreting the market revolution. Although the extended deathbed scene of Little Eva has tended to magnetize critical discussion of this part of the novel, Stowe devotes at least equal space to a series of staged philosophical discussions between St. Clare and Ophelia, themselves a perfect pair of sectionalist political types. St. Clare dominates these conversations, initially educating Ophelia out of her satirically limited northern abolitionist views, which Stowe characterizes as tics of tongue-clucking: "grim with indignation," Ophelia is prone to *Liberator*-headline-style outbursts such as "Perfectly horrible!" and "Shameful! monstrous! outrageous!" For St. Clare's speeches, on the other hand, Stowe practically plagiarizes from Virginian George Fitzhugh, whose iconoclastic proslavery writings, including *A Sociology for the South: The Failure of Free Society* (1854), were in conversation with Marx's *Communist Manifesto* perhaps more seriously than any others in the United States in the early 1850s.[30] Through St. Clare, Stowe asserts that her metropolitan readers *must* attend to the dilemma and the frank horror of the modern South lurking outside the confines of his utopic realm of exception, that they must understand the South not as an isolated and peculiar local problem but rather as an emblematic manifestation of the global ascendance of capitalist modernity.

> The American planter is only doing, in another form, what the English aristocracy and capitalists are doing by the lower classes; that is, I take it, *appropriating* them, body and bone, soul and spirit, to their use and convenience.... [The English laborer] is as much at the will of his employer as if he were sold to him. The slave-owner can whip his refractory slave to death,—the capitalist can starve him to death. As to family security, it is hard to say which is the worst,—to have one's children sold, or see them starve to death at home.

The ideological exploration facilitated by the romantic abstraction of her St. Clare section leads Stowe to state directly what the upcoming Legree section of the novel will narrativize: for her readers living at the centers of Western industrialization, slavery *is* modernity; it is at least their threatened destiny. Southern slave law simply codifies and makes visible the equally despotic, but less transparent, power asymmetry of the industrial capitalist order. Thus to contemplate "the abstract question of slavery" is to comprehend proletarianization and its ramifications: "It takes no spectacles to see that a great class of vicious, improvident, degraded people, among us, are an evil to us, as well as to themselves." And to imagine the injustice coming to a head in violence is to envision not a civil war but rather an American version of the 1848 European revolts of the working classes: "One thing is certain,—that there is a mustering among the masses, the world over; and there is a *dies irae* coming on, sooner or later. The same thing is working in Europe, in England, and in this country."[31]

Despite the clarity of St. Clare's vision of Western modernity and its coming Day of Wrath, Stowe increasingly focuses his soliloquies on his repetitious confessions of inaction: he has failed to become an "actor and regenerator in society"; he "has floated on, a dreamy, neutral spectator of the struggles, agonies, and wrongs of man"; he possesses "only that kind of benevolence which consists in lying on a sofa."[32] St. Clare's characterological "indolence," of course, is of a piece with his tropical identity, a pillar of the climatic determinism through which Stowe structures the entire middle section of the book: "'I never want to talk seriously in hot weather. What with mosquitos and all, a fellow can't get himself up to any very sublime moral flights; and I believe,' said St. Clare, suddenly rousing himself up, 'there's a theory, now! I understand now why northern nations are always more virtuous than southern ones,—I see into that whole subject.'"

Two pages after St. Clare once again "rouses himself up" to imagine starting the revolution he has predicted from his couch—doing his "duty . . . to the poor and lowly . . . beginning with my own servants . . . and perhaps, at some future day . . . for a whole class"—Stowe abruptly administers the long-foreshadowed death blow to his realm. To St. Clare himself, Stowe metes out the most stereotypical Southern-Planter-demise conceivable: he's stabbed "with a bowie-knife" in "an affray . . . between two gentlemen . . . who were both partially intoxicated."

If Stowe in the Shelby section of the novel essentially substitutes time for place, locating the past of her New England childhood in Kentucky, in the St. Clare section she reasserts geography with vigor. The question begged by Stowe's chronotope at the end of the central section of *Uncle*

*Tom's Cabin* then becomes: What northern incarnation of modernity will take over this South predestined by its tropicality for subjugation? Stowe poses this problem to her readers with a tale of two Vermonters-as-masters. On the ruins of St. Clare's insolvent estate, Ophelia uses her newly acquired ownership of the enslaved child Topsy—transferred to her by St. Clare shortly before his death—for good, to protect and educate her lowly dependent. Tom, by pointed contrast, is thrown into jeopardy with the loss of such a paternalistic owner. Left "Unprotected" (the title of chapter 29), Tom is repossessed by the capitalist system that had first clutched him in the form of the trader Haley. Now fully commoditized, he is stored in "The Slave Warehouse" (the title of chapter 30) until his purchase by Simon Legree, a fellow native of Ophelia's Green Mountains. Stowe titles chapter 31—in which she sends Tom, in chains, down the Red River to Legree's infernal plantation—"The Middle Passage," thereby implying that this character who was born into slavery and has been enslaved throughout her plot only *truly* leaves his tropical home and enters U.S. slavery when he passes into the modern industrial dystopia presided over by the dark side of Vermont.

Through the overarching chronotope of the novel, Stowe re-poses the question of U.S. citizenship in the modern age: as not a problem of freedom, but rather as a problem of mastery. Will the modern United States be run by good or evil northern masters? The evil northern masters—the Legrees, the industrial capitalists—have, in Stowe's mind, been ascendant thus far, and so the last act of her novel is set on Legree's preternaturally modern South plantation. Her first description of Legree's realm reasserts the temporal dimension of her chronotope: his god-forsaken estate is simply the industrial destruction of both Shelby's preindustrial village and St. Clare's paradisiacal refuge.

> The estate had formerly belonged to a gentleman of opulence and taste, who had bestowed some considerable attention to the adornment of his grounds. Having died insolvent, it had been purchased, at a bargain, by Legree, who used it, as he did everything else, merely as an implement for money-making. The place had that ragged, forlorn appearance, which is always produced by the evidence that the care of the former owner has been left to go to utter decay.

Legree's plantation completes the fall into the market that has driven the arc of the novel: Haley's threat to the mortgaged Mr. Shelby, the insolvent collapse of St. Clare's last stand—the capitalist concern with profit only, to the "utter decay" of "art," "taste," "comfort," and "goodness"—this threat is fully realized in Stowe's final incarnation of the South. Directly upon the ruins of the moral village order of the Shelby plantation and the manorial noblesse oblige of the St. Clare plantation, Legree has established his own northern industrial city, complete with factory production, prostitution, alcoholism, atheism, and paupers' quarters for the laborers.[33] Tom finds no republican cabin or peasant's "cottage, rude, indeed" here, but rather a Dickensian urban hovel: "a mere shell, destitute of any species of furniture, except a heap of straw, foul with dirt, spread confusedly over the floor . . . trodden by the tramping of innumerable feet."[34]

Legree's bad mastery horrifies Stowe most profoundly as she contemplates how it produces the "lowly" as proletarians, as an underclass who are both miserably exploited and ultimately impossible to control without violence. Her description of the enslaved workers on Legree's plantation serves as Stowe's decidedly elitist portrait of the northern working classes, and in fact eerily echoes the strong rhetoric of her preacher father, Lyman Beecher, on the perils posed to social order by New England's urban poor. As early as the 1830s, when Stowe was still a child in her father's home and church, Beecher had found this emergent class to be "a race of famished, infuriated animals, goaded by instinct and unrestrained by prospective hopes or fears."[35] As Stowe envisions Legree's abased slaves in 1852, she similarly draws upon language of massing, bestiality, and—most horrifying—lack of hegemonic control. "Flocking home" at the end of the shift, the "gang" comprises "sullen, scowling, imbruted men, and feeble, discouraged women, or women that were not women . . . [all exhibiting] the gross, unrestricted animal selfishness of human beings, of whom nothing good was expected or desired." Though Tom dies rather than submit to the new economic order, and though the "neat and respectable" quadroons with "high forehead[s]," Cassy and Emmeline, escape the industrial environs, Legree's atheistic, vicious, and explosive masses remain caught in the maw of his factory-plantation when Stowe resolves her main plotline. When young George Shelby arrives on the Legree plantation just in time to see Tom breathe his last and to give him a proper burial, he is begged for aid by Legree's still living, still suffering workers: "Hard times here, Mas'r! . . . Do, Mas'r, buy us, please!" Despite the presumably world-changing act of martyrdom he has just witnessed in Tom's death, the younger Shelby responds to the continued existence of Legree's realm with the equivalent of throwing his hands in the air: "'I can't!—I can't!' said George, with difficulty, motioning them off; 'it's impossible!'"

As we remember, though, that Stowe had begun the narrative arc of Tom's story with the impotence before the modern market of Shelby *père*, we see the symmetry in her closing with the continued impotence, into the next generation, of Shelby *fils*.[36] The structural symmetry reminds her metropolitan readers that *they*—not southerners white or black—are poised to be the true "actors and regenerators" of the southern story implicitly to come at the end of *Uncle Tom's Cabin*. Having already lived through the market revolution themselves, her readers should understand themselves to be both materially and ideologically poised to command the drama of modernization that now will play itself out on a global stage, in advances ever farther South.

This is the great alchemy of Stowe's evolving southern chronotope throughout the novel, taken as a whole: she transmutes the abasement of industrialization for U.S. citizens into the elevation of empire. In a final chapter of direct exhortation to her readers, Stowe charges them foremost with fighting the bad, Legree-style mastery of capitalist modernity, the fallen industrial condition that immediately surrounds them. "Northern men, northern mothers, northern Christians, have something more to do than denounce their brethren at the South; they have to look to the evil among themselves. But, what can any individual do?" The entire, multifaceted emotional experience of the novel comes to a head with this urgent question about the hidden workings of power and the superhuman scale of system under capitalist modernity—an urgent question which, it is not far-fetched to imagine, may have inspired the title of Nikolai Chernyshefsky's 1863 novel, *What Is to Be Done?*[37] Though Chernyshefsky's novel bears a complex relationship to Lenin's 1901–2 pamphlet of the same title, thinking about this broader modern resonance of Stowe's chronotopic novel brings us back to the question of what it means to understand *Uncle Tom's Cabin* as the great "socialistic" response to the first generation of industrialization in the United States.

Stowe's own answer to her crystallizing question has seemed disappointingly deflating to her critics ever since 1852: "There is one thing that every individual can do,—they can see to it that they *feel right*." We must appreciate, though—as Laura Wexler, Amy Kaplan, and others have insisted—the sheer power of "feeling right" in a nascent imperial context.[38] The injunction is, simultaneously, to feel with moral correctness, and to feel oneself righteous, and Stowe provides her readers with a model of it: her good Vermont mistress, Ophelia, denominated "Miss *Feely*" by her charge—her slave—Topsy. Ophelia's Vermonter alter ego, Legree, is both a factory master and an early version of the Yankee imperialist; his bad mastery of the South opens the possibility for a good mastery, a "right" mastery of it.[39] Shadowing the main plotline in Stowe's final chapters, Ophelia holds out the promise that while metropolitan readers cannot recuperate their lost village life in the modern world, they can recuperate its ostensibly moral hierarchy, by moving outward geographically and managing the modernization of the South. Indeed, Stowe offers "Miss Feely" as the explicit recuperation of the fallen, disempowered Mrs. Shelby of the first section of the novel:

> Who shall detail the tribulations manifold of our friend Miss Ophelia, who had begun the labors of a Southern housekeeper? . . .
>
> South as well as north, there are women who have an extraordinary talent for command, and tact in educating. Such are enabled, with apparent ease, and without severity, to subject to their will, and bring into harmonious and systematic order, the various members of their small estate,—to regulate their peculiarities, and so balance and compensate the deficiencies of one by the excess of another, as to produce a harmonious and orderly system.
>
> Such a housekeeper was Mrs. Shelby, whom we have already described; and such our readers may remember to have met with. If they are not common at the South, it is because they are not common in the world.

Stowe's vision of "extraordinarily commanding" housekeeping here seems to converse with Emerson's desire for a power "omnipotent without violence."[40] Through Ophelia, Stowe holds out to her metropolitan readers the promise that their idealized village paternalism of the past can be reinvented in the modern age as imperial mastery. Her Slave South—her South as a place and a people naturally slavish—finally offers her readers the redemptive possibility of a do-over at the market revolution that has gone awry on their own ground—a chance to get it right on other territory.

This promise of directing a more perfect modernization of the South from the central summit of northern developmental power resonates with a recurrent allusion to the trope of the Holy City—the New

Jerusalem—that Stowe weaves into transitional scenes in her progress through the South. When Haley carries Tom away from the Shelby plantation, Tom meditates upon "these words of an ancient volume . . . 'We have here no continuing city, but we seek one to come; wherefore God himself is not ashamed to be called our God; for he hath prepared for us a city.'" Just before Little Eva reveals to Tom that she is going to die, the two read from the book of Revelations and Tom sings a hymn concluding, "*Bright angels should convey me home, / To the new Jerusalem.*" And as Tom completes the weary journey to Legree's plantation at the opening of "Dark Places," Legree commands him to sing, by yelling "come!" twice. Tom replies with another hymn: "*Jerusalem, my happy home, / Name ever dear to me! When shall my sorrows have an end, / Thy joys when shall—.*"[41] Legree interrupts the hymn before Tom can fulfill the tyrant's own prophecy, that the New Jerusalem shall "come," but Cassy ultimately strikes down Legree, evil genius of the Industrial North, by completing the tripartite incantation: "Come! come! come!"

Through the trope of the Holy City, Stowe follows the English poet William Blake in exhorting citizens of the capital despondent over the costs of industrialization to embrace modernity and build a more perfect metropolis.[42] In his epigraph to *Milton* (1808), Blake confronts the seemingly devolutionary changes wrought upon the English countryside by modernization; yet rather than calling for a return to the pastoral past, he exhorts readers onward to a revolutionary modernization.

> And did those feet in ancient time
> Walk upon England's mountains green:
> And was the holy Lamb of God,
> On England's pleasant pastures seen!
>
> And did the Countenance Divine,
> Shine forth upon our clouded hills?
> And was Jerusalem builded here,
> Among these dark Satanic Mills?
> . . . . . . . . . . . . . . . . .
> I will not cease from Mental Fight,
> Nor shall my Sword sleep in my hand:
> Till we have built Jerusalem
> In England's green & pleasant Land.[43]

The evolving phases of Stowe's southern chronotope cycle through Blake's lines: from the "pleasant pastures" of the Shelby plantation, site of idealized rural nostalgia; to the "dark Satanic Mills" of the Legree plantation, site of industrial dystopia; to, above all, the place possessed collectively in the imagination of the audience: "*England's* mountains green," "*England's* pleasant pastures," "*England's* green and pleasant Land." Stowe's U.S. geographical imagination, though, operates at the juncture between Blake's domestic pastoral and the imperial imaginary that generates a metropolitan comprehension of industrialization by narrating the building of the modern city, from the ground up, on colonial territory.[44] As Stowe exhorts her readers in her "Concluding Remarks," "You pray for the heathen abroad; pray also for the heathen at home."

Of course, there is an inherent irony in all this—the notion that Stowe's readers should combat southern slavery by becoming more perfect masters of the South—and Stowe briefly glances at that irony when St. Clare warns Ophelia, as he signs ownership of Topsy over to her, of this "awful 'doing evil that good may come'!" Structurally, though, Stowe's chronotope urges her readers to take up the modern imperial mission with gusto. Her cycle of falls in the line of Tom's story implies a corresponding cycle of redemptions—literally, purchases—by benevolent masters. Mr. Shelby has, implicitly, redeemed Tom from his birth into slavery at the start of the novel; St. Clare redeems him from his first fall into the market; and, of course, God redeems him when he dies on Legree's plantation. When young George Shelby locates the dying man—"I've come to buy you, and take you home," he tells Tom—Stowe makes her alignment between God's relationship to humans, and the master's relationship to the slave, perfectly explicit. Tom replies, "O, Mas'r George, ye're too late. The Lord's bought me, and is going to take me home." The reader, at this point in the novel, has bought Tom, too, to a certain extent, and the model of Ophelia's redemption of Topsy promises as well that to be a righteous master is, transitively, to be God.[45] A Shelby cannot effect this ultimate redemption; but a true U.S. citizen can, intervening in the cycle of fall and temporary recovery to generate a final progress into imperial modernity, a building of the Holy City on the implicitly expropriated ground of the South. Perhaps now the reported penchant of Union soldiers to carry *Uncle Tom's Cabin* into battle—it was supposedly second in popularity with soldiers only to the Bible—becomes legible. To "feel right" in the terms of this epochal novel is, ultimately, to understand oneself, as a U.S. citizen, to be the agent of the glory of the coming of the Lord, to the benighted Souths of the fallen world.

## Notes

This essay is adapted from *Our South: Geographic Fantasy and the Rise of National Literature* (Cambridge: Harvard University Press, 2010), 169–92.

1. The comment attributed to Lincoln is almost certainly apocryphal, but it has seemed true enough to bear ubiquitous repetition in cultural histories of the nineteenth-century United States. See Joan D. Hedrick, *Harriet Beecher Stowe: A Life* (New York: Oxford University Press, 1994), vii.

2. How Lowell was being portrayed in the antebellum decades is the subject of a number of studies, including Thomas Bender's *Toward an Urban Vision: Ideas and Institutions in Nineteenth-Century America* (Lexington: University Press of Kentucky, 1975) and Brian C. Mitchell's *The Paddy Camps: The Irish of Lowell, 1821–61* (Urbana: University of Illinois Press, 1988).

3. Harriet Beecher Stowe, *Uncle Tom's Cabin; or, Life among the Lowly* (Boston: J. P. Jewett; Cleveland: O. Jewett, Proctor, and Worthington, 1852), 2:184.

4. Karen Halttunen has explored the direct relationship among the writings of the Beecher family between urban and southern gothic, in "Gothic Imagination and Social Reform: The Haunted Houses of Lyman Beecher, Henry Ward Beecher, and Harriet Beecher Stowe," in *New Essays on "Uncle Tom's Cabin,"* ed. Eric J. Sundquist (Cambridge: Cambridge University Press, 1986), 107–34.

5. I take the term from Charles Sellers, who argues that the boom that followed the War of 1812 ignited a generational conflict over the destiny of the Republic, in which democracy was born in tension with capitalism rather than as its natural political expression. Sellers, *The Market Revolution: Jacksonian America, 1815–1846* (New York: Oxford University Press, 1994).

6. Sean Wilentz offers a detailed analysis of this ideological shift in the meanings of republican citizenship under industrialization in *Chants Democratic: New York City and the Rise of the American Working Class, 1788–1850* (New York: Oxford University Press, 1985).

7. Eric J. Foner organizes his study of U.S. history on these lines in *The Story of American Freedom* (New York: Norton, 1999).

8. The vexed ideological relationship of industrial capitalism and slavery in the Anglo-American world has been a subject for intellectual history at least since the publication of Eric Williams's *Capitalism and Slavery* (Chapel Hill: University of North Carolina Press, 1944), which argued that British abolitionists consciously used anti-slavery politics to create ideological hegemony for the industrial order. Williams's thesis was tempered, though not entirely rejected, by later historians, notably David Brion Davis, who found his conclusions too cynical. See particularly Davis's "Reflection on Abolitionism and Ideological Hegemony," in *The Antislavery Debate: Capitalism and Antislavery as Problems in Historical Interpretation* (Berkeley: University of California Press, 1992),

161–79. Philip S. Foner and Herbert Shapiro provide an overview of several decades of subsequent debate in their introduction to *Northern Labor and Antislavery: A Documentary History* (Westport, Conn.: Greenwood Press, 1994), ix–xxx.

9. Perhaps not until Edmund Wilson's *Patriotic Gore: Studies in the Literature of the American Civil War* (New York: Farrar, Straus and Giroux, 1962) did a U.S. critic highlight the aesthetic as opposed to political impact of the novel.

10. William L. Andrews has shown that beginning in the 1840s, European and U.S. literary critics alike cited slave narratives as the first distinctive American literary productions. Andrews, *To Tell a Free Story* (Urbana: University of Illinois Press, 1988), 97–99.

11. The immediate English reception may have had an influence on U.S. understandings of the importance of Stowe's novel. Hedrick, *Harriet Beecher Stowe*, 233–34.

12. Quoted in ibid., 243.

13. Letter from Kingsley to Stowe, quoted in Hedrick (ibid., 234). On more direct connections between the work of antebellum U.S. writers and the Condition of England debates, see Phyllis B. Cole, "The American Writer and the Condition of England, 1815–1860" (Ph.D. diss., Harvard University, 1973).

14. Here I am drawing again on Raymond Williams's crystallizing definition of Dickens's "new kind of novel" in *The Country and the City* (New York: Oxford University Press, 1973). Wilson makes the connections to Stowe's novel explicit (*Patriotic Gore*, 7–8).

15. The Russian fascination with Stowe's novel is an old saw of its reception history; the current Penguin paperback edition gives Tolstoy pride of place on back-cover blurbs ("one of the greatest productions of the human mind").

16. Of Parker's declaration, Priscilla Wald usefully has noted that "there is an irony involved in the transformation of the slave narrative into a national (ist) genre. By appropriating the genre as an emblem of an indigenous American culture . . . the literal slave becomes the emblem of American freedom rather than evidence of American slavery." Wald, *Constituting Americans: Cultural Anxiety and Narrative Form* (Durham: Duke University Press, 1994), 79.

17. I am not the first to notice this progression. See William R. Taylor, *Cavalier and Yankee: The Old South and American National Character* (New York: George Braziller, 1961), 310; and Stephen Nissenbaum, "New England as Region and Nation," in *All Over the Map: Rethinking American Regions*, ed. Edward L. Ayers and Patricia Nelson Limerick (Baltimore: Johns Hopkins University Press, 1996), 57.

18. On the relationship of U.S. painters to the English genre painting movement, see Elizabeth Johns's introduction to *American Genre Paintings: The Politics of Everyday Life* (New Haven: Yale University Press, 1991).

19. Good comparisons may be found in Cruikshank's 1837 illustrations for *Oliver Twist* and Phiz's 1840 illustrations for *The Old Curiosity Shop*.

20. Cruikshank himself was employed by Stowe's London publisher to illustrate the first British edition of the novel. Probably because he was envisioning American slavery from across the Atlantic, Cruikshank used a colonial and tropical visual vocabulary for the novel, rather than creating the sorts of urban scenes for which he was famous and upon which Billings was drawing.

21. Stowe ended the book with an 1820s-era colonizationist plan, sending every

African American character left standing "back to Africa." Hedrick recounts Stowe's distance from antislavery thinkers, and the mad rush of abolitionists to bring her into their camps once her novel became so successful. Hedrick, *Harriet Beecher Stowe*, 235–52.

22. Novelist Caroline Rush had written, "Do [northerners] have no cruel whippings, no torture, no forcing the poor overburdened frame to labor beyond its capabilities[?] In a word, oh! free and happy citizens of the North, have you no slaves in your midst?" [Caroline E. Rush], *The North and the South, or, Slavery and Its Contrasts: A Tale of Real Life* (Philadelphia: Crissy & Markey, 1852), 12.

23. *New York Tribune*, May 23, 1853.

24. Nissenbaum, "New England as Region and Nation," 54–57. Nissenbaum asserts, further, that the "'black' dialect" in *Uncle Tom's Cabin* bears striking resemblance to the New England dialect Stowe employs in her later local-color novels.

25. Philip Fisher, *Hard Facts: Setting and Form in the American Novel* (New York: Oxford University Press, 1985), 120.

26. Ibid., 108–9.

27. See Hedrick's fine analysis of the break in composition at chapter 12 (*Harriet Beecher Stowe*, 218–23).

28. Robert Stepto remarks on the "remarkable admixture of civility and imperiousness" with which Stowe requested "Douglass's assistance in acquiring accurate information about the details of life and work on a southern cotton plantation." Stepto, "Sharing the Thunder: The Literary Exchanges of Henry Bibb, Harriet Beecher Stowe, and Frederick Douglass," in Sundquist, *New Essays on "Uncle Tom's Cabin,"* 135–54.

29. Fisher identifies the "Moral Darwinism" of this central section of the novel as Stowe's sui generis hitting upon Drieserian naturalism fifty years early, but her "conviction that certain forms of life were marginal and could not survive" (*Hard Facts*, 122–23) clearly draws upon a climatological discourse of empire with an ample history.

30. On Fitzhugh's ideological intersections with Marx, see Richard Hofstadter, "John C. Calhoun: Marx of the Master Class," in *The American Political Tradition and the Men Who Made It* (New York: Vintage, 1948), 87–118; and C. Vann Woodward, "George Fitzhugh, *Sui Generis*," in Fitzhugh, *Cannibals All! Or, Slaves without Masters*, ed. Woodward (Cambridge: Harvard University Press, 1960), vii–xlii.

31. Eric Lott has shown how "the American 1848" coalesced, in the Stephen Foster minstrel songs that became its "soundtrack," around the 1848 class revolts in Europe, the South of minstrelsy, and—as the crucial third term—the expansionist dreams of gold-rush California. Out of this crucible, he sees blackface minstrelsy circa 1850 as performing cultural work strikingly analogous to that of Stowe's South as I am defining it: minstrelsy "had become a sectional signifier, a potent popular figure for the North and 'all its emigrations, colonizations and conquests.'" Lott, *Love and Theft: Blackface Minstrelsy and the American Working Class* (New York: Oxford University Press, 1995), 207.

32. On Augustine St. Clare's overdetermined name: with it Stowe indicates that, like St. Augustine, his narration should be understood as his confession. "Clare" further indicates his clarity of vision but also provides a homonym with Stowe's preferred dialect rendering of the word "declare," which makes his philosophical disquisition a latter-day reflection on Jefferson's Declaration. Indeed, to start his discourse with Miss Ophelia,

Stowe has him say, "I'll begin: When, in the course of human events, it becomes necessary for a fellow to hold two or three dozen of his fellow-worms in captivity, a decent regard to the opinions of society requires—" (330).

33. Shelley Streeby has elucidated the imperial dimensions of the conflation between plantation and factory in popular fiction about Mexico published during the Civil War. Streeby, *American Sensations: Class, Empire and the Production of Popular Culture* (Berkeley: University of California Press, 2002), 88–213.

34. In her reading of the direct borrowings from Dickens's *Bleak House* in the novel *The Bondwoman's Narrative*, Hollis Robbins muses on a similar "transformation of Dickens's slum to slave huts." Robbins, "Blackening *Bleak House*: Hannah Crafts's *The Bondwoman's Narrative*," in *In Search of Hannah Crafts: Critical Essays on "The Bondwoman's Narrative"* (New York: BasicCivitas Books, 2004), 80–81.

35. Beecher, "The Perils of Atheism to the Nation" (1835). Wai Chee Dimock quotes these pithy lines in her introduction to *Empire for Liberty: Melville and the Poetics of Individualism* (Princeton: Princeton University Press, 1991), 12.

36. Steven Railton has suggested to me that George Shelby is able to put his father's house in order; when he returns to his home plantation, he manumits the Shelby slaves in a chapter titled "The Liberator." However successful his reform of his own home, though, Stowe shows him to be incapable of imposing the requisite moral order abroad.

37. The connections between Chernyshefsky and *Uncle Tom's Cabin* are many, including the fact that in 1858 he issued the first complete Russian translation of Stowe's novel as a supplement to the literary journal he edited, *The Contemporary*, while serializing his own novel in that venue four years later. Another connection may be traced through Turgenev, upon whom Stowe's influence is well known, and to whose 1862 novel *Fathers and Sons* Chernyshefsky considered himself to be directly responding. On this latter point see Albert Kaspin, "*Uncle Tom's Cabin* and 'Uncle' Akim's Inn: More on Harriet Beecher Stowe and Turgenev," *Slavic and Eastern European Journal* 9, no. 1 (1965): 47–55.

38. The work of Wexler (*Tender Violence: Domestic Visions in an Age of U.S. Imperialism* [Chapel Hill: University of North Carolina Press, 2000]) and Kaplan (*The Anarchy of Empire in the Making of U.S. Culture* [Cambridge: Harvard University Press, 2002]) to disclose the imperial functions of sentimentalism responds to Jane Tompkins's influential argument that the "sentimental power" of Stowe's novel, as in her coauthored domestic manual of 1869, *The American Woman's Home*, derives from its "imperialistic drive," which "flatly contradicts the traditional derogations of the American cult of domesticity as a 'mirror-phenomenon,' 'self-immersed' and 'self-congratulatory'"; instead, Stowe's work lays out (unproblematically for Tompkins, supremely problematically for Wexler and Kaplan) "a blueprint for colonizing the world in the name of the 'family state' under the leadership of Christian women." Tompkins, *Sensational Designs: The Cultural Work of American Fiction* (New York: Oxford University Press, 1985), 144.

39. Leslie Fiedler has argued for the signal significance of Ophelia as "the only other New Englander besides Legree who is close to, if not quite at the mythic center of the novel" and therefore "[the reader's] surrogate in the novel." Fiedler, "New England and the Invention of the South," in *American Literature: The New England Heritage*, ed. James Nagel and Richard Astro (New York: Garland, 1981), 110–11.

40. From Emerson's address on westward expansion, "The Young American" (1844), in *The Complete Works of Ralph Waldo Emerson*, centenary ed. (Boston: Houghton Mifflin, 1903), 1:379.

41. Stowe plays with the words of the English hymn, which dates to the late sixteenth century. On a standard ABAB rhyme, the stanza should traditionally end "Thy joys when shall I see?" rather than, as I am suggesting, a nonstandard (and slant) ABBA rhyme that would end "Thy joys when shall they come?" But Stowe already has purposefully altered the standard second line, which should have caused the opening to read, "Jerusalem, my happy home, / When shall I come to thee?" If Stowe is interested not in Tom's *going* anywhere but rather in the *coming* of the Holy City to the fallen South, she must dispense with that second line as she does, and her bracketing of the unfinished verse with the repeated incantations of "Come!" at the beginning and end of the Legree section powerfully suggests, at least to my ear, the unorthodox conclusion to the traditional stanza.

42. Of Blake, Raymond Williams writes, "[His] forcing into consciousness of the suppressed connections [between country and city] is then a new way of seeing the human and social order as a whole. It is . . . a precise prevision of the essential literary methods and purposes of Dickens. . . . The simplifying contrast is then decisively transcended. It is significant that one of his best-remembered phrases is 'England's green and pleasant land,' but this is not the language of rural retrospect or retreat. The whole purpose of his struggle is, as he says, to build 'Jerusalem / In England's green and pleasant land': to build the holy as against the unholy city" (*The Country and the City*, 149).

43. Blake, *The Complete Writings of William Blake*, ed. Geoffrey Keynes (London: Oxford University Press, 1966), 481.

44. This is Ian Watt's famous reading of Defoe, in "*Robinson Crusoe* as a Myth," *Essays in Criticism* 1, no. 3 (1951).

45. Eric Sundquist's reading is apropos here: "Tom's crucifixion by Legree has powerful emotive consequences but, in the novel, lacks an applicable political meaning; the final deliverance from slavery, as the novel portrays it with no little ironic tension, will come from the paternalistic white God in his good time" (*To Wake the Nations: Race in the Making of American Literature* [Cambridge: Harvard University Press, 1993], 109). This invocation of God as the ultimate actor becomes an enormously political program, I would add, if the reader understands him- or herself thereby *to be constituted as* God.

# 9

................

# Fables of the Reconstruction

## The Citizen as Character

SCOTT ROMINE

Writing in 1940 in *Survey Graphic* magazine, George C. Stoney offered a withering analysis of the poll tax as a barrier to democratic participation in the South. Detailing one repeal effort in Arkansas, Stoney observed that its chances were doomed when "One argument was whispered: 'Do you want to see niggers in the state capital with their feet on the desk?'"[1] Whatever its historical accuracy in terms of the poll-tax controversy, this account depends on an image—black feet on legislative desks—that was apparently powerful to a contemporaneous southern audience and legible to *Survey Graphic*'s readers. Made famous by D. W. Griffith's *Birth of a Nation*, that image finds its origin in Thomas Dixon's *The Clansman* (1905) in a chapter titled "The Riot in the Master's Hall." Set in the South Carolina state legislature during Reconstruction, the chapter describes a white visitor confronting the "pathetic spectacle" of a freedman "throwing his big flat feet in their red woollens up on the desk" and bitterly concluding, "Once more we are a sovereign State—a sovereign negro State."[2]

Besides its durability and apparent power, other properties of this image are noteworthy: as fiction, it is factually embedded in the only legislative house of the Reconstruction era, as C. Vann Woodward observed in 1957, wherein African Americans legislators held political power reflective of their voting strength.[3] To conclude, however, that this image triumphs over history is not to say that it triumphs over historiography, since what Thomas Brown calls "one of the most familiar chapters in the history of American historical literature," the story of Reconstruction prior to the mid-twentieth century, can hardly be credited with offering much resistance to the narrative implicit in Dixon's image. As adumbrated by

Kate Masur, the "mainstream history" of Reconstruction, dominant until
W. E. B. Du Bois and Kenneth Stampp, "looked back on Reconstruction as
a 'tragic era' in which Congress, out of vengeance against the Confederacy,
trampled the Constitution and imposed 'negro rule' on the South."[4] When
Woodward, seventeen years after the *Survey Graphic* article, pointed out
the empirical anomaly of the South Carolina state legislature, he did so in
the clear sense of correcting the record.

Noting that the postbellum era was culturally inclined toward "deterministic theories of the self," Mark Elliott observes that "No subject more
often elicited a deterministic explanation than the failure of Reconstruction."[5] Following this logic, I want to argue that cultural predisposition
toward certain kinds of causal and representational structures exerted a
tenacious pressure on the record of Reconstruction as it emerged from its
on-the-ground realities. Reconstruction had, in other words, a distinctively literary dimension. In attending to that dimension and to the print
practices that materially realized it, I focus particularly on the figure of
the citizen as it evolves in tense relation to figurations of race. In a mostly
hostile reaction to Dixon's *The Leopard's Spots* (1902), an anonymous reviewer in the *New York Times* nonetheless conceded that "The author
does not overstate the evils resulting to both races from the bestowal of
the ballot upon the negro, nor the carnival of insolent misrule attending
negro domination." "It took the good people of the North some time,"
the reviewer continues, "to discover that the negro is not as Mrs. Stowe
imagined him, an Anglo-Saxon bound in black, and not a little sentimental gush characterized the early efforts for his improvement."[6] Deviating
sharply from early accounts of Reconstruction as a project of nation (re)
building organized around sectional difference, the reviewer reiterates
Dixon's insistence on a narrative based in racial difference—that is, as
a story of the "carnival of insolent misrule" following the attainment of
citizenship and civil rights by the negro.[7] That historical lesson, in turn, is
rendered in literary terms—more specifically, as a revelation to northerners that the negro is not what "Mrs. Stowe imagined," an "Anglo-Saxon
bound in black." The intersection here between *citizen* and *character*—
between a legal category of national belonging and literary representations of figures inhabiting that category—constituted, I argue, a central
pivot around which the racial story of Reconstruction gained ascendancy
over the sectional one. More precisely, the relationship between citizen
and character emerges—gradually at first, but with increasing force as the

twentieth century approaches—as one of distance and dissonance: of a gap between, on the one hand, the citizenship inhabited by black characters who do not warrant it, and, on the other, the traumatic denial of citizenship to white characters who do. At one level, textual representations of these gaps reflect historical realities. For many southern whites, the Reconstruction Acts meant disfranchisement; for most African Americans, nominally occupying the category of citizen failed to translate into meaningful citizenship as it was understood by the nation, especially as that understanding was grounded in antebellum conceptions of self-government and racial identity. At the same time, literary accounts of these gaps bring to bear distinctive representational strategies that, I argue, actively shaped the emerging "mainstream history" of Reconstruction as it was rendered legible in new contexts and put to work as a usable history in and for a rapidly evolving nation.

Like all Americans, postbellum authors confronted a scenario in which the category of citizen had been unmoored from long-standing definitions and practices, many of them explicitly racist in nature. As John Ashworth observes in *"Agrarians" and "Aristocrats,"* antebellum Democrats regarded "the suffrage as the superstructure which rested upon equality in both society and politics" and thus were "unable to accommodate a class of secondary or inferior voters." With respect to both Indians and blacks, Democratic theorists such as John Norvell had advocated disfranchisement lest the right to vote be contaminated by its association with inferior groups.[8] Similarly, David Roediger, in his analysis of antebellum labor in *The Wages of Whiteness*, emphasizes the extent to which African Americans were seen not merely as non-citizens but "as *anticitizens*, as 'enemies rather than members of the social compact.'"[9] In the aftermath of the Fourteenth and Fifteenth Amendments it is hardly surprising, then, that so many textual accounts of black citizenship assume an incongruity between the category and those inhabiting it. Time and again in postbellum discourse, representations of African American citizenship appear as critiques of writing—more precisely, of black citizenship as a *merely textual* matter: variations on the trope of the "citizen on paper" are common. Dixon's version of the trope, which refers to the "scratch of a pen in the hand of a madman [that sought] to transform by its magic a million slaves into a million kings" is especially virulent but otherwise unremarkable.[10] More often than not, however, the scratches of pens wielded by journalists, belletrists, and historians worked in the other direction—that is, to segregate the freedman from the symbolic category of citizen and the capacity for self-generated action understood to be entailed in it. By 1902, when Dixon penned his wildly successful "Romance of the White Man's Burden, 1865–1900," he could assume premises that, a few decades earlier, were hotly contested. The discursive field had shifted, not least due to the emergence of the Dunning school of historiography in the 1890s, and would shift further in response to Dixon's own interventions.

Although Dixon's triumph was not merely literary—it had profound cultural and even political effects—it possessed a distinctively literary dimension. By 1902, Dixon was able to compete successfully against other narratives that deployed competing causal, affective, and temporal structures. Notably, it had triumphed over those structures as they appeared in the first novel of Reconstruction, Albion Tourgée's A Fool's Errand (1879), which, as we will see, was acutely aware of its own position in a literary contest about Reconstruction. According to James Phelan, the potential for and expectation of competition is built into the nature of narrative. "If I can go," Phelan writes, "from experience to narrative in multiple ways, then the way I choose can be countered by tellers who prefer different routes" and my awareness of those alternatives shapes the story I tell.[11] In considering how Reconstruction narratives engage in such competition, I want to focus on two discrete but interrelated sites of contestation: character frames and temporal frames. In the field of cognitive narratology, frames (or schemata) are understood, as Marina Grishakova puts it, as governing the "domain of schematic, commonsense knowledge that overlaps with both fictional and nonfictional (referential and nonreferential) types of discourse." Grounded in culture and convention, frames constitute "intuitively grasped patterns of knowledge or schemes of behavior" that store culture-specific, conventionalized information in templates that serve as a tacit ground for conceptualizing and cognitively processing novel situations.[12] As Charles Rice observed in a 1903 article in the Atlantic Monthly, "It is only at long intervals, after great economic or political changes, that new types, new tendencies or modifications of character appear. So it was in reconstruction times after the civil war, and after other landmarks of political, industrial, and social evolution."[13] Although I do not share Rice's assumption of the consonance between type and (actual) character, dissonant frames surrounding race and citizenship in the Reconstruction era necessitated the negotiation of new character frames within a competition that, as I hope to show, ultimately recuperated whiteness as a prerequisite of national belonging.

At a formal level, this process involved a complex alignment of individual characters and what structuralist narratology calls *actants*, deep structural roles uncoupled from discrete characterizations and particularized psychologies.[14] If, as Henry James famously put the matter in *The Art of Fiction*, character is "but the determination of incident," while incident is "but the illustration of character," it is equally true that character, in this individuated sense, is largely peripheral to the broader contest over the story of Reconstruction.[15] Indeed, in order for Reconstruction's outcomes to be understood (as they were) as inevitable, it could not be. Deterministic explanations of Reconstruction's outcomes depended, rather, on *actants* of the kind one finds in Dunning's 1907 landmark study, wherein Reconstruction is glossed as "the struggle through which the southern whites, subjugated by adversaries of their own race, thwarted the scheme which threatened permanent subjection to another race."[16] But while the plot here depends upon a rigorously stripped-down and abstracted configuration of *actants*, it was a configuration that did not happen overnight. Indeed, the story of Reconstruction's story involves a complex interplay of more or less individualized characterizations and actantial roles as the former are slotted into what becomes, over time, a dominant configuration of the latter.

As the emerging Reconstruction narrative consolidated certain character-frames (the carpet-bagger, the scalawag, the traumatized white southerner, the inept freedman) and discarded others, it did so within insistently temporalized frames of reference: *types* were embedded in, and became legible through, *stories*. When the *Atlantic Monthly* closed a year-long series of articles on Reconstruction in 1901, it noted that "The final stage of the long reconstruction controversy seems to close, singularly enough, in the reversal of the very process which marked its inception. Reconstruction began with enfranchisement; it is ending with disfranchisement."[17] Although marking the "final stage" of Reconstruction in the new century was somewhat anomalous, a concern with its beginnings and endings—often, as here, marked with economies of symmetry and reversal—was not. In the most straightforwardly Aristotelian way, many narratives of Reconstruction deploy beginnings, middles, and ends *toward* specific ends. Yet to attach closure to Reconstruction did not mean to declare it a closed matter. To the contrary, the sense of an ending often works to generate affective power in the present and to deploy that power in an effort to envision and realize specific futures. These capacities, in turn, depend on the temporal structures of narrative form. As Mark Currie explains in *About Time: Narrative, Fiction and the Philosophy of Time*, "the model of time which is offered by narrative does its work by crossing the boundary between actual and potential futures to produce a hermeneutic circle between narrative and time, which encourages us to envisage futures on the model of teleological retrospect which narrative encodes." Teleological retrospect—the after-the-fact ordering of events whose significance narrative itself has rendered legible—assumes, according to Currie, a proleptic orientation "as a kind of instruction in the significance of events in the light of later events or outcomes."[18]

Before turning to Tourgée and Dixon and their complex narrative efforts to shape and frame the meaning of Reconstruction, I want to consider briefly a short account of Reconstruction that appeared in 1871. Published in the Boston-based *Every Saturday: A Journal of Choice Reading*, "What to Do with the South" is typical of many early, equivocal accounts of Reconstruction in the northern press. Despite its insistence that there "must be no failure" to the nation's "pledg[e] to the maintenance of all the rights of citizenship granted to the freedmen," the article employs an array of proto-narrative strategies that predict the specific forms that failure would eventually assume. Responding to "the Ku-Klux outrages of the South," the article frames the matter this way: "Given, therefore, the almost entire white population of one section of the country, not only defeated in their 'great expectations' of setting up a proslavery government, but compelled to encounter the emancipation of four millions of chattels, and their endowment with all the rights of citizenship . . . we have the very conditions precedent of a disturbed state of society." Mapping the problem as a sectional one—only *southern* whites are "compelled to encounter" the affront of black citizenship—the anonymous writer temporalizes his account as a matter of outcomes unexpected and expected: the frustration of Confederate "great expectations" produces the "natural sequel" of a "disturbed state of society." This construction is rhetorically proleptic in the sense that it preemptively counters a competing argument—here, that the Klan "outrages" are unexpected, and therefore of great concern—at the same time that it employs narrative prolepsis to imagine the present as future memory. Doubting that "the future historian will be at all surprised at the southern disorders which he will have to set down for the years 1870–71," the author counters the competing narrative that "we have before us the beginnings of another rebellion."[19] Insisting that the matter is closed, this account will have nothing to do with new beginnings.

Within this temporal frame, character-frames operate with equal rigor. To the injury of white southerners compelled to encounter chattels-as-citizens is added further insult. Disfranchised southern whites, the writer explains, have been "subject to the always trying rule for Americans of 'taxation without representation'" and to "the indiscretions and occasional abuse of their privileges committed by the new black citizens of the South, abetted by their white allies, the carpet-baggers, so called."[20] The new black citizens, by contrast, are not *subject to* or *compelled to encounter* anything; effaced entirely is any sense of *black* expectation, frustrated or otherwise. Across sectional lines, what limited intersubjectivity is imaginable limits itself to whites, while black political action is legible only as unthinking ("indiscretions") or abusive. In short, this account imagines what it would feel like to be a white "American" in the South but not to be a black one, much less to be a white "abettor" or "ally" (note how the initial, criminalizing term dominates the second) of the new class of citizens.

In several particulars, then, this contemporaneous—and, to reiterate, highly ambivalent—account of Reconstruction contains several narrative features that would, as we shall see, evolve in distinctive patterns: first, it is rigorously spatialized (as an effort to understand *here* what is going on *there*); second, its structures of feeling assume a normative white subjectivity; third, its temporal shape seeks to shape, in turn, a future course of action; and fourth, it is dependent on character-frames that assume, as a primary set of determinants, the intersection of race and citizenship. I have suggested that those patterns are best understood as competitions, that is, as a matter of some stories or parts of stories winning out over others. Such competition is not purely formal in nature—that is, a matter of better stories triumphing over weaker ones. Although cognitive theory has shown that we are wired for narrative and use narrative for certain tasks—modeling sequences as causal structures, creating expectation based on past experience, accounting for the behavior of others—there is no clear case for anything like an absolute narrative advantage. Narratives do not compete in a vacuum, but within a concretely realized social domain. They do not compete on a level playing field, although they may shape that field in significant ways.

The print world of the late nineteenth century constituted a distinctly uneven playing field. Commenting in 1874 on the state of white opinion observed during his recent southern travels, an anonymous writer in the *Christian Advocate* appraised the situation shrewdly:

"The negro is among us," seemed to be the burden of the cry, "endowed by the Constitution of the United States with all the rights of a free citizen. What shall we do about it? If we let him alone he will become like ourselves, and compel us to recognize his manhood, and his legal equality with us—than which nothing could be more dreadful. We tried to perpetuate his enslavement with the sword, and failed; we next tried to render him an outcast and vagrant by legislation, but were hindered; and since his enfranchisement we have tried to keep him down by the ballot, and there our success is only partial. Let us carry the war into a department into which he cannot follow us; let us bring the press to bear against him, that we may make him odious, after which we may somehow get rid of him."[21]

The operative premise of the white southerner imagined here is that the press constituted a domain ("department") into which the "[negro] cannot follow us." Although the writer opposes the use to which the press will be put—namely, to facilitate the expulsion of "the negro" from a political space wherein manhood and "the rights of a free citizen" would otherwise prove available—he concedes the racially exclusive character of the press whereby that expulsion becomes possible. The grounds for that concession were amply evident in contemporary print practices. The specific occasion for this article was the publication, in the New York–based *International Review*, of E. T. Winkler's "The Negroes in the Gulf States," a thoroughly racist account of Reconstruction framed around two questions: "What should be done with the freedman? In what manner and to what extent could he be invested with citizenship, so that no jeopardy should accrue to the public interest?"[22] Responses to Winkler's article in the northern press reiterated many of his basic assumptions. *The Unitarian Review* rejected Winkler's argument for the "unfitness of the black man for citizenship, and especially fellow-citizenship with the whites," but did so halfheartedly, countering Winkler's accusation that "our poor African brother" is "the lowest of the human races" by assuring its readers that "the Digger Indian, the Comanche, and the Modoc are lower;

also the wild Australian and the cannibal South Sea Islander."[23] Like the *Christian Advocate*, *Zion's Herald* used environmentalist arguments to explain why the "untrained black men have not made, as a whole, good legislators."[24] The *New York Evangelist*, by contrast, even "making allowances" for Winkler's "South side view of the situation," claims that there is "reason to fear that his statements in the main are only too true."[25] But whether contesting or affirming Winkler's conclusions, these accounts consistently position the freedman as the object of a discourse grounded in a normative white subjectivity. The conversations surrounding "What Shall Be Done with the Freedmen?" (to use the *Christian Advocate* title) frame the freedmen as the topic of—and not infrequently, the *problem* occasioning—a conversation not only conducted by (actual) whites but in which whiteness is consistently signaled as a site of utterance and reception. "The negro" may be "among us," or "our poor African brother" may be slandered by Winkler's unjust charges, but the negro never *is* us—that is to say, never afforded the grammatical status of the collective subject, nor imagined as part of the public addressed in and constituted through the discourse.[26] Typically, the negro's exclusion from the discussion turns on his incapacity as citizen; for example, an 1885 *Century* article titled "How Shall We Help the Negro?" notes with "disappointment" that "the negro . . . is utterly incapable of the proper performance of citizen's duty, either at the polls or in the jury-box."[27]

The implications of this discursive exclusion, pervasive in the magazines and newspapers of the period, were profound. Since Benedict Anderson's work in the early 1980s, it has been widely recognized that the relationship between print practices and national "imagined communities" allows strangers to be brought into imaginative relation with each other. As Anderson explains, it is through the dissemination and consumption of print that "fiction seeps quietly and continuously into reality, creating that remarkable confidence of community in anonymity which is the hallmark of modern nations."[28] In his consideration of the relation between print and publics, Michael Warner extends his earlier argument (in *The Letters of the Republic*) that reading printed texts "incorporate[s] an awareness of the indefinite others to whom it is addressed as part of the meaning of its printedness," adding that "in order for a text to be public, we must recognize it not simply as a diffusion to strangers, but also as a temporality of circulation."[29] The temporal, punctual dimension of print is essential to understanding the evolving discourse of Reconstruction, and in particular the discursive flows from high-frequency, local publications (especially newspapers) to periodicals constituting broader publics and, in general, deploying broader temporal frames. The uptake from southern newspapers, which controlled data at its source, to the northern press was explicitly noted in the *Christian Advocate* article cited above. The article traces from southern newspapers via northern newspapers and monthly magazines to "the massive quarterlies" allegations of "the most terrible charges against those 'negro governments,'" as well as depictions of a "scene of horror and ruin all over that 'sunny land' that only the hardest-hearted could fail to pity."[30] Although the flow of representation was hardly as uniform and unilinear as suggested here, the essential characterization of the spatial and temporal dissemination of print stories during and about Reconstruction is sound.

In particular, the use of correspondents, either hailing from or traveling in the South, provided immediate, on-the-ground reports that crucially shaped the emerging narrative of Reconstruction. In a typical instance, the northern journalist Edward Kingsbury's 1868 *Evangelist* article titled "Negro Rule at the South" reported that, upon witnessing the "colored" vote in Brighton, South Carolina, he "could no longer be blind to the fact that soon all the offices would be held, and the laws made, by the colored men in South Carolina." Characterizing the colored men's manifest "lack of capacity to govern or well-provide for themselves," Kingsbury imagines (and limits his imagination to) the "humiliating and deplorable" position of white South Carolinians, a reality confirmed by a white interlocutor who, in bearing witness to white trauma, "said he wished he could speak loud enough for every man in the Union to hear him."[31] The irony, of course, is that even as the man laments his *lack* of access to a public—an imagined community he calls the Union—Kingsbury and the print medium of *The Evangelist* provide him access to strangers enjoined to imagine themselves precisely *as part* of that community, which is figured intratextually and imagined via print as a conversation among white men ("Every man in the Union" does not signal literally).

Although it is beyond the scope of this essay to trace the multiple arcs and trends of print discourse about Reconstruction prior to Tourgée's distinctively literary intervention, suffice it to say that by 1789 a certain consolidation had taken place. As Jennifer Rae Greeson remarks of Reconstruction's "failure," it "is startling, indeed, to recognize how early the judgment on the project of Reconstruction was rendered in U.S. letters."[32]

From its title onward, *A Fool's Errand* announces itself as a quixotic effort in a lost cause even as it deploys causal sequences and character frames in an effort to reverse the verdict of history. It is tempting to argue that the entry of Reconstruction into novelistic space—that is to say, its transition from the conversational, punctual discourses of print journalism to the more capacious and formalized temporal structures of the novel—depended upon a broadly diffused cultural sense that Reconstruction had ended and that history had, in fact, rendered a verdict. Although different temporal structures do indeed figure in *A Fool's Errand*, marking a hard break here is complicated by Tourgée's rigorous and sometimes quite specific engagement with earlier discourses. As it embeds those discourses within a broader narrative arc, Tourgée's novel strives, paradoxically, to use closure to reframe the temporal shape of Reconstruction and the tropes enabling its legibility as failure. In its braiding of plot and history—of "our Fool's story" and "this era of our nation's history"—*A Fool's Errand* characterizes Reconstruction as a "short story . . . full of folly and shame" whose facts "were graven on the hearts of millions with a burning stylus." Tourgée's literary metaphor figures the future as inattentive to the period—he doubts that there is "enough of good springing from its gloom to make it ever tolerable to the historian"—even as he attempts to refocus attention on and refigure the temporal shape of a losing battle in a longer and more potentially hopeful war.[33]

In taking its backward glance, *A Fool's Errand* self-consciously speculates on its usefulness in the future, sending its past and its present forward in anticipatory projection as future memory. At its most local and reified level, this involves an intervention in character frames, most obviously in positioning the novel's hero within the degraded frame of carpetbagger. In an extended and quite brilliant disquisition on the term itself, perhaps the most "perfect and complete . . . epithet" in "all history" (158), Tourgée strives to unsettle and revise the meanings and connotations that had attached themselves to the frame almost immediately upon its appearance in Reconstruction discourse. Strikingly successful in crowding out alternative accounts of the individuals so labeled, "carpet-bagger" allowed a northern disavowal of the Reconstruction project by assigning the figure mercenary motives and characterizing it as morally deficient. Even defenses of the group tended to be halfhearted. Writing five years before Tourgée's novel, Samuel Chapman Armstrong of Hampton Institute described the "carpet-bagger" as a "necessary evil," noting that while

"No other class appeared ready to offer intelligent aid in carrying out the national policy," it "was certain that a better class would have been preferred by the managers." Although the war, Armstrong claims, was "one of principle," "these principles have been represented at the South by unprincipled men."[34] Dispensing with Armstrong's equivocations, Tourgée preserves his agentive logic, noting that "there is no other instance in history in which the conquering power has discredited its own agents, denounced those of its own blood and faith, espoused the prejudices of its conquered foes, and poured the vials of its wrath and contempt upon the only class in the conquered territory who defended its acts, supported its policy, promoted its aim, or desired its preservation and continuance" (161). Acutely attentive to the representational work done by "carpetbagger," Tourgée is equally attuned to the peculiar dissemination of that figure through print. Upon the term's introduction, he explains, "Instantly it spread through the press of the South; and, with its usual subserviency, that of the North followed in its lead, and re-echoed its maledictions" (158).[35]

As Tourgée performs a kind of prophylactic labor on the salient character frames of Reconstruction discourse, he does so through a consistent mediation on distance, and in particular the artificial distance assumed by his imagined North, where spatial separation means inattention and disregard. Of Klan brutality, he explains that "It was not the individual negro, scalawag, or carpet-bagger, against whom the blow was directed, but the power—the Government—the idea which they represented" (229). This formulation *brings home* the violence by rerouting it from individuals who inhabited degraded character frames to the idea of Union itself. Observing that Klan violence "was builded upon an ineradicable sentiment of hostility to the negro *as a political integer*" (229), Tourgée tells a powerful counternarrative of the terroristic response to African American citizenship, thereby responding to the argument of a northern radical who claims the freedmen have failed to "show themselves capable of self-government, able to take care of themselves." "We have prepared him," his correspondent writes, "for the battle of freedom, and it is for him to furnish the manhood requisite for the struggle. . . . Instead of whining over the wrongs they suffer at the hands of the rebels, they should assert themselves, and put down lawless violence" (235). The sentiments expressed here were widely shared; as one writer commented in 1875 of federal interventions in Louisiana, the protection of the freedmen by military force "is far outweighed by the injury of teaching them to look to Washington for whatever they want. To a weak and ignorant race. . . . [it] is not thus that self-government is to be learned."[36] Similarly, a review of Tourgée's novel in *Appletons' Journal* found the correspondent's letter to be "the one piece of really statesmanlike writing in the volume" and faulted the Fool for holding "it up to ridicule, as if its absurdity were self-evident."[37]

But while Tourgée faced a decidedly uphill battle in contesting the frames of citizenship implicit in the correspondent's letter, his own narrative reiterates an incongruity between the freedman's character and his status as citizen. In an early chapter titled "Citizens in Embryo," for example, the Fool is invited to a meeting of the Union League by a freedman named Andy. When he asks who leads the meetings, Andy replies "with ready pride in his new toy," "Wal, sometimes one, an' sometimes anudder, jes' accordin' tu who's scholar enuff tu take de lead" (102). Although the Fool later becomes convinced that the League might serve as a "valuable training-school to the inchoate citizens of the lately Rebellious states," his initial reaction—he finds Andy and his new "toy" "very amusing"—affirms the new citizen's incongruous and "inchoate" status (102). Similarly, the literary convention of Andy's speech—represented in an exaggerated eye dialect wherein "to" is shown as "tu" and "enough" as "enuff"—serves to separate the freedman from the official print language that, as Anderson shows, has often served as a linguistic ground for national consciousness; the convention is all the more striking since the novel rigidly suppresses the phonetic differences between northern and white southern speech.[38]

Tourgée's dissonant frames of freedman and citizen are similarly apparent as the novel mediates on broader historical arcs. Having mastered only the "rudiments of civilization," the Fool explains in a late conversation with his mentor that slaves were "freed almost without exertion upon their part, and entirely without their independent and intelligent cooperation," thus leading them to consider themselves "the special pets of Providence,—a sort of chosen people" (344–45). "This chapter of miracles," the Fool continues, "as they account these wonderful happenings, is always present to the fervid fancies of the race; and, while it has hitherto inclined them to inaction, would be a powerful motive, should it once come, to act in concert with a conviction that their future must be laid in a region remote from the scene of their past" (345). Action *here*, he continues, is made more difficult because they are not "of the same stock as the dominant race," in which case the "line of separation" might "disappear with the lapse of time" (345). Drawing on contemporary biological models of racial difference, Tourgée also reinscribes what one antebellum writer referenced as the "well known distinction between *freeman* and *freedman*," the latter only "*quasi* a citizen."[39] Addressing the question of whether the "African slave of America" can "develop into the self-governing citizen" (343), even this, the most egalitarian novel of Reconstruction, firmly installs the freedman as a passive object in a story of white agency, a discourse limited to white interlocutors.[40]

Indeed, that limitation is crucial to Tourgée's intervention in Reconstruction's temporal contour. Declaring the period closed, he reopens it for future use; he looks back on political Reconstruction as a fool's errand in order to look *forward* to the future of African American civil rights. Casting the conflict in sectional terms as the necessary and forcible superimposition of "the civilization, the idea of the North, upon the South," Tourgée explains Reconstruction's failure as dependent on a false northern assumption of normative *whiteness*—specifically, that "the Southern white man had become identical with the Caucasian of the North" (341). Conceding late in the novel that Reconstruction was a "magnificent failure" as a "logical sequence of the war" and "insofar as it attempted to unify the nation," the Fool insists, too, that it failed "to fix and secure the position and rights of the colored race." "They were fixed, it is true, on paper," he continues, but "No guaranty whatever was provided against their practical subversion, which was accomplished with ease and impunity" (337). Even so, the Fool issues a crucial qualification: "Reconstruction was a great step in advance, in that it formulated a confession of error. It gave us a construction of 'we the people' in the preamble of our Federal Constitution which gave the lie to that which had formerly prevailed. It recognized and formulated the universality of manhood in governmental power, and, in one phase or another of its development, compelled the formal assent of all sections and parties" (338). Precisely because he refuses one ending—the Civil War as the end of slavery, which he claims continues in fact if not in law—he can refuse another: the real history of Reconstruction has not ended because "the struggle between North and South" has "just begun!"; the "irrepressible conflict" yet confronts the nation (338, 340). The desire for an ending—specifically, abolitionism's desire to congratulate itself on "the accomplishment of its mission, . . . on having no more victims to succor" (339)—generates an artificial formalism, a false imposition of closure, that fails to account for the open-ended nature of the historical process.

Tourgée's long view of Reconstruction as a story about citizenship—a view reiterated in the *Atlantic*'s 1901 assertion that Reconstruction began with enfranchisement and was ending with disfranchisement—would prove adaptable to writers with different ideological agendas. Where, for Tourgée, Reconstruction was "a mere incident of a great underlying struggle" *between* sections and civilizations (338–39), Thomas Dixon would view it as an anomalous episode in the nation's progress toward a collective identity grounded in whiteness. As with Tourgée, so for Dixon, Reconstruction constituted a chapter in a much longer story; but for Dixon, the chapter is of lessons learned and forgotten, not of lessons yet to be learned. The ascendance and suppression of "negro rule" during Reconstruction represents, for Dixon, a recurring scenario in American history as the nation repeatedly confronts the question, "Shall the future American be an Anglo-Saxon or a mulatto?"[41] In answering, Dixon figures the black citizen as a contaminant of the body politic, an alien presence that must be eliminated if the nation is to realize its best future.

Although Dixon's most obvious literary opponent in *The Leopard's Spots* is Harriet Beecher Stowe, several of whose characters he recycles, I share Mark Elliott's assessment that the literary strategies and historical arguments of the novel were shaped most forcefully in response to Tourgée.[42] Some of Dixon's reactions are quite local and specific. In one episode, for example, the language of Tourgée's northern correspondent is echoed almost precisely as Dixon shapes an episode wherein freedmen are disfranchised by merely warning them not to vote. Of an upcoming election, a Klan leader informs his subalterns that "Those who come will be allowed to vote without molestation. Any man, black or white, who can be scared out of his ballot is not fit to have one. . . . This is simply a test of manhood" (160). Needless to say, the black vote is sparse, and, as the chapter title tells us, "Civilization Was Saved." Although Tourgée attends closely to white southern humiliation at being forced to confront blacks as fellow citizens, he does so in order to emphasize the *difference* between two civilizations, and the necessity for the civilized one to dominate the one that is actually a "species of barbarism." Dixon, by contrast, deploys white southern trauma in order to teach America what it means to be authentically white. In terms of historical sequence and temporal structure, the novels' divergence is equally pronounced. For Tourgée, Reconstruction follows "logically" from the Civil War as a project of unifying the nation under a new dispensation; for Dixon, it is a separate and "second war" inaugurated in a moment of "profound peace" and waged against a defeated people who had "accepted in good faith the results of the war." This effort to "wipe out the civilization of the South" and to "establish with the bayonet an African barbarism on the ruins of Southern society," Dixon explains, was "a conspiracy against human progress" (194).

Stylistically, however, the two novels could hardly be more different. Although the difference between Tourgée's prose style—ironic, melancholy, wry—and Dixon's anxious, crude melodrama is tonal, tonality shapes the resonance of history. Tourgée writes history with a sigh; Dixon, as Woodrow Wilson would infamously say of *Birth of a Nation*, with lightning. For Tourgée, the history of Reconstruction is a contest between Wisdom and Folly, and he offers his Fool's wisdom as an antidote to the folly of the Wise Men who mismanage Reconstruction from a safe distance, just as he offers his Fool's account of "the way it really was" as a corrective to a record of historical failure distorted by distance, bias, and premature closure. But for Walter Benjamin, in an insight Dixon would have appreciated, "to articulate the past historically does not mean to recognize it 'the way it really was,'" but rather to "seize hold of a memory as it flashes up at a moment of danger."[43] For Dixon, Reconstruction is an especially useful memory to seize hold of in a moment he represented as yet another traumatic encounter between a white nation and the specter of the black citizen.

As I have argued at greater length elsewhere, Dixon's malignant genius manifests itself formally as a melodrama of besieged whiteness. In presenting whiteness under threat, Dixon mobilizes it as a contingent and performative sequence; to be white is to be threatened, but also to respond to the threat.[44] Thus premised, the plot of *The Leopard's Spots* unfolds predictably as a series of iterations of a basic sequence: black citizenship threatens the body politic—often figured, in the novel's erotic economy, as the white female body—and is, consequently, punished or expelled by white agents who secure identity through the act of punishment or expulsion. Reworking Tourgée's chapter on the "Citizen as Embryo" in a chapter titled "The Man or Brute in Embryo," Dixon installs the freedman as the dupe of the Freedmen's Bureau and degrader of white civil rights, a threat that will be removed only when the carpet-baggers are driven from town and the "Black Peril" eliminated. Reconstruction is thus transformed into a series of compulsively staged scenes of abjection, trauma, and violation that, in turn, serve as the origin of white identity. Dixon's story of Reconstruction, then, reduces its plot to the stripped-down morphology Claude Bremond identifies as the deep structure of the folktale—that is, to a narrative cycle from a satisfactory state to state of deficiency and back again through procedures of degradation and improvement, respectively.[45] In Dixon's version, the black anti-citizen appears as the *actant* of degrader, the white "Citizen King" as the *actant* of improver.

But despite the rigorous suppression of historicity necessary to reduce Reconstruction to a simple contest of "the Black against the White" (84), Dixon retains a commitment to the "way it really was." In a prefatory "Historical Note," he writes that "all the incidents used in Book I., which is properly the prologue of my story, were selected from authentic records, or came within my personal knowledge. The only serious liberty I have taken with history is to tone down the facts to make them credible in fiction."[46] What is striking is that, despite Dixon's subordination of historicity to the logics of racial fantasy and horror, contemporary readers so often found the novel either historically credible or even understated.[47] One explanation for this credulity lies in the representation of Reconstruction as it had emerged in professional historiography. In the final article of the 1901 *Atlantic* series dominated by his professional cohort, William A. Dunning explained the "Undoing of Reconstruction" as inevitably following the abatement of "abolitionist fervor" accompanying the war and its Radical aftermath. History had proven, Dunning explained, that the place of slavery "must be taken by some set of conditions which, if more humane and beneficent in accidents, must in essence express the same fact of racial inequality" and the impossible "coexistence in one society of two races so distinct in character as to render coalescence impossible."[48]

This was the kind of history that Dixon could, and did, rewrite with lightning. Recycling Reconstruction for contemporary use, Dixon sought historical coordinates for what Dominick LaCapra calls foundational traumas. In *History in Transit*, LaCapra writes that

every group that is in some significant sense a locus of commitment whose members affirm (and may be pressured to affirm) a collective identity has in its past or in its mythology (often its mythologized past) a trauma that has become foundational and is a source of identity both for those who actually lived through it and in different ways for those born into its aftermath. In perhaps its most politically pointed dimensions, the founding trauma may be a way for a group . . . to reclaim a history and to transform it into a more or less enabling basis of life in the present.[49]

Dixon's configuration of history does precisely such work, mobilizing a mythologized, traumatized past in order to consolidate a national identity shrewdly keyed, as Greeson shows, to an imperialist present looking to the future.[50] In a chapter titled "The New America," the Spanish-American War reveals the nation as overcoming the "Sectionalism and disunity [that] had been the most terrible realities in our national history" and awakening "to the consciousness of her resistless power" (406). This necessitates the expulsion of the Negro from his actantial position as "sentimental pet" or "ward" of the nation (261, 414)—that is to say, from the position used to justify Reconstruction as a Radical project—to a position as contaminant of the body politic. The work of the Klan during Reconstruction, then, becomes a template for the act of expulsion propelling the nation forward as the "Anglo-Saxon race" is "united into one homogeneous mass," having recognized at long last that the "Negro was an impossibility in the newborn unity of national life" (409). (For the South, this is old news.) In a "Speech That Made History," Charles Gaston pronounces that "The Anglo-Saxon is entering the new century with the imperial crown of the ages on his brow" and the lesson of Reconstruction at his disposal. With reference to the Filipino conquest, Gaston observes that "our flag has been raised over 10 millions of semi-barbaric black men in the foulest slave pen of the Orient. Shall we repeat the farce of 1867, reverse the order of nature, and make these black people our rulers? If not, why should the African here, who is not their equal, be allowed to imperil our life?" (435).

Described as "fix[ing] the history of a state for a thousand years" (434), the racial logics of Gaston's speech did not last even a century. Dunning, too, had predicted incorrectly in placing the future of Reconstruction's past alongside America's imperialist project. As he put the matter in his *Atlantic* article, "In view of the questions which have been raised by our lately established relations with other races, it seems most improbable that the historian will soon, or ever, have to record a reversal of the conditions which this process [of the undoing of Reconstruction] has established."[51]

Ironically, the historian who would begin the scholarly process of undoing Dunning's story of Reconstruction had preceded him in the *Atlantic* series. In another irony, W. E. B. Du Bois had opened his essay on the Freedmen's Bureau by similarly positioning Reconstruction alongside imperialism, writing, in language he would reuse two years later in *The Souls of Black Folk*, that "the problem of the twentieth century is the problem of the color line; the relation of the darker to the lighter races of men in Asia and Africa, in America and the islands of the sea."[52] By the time Du Bois returned to the subject in his 1935 study, the transnational field had shifted yet again, as it would continue to do in the postwar years when Cold War politics facilitated a reevaluation of Reconstruction and a renegotiation of what citizenship meant for African Americans. But what confronted Du Bois in 1935, as it had in 1901, was a fable of Reconstruction whose plot had been determined by the color line. Reconstruction had indeed been undone, and its undoing was facilitated by its being *fixed* in print. Considering the "problem" of the freedman (always the *problem*) in 1874, one commentator asserted that "It is not hopefully solving this problem to recklessly and constantly write down the negro."[53] The contemporaneous print record of Reconstruction reveals, however, that to write the negro *was* most often to "write him down"—first, as "the negro," and then, having imprisoned a race inside of a frame, by segregating that frame from the category of citizen. History was said to have rendered its verdict, but the verdict was subject to review.

## Notes

1. George C. Stoney, "Suffrage in the South, Part I: The Poll Tax," *Survey Graphic* 29 (January 1940): 8.

2. Thomas Dixon Jr., *The Clansman: An Historical Romance of the Ku Klux Klan* (New York: Grosset and Dunlap, 1905), 265, 270.

3. C. Vann Woodward, *The Burden of Southern History* (Baton Rouge: Louisiana State University Press, 1960), 100–101.

4. Thomas J. Brown, introduction to *Reconstructions: New Perspectives on the Postbellum United States*, ed. Brown (Oxford: Oxford University Press, 2006), 3; Kate Masur, review of Thomas J. Brown, ed., *Reconstructions: New Perspectives on the Postbellum United States*, H-Civwar, October 2007, http://h-net.msu.edu/cgi-bin/logbrowse.pl?trx=vx&list=h-civwar&month=0710&week=b&msg=zIJvRw0u2muGZayt67fHng&user=&pw= (accessed June 4, 2012).

5. Mark Elliott, *Color-Blind Justice: Albion Tourgée and the Quest for Racial Equality from the Civil War to "Plessy v. Ferguson"* (Oxford: Oxford University Press, 2006), 11.

6. "Mr. Dixon's 'The Leopard's Spots,'" *New York Times*, April 5, 1902, BR10.

7. Here and throughout this essay, I use the racial terminology employed in the text under discussion.

8. John Ashworth, *"Agrarians" and "Aristocrats": Party Political Ideology in the United States, 1837–1846* (Cambridge: Cambridge University Press, 1987), 221–22.

9. David R. Roediger, *The Wages of Whiteness: Race and the Making of the American Working Class* (London: Verso, 1991), 57.

10. Thomas Dixon Jr., *The Leopard's Spots: A Romance of the White Man's Burden, 1865–1900* (New York: Doubleday, Page, 1902), 438.

11. James Phelan, "Narratives in Contest; or, Another Twist in the Narrative Turn," *PMLA* 123 (2008): 168.

12. Marina Grishakova, "Beyond the Frame: Cognitive Science, Common Sense and Fiction," *Narrative* 17 (May 2009): 189.

13. Charles Rice, "Libin: A New Interpreter of East Side Life," *Atlantic Monthly*, February 1903, 256.

14. Originating in the work of Vladimir Propp and A. J. Greimas, *actants* enabled structuralist efforts to locate and identify the minimal units of narrative. My concern here, less theoretical than pragmatic, is to identify and describe particular intersections between characters and *actants* (or "character-positions"); I use the term "character-frames" to describe these intersections.

15. Henry James and Walter Besant, *The Art of Fiction* (Boston: Cupples, Upham, 1885), 69.

16. William Archibald Dunning, *Reconstruction: Political and Economic, 1865–1877* (New York: Harper and Brothers, 1907), xv.

17. "Reconstruction and Disenfranchisement," *Atlantic Monthly*, October 1901, 343.

18. Mark Currie, *About Time: Narrative, Fiction and the Philosophy of Time* (Edinburgh: Edinburgh University Press, 2007), 21, 22.

19. "What to Do with the South," *Every Saturday: A Journal of Choice Reading*, April 22, 1871, 362.

20. Ibid.

21. "What Shall Be Done with the Freedmen?" *Christian Advocate*, August 22, 1874, 276.

22. E. T. Winkler, "The Negroes in the Gulf States," *International Review* 1, no. 5 (1874): 577. Although hardly original, Winkler's racist construction of "the Negro" (or "the African") is crucial to his political critique of Reconstruction policy. Possessed with a "mercurial and shiftless temper," a propensity for theft, a disregard for "personal purity," and a superstitious temperament, the Negro demonstrates, according to Winkler, that "the thin varnish of civilization and sentiment cannot conceal the barbarism of the race"; see 581–85.

23. M. P. L., "Of Things at Home," *Unitarian Review and Religious Magazine* 3 (April 1875): 412.

24. "Freedmen and Their Detractors," *Zion's Herald*, reprinted in *Christian Advocate*, September 10, 1874, 289.

25. "A Sad Picture of the South," *New York Evangelist* 45 (September 1874): 2. Although

Winkler's southernness is here presented as the potential cause of bias, it is also as a source of authority: Winkler's statements "deserve special attention, because of his opportunities for observation."

26. "What Shall Be Done with the Freedmen?" 276; M. P. L., "Of Things at Home," 412.

27. T. U. Dudley, "How Shall We Help the Negro?" *Century Illustrated Magazine*, June 1885, 273.

28. Benedict Anderson, *Imagined Communities: Reflections on the Origin and Spread of Nationalism* (London: Verso, 2006), 36.

29. Michael Warner, "Publics and Counterpublics," *Public Culture* 14 (2002): 65–66.

30. "What Shall Be Done with the Freedman?" 276.

31. E. Kingsbury, "Negro Rule at the South," *New York Evangelist* 39 (May 1868): 2. Empathy with white southerners could take extreme forms. *The Old Guard*, a New York–based journal that during the war had shown distinct Copperhead tendencies, published in 1869 a letter purportedly written to Ulysses S. Grant. Commenting on the scarcity of meat, the letter suggests that "this vexed question of reconstruction enables us to settle the difficulty"—specifically (in a clear nod to Swift's "Modest Proposal") by butchering southerners for human consumption. See "Intercepted Letter," *The Old Guard* 7 (August 1869): 612.

32. Jennifer Rae Greeson, *Our South: Geographic Fantasy and the Rise of National Literature* (Cambridge: Harvard University Press, 2010), 254.

33. Albion W. Tourgée, *A Fool's Errand, By One of the Fools* (New York: Ford, Howard, and Hulbert, 1880), 112. Text hereafter cited parenthetically.

34. S. C. Armstrong, "Reconstruction," *Friends' Review: A Religious, Literary and Miscellaneous Journal* 28 (November 1874): 235. Armstrong's attention to white southern sensibilities is noteworthy. Noting the dangers of a "wide separation of sympathies" between the North and its southern "brethren," Armstrong concludes that, despite the "humiliat[ion] to the South" caused by negro citizenship, "The negro was entitled to citizenship," which therefore "could be tolerated as a necessity."

35. Tourgée's unsuccessful effort is perhaps best illustrated by John Hope Franklin's 1961 introduction to the novel, which explains that "While Tourgée may be classified as a carpetbagger, it is improper to group him with those settlers from the North . . . who expected to get something for nothing from the South." Franklin, "Albion Tourgée, Social Critic," in *A Fool's Errand*, by Albion W. Tourgée (Cambridge: Belknap Press, 1961), x.

36. "The Lesson of New Orleans," *Christian Union* 11 (January 1875): 50.

37. C. H. Jones, "Sectional Fiction," *Appletons' Journal: A Magazine of General Literature*, December 1880, 565.

38. For discussion of the relationship between vernaculars and "national print-languages" see Anderson, *Imagined Communities*, 43–46. The relationship between print-dialect and the horizons of the national imagined community has received extensive analysis relative to the genre of local color in late-nineteenth-century America; see especially Richard Brodhead, *Cultures of Letters: Scenes of Reading and Writing in Nineteenth-Century America* (Chicago: University of Chicago Press, 1993), 107–41.

39. D. J. M., "Civil Liberty and Self-Government," *Southern Quarterly Review* 9 (April 1854): 312.

40. This limitation is less pronounced in Tourgée's second novel, *Bricks without Straw* (1880). That novel, however, is, in comparison with *A Fool's Errand*, less keyed to the historical coordinates of Reconstruction.

41. Dixon, *The Leopard's Spots*, 159. Text hereafter cited parenthetically. Iterations and variations of this question appear throughout the novel; see also 97, 198, 242, 333, 383, 433, 438.

42. Elliott, *Color-Blind Justice*, 18.

43. Walter Benjamin, "Theses on the Philosophy of History," in *Illuminations* (New York: Shocken Books, 1969), 255.

44. See Scott Romine, "Thomas Dixon and the Literary Production of Whiteness," in *Thomas Dixon and the Birth of Modern America*, ed. Michele K. Gillespie and Randal L. Hall (Baton Rouge: Louisiana State University Press, 2006), 124–28.

45. Claude Bremond, "Morphology of the French Folktale," *Semiotica* 2 (1970): 251.

46. As Elliott notes, one of more fabulous historical fabrications in *The Leopard's Spots* is a plan, proposed by a Negro legislator, to have Confederate marriages annulled in order to facilitate racial amalgamation. According to Dixon, Congress threatens news agencies in an effort to keep this information from "being circulated throughout the country" (114). See Elliott, *Color-Blind Justice*, 18–19.

47. For a review of reactions to the novel, see Romine, "Thomas Dixon," 146–49. See also Elliott, *Color-Blind Justice*, 19–20.

48. William Archibald Dunning, "The Undoing of Reconstruction," *Atlantic Monthly*, October 1901, 449.

49. Dominick LaCapra, *History in Transit: Experience, Identity, Critical Theory* (Ithaca: Cornell University Press, 2004), 57.

50. Greeson, *Our South*, 278.

51. Dunning, "The Undoing of Reconstruction," 449.

52. W. E. Burghardt Du Bois, "The Freedmen's Bureau," *Atlantic Monthly*, March 1901, 354.

53. "Freedmen and Their Detractors," 289.

# 10

.....................

# White Supremacy and the Question of Black Citizenship in the Post-Emancipation South

DARYL MICHAEL SCOTT

With the Reconstruction Acts and the ratification of the Fourteenth and Fifteenth Amendments, the legal ambiguity surrounding the national citizenship of free persons of African descent vanished, and for the first time most of those who had lived in the antebellum South could aver that they were now legally citizens of their states and the American nation. This triumph of civic or liberal nationalism did not please everyone, especially Southerners (whites born or assimilated into southern culture).[1] After all, this revolution in American citizenship took place in the wake of military defeat and with the possibility of further federal action. Southerners watched from the political sidelines in dismay and sometimes fear as the general government and state conventions also granted voting rights to the new citizens. Virtually no Southerners thought that they had granted blacks state citizenship, which they viewed as a necessary condition for federal citizenship.[2] If the war had brought home to Southerners that their states would not be sovereign, the Radical Reconstruction amendments, in their estimation, stripped them of home rule. Despite white supremacy campaigns that excluded blacks from the political community and extracted the marrow from their citizenship, scholars have nonetheless tended to treat the new fundamental laws as an accomplished, if imperfect, fact rather than a dead letter in the American South.

As a consequence, the history of the post-emancipation South has been written from the perspective of federal pronouncements rather than on-the-ground realities. Their official badges of citizenship notwithstanding, persons of African descent struggled for generations against ethnoracial nationalism. Recognizing a gap, scholars have often referred to blacks as second-class citizens, a status unknown under the law. This compromised language underwrites the nearly universally held view of America as the quintessential example of civic nationalism and distorts global understandings of the history of nationalism.[3] When white supremacy is explored as an ideology as well as a condition, its ethnoracial nationalism becomes clear and the central claim of American exceptionalism is shown to be its most enduring myth.[4]

# I

Over the last two generations, historians have espied black nationalism everywhere and white nationalism virtually nowhere.[5] From liberals to Marxists, historians have portrayed slaves and mainstream leaders such as Booker T. Washington and W. E. B. Du Bois as black nationalists along with Marcus Garvey and the Nation of Islam.[6] Steven Hahn has explored both black and white agrarian movements in the South and found racial nationalism only among the former—even though the rural blacks he studied aimed at inclusion in the American political community.[7] In most studies of nationalism, such movements for political inclusion, despite group solidarity, would be treated as expressions of civic nationalism. The American scholarly community has treated black nationalism as sui genus, which largely explains why it has been a cipher in the broader discourse on nationalism. The usual core definition of nationalism— movements for and maintenance of political sovereignty over a territory, or at least self-rule in a multinational state—is applied to neither blacks nor whites. When this widely accepted definition is applied, white nationalism has been bountiful in America and black nationalism has been relatively minor. American historiography is inside out.

Ethnoracial nationalism differs from its civic counterpart in making racial or ethnic identity the basis for belonging to the nation.[8] For ethnoracial nationalists, a nation must be racially if not ethnically homogeneous, and while the presence of racial or ethnic aliens might be tolerated in the homeland, they cannot be part of the political community. As long as few blacks were free, America's view of itself as a people based on ideals remained largely undisturbed. Yet, the growing free black population in the North and the abolitionist movement brought the question to the fore. With the rise of the movement to colonize free blacks, integral

nationalism, attenuated as it was, appeared in the United States generations before it arrived in Europe. Leading statesmen such as Thomas Jefferson, Henry Clay, and Abraham Lincoln envisioned an America free of
blacks.[9] Prior to the war, civic nationalism prevailed only in a few states
in the Northeast, and no major political party, especially the Republicans,
championed the idea of blacks as citizens of either their states or the federal government. Born of the desire to keep the West free and white, the
Republican Party became the unlikely champions of civic nationalism.[10]

Full-bodied expressions of civic ideals, the Fourteenth and Fifteenth
Amendments to the Constitution represented America's version of official nationalism. Hugh Seton-Watson and Benedict Anderson have
shown how the dynasties of Europe responded to the popular ethnoracial nationalisms coursing through the continent by constructing official
nationalisms that naturalized the foreign rulers and the polyglot peoples
and races who composed their empires. America, of course, had no crown
seeking to maintain its legitimacy, and no empire to bring into the fold.[11]
Yet America's new official nationalism, like those in Europe, countered
the popular ethnoracial understandings of the nation by attempting to
make citizens of alien races. In having to contend with its own old regimes
in the South and West, Republicans had all of the challenges of those
seeking to implement radical change. "The model of official nationalism,"
writes Anderson, "assumes its relevance above all at the moment when
revolutionaries successfully take control of the state, and are for the first
time in a position to use the power of the state in pursuit of their vision."[12]
Shaped by the abolitionist movement, the vision of the Radical Republicans would prove difficult to implement and impossible to maintain.
The Democratic Party forthrightly opposed black citizenship, and the U.S.
Supreme Court would become the brake against the rapid advance of civic
ideals imposed from above. The Republican Party succeeded in gaining
approval of the new nationalism in the North, placing the states and the
whites of the region on the path to accepting blacks as citizens. However
derived, the acceptance of an ethnoracial group's inclusion by other citizens, not legal declarations, is the true measure of civic nationalism.[13]

In the South, the river refused to bend toward civic nationalism. Transforming free blacks and the former slaves into citizens did not sit well
with most Southerners. They thought of America as a white nation and,
unlike Northerners, were expected to accept large percentages of blacks
as members of their political communities. To prevent federal military

intervention, Southerners rarely assaulted the language of civic nationalism head-on and instead adopted phrases such as "keeping the Negro in
his place" and "the South is a white man's country." In his famous essay
on white supremacy as the South's central theme, the Southerner Ulrich
B. Phillips relied on their language to make his case, silencing its contradiction to American ideals. Subsequent historians, revisionists and post-
revisionists alike, have rejected Phillips's static and decidedly southern
interpretation. For both schools of conflict historians, the debate has been
over whether racism or class conflict has been the central theme, obscur-
ing white nationalism in the American South.

## II

Historians have thought of racism as the sole ideology of white supremacists.[14] Only Guion Johnson has explored white supremacy as an ideology,
and even she invoked racism as its justification.[15] Though they mingle
together well, white supremacy and racism are distinct ideologies. White
supremacy had a separate origin, a unique set of ideas and beliefs, and its
own long life. Racism mixes well with an assortment of other ideologies,
ranging from nationalism to communism. Although they are opponents
of white supremacy, many civic nationalists have also been inveterate racists. One pointed example must suffice. Radicals like Ohio's senator Benjamin Wade could countenance black citizenship but could hardly suffer
personal interactions with black people. In 1851, shortly after arriving in
Washington, Wade complained about the smell of blacks. His meals were
"all cooked by niggers until I can smell and taste the nigger." As late as
1873 the civic nationalist complained that he wanted a European servant
"because he was 'sick and tired of niggers.'"[16] The struggle to preserve the
Union compelled most Republicans to blend civic nationalism with their
racism and to see blacks as part of the imagined community, however
inferior and personally offensive they thought them to be.

It is more than coincidental that white supremacy developed as a popular ideology only with the advent of Radical Reconstruction as a response
to what Southerners perceived as the "black supremacy." As the Southerner Edward Allen Pollard phrased it, "Military rule and Negro Supremacy become the short definition of 'Reconstruction.'"[17] Black supremacy
conjured up the imagery of the Revolution of Saint-Domingue and Des-
salines' integral black nationalism, his slaughter and exclusion of whites

from citizenship, making Haiti a black supremacy.[18] It was the struggle against "Negro Rule" or "black supremacy," however removed from reality, that gave birth to white supremacy as the ideology of Southerners' resistance.

The core of the ideology of white supremacy was the straightforward nationalist belief that Southerners, along with other whites, should govern themselves and all non-white people in what they considered to be their homeland. Southerners fashioned and articulated white supremacy in response to their sudden, dramatic loss of power over their own lives and destiny. It is not easy to view the world from the eyes of oppressors, but it is necessary to comprehend what it meant to Southerners to lose their supremacy and be put under what they considered the supremacy of another race. In January 1868 a conservative committee in Alabama called for a day of prayer to ask God that the state be delivered "from the horrors of negro domination." Not counting on divine intervention, the committee petitioned their conquerors in Congress to make white Yankees their overlords: "Continue over us, if you will do so, your own rule by the sword. Send down among us honorable and upright men of your own people, of the race to which you and we belong. . . . But do not, we implore you, abdicate your rule over us, by transferring us to the blighting, brutalizing, and unnatural dominion of an alien and inferior race, a race which has never exhibited sufficient administrative ability for the good government."[19] In the minds of Southerners, the world had been turned on its head—inferior black aliens had been given a supremacy over them. Here was the ethnoracial nightmare of Thomas Jefferson's prophecy of blacks pitted against whites in a war of extermination. Southerners did not recoil in fear for long. They constructed *an ideology* of white supremacy, and created a movement to restore the *condition*.

For the historian Barbara J. Fields, when Southerners invoked the phrase "white supremacy" they were not doing much more than mouthing a slogan that signified very little, was devoid of belief, and aimed at uniting whites through calculated imprecision.[20] In political discourse there was nothing opaque about the concept of white supremacy, though the words may seem vacuous to the modern mind tutored to dismiss biological notions of race and unfamiliar with the political concept of supremacy. The slogan encapsulated its advocates' ideological core—their belief that whites should govern blacks—and reflected their will to rule the states that constituted what they considered *their* homeland. It was a rejection of the new official nationalism that attempted to make black citizens, persons who shared in American sovereignty, had a claim to respect, and enjoyed a mutuality of rights, obligations, and duties. As an ideology, white supremacy was an affirmation of Chief Justice Taney's 1857 ruling that blacks were not citizens with inalienable rights. Like all nationalist ideologies, white supremacy did not address the nature of the social relations of those deemed the people, and it served the class interests of the poor whites the least. Yet in relation to blacks, it, like all nationalisms, defined *who* constituted the people, *who* should govern, *who* should hold positions of authority, and *who* should be the beneficiaries of state goods and services. Intrinsically, racism makes no such demands, but nationalisms do.

Rather than returning to war against the central state for its official nationalism, Southerners pummeled its would-be beneficiaries, often gratuitously, making it clear that they meant to govern themselves and blacks. Simultaneously, they professed their loyalty to the general government and implored Northerners to share their ethnoracial vision of the American people. In North Carolina, as white Republicans abandoned the party with the passage of the Civil Rights Act of 1875, one announced that he did so "for the preservation of constitutional government and the purity and salvation of the Anglo-Saxon race of our great land." As Southerners waged their battle for Redemption in South Carolina, southern papers carried a letter of a white woman from Hamburg, the scene of the notorious massacre of blacks, decrying the lack of racial loyalty among Northerners: "The North generally is so much more attached to the African than to the Anglo-Saxon race, that it will believe everything for the former and everything against the latter."[21] As the sociologist Craig Calhoun has put it, "nationalism is the rhetoric or discourse in which attempts are made to establish who the relevant people are."[22] In the aftermath of military defeat, confronted by civic nationalism, Southerners swallowed their Confederate pride, pined about their Lost Cause, and pursued the new cause of white Americanism.[23] In the plainest language, "white supremacy," they insisted on home rule under white patriarchy.

Rarely has an ideology been so clear and its resulting policy prescriptions so straightforward. White supremacists believed blacks should not have the right to vote, serve on grand juries, or hold elected offices and other positions of authority. These and more inalienable rights were taken when possible and granted only when necessary to placate the central state. Increasingly barred from trial juries, black people found their property, liberty, and lives in the hands of people who rejected their citizenship. Throughout Reconstruction and after, the election and appointment of blacks to official positions, including postal positions, roiled Southerners, and the most hard-core nationalists challenged black education altogether. As a nationalist ideology fashioned to meet the new crisis of the official nationalism, white supremacy called for a return to the antebellum status quo in which free blacks were not citizens.

Southern elites had no need to invent a white nationalist tradition. Its potency arose from asking Southerners, a preexisting, self-governing community, to band together as a people and recover the power that had just been taken. Rights lost are often more powerful than rights denied. Whites had governed themselves and blacks, slave and free, for generations. Only a decade before, northern Democrats had coined the phrase "white supremacy" and made it part of national debates, and the Supreme Court had affirmed it. As ideologies go, white supremacy must have seemed awfully natural, much more so than the central state's *naturalization* of a race of aliens by constitutional amendment or any proposed interracial alliances based on civic ideals. In their civic nationalism it was the radicals who sought to invent tradition, and consensus and conflict historians have followed suit, reading black citizenship back into the Declaration of Independence.[24]

So misunderstood is white supremacy that it is often confused with attitudes of superiority.[25] Historically, supremacy had nothing to do with attitudes and everything to do with the affairs between groups competing for sovereignty, especially over a given territory. It was commonly used during the eighteenth and nineteenth centuries as European powers, independent republics, indigenous peoples, and slaves vied for freedom and liberty, on the one hand, and for sovereignty on the other. Supremacy concerned power and authority, the power of one people or entity to impose its will on another. It denoted the power relationship between kings and their subjects, the pope and the emperors of western Europe, and republics and their rivals. When a supremacy appeared to be challenged, those exercising it demanded that their subordinates acknowledge their inferior power position. The pope demanded that the kings of Europe acknowledge his supremacy; the king of England demanded it of the colonies; and the United States demanded it from Indian tribes.[26] And in the post-emancipation South, the overwhelming majority of Southerners demanded it from blacks. In his authoritative American dictionary, Noah Webster defined supremacy as a "state of being supreme or in the highest station of power; highest authority or power." Given that supremacy was about power, both raw and refined, he needed only one word—suprem-acy—to define sovereignty.[27]

It is thus hard to imagine an ideology more outside the pale of civic nationalism than one that calls for one race to exercise sovereignty over all others. Within a nation-state, struggles for supremacy or sovereignty most often took place between descent groups, explaining the tendency of antebellum Southerners to see themselves increasingly in ethnic terms. Rarely has supremacy been part of the discourse of gender and class con-flict, for the women and the poor of the same race have always been con-sidered members of the nation, regardless of their palpably inferior rights. A nation consists of persons who recognize each other's equal status in the political community, regardless of the low regard one might have for others' race, ethnicity, or gender and their standing in shaping the nation's destiny. Holding together disparate peoples has ever been the challenge of nations based on civic ideals.[28] Most Southerners rejected blacks as co-nationals. They felt no sense of kinship and fraternity with blacks, not to mention mutual obligations and duties. To borrow a phrase from Bene-dict Anderson, "horizontal comradeship" with those identified with the black race remained an anathema to most Southerners.[29] In a nation-state founded on the idea that the people were the sovereigns, citizens were those who *shared in* rather than *vied for* sovereignty. Rights alone do not make the citizen.

Within a nation-state, movements for supremacy between ethnoracial groups are nothing less than struggles to define or redefine the people. In the broad scope of nationalism, struggles for supremacy are of great importance, for they signal a nation lost, a nation-state badly formed, or a new one born in and of blood. Lincoln's horribly violent quest for "a more perfect union" is a case in point, and the thoroughness of their defeat placed Southerners on the path of becoming the most patriotic Ameri-cans, reducing their nascent ethnic identity. In multiethnic or multiracial states, ethnoracial wars or cleansings are the source of constant fear, and the late-nineteenth-century South brimmed with prophecies of race wars and endured numerous armed skirmishes. The existence of an ideology of white supremacy articulated by a major political party is prima facie evidence that the official nationalism, the Radical Republicans' version of a better union, had not taken hold. Having survived one threat from a competing nationalism, the general government faced another.

## III

As ethnoracial nationalists bent on self-rule, the Redeemers included all Southerners who participated in the movement, not just the politicians elected to office. In their thinking, home rule for Southerners could be achieved by rendering blacks politically inert first through solidarity and violence and ultimately by asserting the powers provided states in America's federalist system. Federalism mattered. Accepting the official nationalism at face value, historians have treated the Southerners' struggle to "redeem" their states as merely a violent phase of electoral politics in which the status of black citizenship was not at stake.[30] So buried is the ethnoracial nationalism of Redemption, so ignored is the broader social movement that those who are less familiar with the history of American South might think that blacks, too, were considered Southerners and that they, too, redeemed their states from Yankees. Yet Redemption had meaning for Southerners precisely because it was *their* collective struggle for home rule against Yankees *and* blacks. Redemption was particularism writ large, a veritable ethnoracial movement that broke the central state's will to make its official nationalism a reality. Writing in 1890, one Redeemer from Mississippi summed up their eight-year struggle against Reconstruction through secret organization: "We pledged ourselves to be true to the Constitution of the Union, but at the same time, to maintain the supremacy of white civilization. We met by stealth, in secluded room, with curtained windows and shaded lamps, speaking at low breath, because well we knew that discovery meant imprisonment in some Northern fortress. In eight years a returning sense of justice in the North, enabled the people of the South to take charge of their own governments again."[31] The triumph of the Redeemers and the Compromise of 1876 marked the central state's first betrayal of the Negro and the rebirth of the abolitionist myth of black citizenship.

Voting statistics notwithstanding, black citizenship moved from farce to fiction during the course of the late nineteenth century. In pockets of the Upper South blacks participated as free actors in the political community, but even there Redemption entailed limiting their ability to influence statewide policies.[32] Except in counties where they held supermajorities, blacks in the Deep South lost the exercise of free suffrage through violence, labor coercion, election-law trickery, and bribes. Voluntary black Democrats, graciously allowed by the ruling race to vote for the white man's party, were forbidden to participate in the selection of candidates and quickly denied the opportunity to govern.[33] Between 1890 and 1908, black participation in political life became fiction as the central state turned its head and allowed Southerners to trample on the Reconstruction amendments through an array of "color-blind" measures enacted by self-proclaimed white supremacists. Everywhere but in America such a fundamental discrimination that removes the political free agency and participation of one people and places them under the supremacy of another would typically be treated as ethnoracial nationalism. In America it is reduced to but one more example of racism, flattening out the historical reality of blacks in both regions and yet not seen as erasing the nation.[34]

In the interim between Redemption and legal disfranchisement, a period of less than fifteen years in many cases, historians have stressed the possibility for progressive change, employing the term "fluid" as a metaphor to describe the malleability of race relations. Advanced by C. Vann Woodward, the fluidity thesis is a rejection of both U. B. Phillips's static order of white supremacy, the liberal historians' unabated racism, and Rayford Logan's slow descent to a nadir. For Logan and the liberal students of racism there was no indigenous southern alternative to racial oppression; only the federal government could have prevented Southerners from stripping blacks of their rights.[35] In contrast, Woodward believed that Populism, a homegrown movement, represented a viable alternative to the rigid, state-enforced racial order that followed. While his Southerners were racists, he believed political conflict could transform them and lead blacks and whites toward a new yet unimagined racial order.[36] Woodward's interpretation, especially his timing of segregation and the potential of Populism, has ever had its dissenters among those who view southern racism as all-consuming and the South as unchanging.[37] Yet it engendered a romance among historians that has endured and prospered as the opposing schools have weakened. It has inspired a generation of neo-Woodwardians, whose divining rods have led them to focus on the Upper South, where the fluidity thesis works best. Virtually all concede that the period was no "golden age" of black-white relations but insist that despite violence and racism, interracialism lived, making progressive change possible.[38] Were one to map the terrain of white nationalism in the aftermath of Redemption, sections of both states were relative bastions of civic nationalism, places where white men did not wholly govern themselves (and everyone else) and uppity, middle-class Negroes proliferated.[39] In the Deep South, primarily in large cities, union interracialism kept civic ideals alive in their organizational structures. Their commitment to racism and the party of white supremacy notwithstanding, white workers discovered that some degree of power sharing with black workers was necessary for unionism to function.[40] The consequence of focusing on the Upper South and Deep South urban unionism is that the margins of black-white relations have overwhelmed the center of the narrative. In 1900 a full 80 percent of blacks in former Confederate states lived in the cotton South. Yet the nine states that constitute that enormous, dry, and arid desert of white nationalism appear as specks on the historian's conceptual horizon.[41]

If the students of racism have painted Southerners with too broad a brush and been blind to change, the Woodwardians have overstated the amount of racial fluidity, understated or dismissed its viscosity, and misidentified its main source. Slowly but steadily, the white supremacist regimes of the Bourbons were forced by competing elites within the White Man's Party to eviscerate the official citizenship of African Americans. They outlawed and punished interracial marriages, instituted racial segregation as they expanded state institutions, disarmed most black rifle clubs that provided self-defense, pushed black appointees and elected officials from offices, removed blacks from juries that decided the fate of their persons, property, and liberty, and increased the flow of the disempowered race into county chain gangs and the state-run convict-lease systems.[42] Enforced by counties, vagrancy laws, color-blind in letter only, tied blacks to farming, if not to a given parcel of land.[43] Neither working-class allies nor the pledges of paternalist Redeemers in high office could protect blacks and alter the downward flow.

Draconian laws and institutions notwithstanding, popular white nationalism was the central feature of the redeemed South. Once blacks ceased to be someone's property, Southerners, as individuals and a group, felt empowered to discipline and punish them for violations of laws and Southern(ers') customs. What may be called Negrocide or Africide, the act of killing blacks without cause or compunction, has never been studied, let alone its frequency assessed. It is likely that Negrocide often reflected racist hatred, but it is as likely that such killings at times involved an integral nationalist desire to rid the South of blacks. Whites known as regulators or whitecaps also meted out extralegal punishment against blacks, as well as whites, for violating Southern(ers') customs, including interracial relationships. They chased blacks off their land, forced others into labor contracts, and cleansed still others from their counties.[44] As a group behavior that flouted the power of the state, lynching was the ultimate form of white popular sovereignty. When taken as a whole, they reflect the will of whites to govern themselves and the blacks in their homeland.

Given that the authority of southern states to enforce the will of Southerners was hindered by the central state, measuring fluidity without exploring its viscosity can be exceedingly misleading. This is especially so since the Redeemers inherited a constitutional order created by civic nationalists. On the other hand, the sources of friction in society—whether on the basis of class or race—were local and often reflected a displeasure with both race and class relations. Between elections, civic and ethnoracial nationalists struggled to make the South reflect their ideologies in the fields, factories, town squares, and city streets. Never trusting the Bourbons whom they perceived as coddling blacks, Southerners took it out on the black community, despite their tendency to fight back. And it was an ongoing battle that often involved harsh verbal exchanges, jostling in public, violent skirmishes, gunplay, riots, and pogroms. White supremacists chafed against the laws, local and national, that sought to pump civic ideals into black-white relations, leading many to adopt ultrademocratic, extralegal means of controlling blacks and whites who ran afoul of their ethnonationalist vision. From emancipation into the twentieth century, popular white nationalism imbued black-white relations with the viscosity and combustibility of heavy crude oil, and racial fires ignited constantly.

In the age of popular white nationalism, being a white supremacist involved much more than enjoying white privileges, which has been too often the focus of whiteness studies. In the form of popular nationalism, whiteness may have provided a psychological wage, but it also demanded a personal tax.[45] Subscribing to white supremacy entailed ethnoracial duties and obligations, calling for ad hoc services to police and protect Southern(ers') customs, *their* white women, and their supremacy.[46] Possessive and masculinist as conservative nationalisms tend to be, white nationalism saddled white men with burdensome and dangerous responsibilities. Belonging could mean participating in lynchings and riots, mobilizing late at night to quell alleged black "insurrections," engaging in race wars, serving in posses to hunt recalcitrant blacks, enlisting in bands of regulators, and planning pogroms mislabeled as riots.[47] Keeping Negroes in their place could alter the pattern of one's life. Those who volunteered for racial service could and sometimes did die carrying out their ethnoracial missions, for late-nineteenth-century blacks had a disturbing habit of arming themselves and fighting back. For reasons ranging from cowardice to heroic adherence to civic ideals, some Southerners refused to shoulder the burden of racial duty; this other South, when the question of social equality is put aside, was far more numerous than the handful of committed racial egalitarians.[48] They lived under the social stigma of being traitors and nigger lovers, and they, too, faced the possibility of nocturnal visits from whitecappers, who saw policing wayward whites as part of their charge. No small wonder that the vast majority of Southerners closed ranks, or remained silent. Popular white nationalism and the viscosity it engendered was the central feature of the fluid age of Redemption.

The unfixed nature of affairs in the Redeemers' racial order was more in laws than Southerners, more in the limits of internal and external controls than the desire of Southerners to be racial sovereigns. Violations of their cultural norms occurred with what most Southerners considered alarming frequency. For every white woman who took a black lover, there were hundreds of Southerners who wanted none of it in their homeland. For every planter who dragooned blacks to vote for his preferred Democratic candidate or watched autonomous blacks vote Republican or Populist, there were hundreds of outraged Southerners who believed blacks had no place in white people's political affairs. For every black politician or appointee who clung to office, many Southerners longed to have them purged. Far from being nobodies, many of these Southerners were persons of standing, and most brandished redeemer credentials themselves. Pitchfork Ben Tillman, to name one prominent example, waged his war for disfranchisement from 1876 until he obtained his objective in 1895, bruiting his participation in the Hamburg Riot. Maintaining norms with an inadequate state apparatus or with a weak-willed party in power is often a vicious, bloody business, requiring more popular vigilance than volunteers can always muster. Under such conditions, interracial coitus happened, black votes were cast, uppity Negroes got saucy, and black

vagrants exercised their right of locomotion and frightened Southerners on dark, lonely roads. Breaches had to be tolerated unless and until
popular white nationalists put the Negro back in his place. Historians
have emphasized the threat to Bourbon rule from the left and have largely
ignored the factional fighting within the ranks of the White Man's Party
and white supremacists in general. This was the flammable nature of the
fluid relations between blacks and whites during the long decade of the
1880s, stretching from the late 1870s and in places to the early 1890s.

In no former Confederate state did the civic nationalism of the Republicans, Readjusters, and Populists ever come close to breaking the grip of
the ideology of white supremacy over Southerners by enlarging and maintaining their ranks. Even in North Carolina, where Populists fused with
Republicans, the exercise of civic ideals that placed blacks in positions of
authority over whites violated a cardinal principle of white supremacy
and led to a backlash that culminated in the Wilmington Pogrom and
disfranchisement.[49] Black voting was bad enough; Negroes in power was
insufferable. Rayford Logan understood best that the central state, not
southern wellsprings, had irrigated the former Confederate states with
laws based on civic ideals and that its hand controlled the spigot. In pursuit of sectional reunion and empire, the federal government betrayed
all civic nationalists in the South, unionists, agrarians, and the "better
classes" of both races. Its retreat from civic nationalism best explains the
ultimate triumph of statist white nationalism in the South and the array
of laws that transformed "official" citizens into the hapless subjects of local
and state governments.

Completing the movement to remove blacks from the political community through color-blind disfranchisement, the Progressives, a new
generation of white supremacists, relied more on government and experts
to create a new white nationalist order that was less dependent on popular
mobilization. Under their regimes, affairs with blacks would be managed
primarily by laws, bureaucracies, sheriffs, and deputies.[50] Ensconced in
the new interpretation of American federalism, white supremacy as a condition was again secure without constant reinforcement of the common
Southerner. Disfranchisement left blacks to infrapolitics; state mandated
and fully rationalized, segregation hemmed blacks in socially; sanctioned
and mandated discrimination in employment kept most economically
poor; and exclusion from juries made their property and liberty fragile.
Indeed, race relations became rigid rather than fluid, and with the fluid

went most of the viscosity. With white supremacy as an unchallenged ideology of governance and a universal condition, whiteness moved toward pure privilege as the new century progressed.

Historians have turned Jim Crow or segregation, the least-oppressive feature of the white supremacist regimes, into a metonymy for an entire system of oppression. John Cell went so far as to call segregation the ideology of the period.[51] Yet to reduce white nationalists to segregationists is to mistake their method for their madness, a single policy for their ideology. Although Barbara Fields rejects white supremacy as an ideology, she is right to point out that segregation was "an act of political power."[52] White supremacists *imposed* segregation on blacks. In theory it could have been a democratically derived, pluralist policy, as it had been in education during radical Reconstruction. In fact, however, Progressive Era white supremacists, taking their cue from the Supreme Court, made segregation all-pervasive once they had disfranchised blacks and thereby removed them from the field of politics. It was an exercise of the sovereignty of Southerners and reflected the will of the white people, not simply the demagogues voted into office.

To argue that most Southerners, when left to their own devices, rejected governance by civic ideals is neither to deny class conflict nor to overlook progressive efforts flowing from the structural legacies of Reconstruction.[53] Interracial unionism could thrive to the degree that it confined itself to the workplace, and so too could the agrarian movement as long as it stayed clear of politics.[54] Dividing the farmers' movement, the Populists aimed for more, and so they often offered blacks more. They launched a frontal assault on ethnoracial nationalism and established a region-wide, homegrown version of civic nationalism. The movement embraced blacks as members of the political community who could vote and hold positions of power over white citizens.[55] Though it treated blacks as junior partners, southern Populism would have provided a counterbalance to white nationalism and deprived its proponents of supremacy. And that was the problem. They asked Southerners to cease to be a self-governing people and accept blacks as part of *the people* who would shape the future. Most Southerners rejected their appeal to place class over ethnoracial ties, and the white Populists found themselves social pariahs for embracing civic nationalism. When their movement failed, the Populists did not capitulate to racism, as Woodward asserted. Like the white Republicans before them, they had never quit their racism. It was the ideology of white supremacy that they had abandoned, and it was to white supremacy that they surrendered.[56]

## IV

Under white nationalism, African Americans in the South were at once the "official" citizens of the general state and unofficial subjects of the southern states. Like their ethnoracial counterparts in northern states, they faced racism, but unlike them they took virtually no part in the political community and lived under the laws imposed on them by the sovereign race. In many ways, the political units of black subjugation were more important than their standing before the general government. Counties and states exercised power over property and social welfare, education and opportunity, taxation and service, liberty and death. If juries rather than mobs would increasingly decide the fate of blacks, it would be the white man's decision and *his* alone.[57] Blacks occupied a space so far outside of Southerners' "circle of we" that officials often stopped recording black marriages and deaths, and like true subjects they were prevented altogether from serving in the state-based National Guard and police forces.[58] In the pursuit of happiness and the avoidance of persecution, being a Georgian or Virginian was far more important than being an American.

Recognizing white supremacy as a nationalist ideology enriches our understanding of American nationalism by evincing that ethnoracial nationalism was an ideology of governance, not simply a discursive and representational cultural phenomenon. If state-based white nationalism proves the history of American civic nationalism to be partially a myth, its demise reveals discontinuity in both the South and the United States. To rediscover the lost world of white nationalism is to reveal as much racial progress as oppression. The aim is not to equate Southerners with Nazis, nor to pose the civic nationalism of the North as a racial promised land. Although exploring white supremacy as an ideology and a practice presents a late-nineteenth-century South that fully incorporates political will and violence back into discussions of racial malleability, it also points to progress in civic ideals, including black voting, after the demise of the white primary.

As an ideology, white supremacy had an existence too brief to serve as the central theme of southern history, and yet too potent and dynamic to serve as a backdrop for studies of racism or class conflict.[59] The metonymy of segregation has obscured the decline of white supremacy as a hegemonic ideology and a condition. Almost a decade before the assault on segregation, civic nationalists, laboring across racial and class lines, challenged and in places defeated white supremacists in the urban South.[60] After World War II the majority of Southerners were more committed to segregation and racism than to any brand of white nationalism. By studying how civic and ethnoracial nationalism competed for the hearts and minds of Southerners, we can better understand how civic ideals finally sprouted in a bed of racism and how America's central myth of civic nationalism became a belated reality.

## Notes

I would like to thank Allison Dorsey, Robert J. Norrell, and James B. Oakes, along with the editors, for their critical readings of this essay.

1. This essay capitalizes the term *Southerner*. During this period, whites in the South viewed themselves and were viewed by others as a people, and they most often used *Southerner* as a proper noun to distinguish themselves from others. Because they mobilized politically and organized socially on this basis, it would distort history to erase their peoplehood by treating all who lived in the South as Southerners or using the term as a common noun. Moreover, by underscoring their peoplehood, we highlight what it meant to non-Southerners to be so excluded.

To recover the world of white nationalism, it is necessary to revert back to the original meaning of certain terms. Today, referring to blacks as Southerners is standard usage, along with using the term as a common noun. A product of civic nationalism, this usage distorts the past by erasing the fundamental division between blacks and whites in the South and removing the ethnic dimension of white identity.

2. See Dan T. Carter, *When the War Was Over: The Failure of Self-Reconstruction in the South* (Baton Rouge: Louisiana State University Press, 1985); William C. Harris, *Presidential Reconstruction in Mississippi* (Baton Rouge: Louisiana State University, 1967), 122.

3. The absence of studies of white nationalism in America simply reflects the continued influence of the consensus school of American historiography despite a half-century of revisionism. Louis Hartz and his post–World War II contemporaries boasted that the United States was exceptional, contrasting it with the ethnoracial origins and tendencies of European nations. Foreign observers from Alexis de Tocqueville to Gunnar Myrdal, from Hans Kohn to Eric Hobsbawm, have shared this view. Kohn bruited that the United States was held together by "an idea, the idea of liberty under the law as expressed in the Constitution." Hobsbawm has written, "The revolutionary concept of nation as constituted by the deliberate political option of its citizens is, of course, still preserved in a pure form in the USA. Americans are those who wish to be." Hans Kohn, *Nationalism: Its Meaning and History* (1965; reprint, New York: D. Van Nostrand, 1971),

19–20. E. J. Hobsbawm, *Nations and Nationalism since 1780: Programme, Myth, Reality* (New York: Cambridge, 1992), 88. See also Walker Connor, *Ethnonationalism: The Quest for Understanding* (Princeton: Princeton University Press, 1994), 47–51; and Anthony D. Smith, *The Ethnic Origins of Nations* (Oxford: Blackwell, 1937), 150. This view persists even as scholars began to recognize that even civic nation-states have bouts of ethnoracial nationalism. Anthony D. Smith, *National Identity* (1991; reprint, Reno: University of Nevada Press, 1993), 13; see also Craig Calhoun, *Nationalism* (Minneapolis: University of Minnesota Press, 1997), 89, 91–92.

4. In recent years, scholars have come closer to exploring white nationalism in American history. Rogers Smith explores what he calls the ascriptive nature of citizenship in American political culture, and Gary Gerstle has written of an ethnoracial tradition in American political culture, focusing on national figures and culture rather than movements, state and local politicians, and policies. He has, however, introduced the dichotomy between civic and racial nationalism to U.S. historiography. Rogers M. Smith, *Civic Ideals: Conflicting Visions of Citizenship in American History* (New Haven: Yale University Press, 1997); Gary Gerstle, "Race and the Myth of the Liberal Consensus," *Journal of American History* 82 (September 1995): 579–86, and *The Crucible of Race: Race and Nation in the Twentieth Century* (Princeton University Press, 2001). More recently, a few scholars have been willing to call white nationalism by its name. Paul Ortiz, *Emancipation Betrayed: The Hidden History of Black Organizing and White Violence in Florida from Reconstruction to the Bloody Election of 1920* (Berkeley: University of California Press, 2005), 85; Robert J. Norrell, *Up from History: The Life of Booker T. Washington* (Cambridge: Belknap Press of Harvard University Press, 2009), 49; and Matthew J. Clavin, *Toussaint Louverture and the American Civil War: The Peril of a Second Haitian Revolution* (Philadelphia: University of Pennsylvania Press, 2010), 161.

5. The list of scholars who have affirmed the existence of black nationalism in America while not seeing signs of white nationalism is long, including scholars writing from various perspectives and disciplines. Eugene D. Genovese, "The Legacy of Slavery and the Roots of Black Nationalism," *Studies on the Left* 6 (November–December 1966): 418; Walker Conner, *Ethnonationalism: The Quest for Understanding* (Princeton: Princeton University Press, 1994), 49.

6. While blacks have produced nationalists and nationalisms that are in keeping with widely used definitions, the term has been used expansively to cover what should typically be considered ethnoracial politics and racial solidarity. The expansive definition is a by-product of the Black Power movement. See John H. Bracey, August Meier and Elliott Rudwick, eds., *Black Nationalism in America* (Indianapolis: Bobbs-Merrill, 1970); Sterling Stuckey, *The Ideological Origins of Black Nationalism* (Boston: Beacon Press, 1972); and William Jeremiah Moses, *The Golden Age of Black Nationalism, 1850–1930* (New York: Oxford University Press, 1988).

7. Steven Hahn, *The Roots of Southern Populism: Yeoman Farmers and the Transformation of the Georgia Upcountry, 1850–1890* (New York: Oxford University Press, 1984) and *A Nation under Our Feet: Black Political Struggles in the Rural South from Slavery to the Great Migration* (Boston: Belknap Press of Harvard University Press, 2005), 5–9.

8. Even scholars who reject ethnoracial identities as being determinative of the

formation of any modern nations recognize the challenge of such identities to national formation. See Calhoun, *Nationalism*, 48–49.

9. No attempt is made here to equate America's dominant integral nationalism during the nineteenth century with the full expressions of the twentieth. No major leader envisioned a state to which individuals had to subordinate themselves for the national good. American leaders, however, were divided over whether national fraternity could exist between racially diverse nations or within a racially heterogeneous nation. While the colonization of blacks and the exclusion of Asians were relatively humane, these policies reflected the ideas of integral nationalism. For political leaders in favor of colonization, see Eric Foner, "Lincoln and Colonization," in *Our Lincoln: New Perspective on Lincoln and His World*, ed. Foner (New York: Norton, 2008), 135–66.

10. Eric Foner, *Free Men, Free Soil, Free Labor: The Ideology of the Republican Party before the Civil War* (New York: Oxford University Press, 1995).

11. Hugh Seton-Watson, *Nations and States: An Enquiry into the Origins of Nations and the Politics of Nationalism* (Boulder: Westview Press, 1977), 148; and Benedict Anderson, *Imagined Communities: Reflections on the Origin and Spread of Nationalism* (London: Verso, 1991).

12. Benedict Anderson, *Imagined Communities: Reflections on the Origin and Spread of Nationalism*, rev. ed. (London: Verso, 2006), 159.

13. Ernest Gellner, *Nations and Nationalism* (Ithaca: Cornell University Press, 1983), 7.

14. Their interpretive differences notwithstanding, George M. Fredrickson and Barbara Fields treated racism as the ideology of Southerners. Fredrickson saw white supremacy as a condition, while Fields explicitly rejected it as an ideology. Others like John Cell thought of white supremacy as an ethos. To be sure, some leading scholars such as Glenda Gilmore have seen white supremacy as an ideology but not explored it as such. See George M. Fredrickson, *The Black Image in the White Mind; the Debate on Afro-American Character and Destiny, 1817–1914* (New York: Harper & Row, 1971), 187–93; Barbara J. Fields, "Race and Ideology in American History," in *Region, Race, and Reconstruction: Essays in Honor of C. Vann Woodward*, ed. J. Morgan Kousser and James M. McPherson (New York: Oxford University Press, 1982), 143–77; John Cell, *The Highest State of White Supremacy: The Origins of Segregation in South Africa and the American South* (New York: Cambridge University Press, 1982), ix; Glenda Gilmore, *Gender and Jim Crow: Women and the Politics of White Supremacy in North Carolina, 1896–1920* (Chapel Hill: University of North Carolina Press, 1996), 199.

15. Guion Johnson, "The Ideology of White Supremacy, 1876–1910," in *Essays in Southern History*, ed. Fletcher Melvin Green (Chapel Hill: University of North Carolina Press, 1949), 124–56.

16. Quoted in V. Jacque Voegeli, *Free but Not Equal: The Midwest and the Negro during the Civil War* (Chicago: University of Chicago Press, 1967), 180–82.

17. Edward A. Pollard, *The Lost Cause Regained* (New York: G. W. Carleton, 1868), 81.

18. "Slavery in the United States," *Southern Quarterly Review* 12 (July 1847): 105; Henry Brougham, *Opinions of Henry Brougham, Esq. on Negro Slavery with Remarks* (London: Whitmore and Fenn, 1826), 24; George C. Rable, *But There Was No Peace: The*

*Role of Violence in the Politics of Reconstruction* (Baton Rouge: Louisiana State University Press, 1978). For the role of the Haitian Revolution in the Civil War, see Clavin, *Toussaint Louverture.*

19. "Alabama," *American Annual Cyclopedia and Register of the Important Events of the Year 1868*, vol. 8 (New York: D. Appleton, 1873), 15–16. For other examples of whites recoiling in fear, see "The State Elections to Virginia: Negro Supremacy the Danger Ahead," *New Orleans Times-Picayune*, November 2, 1867, 2; "An Address to the People of Georgia and the United States," *Macon Weekly Telegraph*, January 10, 1868, 2; "South Carolina Conservative Convention: Address to the People" *Macon Weekly Telegraph*, November 22, 1967, 3; William C. Harris, *The Day of the Carpetbagger: Republican Reconstruction in Mississippi* (Baton Rouge: Louisiana State University Press, 1979), 14.

20. In Fields's estimation, slogans are devoid of beliefs and aim at manipulation, while ideologies are not. She has underestimated slogans. Liberty, freedom, and equality are also slogans with ambiguous meanings, and they, too, have served to rally people across the social fissures of race, class, and gender precisely because they represent deep-seated beliefs communicated in a concise form that is easily unpacked and understood by members of the culture. Fields, "Race and Ideology in American History."

21. "Old Rip on Civil Rights," *Macon Weekly Telegraph*, February 16, 1875, 2; Private Letter from a Lady to a Northern Friend, "South Carolina Horrors: Some Frightful Results of Carpet-Baggers' Rule," *Augusta Chronicle*, September 9, 1876, 1.

22. Calhoun, *Nationalism*, 123.

23. Nina Silber, *The Romance of Reunion: Northerners and the South, 1865–1900* (Chapel Hill: University of North Carolina Press, 1993), 140–50.

24. On the perils of historians and nationalism see David M. Potter, "The Historian's Use of Nationalism and Vice Versa," *American Historical Review* 67, no. 4 (1962): 924–50.

25. James M. Beeby states that Populists "were white supremacists who believed in the 'natural superiority' of whites" and goes on to say that they supported black political inclusion. James M. Beeby, *Revolt of the Tar Heels: The North Carolina Populist Movement, 1890–1901* (Jackson: University Press of Mississippi, 2008), 8–9. See also Carl N. Degler, *Place over Time: The Continuity of Southern Distinctiveness* (Baton Rouge: Louisiana State University Press, 1977), 125.

26. "President of the United States, Communicating Sundry Papers Relating to Indian Affairs," December 11, 1826, Serial Set Vol. No. 149, Session Vol. No. 2; Report: H. Doc. 9 (Washington, D.C.: Gales & Seaton, 1826), 6. See also "Treaty with the Siounes and Ogallalas," in Treaties with several tribes. Communicated to the Senate, January 11, 1826, American State Papers 08; Report: Publication No. 226 (Washington, D.C., 1826), 895.

27. Noah Webster, *An American Dictionary of the English Language Abridged*, rev. ed. (New York: Harper and Brothers, 1844), 774, 812.

28. Anthony D. Smith, *National Identity* (Reno: University of Nevada Press, 1991), 91. Voting was neither a necessary nor sufficient condition of citizenship in the United States—aliens often exercised that right. James H. Kettner, *The Development of American Citizenship, 1608–1870* (Chapel Hill: University of North Carolina Press, 1978), 231n; Al-

exander Keyssar, *The Right to Vote: The Contested History of Democracy in America* (New York: Basic Books, 2000), 32.

29. B. Anderson, *Imagined Communities* (1991 ed.), 7.

30. For prominent examples of Redemption treated from the vantage point of party politics, see Eric Foner, *Reconstruction: America's Unfinished Revolution, 1863–1877* (New York: Oxford University Press, 1984); Michael Perman, *The Road to Redemption: Southern Politics, 1869–1879* (Chapel Hill: University of North Carolina Press, 1984), xiv, 170.

31. Letter to the Editor, "Mr. Gibb's Reply," *Clarion Ledger*, January 16, 1890, 8.

32. J. Morgan Kousser emphasizes ongoing black political participation, but his quantitative methods assume free choice while qualitative evidence suggests that the black vote was controlled. J. Morgan Kousser, *The Shaping of Southern Politics: Suffrage Restriction and the Establishment of the One-Party South, 1880–1910* (New Haven: Yale University Press, 1974); Eric Anderson, *The Black Second: Race and Politics in North Carolina, 1872–1901* (Baton Rouge: Louisiana State University Press, 1981).

33. George Tindall, "The Campaign for the Disfranchisement of Negroes in South Carolina," *Journal of Southern History* 15 (May 1949): 214–15.

34. On racism erasing nation-ness, see B. Anderson, *Imagined Communities* (1991 ed.), 148.

35. Rayford W. Logan, *The Betrayal of the Negro, from Rutherford B. Hayes to Woodrow Wilson* (New York: Collier Books, 1965).

36. C. Vann Woodward, *The Strange Career of Jim Crow* (New York: Oxford University Press, 2001).

37. Joel Williamson, *After Slavery: The Negro in South Carolina during Reconstruction, 1861–1877* (Chapel Hill: University of North Carolina Press, 1965); Howard N. Rabinowitz, "From Exclusion to Segregation: Southern Race Relations, 1865–1890," *Journal of American History* 63 (September 1976): 325–50; and Leon Litwack, *Trouble in Mind: Black Southerners in the Age of Jim Crow* (New York: Vintage, 1999).

38. Gilmore, *Gender and Jim Crow*; Jane Dailey, *Before Jim Crow: The Politics of Race in Postemancipation Virginia* (Chapel Hill: University of North Carolina Press, 2000); Kent Redding, *Making Race, Making Power: North Carolina's Road to Disfranchisement* (Champaign: University of Illinois Press, 2003); Janette Thomas Greenwood, *Bittersweet Legacy: The Black and White "Better Classes" in Charlotte, 1850–1910* (Chapel Hill: University of North Carolina Press, 1994), 3, 78, 150. Scholars have been less sanguine about fluidity in the cotton South. Neil R. McMillen, *Dark Journey: Black Mississippians in the Age of Jim Crow* (Urbana: University of Illinois Press, 1989), 4.

39. Leslie Brown, *Upbuilding Black Durham: Gender, Class, and Black Community Development in the Jim Crow South* (Chapel Hill: University of North Carolina Press, 2008); Gilmore, *Gender and Jim Crow*; Greenwood, *Bittersweet Legacy*.

40. Daniel Letwin, *The Challenge of Interracial Unionism: Alabama Coal Miners, 1878–1921* (Chapel Hill: University of North Carolina Press, 1998), 130–31.

41. Bradley G. Bond, *Political Culture in the Nineteenth-Century South: Mississippi, 1830–1900* (Baton Rouge: Louisiana State University Press, 1995); Stephen Kantrowitz, *Ben Tillman and the Reconstruction of White Supremacy* (Chapel Hill: University of North Carolina Press, 2000).

42. For the struggle to police sex between black men and white women, see Martha Hodes, *White Women, Black Men: Illicit Sex in the Nineteenth-Century South* (New Haven: Yale University Press, 1997), 123–206; Charles Frank Robinson II, *Dangerous Liaisons: Sex and Love in the Segregated South* (Fayetteville: University of Arkansas Press, 2003), 129. Little work has been done on the composition of juries, but it factored in the Redeemer-era exodus from the South, and it is known that in many counties blacks never sat on them. Gilbert Thomas Stephenson, *Race Distinctions in American Laws* (New York: D. Appleton, 1910); George Washington Cable, *The Silent South: Together with the Freedman's Case in Equity and the Convict Lease System* (New York: Scribner, 1885), 91–93; United States Senate, *Report and Testimony of the Select Committee of the United States Senate to Investigate the Causes of the Removal of the Negroes from the Southern States to the Northern States*, Part II, Reports of Committees of the Senate of the United States for the First and Second Sessions of the Forty-Sixth Congress, 1879–1880, Volume 3 (Washington, D.C.: Government Printing Office, 1880); Edward L. Ayers, *Vengeance and Justice: Crime and Punishment in the 19th-Century American South* (New York: Oxford University Press, 1984), 185–222; and Matthew J. Mancini, *One Dies, Get Another* (Columbia: University of South Carolina Press, 1996).

43. Jonathan M. Bryant, *How Curious a Land: Conflict and Change in Greene County, Georgia, 1850–1885* (Chapel Hill: University of North Carolina Press, 1996), 156–57.

44. Before the term "whitecapping" was coined in the late 1880s, the practice of chasing blacks off the land was well established and referred to by different names, including loosely used terms such as "bulldozing" and "regulating." Though the practice is understudied, most scholars view it as starting in the 1890s. Hahn, *A Nation under Our Feet*; Joel Williamson, *The Crucible of Race: Black-White Relations in the American South since Emancipation* (New York: Oxford University Press, 1984), 114; Charles L. Flynn, *White Land, Black Labor: Caste and Class in Late Nineteenth-Century Georgia* (Baton Rouge: Louisiana State University Press, 1983), 55.

45. Born of a passing observation of W. E. B. Du Bois, whiteness studies effectively resume the social psychologist John Dollard's quest to understand what whites gained psychologically from racial oppression while ignoring Dollard's companion concern with psychological losses. Early labor historians who initiated this historiographical movement were well aware of what whites lost politically and economically in failing to reach out across the color line, but, as George Lipsitz warned, many scholars, especially in cultural studies, have failed to pay enough attention to social structure. In almost all cases, scholars have overlooked the personal sacrifices attendant to whiteness inherent in popular ethnoracial nationalism when "the other" refuses to submit. See John Dollard, *Caste and Class in a Southern Town* (New Haven: Yale University Press, 1937); George Lipsitz, "The Possessive Investment in Whiteness: Racialized Social Democracy and the 'White' Problem in American Studies," *American Quarterly* 47 (September 1995): 37: David R. Roediger, *The Wages of Whiteness: Race and the Making of the American Working Class* (London: Verso, 1991).

46. Whiteness studies have overlooked the duty and obligations of whites. Grace Elizabeth Hale, *Making Whiteness: The Culture of Segregation in the South, 1890–1940* (New York: Vintage Books, 1998).

47. Since the rise of modern social science, scholars have debated definitions of riots, and their definitions have been colored by ideological biases. There has been a consensus, however, on the spontaneous, unplanned nature of riots. Despite this, historians have continued to refer to planned, organized pogroms against blacks as riots. For the planning behind the Wilmington Pogrom of 1898 see Helen G. Edmonds, *The Negro and Fusion Politics in North Carolina, 1894–1901* (Chapel Hill: University of North Carolina Press, 1951), 166–67. On spontaneity in rioting see Gary T. Marx, "Issueless Riots," *Annals of the American Academy of Political and Social Science* 391 (September 1970): 24.

48. Measuring racial liberalism by the standards of Reconstruction or the post–World War II era, scholars have often overlooked Southerners who took seriously the idea of black citizenship. Carl N. Degler, *The Other South: Southern Dissenters in the Nineteenth Century* (Boston: Northeastern University Press, 1982).

49. Edmonds, *The Negro and Fusion Politics.*

50. J. Douglas Smith has coined the term "managed race relations" to describe the shift away from violence. He argues that Virginia differed from other states in this regard. His general insight is invaluable, but I believe "managed race relations" was less about interpersonal relations than government policies, including and especially de jure segregation itself. J. Douglas Smith, *Managing White Supremacy: Race, Politics, and Citizenship in Jim Crow Virginia* (Chapel Hill: University of North Carolina Press, 2002), 4–5; William A. Link, *The Paradox of Southern Progressivism, 1880–1930* (Chapel Hill: University of North Carolina Press, 1992), 59–63.

51. Cell, *Highest Stage of White Supremacy*, x.

52. Barbara J. Fields, "'Origins of the New South' and the Negro Question," *Journal of Southern History* 67, no. 4 (2001): 820.

53. Eric Arnesen, *Waterfront Workers of New Orleans: Race, Class, and Politics, 1863–1923* (Urbana: University of Illinois Press, 1994); Joseph Gerteis, *Class and the Color Line: Interracial Class Coalition in the Knights of Labor and the Populist Movement* (Durham: Duke University Press, 2007).

54. Peter Rachleff, *Black Labor in Richmond, 1865–1900* (Urbana: University of Illinois Press, 1989), 158–78.

55. William Ivy Hair, *Bourbonism and Agrarian Protest: Louisiana Politics, 1877–1900* (Baton Rouge: University State University Press, 1969), 222–23.

56. C. Vann Woodward, *Tom Watson: Agrarian Rebel* (1938; New York: Oxford University Press, 1963).

57. In her study of rape trials, Lisa Lindquist Dorr has shown that white solidarity frequently did not govern jury decisions. While white nationalism prevailed, racism at times lost out. Lisa Lindquist Dorr, *White Women, Rape, and the Power of Race in Virginia, 1900–1960* (Chapel Hill: University of North Carolina Press, 2004).

58. Barry M. Stentiford, *The American Home Guard: The State Militia in the Twentieth Century* (College Station: Texas A&M University Press, 2002), 15.

59. U. B. Phillips, "The Central Theme of Southern History," *American Historical Review* 34 (October 1928): 31.

60. Jennifer E. Brooks, *Defining the Peace: World War II Veterans, Race, and the Remaking of Southern Political Tradition* (Chapel Hill: University of North Carolina Press,

2004), 127–28; Robert Rogers Korstad, *Civil Rights Unionism: Tobacco Workers and the Struggle for Democracy in the Mid-Twentieth-Century South* (Chapel Hill: University of North Carolina Press, 2003), 136–39. Concerned with the pace of change, scholars have often glossed over the amazing fact that political exclusion often took place with bloodshed and re-inclusion rarely did. William R. Keech, *The Impact of Negro Voting: The Role of the Vote in the Quest for Equality* (Chicago: Rand McNally, 1968), 105; Steven F. Lawson, *Black Ballots: Voting Rights in the South, 1944–1969* (New York: Columbia University Press, 1976), 130–34. Laurie Green shows that in the case of Memphis black political inclusion and influence came even earlier than the New Deal. Laurie B. Green, *Fighting the Plantation Mentality: Memphis and the Black Freedom Struggle* (Chapel Hill: University of North Carolina Press, 2007), 36.

# 11

........................

# Tolentino, Cable, and Tourgée Confront
# the New South and the New Imperialism

PETER SCHMIDT

Although some investigation has been undertaken over the last several decades of the possible connections between the strange career of Jim Crow at home and U.S. expansionism abroad in the post-Reconstruction era, we are still in the early stages of thinking *historically* about this moment. In my book *Sitting in Darkness* I made the rather counterintuitive argument that even though Reconstruction was dead after 1877 there may be profound parallels between Reconstruction's goals of transforming the post-slavery plantation South and the equally ambitious schemes driving the so-called Age of Empire beginning in the 1890s to modernize the United States' newly acquired colonies in the Caribbean and the Pacific.[1] Emboldened by the profitable post-Reconstruction alliances between northern capital and the southern post-slavery plantation economy, in which new sharecropping practices ensured control of cheap labor, the United States in the 1890s looked to acquire and exploit other plantation economies in the Caribbean and the Pacific, including Hawaii and the Philippines. The United States' new colonialism reconstructed Reconstruction in two primary ways: first, by developing a revisionist history of the postwar era that emphasized the dangers of an inferior race dominating a superior one; and second, by adapting Reconstruction narratives and procedures for citizen building and citizen control in a transnational context under the newly coined slogan of the "white man's burden." As Saidiya Hartman and others have shown, the domestic "uplift" practices of Reconstruction that allegedly formed citizens-to-be worked primarily as ideologies of subjection and containment, though its rhetoric often stressed liberation and development.[2] Trying to synthesize C. Vann

Woodward[3] and Hartman, I argued that white rule in the "Redeemer" New South actually continued rather than renounced key elements of both the discourses and practices of Reconstruction. One of our tasks as historians is to develop ways of testing whether or not Jim Crow developments at home and colonialist infrastructures abroad in the 1890s and after were mutually constitutive—that is, constructed during the same historical period and justified using similar arguments. A few blacks and many whites—southerners and northerners, especially Unionists who had experience with black troops or blacks during Reconstruction—affirmed their patriotism for the newly united nation by offering their services as racial experts for the United States' new colonial enterprises. As historians, though, we should not neglect those voices that questioned whether the emerging new racial order at home and abroad jeopardized citizens' rights and constitutional democracy, particularly those rights encoded in the Fourteenth and Fifteenth Amendments passed during Reconstruction. Including dissenters who held progressive civic nationalist views will help prevent reifying the New South's beliefs regarding race or the new imperialism into a single, fixed position. White or black southerners' attitudes about race were neither consistent nor unified—which may have been one reason why so many efforts were made to enforce conformity among whites. Similarly, there was no southern unanimity either pro or con on the new imperialism. Even as rabid a believer in white supremacy as Thomas Dixon could be wildly contradictory on this issue, particularly in his fiction.[4] In assessing New South views on citizenship at "home" and "abroad," historians should present the range of competing views that existed and give us good working hypotheses about how those differences were generated and how they functioned.

Fictional texts that circulated during the early Jim Crow colonial era have much to teach us regarding all these issues, and not just because many were widely read and influential. Key texts discussed here, particularly Tourgée's and Cable's, have important arguments to make about the problematic history of civil rights in the South that should be part of any story we narrate about southern Progressivism. Tolentino and Cable will also allow us to add a *transnational* dimension to our studies of southern Progressivism's long, fragile, and paradoxical history. For after 1898 arguments for reform in the South often had both their diagnoses of problems and their proposals for solutions intertwined with similar arguments for reform projects in the "other" South, the new U.S. colonies in the Caribbean and the Pacific. As historians, however, we must be able to distinguish between reforms that advanced democracy and those that presented domination wearing a new guise. All three authors here considered argue eloquently that there cannot be an accurate measure of Progressivism unless we focus on the difference between creating *subjects* and *citizens*.[5]

Imaginative works such as novels and plays present unique challenges to historians who may be inclined to use them as documentary evidence. This essay will ponder some reasons why we should not ignore fictional texts and will offer some suggestions about how to handle the dangers and opportunities such works present, first by discussing Aurelio Tolentino's 1903 play *Yesterday, Today, and Tomorrow*, about the Philippine independence movement; then George Washington Cable's sadly neglected last novel, *Lovers of Louisiana (To-Day)* (1918); and finally Albion Tourgée's masterpiece, his second novel, *Bricks without Straw* (1880), about the rise and fall of Reconstruction in North Carolina and throughout the South. The order in which these texts are discussed scrambles chronology a little, but I hope the reader by the end will agree that moving from Tolentino to Tourgée makes sense. These writers disagree in fascinating ways from how the emerging racial order of their era defined citizenship rights and responsibilities in the United States' new imperial era. But to appreciate their works' power we must focus on aspects of their *form* as well as their content and context. My examples of form informing content will be transformative figures of speech in Tolentino, historical and literary allusions both overt and hidden in Cable, and Tourgée's narrative about the proximate versus ultimate causes for Reconstruction's demise.

## Aurelio Tolentino's Anti-Imperial Archive in *Yesterday, Today, and Tomorrow*

First, let's consider how figures of speech give us a rich way of conceptualizing how narratives work and why interpretations of them may productively clash. Plot paraphrase can be particularly powerful in analysis so long as it focuses on how to understand the plot's central dramatic tensions and their resolution (or lack of one). Yet narratives also often comment on themselves within the story even as it is unfolding. Such metafictional moments provide a way for an audience to generate hypotheses in the midst of a story about that tale's direction and meanings. I'll focus here on the climax of Tolentino's play, which offers a governing analogy both for its "whole" and for how and why members of the audience interpreted this moment differently in ways that are historically significant. These comments about reading generative metaphors or analogies are also applicable to other authors and texts.

Tolentino's *Yesterday, Today, and Tomorrow* was performed in Tagalog in Manila in 1903. At the play's climax, Bagonsibol, a female figure representing the United States, is confronted by rebels onstage. Behind them there is a curtain filled with figures representing the whole of the Filipino army, including its infantry, artillery, and engineers, flanked by Filipina women in Red Cross uniforms. The rebels petition the United States to grant the Philippines its sovereignty. But Bagonsibol replies, "It cannot be."[6] This provokes an impassioned speech from a rebel that invokes America's own revolutionary war for independence from a colonial master: "consider that the liberty which I long for thou didst also long to obtain from him who was thy master" (i.e., England). When this appeal also fails, Filipino children then appear onstage "carrying a large book," "the record of our unhappy people" (332). They give it to America, but the book "falls from her hands" to the ground. Out of the book, however, swirls a giant version of the banned flag of the free Philippines. According to a footnote in the 1905 English translation, this banner abruptly covered the American flag onstage—and it was at this point that the "Americans and Spaniards in the theater rushed upon the stage" and shut the play down. Many of these angry members of the audience surely couldn't follow the play's speeches in Tagalog, but they thought they understood perfectly well the trope of a book becoming a Philippine flag covering the American flag, and they were also alarmed because at this climax Filipinos in the audience began cheering "violently" (332–33). What occurred in the script of the play's conclusion, never performed? America's decision to relent and grant the Philippines independence. The Filipino army she could oppose, but an army of children she could not.

Hardly a realistic depiction of the war in the Philippines as it transpired after 1898. In fact, the play was never performed again and its author was jailed for sedition—not quite the happy ending Tolentino tried to script. Yet the book the children present in the play *textually inscribes* an eloquent metaphor for many Filipinos' intense yearnings for independence. The book treats those feelings as a written record that transforms text into the texture of the flag of the new republic. Covering the U.S. flag, their statement places their own act of rebellion within the historical lineage of the American Revolution and demands that Filipinos be treated as citizens in a new republic, not colonial subjects who have just changed masters. In short, Tolentino employs arguments central to the U.S. tradition of civic nationalism in order to argue for the Philippines' own rights to national sovereignty.

As I described in *Sitting in Darkness*, the U.S. government decided that an archive of Philippine culture needed to be created, and it authorized a minor bureaucrat, Arthur Stanley Riggs, to assemble as part of that archive a volume titled *The Filipino Drama*, including Riggs's translation into English of the complete *Yesterday, Today, and Tomorrow*.[7] In his 1905 volume, Riggs worked assiduously to reframe this moment when the "record" of a people tired of being colonized is presented to America so that it will be read in a way precisely opposite from what Tolentino intended. Tolentino invoked the American Declaration of Independence and Revolution as a "mirror" (333) that should reflect America's actions in the Philippines, but Riggs's introduction stressed the play's mysticism and violence, arguing that these are "typical of the ferocity of such peoples only as, half-civilized, [they] carry their ancient spirit of savage barbarity . . . and let it burn hotly through . . . the perilously thin veneer of quasi-civilization" (278). He ascribed utmost powers of seduction and sedition to Tolentino, saying that had he not been imprisoned "the fertile brain of the agitator-tool would have brought forth" (278) a sequel to *Yesterday, Today, and Tomorrow*. Yet Riggs then also immediately tried to downplay Tolentino's competence as a revolutionary playwright, insinuating that reliable native informants confided to him that the average Filipino couldn't follow Tolentino's plays, particularly their long speeches (278–79). Riggs suggested Filipinos were also unable to comprehend the United States' long-term good intentions. According to Riggs, the United States would not act as a Spain-like colonial despot but rather as a tutor educating Filipinos to take their first steps on the long road to civilization and—eventually—independence and Philippine citizenship.

Highlighting and analyzing Riggs's contradictory constructions of the "native," we may map how colonialist discourse works to frame natives as both uneducated and infinitely cunning. "White man's burden" discourse both promotes a developmental narrative—natives moving gradually into modernity guided by an imperial power—and undercuts that narrative with suggestions that any acquired "civilized" traits will be, in

Riggs's terms, a mere "veneer" masking dangerous, untouchable barbarity. We also need to look for traces of a *counter-archive* in such colonial texts, wherein the "natives" talk back and present themselves as anything but savages unable to understand the choices before them or the meaning of the U.S. Declaration of Independence and its Constitution and Bill of Rights. Indeed, Tolentino proves savagely adept at parodying the self-justifying rhetoric of colonial discourse: "I have not acceded to thy desires [for freedom] because I love thee," Tolentino's America says, patronizingly; "thou hast not yet sufficient strength to sustain thine own rights" (331). The playwright eloquently voices the counter-narrative to American imperial discourse, even though Tolentino's appeal is encased in Riggs's stilted translation: "consider that the liberty which I long for thou didst also long to obtain from him who was thy master" (332). Ironically, the U.S. colonial archive, by authorizing a translation of and commentary on Tolentino's play, thus catalogues both the colonizers' contradictory perceptions of the Filipinos and textual evidence that challenges the colonizers' key self-justifying claims.

Tolentino's *Yesterday, Today, and Tomorrow*, along with Riggs's notes and critical framework, are rarely included in syllabi covering either U.S. colonialism or the literary history of the period, much less those on the history of Jim Crow or debates about the civil rights of those in the new U.S. colonies.[8] Yet this text proves an intriguing instance of how by investigating colonial archives in the 1890–1920 period we may begin to generate a comparative analysis between "uplift" and containment (even terroristic) actions and discourse in the United States' new colonies and developments at home. The period is marked by sedition laws, military offensives, and segregation in the colonies abroad, paralleled in the United States by vigilante lynchings, segregation, and (in 1918) a powerful new Sedition Act that applied to all U.S. residents, not colonials. Ambitious Reconstruction-like federal plans to upgrade educational systems and permit limited voting and civil rights were debated and then implemented in the new colonies, whereas in the States the rise of Jim Crow segregation placed blacks in citizenship limbo, with the rights guaranteed them by the Fourteenth and Fifteenth Amendments largely made fictional.[9] Inverting colonialist binaries of civilized and savage and claiming universal citizenship rights on the global stage, Tolentino's play raises profound questions about the relations between humans conceived as free, autonomous subjects and any institution—U.S. colonial or Filipino—that claims to represent their rights. In Etienne Balibar's terms, commenting on Kant's notion of universal rights and world citizenship, "the 'citizen' belonging to any human institution and *subjected* to it, but particularly to the legal state..., can 'belong' to that institution and state as a *free and autonomous subject only* inasmuch as every institution, every state, is conceived as a partial and provisional representative of *humanity*, which in fact is the only absolute 'community,' the only true 'subject of history'" (italics and quotation marks are Balibar's).[10]

As Michael O'Brien shows in his essay in this volume, there's a tension between human and citizenship rights built into the wording of the Fourteenth Amendment. Tolentino, Cable, and Tourgée prove invaluable for further discussion of this point because, following Kant and anticipating Balibar, they argue that a citizen's rights do not conflict with natural rights; rather, they must be *grounded* in them. That is, in their view civic nationalism is fragile indeed if it involves no recognition that transcendent human rights—what the American revolutionaries called the natural rights of man—can *never* be fully embodied in or represented by flawed human institutions like a constitutional state or the merely legal definition of a citizen's rights and immunities, though both are certainly valuable.

## "Burden Enough for Any White Man": George Washington Cable's Anti-Imperial Irony in *Lovers of Louisiana*

Another key element of imaginative narratives is their use of allusion, that is, the citation of a work, a person, an event, or another element in either another virtual world or in the past or present world that passes for our "real" one. Allusions may be very direct, what some call name-dropping, or they may be quite indirect and covert, what we might call name-coding or name-shielding. In the latter case, detective work must be undertaken to trace what is being alluded to, why it's important, and why it was disguised. Tracking down an allusion and making a case for its importance to the primary text is just the beginning. After that the real work of interpretation begins. Once the source material alluded to is found and pondered, then we have to ask how our reading of that new material should affect our interpretation of the primary text. Determining what is relevant and how to apply it is actually a layered set of interpretive moves, all potentially controversial or even wrong. But therein lies the power and interest of allusions, for like an in-text analogy that provides a new interpretive

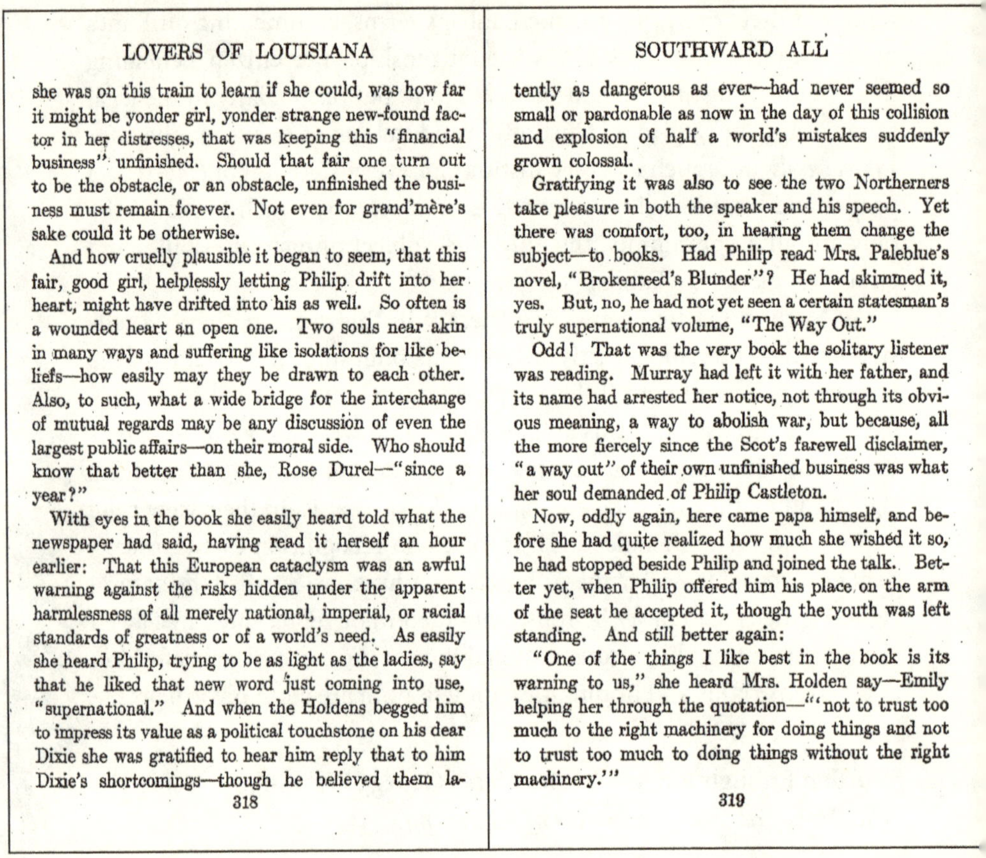

LOVERS OF LOUISIANA

she was on this train to learn if she could, was how far it might be yonder girl, yonder strange new-found factor in her distresses, that was keeping this "financial business" unfinished. Should that fair one turn out to be the obstacle, or an obstacle, unfinished the business must remain forever. Not even for grand'mère's sake could it be otherwise.

And how cruelly plausible it began to seem, that this fair, good girl, helplessly letting Philip drift into her heart, might have drifted into his as well. So often is a wounded heart an open one. Two souls near akin in many ways and suffering like isolations for like beliefs—how easily may they be drawn to each other. Also, to such, what a wide bridge for the interchange of mutual regards may be any discussion of even the largest public affairs—on their moral side. Who should know that better than she, Rose Durel—"since a year?"

With eyes in the book she easily heard told what the newspaper had said, having read it herself an hour earlier: That this European cataclysm was an awful warning against the risks hidden under the apparent harmlessness of all merely national, imperial, or racial standards of greatness or of a world's need. As easily she heard Philip, trying to be as light as the ladies, say that he liked that new word just coming into use, "supernational." And when the Holdens begged him to impress its value as a political touchstone on his dear Dixie she was gratified to hear him reply that to him Dixie's shortcomings—though he believed them la-

318

SOUTHWARD ALL

tently as dangerous as ever—had never seemed so small or pardonable as now in the day of this collision and explosion of half a world's mistakes suddenly grown colossal.

Gratifying it was also to see the two Northerners take pleasure in both the speaker and his speech. Yet there was comfort, too, in hearing them change the subject—to books. Had Philip read Mrs. Paleblue's novel, "Brokenreed's Blunder"? He had skimmed it, yes. But, no, he had not yet seen a certain statesman's truly supernational volume, "The Way Out."

Odd! That was the very book the solitary listener was reading. Murray had left it with her father, and its name had arrested her notice, not through its obvious meaning, a way to abolish war, but because, all the more fiercely since the Scot's farewell disclaimer, "a way out" of their own unfinished business was what her soul demanded of Philip Castleton.

Now, oddly again, here came papa himself, and before she had quite realized how much she wished it so, he had stopped beside Philip and joined the talk. Better yet, when Philip offered him his place on the arm of the seat he accepted it, though the youth was left standing. And still better again:

"One of the things I like best in the book is its warning to us," she heard Mrs. Holden say—Emily helping her through the quotation—"'not to trust too much to the right machinery for doing things and not to trust too much to doing things without the right machinery.'"

319

Figure 11.1. From George Washington Cable, *Lovers of Louisiana (To-Day)*.

map, such as the book-archive discussed in Tolentino, allusions too may come embedded with interpretive clues that function as powerful gifts for the adventurous detective-reader.

There is not space here to discuss in much detail Cable's fascinating novel *Lovers of Louisiana* (1918), so for my touchstone sample of it I've chosen a particularly intriguing passage in which the heroine, Rosalie Durel, eavesdrops on others, including her erstwhile lover, Philip Castleton, and a romantic rival as they discuss the causes of World War I (see fig. 11.1).[11]

Cable wrote his last novel in his seventies, as World War I was unfolding. As its characters discuss contemporary events while they journey home by train to Louisiana, the passage in question appears to make its primary allusions quite obvious. A newspaper article about lessons to be learned from the "cataclysm" of World War I has been read by some of the protagonists, who find that it reminds them of "a certain statesman's truly supernational volume, 'The Way Out'" (319). This title and the word *supernational* leap out here as providing clues to track down. We get several more embedded in the narrator's paraphrase of the gist of the newspaper piece as understood by Rosalie: "this European cataclysm was an awful warning against the risks hidden under the apparent harmlessness of all merely national, imperial, or racial standards of greatness or of a world's need" (318). Moreover, in an especially interesting move, the novel's hero, Philip Castleton—who just happens to be a historian teaching at the newly founded Tulane University—suggests that given World War I and the "explosion of half a world's mistakes suddenly grown colossal," the criticisms that he has leveled at his beloved Dixie ought to seem rather "small or pardonable" in comparison. What were those criticisms? That the South's refusal to allow its black citizens to exercise their civil rights as guaranteed by the Constitution's Fourteenth and Fifteenth Amendments not only hurts southern progress but jeopardizes the United States' standing moral stature just at the moment when it seeks to play a leadership role on the world stage. Just as controversially, Philip critiques southern political culture for its assumption that all public criticism of the South is traitorous.

Cable's linkage of the injustices of Jim Crow with the causes of World War I here is rather audacious: the narrator suggests that although such policies may be justified by "racial standards of greatness"—a phrase that may be glossed as a euphemism for the "white man's burden" to "civilize" but also control people of color—such systems of dominance masquerading as uplift may eventually explode in racial warfare in the United States. Implying that the white man's burden was dangerous for the South was shocking enough for 1918, but the suggestion that a European war had colonialist causes was even more startling: to what could Cable, through the character of Philip Castleton, be alluding?

Let's address first the more straightforward moves of the passage. Who might be the "statesman" mentioned, associated with warnings that groups or nations pursuing their own selfish interests are a prescription for global disaster? One obvious reference here would be to President Woodrow Wilson, whom we know from Cable's biographers that he admired. In a speech in Des Moines, Iowa, in 1916, that received national publicity while Cable was beginning work on his new novel, Wilson argued that only an "international tribunal" would be able to guarantee the terms of whatever peace agreement emerged at the end of the current European war.[12] And in his famous "Fourteen Points" speech to Congress in January 1918, the president suggested that the United States' motives in entering the war were that the world be "made safe for every peace-loving nation which, like our own, wishes to live its own life, determine its own institutions, be assured of justice and fair dealing by the other peoples of the world as against force and selfish aggression. All the peoples of the world are in effect partners in this interest, and for our own part we see very clearly that unless justice be done to others it will not be done to us."[13]

According to the National Union Catalogue listings for books in English published before 1955, no volume titled *The Way Out* was ever published, certainly not by Woodrow Wilson. Cable has disguised his allusion to Wilson under an invented text, relying on the words "statesman" and "supernational" and the general idealism of the summarized texts to give his readers in 1918 enough clues so that they would be able to link to the Progressivist southern president the views expressed in the scene about an international agency needed to prevent future world wars.

Yet there remains an anomaly here worth pondering more carefully, for I think it provides us with a different clue. The passage's emphasis on "the risks hidden under the apparent harmlessness of all merely national, imperial, or *racial standards of greatness*" (my italics) is remarkable because of its warning that imperial and national claims to greatness often have a suspect racial component. Such a note hardly seems Wilsonian. If we then search the rest of Cable's novel looking for passages that would give us guidance as to how to interpret this phrase, one in particular begs for closer consideration. This is an earlier scene that also includes a public discussion about the United States' proper international role in the post–World War I world. A Scotsman named Murray exploring New Orleans for the first time has befriended Cable's protagonists, and at one point he launches into a discussion regarding how much the former colony and newly imperial nation has to learn from the United Kingdom. Murray admits Britain has made serious errors in managing its colonial empire, but he maintains that introducing limited electoral democracy for property owners of color in all the colonies, not just Bermuda, must be Britain's primary goal.

Listen first to Cable's narrator's ironic summary of Murray's tactics: he "spent his wiliest efforts preaching the abominable gospel of government by peaceable counterplay of rival political parties enjoying equal rights" (223). Cable's third-person narrative voice here and elsewhere ironically mimes the speech of conservative white southerners, using what we literary historians call "free indirect discourse" to dub all such discussion of blacks' or colonists' rights an "abominable gospel." Cable signals that he's using irony by opening this scene with the narrator tartly calling Murray "burden enough for any white man" (222), a trope that wittily turns on its head Kipling's newly coined pro-imperial cliché of the white man's burden to uplift non-Western civilizations.[14] In Cable's wry reversal of Kipling's coinage, the "burden" that must be undertaken here signifies listening to Murray's eloquent diatribe questioning some of the central premises of pro-imperialist discourse. And Murray audaciously applies that rhetoric not just to U.S. policies abroad but to its actions at home. His speech rendered not via a narrator's arch summary but in Murray's own lively Scottish burr, Murray argues that there are profound parallels between blacks restive in the U.S. South and colonized peoples worldwide. The question of political rights for the colonized abroad and blacks in the United States under Jim Crow is not dead and settled, in Murray's view, but "'tis but possuming. Lorrd! Ye can't *neglect* it to death; the neglect of all America can't kill it. It's in the womb o' the future and bigger than Asia, Africa, and America combined. Ye'll do well to be friendly wi' its friends and trreat it kindly while it's young and trractable" (223).

It's hardly surprising, of course, that a Scotsman might have particularly strong views about the dangers of being colonized. It's also true, admittedly, that Murray's rhetoric is not absolutely anti-imperial. As Murray develops his theories in other scenes in the novel, he stresses his faith that Britain's colonial policies are enlightening and whitening (27) its colonized peoples so that they will soon earn the franchise and become masters of their own destinies, citizens rather than dependent colonial subjects. But unlike Tolentino's Bagonsibol (America), Murray is emphatic that a movement toward democratic rights must begin *now*, not at some indefinite date in the future.

These scenes and Cable's *Lovers of Louisiana* as a whole demonstrate the facts of black-white interdependency and the ethical and practical disasters that await the South and the United States if black civil rights continue to be denied. Further, blacks' struggles in the South are linked to global movements for the rights of colonized peoples. At such a moment, surely, Cable's text hardly sounds Wilsonian. This 1918 novel enacts contemporary debates about colonialism, not to mention anxieties swirling in both the South and the United States as a whole about the "womb of the future" when it came to racial relations, black citizenship rights, and the civil rights of those in Puerto Rico, Cuba, Hawaii, the Philippines, and elsewhere.

I would argue that Cable's vision of the global civil rights of people of color gestating in the "womb of the future" comes from another source who is decidedly not President Wilson, W. E. B. Du Bois—in particular, an article titled "The African Roots of the War" that appeared in 1915 in the *Atlantic Monthly*, a journal Cable knew well.[15] Du Bois claimed that the real cause of the war was competing imperial attempts by European nations to exploit African labor and natural resources to enrich themselves and appease class conflicts and economic crises at home. Du Bois prophesied that a conflagration worse than World War I would come if Europeans continued to refuse democratic rights to colonized peoples. Such a position is certainly more radical than Murray's and Cable's, for those gentlemen tend to think in terms of the white man's burden and the dangers that would come if uplift and democratization programs were not successful, whereas Du Bois is considerably more apocalyptic about the threat, while also stressing the rights and agency of peoples of color. Like Tolentino, Du Bois treats people of color as rightful heirs of democracy, not largely passive recipients of whites' largesse. But Du Bois's and Cable's vision comes together via a shared understanding that World War I raised global questions about the citizenship rights of colonized peoples, as well as for those who were formerly enslaved.

With a transnational, postcolonial focus unique in Cable's canon, *Lovers of Louisiana* is also enlivened by its comedy-of-manners treatment of the awkward courtship of the Creole heroine Rosalie Durel and the "Américain" hero Philip Castleton. Indeed, in the touchstone passage from the novel first discussed, the phrase "the way out" as it is understood by our heroine signifies not just a possible solution to global cataclysm but also a way (she hopes) to resolve her own muddled romance with Philip Castleton and the tension it is causing between their very different families ("'a way out' of their own unfinished business was what her soul demanded of Philip" [319]): both politics and romance are adroitly braided together via Cable's plot. Like any substantive novel of manners, *Lovers of Louisiana* chronicles personal and clan drama as well as the emergence of a new social order—in this case, Creole/American alliances realigning the social networks of modern industrial New Orleans. The novel also has a fascinating subplot involving its black characters, particularly a bookstore owner and archivist named Ovide Landry. Cable's last work richly depicts the complex financial and social interdependency of blacks and whites occurring daily hidden beneath the fictions of Jim Crow segregation.

In sum, Cable's novel challenges any easy generalizations we might be tempted to make about how white southerners after 1898 suavely translated their alleged racial expertise into support for Jim Crow at home and the nation's new imperialism abroad. *Lovers of Louisiana* also troubles our received sense of the proper "canon" of Cable texts, wherein only Cable's portraits of antebellum "Old Creole" Louisiana, and/or perhaps excerpts from his essays in *The Silent South* or *The Negro Question*, are occasionally included in course syllabi or anthologies.[16] Fine as those pieces are, the time has come to recognize the centrality of Cable to studying the South's role in the United States' Jim Crow colonial era.

It is now relatively common to teach U.S. southern history (including its literary history) as part of the "global South," the broader history of plantation slavery and post-slavery societies linked to the industrializing West. When doing so we should remember that Cable's out-of-print[17] *Lovers of Louisiana (To-Day)* contrasts instructively with Thomas Dixon's *The Leopard's Spots* and *The Clansman* as one of the most intriguing examples before Faulkner of a New South text that adroitly places its representation of the post–Civil War United States in the context of both global history and the "local" complexities of citizenship/civil rights debates and changing clan, class, and race dynamics.

## Albion Tourgée on Subjects versus Citizens: *Bricks without Straw*

I have emphasized rhetorical strategies that Cable's and Tolentino's texts employ to challenge orthodox pro-imperial discourse in the late nineteenth and early twentieth centuries. That discourse, eloquently distilled by Kipling in his 1899 poem "The White Man's Burden," stressed uplifting oppressed peoples into the light of modernity as a burden or "harness" to be honorably taken up by the Anglo-Saxon race. But in practice such language justified creating new post-slavery or postcolonial *subjects*, not citizens—"Your new-caught, sullen peoples, / Half-devil and half-child," Kipling called them, referring to Filipinos newly under U.S. sovereignty. For an incisively different angle on debates about citizenship and identity, we may turn to Albion Tourgée, particularly his 1880 novel *Bricks without Straw*, which has just been reissued by Duke University Press in a splendid new edition with an introduction by Carolyn L. Karcher.[18] Almost two decades before the United States' war with Spain and attendant debates about the civil rights of the colonized, Tourgée in his fiction considered deeply the issue of how to bring democracy to the post-slavery South. Focusing on both the promise of Reconstruction and its tragic demise, Tourgée traced how the return of white supremacist rule in the allegedly "New" South forged a society that retained many features of the slave South except slavery, including rigid social stratification caused by oligarchal rule marginalizing many whites as well as all blacks.

Fictional universes necessarily have a complicated relation to historical facts as we know them. They may give us counterfactual versions of history, or they may instead seek to present new interpretations of the facts we think we know. They may also seek to imagine what the known facts cannot tell us. As the contemporary southern novelist Ellen Douglas has said, in her provocative autobiographical novel *Truth: Four Stories I Am Finally Old Enough to Tell* (1998), when family tales or official chronicles claim to present "the truth" about the past, their apparent facts tell us only so much. There is always something important left unexplained—questions about causes and motives and chronology and consequences, mysteries ultimately about the *meaning* of it all. Sometimes the facts that we are left with even seem to suggest contradictory interpretations of what happened and what it might portend. In no way does Douglas mean to denigrate the historian's job of fact seeking or truth telling. But the novelist's job, she suggests, is to go beyond what can be known for certain and to mark the silences, the omissions. It is then also to plunge into those empty spaces and emerge not with a single narrative about what might have happened but a cluster of conflicting stories and possibilities that plausibly render not just different interpretations but the reasons why people remember differently.[19] Fictional texts may even prove eccentric to their era but prophetic of the future, sketching revisionary truths that are validated by professional historians only decades later. Tourgée's *Bricks without Straw* presents just such a case.

In making her observations, Douglas was perhaps alluding to Tolstoy, who famously (or notoriously) proclaimed in *War and Peace* that recoverable historical facts "tell [us] nothing, explain nothing."[20] Tolstoy of course was hardly shy about presenting a theory of history behind the particular story he had to tell, for in 1869 he published not just his epic portrait of why Russia defeated Napoleon's army but—especially in part 2 of his epilogue and then the appendix that concluded *War and Peace*—not one but two contradictory theories of history that he believed must function in dialectical tension in order to shape history's telos, the "goal towards which peoples and mankind move" (1180). The first historical force Tolstoy conceptualized was an early version of what today we somewhat disingenuously call "history from the bottom up," a vision of historical change that does not focus solely on ruling elites. The second element in Tolstoy's dialectic of history was a claim about the *contingency* of all historical narratives, and thus the necessity for skepticism, complexity, contradiction, and a sense of irony. In particular, Tolstoy urged a focus on how people when they act generally think they are free and rational but are influenced or predetermined by laws governing group behavior they cannot fully understand.

Though hardly a novelist of Tolstoy's stature, Tourgée too understood the historical novelist's job to be deeply revisionary and dialectical. In his first two novels, *A Fool's Errand*[21] and *Bricks without Straw*, published in 1879 and 1880, respectively, Tourgée sought to provide a different interpretation, a new telos, regarding why Reconstruction failed in the South, along with a plea that if Reconstruction's goals were rejected by the nation then the ideals of the United States itself would be in danger. U.S. constitutional democracy, like Reconstruction, is revealed by Tourgée's Reconstruction novels to have been made of "bricks without straw," dangerously weak internally because of flaws in its design, materials, and workmanship. Tourgée's thesis in *Bricks* is a two-part one, the first focusing on postwar events and their proximate causes in North Carolina, the second focusing on his theory of an ultimate cause. The novel maps a perfect storm of proximate causes for Reconstruction's collapse, including internal weaknesses in Reconstruction programs themselves, the refusal of the federal government to counter terrorist violence, and white racists' ability to exploit fears not just of black power and black citizenship but also of the black-white coalitions created during Reconstruction. Although North Carolina's oligarchy-controlled political culture harmed the majority of whites as well as blacks, attempts to change this power structure via the new North Carolina constitution of 1868—many of whose provisions were authored by Tourgée himself as a delegate to the constitutional convention—were vitiated in 1875. Indeed, it was the blatant rewriting of the text of the 1868 North Carolina constitution by the conservatives in 1875 that largely provoked Tourgée to turn to contesting in the field of fiction what had been lost in the field of history.

At the conclusion to *Bricks without Straw,* Tourgée presents his analysis of the ultimate cause for Reconstruction's failure via a long speech by one of the southern elites, Hesden Le Moyne, who betrayed his class and sided with the Reconstructionists. That cause is the absence of robust *local* democratic cultural traditions throughout the South, embodied in its high rates of illiteracy and a lack of a township-meeting tradition and elections. Only in such meetings, Le Moyne asserts, may a people transform themselves from subjects controlled by others to citizens who understand the responsibilities of self-rule. Instituting the local election of township officials (rather than their appointment by a ruling party) was one of the crucial reforms written into the 1868 North Carolina constitution at Tourgée's insistence but stripped from it in 1875. In Le Moyne's words: "In every state in which the township system really prevailed, slavery was abolished without recourse to arms. . . . [Further,] in the states in which the township system did not prevail in fact as well as in name, the public school system did not exist, or had only a nominal existence; and the proportion of illiteracy in those states as a consequence was, *among the whites alone,* something like four times as great as in those states in which the township system flourished" (423; Tourgée's italics).

Le Moyne goes on to trace the origins of the township system in European borough systems, especially the Anglo-Saxon "Hundreds," and to stress that he has good company in claiming the township's overriding importance for developing democracy—Alexis de Tocqueville in *Democracy in America* (volume 1, chapter 5).[22] Having neatly surveyed township divisions is much less important in Le Moyne's view than developing an internalized democratic culture where the inhabitants are organized into self-governing units and learn to discuss and debate governmental decisions (424–25). "The South is to-day and always has been a stranger to local self-government," favoring instead an oligarchal system whereby statewide elections were held but party elites essentially determined important local officials such as justices of the peace, constables and sheriffs, school boards, election officials, and the county commissioners who made financial decisions for the county (425).

In short, when applied to the events of 1865–77 in the South, Tourgée's startling theory of history finds that large events can be explained by looking at how southern political culture functioned at the most local of levels. His novel works equally powerfully as micro-analysis and macro-mapping of major historical developments. As a Reconstruction judge in North Carolina, Tourgée lamented the lack of vigorous intervention by President Grant and others, for he saw that without federal protection Reconstruction reformers and their reforms were vulnerable to counterattack. And he was proved right. Written in grief, anger, and hindsight, *Bricks without Straw* emphasizes tragically lost opportunities, not just history as a predetermined narrative. Tourgée's novel demonstrates how many black and white southerners and northerners worked together in North Carolina to build from scratch local and statewide democratic practices until, without federal protection, they had much of their work systematically overwritten and destroyed by the return of racist and oligarchal rule. In the process, much property forcibly changed hands and many lives were lost.

Given the ambition of Tourgée's *Bricks without Straw* and the prominence of its claims about the township system, it's odd that Tourgée's ultimate-cause thesis about townships and the demise of Reconstruction has not been carefully evaluated by historians. Of course one reason may be that Tourgée is wrong, or at least too simplistic. But it's hard to find mention of his claims, much less a careful testing of them, in the many texts by recent historians who (ironically enough) follow in Tourgée's footsteps and attempt to present us with a comprehensive narrative explaining the fate of Reconstruction and its meaning for America. Carolyn Karcher's extensive and valuable introductory essay in her new edition of *Bricks without Straw* doesn't explore Tourgée's township thesis.[23] Mark Elliott, Tourgée's most recent biographer, does stress township electoral changes as one of the many reforms Tourgée helped add to the 1868 constitution: "the Republicans . . . divided counties into townships to be governed by popularly elected officials, school boards, and justices of the peace. Property qualifications for political office were abolished."[24] Elliott has also done lucid detective work tracing the many correspondences and divergences between characters and events in *Bricks without Straw* and the historical record.[25] But more needs to be done to evaluate the validity of Tourgée's township thesis.

Consider Eric Foner's magisterial *Reconstruction*. Foner stresses how profound were the changes that Reconstruction reforms introduced at the local level—no doubt one reason why their challenges to oligarchy were so systematically attacked. Writing about Reconstruction Mississippi, Foner has said that "in virtually every county with a sizeable black population, blacks served in at least some local office," and some obtained county positions such as supervisor or sheriff.[26] Foner's history is well known for demonstrating how black schools, fire companies, and other local organizations provided leadership training for the new black officeholders, as did, eventually, the new black colleges (cf. 359). But when Tourgée is mentioned, Foner oddly calls him merely a "Carpetbagger Judge" (430), and when Tourgée's *A Fool's Errand* is cited Foner suggests that Tourgée mainly depicted blacks as helpless (436). In fact, however, in both *Fool's Errand* and, especially, *Bricks without Straw*, Tourgée with eloquence and detail not only chronicles where blacks gained their leadership training; he makes the same connection that Foner did more than a century later between blacks' initiative, Reconstruction's attempts to build public school systems for the first time in the South, and the emerging story of blacks and (some) whites working together to try to jump-start a new, robust, and local democratic culture in the South.

Paul Escott's *Many Excellent People: Power and Privilege in North Carolina, 1850–1900*, similarly, contains excellent analyses of the interactions between village and county and state political systems before and after the war, finding many continuities between them. His conclusions regarding antebellum local North Carolina governments even use some of Tourgée's very words—"oligarchic, undemocratic"—to describe how locals ceded power to county and state authorities.[27] Escott's analysis of Redeemer "reforms" of the North Carolina Reconstruction constitution in 1875 also essentially confirms Tourgée's claims in *Bricks without Straw*. After chronicling how the social and financial position of county officers changed markedly for both blacks and whites during Reconstruction, revealing that a much less elite circle of white tradesmen and farmers gained political power, not just wealthy plantation owners and judges, Escott notes that it "is easy to see why the Democratic offensive was aimed so directly at local government. Control of county affairs had been the foundation of North Carolina's aristocratic social order; local gentry who made the decisions about roads, schools, and tax rates . . . had easily dominated politics at higher levels."[28] Escott concludes that although racist fears were often central to Redeemer rhetoric, we must not underestimate how *class* tensions among whites—and the white oligarchy's fears that nonelite whites' coalitions with blacks would cause both groups to aspire for more power—also drove the urge to eviscerate Reconstruction reforms. These key points in Escott's 1985 study were first extensively developed by Tourgée in 1879–80. Yet Tourgée is not once mentioned in Escott's book as one of the "many excellent people" to be studied to understand power and privilege in North Carolina in the nineteenth century.

My point is hardly to lambast Escott or Foner, for the merits of their studies stand eloquently on their own. Rather, I lament the counterproductive split between literary and social historians here revealed by Tourgée's partial eclipse. I also lament the ways in which a researcher as comprehensive as Karcher appears not to be that interested in Tourgée's township thesis explaining the deep cause of Reconstruction's demise and the foundation on which any future real "New South" citizenship reforms must be built. Such neglect of a key part of the agenda of Tourgée's best novel is indeed perplexing. After all, the literary commentators eloquently depict Tourgée's unstinting belief in the power and responsibility that *fiction* possesses to expose fictional histories that pass for true in the "real" world so as to provide us with alternative testimony and counter-narratives.

So, in Tourgée's case, what's the solution? I would suggest two Reconstruction reforms for our own research and teaching practices as historians. First and most obvious, literary and social historians need to read each other's works more comprehensively. The literary folks need to pay more attention to how the authors they prize for their individuality should also be understood as part of their era, in the context of much larger social networks and group struggles. But we also should consider introducing more fiction (when relevant) into our history classes, and more of history's controversies into our literature classes. When teaching classes on Reconstruction and post-slavery citizenship issues, for instance, why not assign some key scenes from Tourgée's *Bricks without Straw*, using Karcher and Elliott perhaps as a guide, so that students can read scenes of blacks and whites discussing together Reconstruction's ideals, or sharing the pain of its destruction? Let's also give them a little of Le Moyne's (and Tourgée's) thesis about why Reconstruction failed and why that failure was not local but a threat to the very ideals of U.S. democracy itself— then encourage students to debate Le Moyne's and Tourgée's ideas while turning to de Tocqueville and contemporary historians for evidence and counterevidence. Tourgée's novel need not even be assigned in its entirety; it's eminently easy to excerpt because it's very episodic, built up via a series of set-piece dramas that can stand on their own if minimal background is provided. Of course the complete Karcher edition of *Bricks without Straw* will work on a syllabus too: it's a dramatic story well told, with helpful scholarly notes.

My second suggestion regarding Tourgée returns me to my thesis, which is that, when considering imaginative works, we must attend to their *form*, not just their plots and overt claims they may make about empirical historical events. Focusing on key metaphors and compound allusions (as discussed with Tolentino and Cable) would be a good beginning, as would being sure that when U.S. southern history is taught we do not excise regional or U.S. developments from their larger imperial and global historical contexts. But we need also to attend to how a narrator and the book's structure may add important layers of irony and hidden critique (Cable); how what characters do and say vividly places before us history's dramatic clashes of ideas (all three authors); and how dissenting authors and texts eclipsed from the canon of works usually featured in our syllabi can reform how we understand the entire period to which they belong (Tolentino, but Tourgée and Cable too). Tourgée created his novels in the same way that he shaped his 1880 tract against the Ku Klux Klan (*The Invisible Empire*): as a powerful compendium of suppressed voices testifying to alternative ways of interpreting U.S. history.[29] Plus, like Cable, Tourgée attempted to build into the very structure of his novel dialogue and debate that had to take place in the public sphere if postwar U.S. democracy would be healthy. At considerable cost to their reputations and their personal lives, Cable and Tourgée spent a lifetime agitating for a wider range of voices and viewpoints to be honored in public discussion in the South. Sentimental romance, tragedy, melodrama, legal disquisition, Socratic dialogue, personal testimony, and set-piece speeches and debates—these are just a few of the rhetorical formats that Tourgée employed in *Bricks without Straw* to change his readers' understanding (read: ignorance) of recent U.S. history. I've analyzed here just one of Tourgée's effective rhetorical techniques in *Bricks without Straw*, the debate he stages over whether the lack of a township-meeting tradition meant that southern post-slavery democracy was bound to fail. It is true that Tourgée usually stacks the deck in favor of some characters and against others. In the township debate in *Bricks without Straw*, the author clearly favors Hesden Le Moyne and revels as he vanquishes all arguments against his position. As Anna Julia Cooper, an admirer of Tourgée, quipped in *A Voice from the South* (1892), all his heroes "are little Tourgees—they preach his sermons and pray his prayers."[30] But if we understand Tourgée's work properly, we will see that the powerful forces arrayed *against* Tourgée's arguments in the post-Reconstruction New South drove him to construct fictional texts that functioned as vociferous counterarguments from "below"—revisionist interventions into received history in the best Tolstoyan tradition.

Tolentino, Cable, and Tourgée also teach readers to cultivate a powerful but not cynical *skepticism* toward grand historical narratives. Between these two forces—empathy for the underdog and skepticism toward any narrative that purports to be the "whole" truth—it's possible to generate a really productive Tolstoyan dialectic in the historical study of citizenship and identity in the new colonies and the nineteenth-century U.S. South, including our interpretation of key imaginative works that responded to that history and attempted to change it. Tolentino, Cable, and Tourgée wrote eloquently about how participatory democracy in their era was ignorant of its own history. Instead, these authors showed dominant narratives of citizenship to be full of repressions, contradictions, denials, hypocrisy, and outright lies perpetrated by violence. Yet all three refused to call dead the United States' self-negating and contradictory discourses and practices of citizenship. If anything, they understood that the freedoms citizenship could confer had not yet been fully born. It is as if those children in Tolentino's almost-lost play are still holding out that "large book" for us to take and read rather than censor or forget. Learning from these texts, we may discover that what they have given us is not just a chronicle of loss but also a story of forms of citizenship and memory yet to be fully lived.

## Notes

1. Peter Schmidt, *Sitting in Darkness: New South Fiction, Education, and the Rise of Jim Crow Colonialism, 1865–1920* (Jackson: University Press of Mississippi, 2008).

2. Saidiya V. Hartman, *Scenes of Subjection: Terror, Slavery, and Self-Making in Nineteenth-Century America* (New York: Oxford University Press, 1997).

3. C. Vann Woodward, *Origins of the New South, 1877–1913* (Baton Rouge: Louisiana State University Press, 1951); C. Vann Woodward, *The Strange Career of Jim Crow*, 3rd rev. ed. (New York: Oxford University Press, 1974).

4. Thomas Dixon, *The Leopard's Spots: A Romance of the White Man's Burden, 1865–1900* (New York: Doubleday Page, 1902); Thomas Dixon, *The Clansman: An Historical Romance of the Ku-Klux Klan* (New York: Doubleday Page, 1905).

5. Building on Woodward's *Origins of the New South*, Grantham's and Link's books on southern Progressivism illuminate the tradition's tensions and mixed legacies as well as

its accomplishments. For a more recent study that fully considers how analyses of southern problems and solutions were inextricably connected to U.S. *colonialist* discourses and practices, see Jatalie J. Ring's *The Problem South: Region, Empire, and the New Liberal State, 1880–1930* (Athens: University of Georgia Press, 2012). Dewey W. Grantham, *Southern Progressivism: The Reconciliation of Progress and Tradition* (Knoxville: University of Tennessee Press, 1983); and William A. Link, *The Paradox of Southern Progressivism* (Chapel Hill: University of North Carolina Press, 1992).

6. Aurelio Tolentino, *Yesterday, Today, and Tomorrow*, in *Filipino Drama*, ed. Arthur Stanley Riggs (1905; rpt. Manila: Ministry of Human Settlements, Intramuros Administration, 1981), 332. Page numbers hereafter given parenthetically in the text.

7. Riggs, *Filipino Drama*, 276–333.

8. Tolentino's and Riggs' contributions to the U.S. colonial archive are difficult to access today. To read the play, I used interlibrary loan; the copy lent to me, from a 1980s reprinting done in Manila but only sporadically available in United States, came from the Philippines Consulate library in New York City. I have made a pdf of Riggs's translation of and commentary on Tolentino's *Yesterday, Today, and Tomorrow* available on my Web site, linked to my book *Sitting in Darkness*: http://www.swarthmore.edu/Humanities/pschmidl/scholarship.html. For further discussion of Tolentino and Riggs see my *Sitting in Darkness*, 144–50.

9. For more on these developments see my *Sitting in Darkness*, 99–125.

10. Etienne Balibar, "Subjection and Subjectivation," in *Supposing the Subject*, ed. Joan Copjec (New York: Verso, 1994), 7.

11. George Washington Cable, *Lovers of Louisiana (To-day)* (New York: Scribner, 1918), 318–19. Page numbers hereafter given parenthetically in the text.

12. The word "supra-nationalism" is used to describe Wilson's position in Mark Weston Janis, "How 'Wilsonian' was Woodrow Wilson?" *Dartmouth Law Journal* 5, no. 1 (2007): 12 (see also 12 n. 47), http://lsr.nellco.org/uconn wps/75 (accessed September 26, 2010).

13. Wilson, "Fourteen Points Speech" (1918). Available at http://usinfo.org/docs/democracy/51.htm (accessed September 26, 2010). The excerpt quoted is from the second paragraph of the speech.

14. Here are the first and final stanzas of Kipling's famous poem, first published in 1899 to urge that the United States replace Spain as ruler of the Philippines. Kipling's poem hardly envisages civil rights at the heart of the colonial program; rather, it stresses that the colonists' efforts to reform the uncivilized behavior of the colonized will be met with scorn from both the natives and rival empires:

> Take up the White Man's burden—
> Send forth the best ye breed—
> Go bind your sons to exile
> To serve your captives' need;
> To wait in heavy harness,
> On fluttered folk and wild—

Your new-caught, sullen peoples,
Half-devil and half-child.

. . . .

Take up the White Man's burden—
Have done with childish days—
The lightly proferred laurel,
The easy, ungrudged praise.
Comes now, to search your manhood
Through all the thankless years
Cold, edged with dear-bought wisdom,
The judgment of your peers!

   Rudyard Kipling, *Poems, 1886–1929* (London: Macmillan, 1929).

15. W. E. B. Du Bois, "The African Roots of the War," *Atlantic Monthly*, May 1915, 707–14.

16. George Washington Cable, *Old Creole Days* (New York: Scribner, 1879); George Washington Cable, *The Grandissimes: A Story of Creole Life* (New York: Scribner, 1880); George Washington Cable, *The Silent South* (New York: Scribner, 1885; expanded edition, 1889); George Washington Cable, *The Negro Question* (New York: Scribner, 1890).

17. *Lovers of Louisiana (To-Day)* is available for free online, via Google Books.

18. Albion Tourgée, *Bricks without Straw: A Novel*, ed. Carolyn L. Karcher (1880; reprint, Durham: Duke University Press, 2009). Page numbers hereafter given parenthetically in the text.

19. See Ellen Douglas, *Truth: Four Stories I Am Finally Old Enough to Tell* (Chapel Hill: Algonquin Press, 1998). For a fine introductory discussion of Douglas's career as an intrepid exploration of the borderline between truth and fiction, I recommend Panthea Reid, "Invention and Truth: Ellen Douglas and *Truth*." *Virginia Quarterly Review* 75 (Summer 1999): 583–89, http://www.vqronline.org/articles/1999/summer/reid-invention-truth. The epigraph Douglas chose for *Truth* is also relevant. It is from Robert Penn Warren's *Brother to Dragons*, a verse novel that, like Douglas's *Truth*, reinterprets the past by giving space to a greater variety of voices: "Forgetting is just another kind of remembering." Robert Penn Warren, *Brother to Dragons* (New York: Random House, 1979).

20. Leo Tolstoy, *War and Peace*, trans. Richard Pevear and Larissa Volokhonsky (New York: Knopf, 2007), 1220.

21. Albion Tourgée, *A Fool's Errand* (1879; reprint, New York: Fords, Howard, and Hulbert, 1880).

22. Alexis de Tocqueville, *Democracy in America*, vol. 1, ed. Phillips Bradley (New York: Random House/Vintage, 1945).

23. Carolyn L. Karcher, introduction to Albion Tourgée, *Bricks without Straw*, ed. Karcher (Durham: Duke University Press, 2007), 1–64.

24. Mark Elliott, *Color-Blind Justice: Albion Tourgée and the Quest for Racial Equality from the Civil War to "Plessy v. Ferguson"* (New York: Oxford University Press, 2006), 130.

25. Following Elliott's lead (*Color-Blind Justice*, 116–17 and 344 n. 64), Karcher has

found a possible source for some of the ideas in Hesden's speech (*Bricks without Straw*, 444 n. 116). They may be attributable to Tourgée's friend Thomas Settle Jr. in his 1876 campaign for governor of North Carolina. For more on Settle, whose papers are in the Southern Historical Collection at the University of North Carolina, see Jeffrey J. Crow, "Thomas Settle, Jr., Reconstruction, and the Memory of the Civil War," *Journal of Southern History* 62 (November 1996): 689–726. For Elliott's analysis of Tourgée's role in the 1868 North Carolina constitutional convention, and the conservative criticism he received, see especially 123–33.

26. Eric Foner, *Reconstruction: America's Unfinished Revolution, 1863–1877* (New York: Harper and Row, 1988), 356. Page numbers hereafter given parenthetically in the text.

27. Paul D. Escott, *Many Excellent People: Power and Privilege in North Carolina, 1850–1900* (Chapel Hill: University of North Carolina Press, 1985), 15–16, 20. Escott's points regarding antebellum democracy in North Carolina are at variance with those of earlier southern historians such as Cash and Green, who argued there was growing democratization in southern politics in the Jackson era and after, in contrast to the planter-domination thesis of Phillips. For more on these debates, see David Brown's essay in this volume. Brown's focus on the limited political influence of southern white non-elites in the antebellum period provides some support for Tourgée's claims. Tourgée, Escott, and Brown concur regarding North Carolina: as Brown puts it, elites in North Carolina "were arguably the most successful of all the Upper South states in resisting change." Brown's analysis of state-by-state conditions, however, also suggests that Le Moyne's and Tourgée's generalizations about township democracy *throughout* the South may be too broad.

28. Ibid., 167.

29. Albion Tourgée, *The Invisible Empire* (1880; reprint, New York: Gregg Press, 1968).

30. Anna Julia Cooper, *A Voice from the South*, ed. Mary Helen Washington (1892; reprint, New York: Oxford University Press, 1988), 189.

# Epilogue

......................

# Place as Everywhere

## On Globalizing the American South

MICHAEL O'BRIEN

Two recent, interconnected, and intriguing developments have been the projects of globalizing southern history and that literary scholarship which has come to be called the New Southern Studies. Both are worth encouraging, but also merit scrutiny, and both are of help in making sense of the problem of citizenship. The former is of direct relevance to the nineteenth century; the latter has for the most part been preoccupied with the twentieth or, at least, the status of the South since the defeat of the Confederacy.

At the heart of the former project are economic historians and occasionally sociologists, who have been making a case for the deep engagement of the southern economy and its attendant social relations in a wider global market. At first this case was preoccupied with recent and contemporary markets, with Japanese car manufacturers in Alabama or with Chicano migrant workers in North Carolina, and hence initially tended to assume that this marked an unprecedented moment in southern culture. By these lights, the pre-1941 South was a world that, though it exported people to the rest of the United States, was otherwise isolated and backward, and this condition stretched back to the Civil War, if not further. There is a Gothic image of the South after the Civil War articulated by Thomas Wolfe in *The Web and the Rock*, an image that might seem apposite:

There was an image in George Webber's mind that came to him in childhood and resumed for him the whole dark picture of those decades of defeat and darkness. He saw an old house, set far back from the travelled highway, and many passed along that road, and the troops went by, the dust rose, and the war was over. He saw an old man go along the path, away from the road, into the house; and the path was overgrown with grass and weeds, with thorny tangle, and with underbrush until the path was lost. And no one ever used that path again. And the man who went into that house never came out of it again. And the house stayed on. It shone faintly through that tangled growth like its own ruined spectre, its doors and windows black as eyeless sockets. That was the South. That was the South for thirty years or more.[1]

This is a quotation I used in my first (and very bad) article on the South. I can now see, looking back, that I was to become overly impressed with the notion of experiencing the changes these economic and social historians came to describe. Somehow I seemed one of the many people penetrating the tangled growth, and there, in a back bedroom, I found the eyeless sockets of Allen Tate, among other dank skeletons.[2] The process of renovating the house seemed to come in stages. So, when I was twenty and first visited the South, I was a curiosity whom the locals examined with politeness and puzzling Anglophilia, because they saw so few strangers. So, when I went to teach at the University of Arkansas in 1980, I was a small part of a wider in-migration and strangers were becoming more common. So, later, when I went to southern historical conventions, I began to encounter other Europeans, at the same moment that I went to Genoa and encountered southerners abroad. So, much later, there came to be conferences, like those that were the inception of this book, which took the existence of a transnational conversation about the South for granted. It is a beguiling historical construct, this vision of a movement from isolation to engagement, and the construct is not groundless. However, the economic historians have, more recently, shifted their focus and often now remind us that Thomas Wolfe's image is deeply misleading, that at best his shuttered mansion existed very briefly and exceptionally, and that the entanglement of the South with international markets has been fairly continuous since the seventeenth century, that in-migration has long been a characteristic southern experience, that multiculturalism has long been a norm, that foreign investment in the southern economy has long been commonplace, and that the economic changes that began in the 1940s and accelerated in the 1970s should be seen less as an unprecedented innovation and more as the resumption of normal service, though within the framework of a dynamic world economic system that has much changed since 1607. Peter Coclanis, in particular, has been cogent on these matters.[3]

For the New Southern Studies, newness seems to matter more than it does to the economic historians, who like to see themselves as bearers of old news, too long forgotten. New Southern Studies strikes me as the more complicated of the two projects, in part because it is more interdisciplinary and so has more balls to keep in the air, in part because southern literary studies has long been marked by the anxiety of influences, generational conflicts, multicultural sensitivities, and the bemusing if exhilarating premises of postmodernism and postcolonialism. The economic historians have been little influenced by any of this and could have written what they have written without Jacques Derrida, or Edward Said, or magical realism ever having existed. And this seems to hold true of works of sociology, too, especially James Peacock's *Grounded Globalism*, which evidences an amiable empiricism of an older school. However, books like Jon Smith and Deborah Cohn's *Look Away! The U.S. South in New World Studies*, Scott Romine's *The Real South: Southern Narrative in the Age of Cultural Reproduction*, Suzanne Jones and Sharon Monteith's *South to a New Place*, and Martyn Bone's *The Postsouthern Sense of Place in Southern Fiction* are unimaginable without Derrida, Said, and the rest.[4] So we are not dealing with a single debate, but with two debates that happen to overlap and unstably share a few concepts.

One of the merits of the New Southern Studies is a quirky independence of mind and style, so it is difficult to discern a wide-ranging consensus about presumptions. Still, some propositions do seem apparent. The practitioners of this discourse share the postmodernist mistrust of essence and the postmodernist trust in constructive acts of imagination and will. So, they see no such thing as a natural southern community, as described by John Crowe Ransom, but only imagined communities, plural and hybrid. By the same token, place is not a social premise but a usable fiction, sometimes an unusable fiction. There is a sense that the South is best understood not by seeing it as connected to American culture and the North, its traditional counterpoints, but as one among many cultures, some in the New World, some in the Third World, some regional cultures in the developed world. This new configuration is thought to be plausible for a variety of reasons. Occasionally it is plausible because of mutualities of intellectual and literary influence—Gabriel García Márquez reading William Faulkner, for example. Sometimes it is thought to arise from a mutuality of experiences—having been plantation cultures, having suffered military defeat, being postcolonial, having a shared sense of marginality (which can run so deep as to merit the term *trauma*). Comity of experience seems, especially, to matter. As Cohn put it in 1999, she studies "convergences, similar features and strategies that have developed as responses to analogous sociopolitical and historical circumstances."[5]

Perhaps Melanie Benson has best summarized what the New Southern Studies wishes us to understand. "[This] wealth of critical activity," she writes, "has reconceptualized the South, often postcolonially, as a particularly diverse container of settlement and racial histories, stretching its purview to the global, Latin American, and Caribbean 'Souths' with which it shares histories, cultures, and legacies of economic and racial domination. . . . [T]he South [is] inherently and historically transnational."[6]

For all that, insofar as these are postmodern literary scholars, they are less committed to the constraints of the historical imagination than was common among southern literary critics in, say, 1960. So they seem to assert the right to seek out unexpected juxtapositions, which may or may not be demonstrable to the dogged historicist. Since the fragmentary is of the postmodernist essence, if I may hazard an oxymoron, it would be inconsistent to demand consistent patterns and tight logics from the New Southern Studies, which believes in the constitutive power of the imagination.

Here, no doubt, lies the deepest heterodoxy of this school, when judged by the standards of older traditions of southern thought, which stretch back to the Agrarians, but also to the beginnings of the nineteenth century. For nothing marked those traditions more than the desire to find order, establish synthesis, make binding patterns, and establish boundaries. Society, history, and place were thought to be meaningless unless specific. Community was us, not you. Place was here, not there. Self was me, not you. This was not an ideologically partisan desire, though in its later stages it seemed superficially to come more often from conservative thinkers like Donald Davidson. But, in truth, it came as much from George Washington Cable or C. Vann Woodward. What all these southerners shared was a powerful sense that, in the balance between freedom and constraint, there was more weight on the side of constraint. We are what our place has made us, we are what history has made us, we must choose what has

Epilogue: Place as Everywhere: On Globalizing the American South · 275

been chosen. To be sure, we might dissent and prefer Angelo Herndon to Tom Watson or W. E. B. Du Bois to Booker T. Washington, but there was assumed to be small maneuvering room, because the pressure of society and history was so great—great as a nightmare from which one wished to awake or great as a tradition one wished to celebrate—but always great.

I have argued elsewhere, in various places and with no great originality, that these southerners were offering a local variant of the larger paradigm of romanticism, that modernism was in turn a bleaker version of romanticism, and that postmodernism is a further variant, though one that has lightened the mood. Here it will be pertinent not to stress the continuities but to highlight how much difference that recent lightening of the mood has made. The older traditions of romanticism and modernism, with varying degrees of explicitness, usually had religious purposes. Wordsworth, Hegel, Michelet, Schleiermacher, Eliot, all saw God as an indispensable referent. If we were trapped by society and history, it was because this was God's purpose, God's trial, or God's gift. One characteristic of postmodernism, however, is its indifference to God. Nietzsche, at least, thought God was worth killing, but postmodernists do not often think he is worth mentioning. At best, God is bundled up with many other metanarratives, about which there is incredulity. This indifference helps to explain the postmodernist enthusiasm for the disparate and fragmentary. It was the deep, awful fear of the older traditions that admitting to a loss of pattern would lead to a loss of faith, the death of God, atheism, disorder, and ignorant armies clashing at night. If you do not care a whit for God and the afterlife, a loss of pattern can be transmuted into the possibility of freedom.

Freedom has been a central theme of recent American and southern thought. I do not mean by that only what one might conventionally designate as the traditions of American political and civic freedom, such as can be found in the Bill of Rights, the Fourteenth Amendment, and the values expressed in the civil rights movement and its various spin-offs—the freedom to vote, the freedom to have an abortion, the freedom to express a sexuality, and so forth. More fundamentally, there has been an idea, amounting to a belief, that individuals not only *should be* free to choose but that individuals *are* free to choose. An extraordinary amount of the scholarship of recent decades has concentrated on locating moments of freedom, in time and space, and on stressing the humane possibilities inherent in contingency.[7]

The scholars of globalization differ widely about freedom. There have been many neoliberal economists who have claimed that globalization offers the final freedom for economic man, in that, by it, he or she is enabled to leap free of the local constraints of regulating nation-states. For such thinkers, the freedom of the market must, finally, be the freedom of the global market, and in the long run there will be more prosperity around the globe because of that freedom. Other economists, or rather other social thinkers who have interested themselves in economic matters—the distinction is necessary because, in our time, hard economists have lost interest in the humane traditions of Adam Smith, David Ricardo, Karl Marx, and John Maynard Keynes—have been more gloomy. They see little but danger in unregulated freedom, and they stress how the freedom of the market has created an abundance of human misery—sweatshops in Thailand, imprisoned Filipino maids in Riyadh, sex trafficking in Rome, cheap labor everywhere, money that flits irresponsibly and destructively around the globe and the Internet. By their lights, there is little hope of human freedom in globalization—indeed, globalization can be seen as extinguishing what might meaningfully be regarded as freedom. In the 1980s and even into the 1990s, the former school was predominant. Now, with the world economic crisis, the latter school looks likely to dominate the debate for the foreseeable future.

I have been struck, in reading the New Southern Studies, that its scholars seem curiously, if only implicitly, closer to the neoliberal position than they might prefer. Not that they are indifferent to sweatshops and sex trafficking—quite the reverse, in fact. Martyn Bone, for example, in *The Postsouthern Sense of Place*, is anxious to "take a stand . . . against the exploitative forces and purely economic definitions of 'globalization' or 'transnationalism,' and for radically revised conceptions of community and solidarity."[8] Still, most of the New Southern scholars seem to assume that globalization, though its economics might often be pernicious, may have social consequences that may, if we are lucky, tend to increase human freedom. The dissolving of boundaries, the movements of peoples, the juxtaposition and mingling of cultures, the hybridity of discourses— these are portrayed as promising developments, because they multiply choices and contingencies, and they weaken coercive authorities. To some extent, I sympathize with this standpoint.[9] Still, there is a problem and it runs deep. Whatever Alexander ("whatever is, is right") Pope may have claimed, let alone Hegel, the moral and the real are not synonymous and, for good or ill, the world is not a thing our imagination can freely construct, because we are made by the world even as we make it. There is the individual, but also the social. So the New Southern Studies may be more invested in individualism than it realizes, if only because it is so anxious to distance itself from organic communitarianism. The individual consciousness, not the social, does seem to be its basic unity of analysis. Richard Gray, whose qualifications as a paid-up member of the New Southern Studies might be regarded as doubtful, states the problem in his recent Lamar lectures, where he writes: "Just as each *southerner* is irrevocably private, an individual and yet implicated in history, connected to a complex web of *social* relations . . . so each southern *writer* works within a map that locates him or her as both autonomous and engaged, separate yet involved in a vaster regional and transregional geography of speech."[10]

Nothing is more social than citizenship, one of this book's topics and pertinent to globalization, not least because citizenship is deeply implicated in the nation-state, an entity for which the New Southern Studies has expressed little enthusiasm, as a compelling instance of the "organic culture which is gone for good."[11] As Kathryn McKee and Annette Trefzer have put it, many proponents of the New Southern Studies think it needful to reject "the structuralist principles that guided state formation" and, instead, "unmoor the South from its national harbor," so that it may become "a floating signifier in a sea of globalism."[12] Jon Smith and Deborah Cohn have spoken of a desire to "avoid modernity's fetishization of the nation-state and the imagined community," and they recommend that we look away, not just from the northern United States, but even from the United States.[13] Leigh Ann Duck's *The Nation's Region: Southern Modernism, Segregation, and U.S. Nationalism* (2006) is deeply informed by a skepticism about American exceptionalism and explores the instabilities of regional and national discourses, as well as what she calls the "model of binding and determinate group identification."[14] Melanie Benson has written of "the delusions of exceptionalism."[15] Martyn Bone wants us to develop a "critical, global 'sense of place,'" presumably in preference to that sense that is regional or national.[16] Even James Peacock, that most benign of commonsensical authors, politely averts his gaze from the American nation-state; the happy migrants inhabiting his pages seem to flow over borders with as much ease as though wandering over so many suburban lawns to reach a church picnic.

This logic can work in many ways. One might focus on the unmoored South and ignore the rest of the United States, for example, or you might focus on the rest of the United States and ignore the South. The latter is the intellectual strategy of Jennifer Rae Greeson's *Our South: Geographic Fantasy and the Rise of National Literature*, which argues that the South, in the late eighteenth and nineteenth centuries, played only an oblique role in the American national narrative. This was so, not merely because many northern writers of cultural authority regarded the South as un-American, but because, in fact, the South itself played no significant role in the making of American literary culture, other than as a blank canvas on which Americans projected their fantasies, and did not belong to "the metropolis—the center of cultural production, the cultural capital." Hence she feels she can rigorously say: "I leave to the side questions of 'southern identity,' and do not attempt to account for the points of view of people living in southern states, except as those people come to engage in the dominant metropolitan discourse."[17]

I am no great fan of the nation-state and even less so of nationalism, but few phenomena are more important in modern history. Amid the vast body of writing on the modern state, there is a pertinent body of scholarship about the relationship between globalization and the nation-state, which is worth bringing into this debate about the South. Notable are the various works of Saskia Sassen, works that do not seem to have had much if any influence on how southern historians and literary critics have approached globalization. Peacock, it is true, does glancingly refer to her stress upon cities as sites for globalization, but Sassen seems to be absent from the texts, footnotes, and bibliographies of the New Southern Studies.[18] This seems a pity, because, although Sassen's prose is murky, her analyses are often trenchant, especially in *Territory, Authority, Rights* (2006).[19] To some extent, the historical part of her analysis is conventional and unsurprising. She describes how medieval culture was fragmented and local, then how from the seventeenth century the nation-state began to supersede these particularities and gather to itself a broad range of sovereign powers—legal, economic, cultural, political. If anything, she is less impressed by the existence of economic globalization before the twentieth century than many modern historians, especially Chris Bayly in *The Birth of the Modern World, 1780–1914*.[20] More valuable is how Sassen sees the period since 1945. Her major argument is that the global economic system established at Bretton Woods, which created the International Bank for

Reconstruction and Development (latterly enfolded into the World Bank) and the International Monetary Fund and fixed currency exchange rates, should be regarded not as a supersession of nation-states but as a system sponsored by and largely controlled by nation-states, or, at least, a small number of developed nation states. Second, she contends that this system began to collapse in the 1970s, when nation-states, sometimes intentionally in the name of deregulation, sometimes unwillingly, began to lose control of the movements of capital, and a realm of globalized capitalism came to exist in parallel to those financial structures still under the control, more or less, of national governments. However, she does not see globalization as a lawless realm, filled with freebooters who wander the globe in search of profit, cheap labor, and plunder, freebooters who have sufficient fiscal muscle to ignore nation-states. Rather, she thinks globalization has its own structures, now powerful enough to interact with nation-states, often to the point of changing national policies. We are no longer in the world of 1945, when nation-states dictated the terms of globalization, but neither are we in a world where globalization can freely dictate the terms of nationality. Rather, we are in a poised and dialectical world where nationality is unintelligible without globalization, but—this is relevant to the New Southern Studies—globalization is unintelligible without nationality.

What are these global structures? Most obvious are the corporations with a global reach, available to be seen as freebooters. But there are many other transnational, international, and non-national structures—the United Nations, the World Bank, the International Monetary Fund, and the World Trade Organization, as well as regional institutions like the European Union. Falteringly, there are legal institutions, notably the International Criminal Court, the International Court of Justice, and the European Court of Justice. There are articulations of international law, such as the UN's Declaration of Human Rights (promulgated in 1948) and the European Union's Charter of Fundamental Rights (2000). Sassen makes much of the innumerable informal organizations and NGOs who work internationally but negotiate habitually with nation-states and international organizations—Greenpeace, Amnesty International, Oxfam, the Red Cross, Médecins Sans Frontières, and the like.

Clearly, these global and regional structures unevenly affect the lives of individual citizens and those with no citizenship. For the most part, these structures are instruments of the powerful to control the lives of the less powerful or powerless. So only politicians from failed states get hauled before the International Criminal Court, only the human rights intelligible to Western states are encoded in the Declaration of Human Rights, only weak economies need take orders from the International Monetary Fund, and so forth. However, the case of the European Union, at least, modifies this assertion, for this is a bargain among the powerful, who see cooperation as a means to greater power, or at least to greater prosperity.

So globalization is not a counterpoint to nationality and not a formless sea that offers an escape from the oppressions of place, landscape, community, and nation. The global world has its own imagined communities, binaries, and structures of entrapment and freedom. Now, you may prefer to identify with these global patterns, in contradistinction to national ones, but it is doubtful that you thereby gain freedom.

But where does the United States sit in these global patterns? In one sense, the United States is deeply enmeshed, in ways that southern economic historians and literary scholars well understand, because Americans, including southerners, have created and exported so many international corporations and have imported so much labor, legally and illegally. In another sense, the position of the United States is anomalous. In most parts of the world, the nation-state is only one among the governmental and nongovernmental institutions that structure the lives of individuals. In much of Africa, as elsewhere, nation-states tenuously exist and institutions like UNESCO and Oxfam are deeply important. At the other end of the scale, in Scotland, for example, a citizen deals with at least three levels of government (the devolved Scottish parliament, the British government in Westminster, and the European Union), and this experience is common for many Europeans, who have uneasily habituated themselves to divided sovereignties and multiple jurisdictions. This is not utterly different from the structures of American federalism, except that the United States, since the Civil War, has established a firm hierarchy among these levels and the Europeans have not, or very unstably.

What has become peculiar about the United States is that it has remained largely insulated from this commonplace global condition of not experiencing a unified nation-state as the precondition for civil life. Americans send money to the United Nations and the World Bank, but one would be hard put to see how, in any significant way, the lives of American residents are influenced by decisions made by the United Nations and the World Bank. Almost all NGOs, apart from those interested in ecological matters, do not operate within American borders, save for fund-raising purposes. Further, the United States has in recent years refused to join a number of international organizations and ventures. It never signed the Kyoto Treaty, it has refused to ratify the treaty that created the International Criminal Court and disavows the court's jurisdiction over American citizens, and, during the administrations of the younger Bush, it formally withdrew from any binding sense of obligation toward even the Geneva Conventions. It has grown semi-detached from the United Nations. The U.S. Supreme Court, though over the dissent of a small minority of justices, does not acknowledge that international law has a pertinence to American constitutional law. With the exceptions of North Korea and perhaps China, one would be hard put to name a country that is more resolutely committed to the sovereign prerogatives of the nation-state than the United States, and more feebly committed to internationalism. The only exception may be NAFTA, but that is a pale abridgment of national sovereignty in comparison to the abridgments intrinsic to the European Union. For most Americans, the global, the transnational, and the international are only instrumentalities for the American nation-state and its citizens, and hence hardly ever involve reciprocity. For most Americans, to use M. H. Abrams's old phrase, the world is a mirror and not a lamp, despite or because of Barack Obama's diffident attempts to suggest otherwise.

A proponent of the New Southern Studies might, at this point, say that this peculiar strength of the American nation-state is why he or she would wish to flee its oppressive authority, why she or he would wish to venture upon the bracing seas of globalism. Well, maybe, but it does seem to me that much of the fiction, critical writing, and social theory that recommends a globalism of the imagination—especially that emanating from Latin America—comes from cultures where states are weak, nationality is contested, and the postcolonial condition is often freshly apparent, and hence comes from cultures very differently placed from the United States and its southern region. By contrast, American and southern commentators, used to living in so strong an institutional framework, tend overmuch to see the global world as formless. With the exception of Peacock's work, the institutions of globalism to which I have just referred are absent from the texts of the New Southern Studies, and are even absent from the studies of the economic historians, who tend most to focus on the centripetal, on how globalism has affected the American labor market, especially through immigration. Almost all of James Cobb and William Stueck's *Globalization and the American South*, for example, is preoccupied with the centripetal. The titles of many essays tell the story: "Globalization, Latinization, and the *Nuevo* New South," "Asian Immigrants in the South," "From Southeast Asia to the American Southeast: Japanese Business Meets the Sun Belt South," "Another Southern Paradox: The Arrival of Foreign Corporations—Change and Continuity in Spartanburg, South Carolina." More marginal to this narrative is not how globalization has changed the South but how the South through the mechanisms of globalization has changed the world.

So my sense is that, because of the peculiarity of the American condition, the New Southern Studies, in turning away from the nation-state, is turning away from more than would be the case for, say, a Colombian scholar or even a British one and so may be leaving more unexplained. This is not to say that the nation-state should be restored to its status as the omnicompetent point of reference, the singular framework, but it is to say that there is no fixed pattern in the balance between the institutions of the nation-state and the institutions of globalism, and that the balance or imbalance varies from country to country. As it happens, the United States and its southern region are at that end of the spectrum where the nation-state is strong and the influence of global institutions is weak, yet many southern scholars are drawing their theoretical premises from the middle or other end of the spectrum. This poses an intellectual problem.

Why are the New Southern Studies so interested in evading the topic of the American nation-state? The postmodernist theoretical position is clear enough, but the cultural politics are more elusive. There is much talk of boredom, that the old themes are hackneyed to the point of tedium. There is some talk of repudiating the New England paradigm for understanding American culture, not by substituting a southern paradigm or gaining coequal status in the making of paradigms but by abandoning the national cultural paradigm, *in toto*. This can look suspiciously like taking your ball and going home when you are losing a game. But, it may be more a statement that the game has grown tedious, that it is time to stop playing baseball and start playing . . . well, what? Pelota? Or there may be a deeper strategy. Sometimes it seems to be argued that the North is playing the old game of dominating the nation, but this means it has failed to notice that there is a new game in town, the global game. So the hope seems to be that Harvard graduates will smile and say complacently that they control American culture and society, while Vanderbilt graduates, in due course, will be able to smile and say complacently that they have helped to make the world, besides which American cultural politics are small beer. If this inference is right, it becomes unclear whether this is a cosmopolitanism designed to earn standing within a national culture or a cosmopolitanism that wishes to abandon a national culture.[21]

Yet there is a deeper issue, perhaps more troubling, to do with the matter of centrality and marginality, the logic that this new scholarship repudiates. After the Civil War the South was regarded by other Americans as marginal, and white southerners responded by either following the logic of the New South movement and trying to join the mainstream or, following the logic latterly articulated by the Agrarians, claiming a distinct moral equivalence or superiority. In both cases, southerners discerned a distance between themselves and the actions of the American nation-state. In the case of black southerners, that distance was more or less absolute. But, since the 1960s, the distance has dramatically closed and even been erased, because the South assumed a full share of American political power and even of cultural power through its religion, music, and literature. Between 1963 and 2009, southerners occupied the White House for eighteen years, westerners for thirteen, Texans (hard to classify but semi-southern) for twelve, and northerners for barely three—and that by accident. To be sure, the elder Bush was a New Englander by birth, education, and temperament, yet a Texan in politics. No politician from Maine, outside the agreeable fantasy of *The West Wing*, could have become president, any more than Woodrow Wilson would have reached the White House if he had not migrated from Virginia to New Jersey. Southern political power, likewise, has been decisive in the House and the Senate, and influential upon American jurisprudence.

This being so, it is unclear what it might mean to assert that southern culture should or might be unmoored from the American nation-state, when one considers that southern culture has become intrinsic to the American nation-state, as intrinsic as it was in the years between George Washington and James K. Polk. Whatever the United States has done in the last half-century—good, bad, and indifferent—is ineluctably the South's responsibility, not alone, but significantly. Hence a cultural decision to ignore the nation-state could be understood as an evasion of responsibility for that half-century and might lead to an inability to recognize and describe a central theme of recent southern history and culture, which is not the region's dispossession but the region's profound entanglement with power, exercised nationally and internationally. To reconfigure the South now as the natural companion of the dispossessed, the marginal, and the postcolonial seems, when viewed in this light, a paradoxical venture.

What of citizenship, the theme of this book? What I observed earlier about the positioning of the United States in the global order may be applied, though less stringently, to citizenship and its connected problem, rights. To understand this, it helps to go back to the origins of the American republic. In theory, in the beginning, it was presumed that natural rights, as a gift from God, were intrinsic to the human condition and that Americans, in promulgating the Declaration of Independence and enacting the Bill of Rights, had merely made themselves into a people who articulated what should be common to all human beings, and what would become common. But, in practice, Americans came to enfold the idea of natural rights into the prerogatives of citizenship, a tendency much amplified when the Fourteenth Amendment displaced citizenship from the states to the federal government and, with some ambiguity, offered the equal protection of the laws to citizens, but not necessarily to non-citizens, and hence placed a distance between American constitutional law and natural rights, intrinsic to citizen and non-citizen alike. I say with ambiguity, because the first clause of the second sentence of section 1 of the Fourteenth Amendment is insistent upon the centrality of citizenship—"No State shall make or enforce any law which shall abridge the privileges or immunities of citizens of the United States"—but it is not clear whether the next clauses—"nor shall any State deprive any person of life, liberty, or property, without due process of law; nor deny to any person within its jurisdiction the equal protection of the laws"—apply only to citizens or, instead, to anyone resident in the United States. The latter interpretation would provide grounds for thinking the Constitution was respectful of natural rights, not merely of civil rights. However, with rare exceptions, American courts have opted for the narrower interpretation. Citizens have rights, non-citizens do not, or only as a revocable courtesy. It has been logical, therefore, that non-citizens should often have made great efforts to gain access to citizenship, because it has meant entering a magic circle. (It is one of the paradoxes of modern history that monarchies, who had only subjects, were in this regard less exclusionary than democratic republics, who had citizens and non-citizens of unequal condition.) This premise of the desirability of citizenship helped to make those great American metanarratives—the stories of immigration and assimilation, African American emancipation, women's rights. They all tell of the movement from non-citizenship to citizenship, and hence from darkness to light, from exclusion to belonging. We are asked to believe that these are encouraging stories, that this is how it is supposed to work.

It is important to remember that, during the American Revolution, it became necessary to invent the idea of voluntary allegiance. Under British law, since individuals were subjects and not citizens, their allegiance to the Crown was not a matter of choice. In search of a rationale for severing that allegiance, Americans opted for the social contract, and hence becoming a citizen become a matter of voluntary choice, as it still is. Anyone who is an American citizen can fill in a form foreswearing his or her allegiance, and the American government is obliged to let that person go. On the other hand, Elizabeth II—queen of the United Kingdom of Great Britain and Northern Ireland, Canada, Australia, New Zealand, Jamaica, Barbados, the Bahamas, Grenada, Papua New Guinea, the Solomon Islands, Tuvalu, and Saint Lucia, Supreme Governor of the Church of England, Duke of Normandy, Lord of Man, and Paramount Chief of Fiji—feels no such obligation. But one implication, not necessary but habitual, of the American doctrine of voluntary allegiance became that Americans were obliged to have only one allegiance. To become an American was to cease to be a Prussian or whatever. It was to become, for example, part of the ritual of American citizenship ceremonies in the late twentieth century that new citizens should solemnly hand over their old passports. The oath one has to take reads, in part, "I hereby declare, on oath, that I absolutely and entirely renounce and abjure all allegiance and fidelity to any foreign prince, potentate, state or sovereignty, of whom or which I have heretofore been a subject or citizen; that I will support and defend the Constitution and laws of the United States of America against all enemies, foreign and domestic . . ." and so forth.[22] This made being an American an exclusionary condition; to become an American citizen was to cease to be, not only a non-citizen, but a non-American.

Curiously, citizenship is one of the few areas in which the United States has yielded legal ground to the forces of globalization and, however mildly, abridged its otherwise iron insistence upon American national sovereignty. For the United States does now tolerate dual and multiple allegiances, though very reluctantly. As the official web page of the State

Department puts it, with polite dishonesty: "The U.S. Government recognizes that dual nationality exists but does not encourage it as a matter of policy because of the problems it may cause. Claims of other countries on dual national U.S. citizens may conflict with U.S. law, and dual nationality may limit U.S. Government efforts to assist citizens abroad."[23]

Embedded in this issue is a dissonance between civil rights and human rights. Nothing has been more characteristic of the effort to control and civilize globalization than an insistence upon human rights. Hannah Arendt once argued that it became "the consensus of opinion" in the nineteenth century, as an implication of the French Declaration of the Rights of Man, that "human rights had to be invoked whenever individuals needed protection against the new sovereignty of the state and the new arbitrariness of society."[24] It followed that human rights are in tension with citizenship, for civil rights belong to citizens, while human rights belong to everyone, including the stateless and quasi-stateless. But, because those who possess human rights but not civil rights are mostly weak or powerless, it has also followed that human rights have been seldom respected. For Arendt, especially as a Jew at a time when Jews filled the ranks of the stateless, this was a matter for profound regret, though her solution was to move toward community and the state.

It has been the traditional response of Americans, including southerners, to resolve this problem by extending the magic circle of citizenship or—this has been the other side of the same coin—by restricting or eliminating the number of non-citizens, especially by restricting immigration. One effect of globalization is to make these solutions more implausible. There is too much migration, too much hybridity, too many diasporas, and this has led to a slackening of interest in the civic bargain of singular citizenship, even of citizenship itself. This has happened up and down the social scale. At the top end there are people like Rupert Murdoch, an Australian who acquired an American passport not because he wished to be a citizen of the American republic but because it advanced his economic purposes. In the middle there are what Sassen calls "transnational networks of government officials" and social activists.[25] At the bottom there are low-wage migrants, who might move from a province of Mexico where the state little intruded upon their lives, to Atlanta, where the state prefers to ignore them; these migrants can feel little reason to engage with the implausible abstractions of citizenship.

Here there is a dilemma. Nothing is more central to southern history and literary studies than the metanarrative of civil rights, understood as a progress. Yet, from the standpoint of globalization, civil rights can be understood as an enemy, because the idea of civil rights privileges citizenship over non citizenship and habitually denies human rights. Liberal proponents of the global, when seeing this dilemma, respond by striving to amplify human rights and trying to lodge in the international system an ethical structure that might be indifferent to passports and allegiances, that might be portable between cultures, and that might nonetheless receive social justice from those nation-states that migrants and the stateless might, however fleetingly, inhabit. For some theorists this is a matter of superseding citizenship as ordinarily understood, while for others it is a matter of transforming citizenship from the exclusionary to the inclusive, of "denationalizing" citizenship, or of devising a "postnational citizenship."[26] Not astonishingly, neither effort is going very well, given the weakness of international juridical bodies, given that assertions of human rights tend only to gain traction by working through nation-states, and given that such states are governed by citizens, fairly exclusively in the interests of citizens. It is still more discouraging to reflect that almost all the institutions of globalization, whether liberal or conservative, are non-democratic and that even human rights, enforced internationally, lack democratic sanction, except very obliquely. Corporations, NGOs, and international bureaucracies do not have voters. As James Tully has recently put it, "Effective political power can no longer be assumed to be located in representative governments alone. It is dispersed—shared, negotiated and contested by diverse agencies at the local, regional, national and international level. The systems of formal representative democratic government persist, of course, but they are crossed by complex economic, organisational, administrative, legal and cultural processes and structures that limit and escape their efficacy and grasp."[27]

Jimmy Carter notwithstanding, one of the great enemies of international human rights in the last generation has been the American South. Given the South's sense of self, both liberal and conservative, it is hard to see how it could have been otherwise. So the dilemma is very great, because it may follow that, if a scholar is serious about globalizing southern history, he or she may need to transform its narrative. The old story of civil rights as a story of progress may have to be thrown away, to be replaced with narratives in which southerners, black and white, are shown to have struck a bargain of citizenship that became a blind alley, from the dark corners of which the South looked out upon a world unintelligible to its civic presumptions. Or, if things turn out better than there is any reason to expect, there may come to be narratives in which southern commitments to civil rights wisely came to elide into a commitment to human rights. But neither scenario seems likely, because the southern metanarrative of civil rights is so fundamental and explicit, and the southern commitment to the American nation-state is so intrinsic. Yet this may mean that southerners will find it difficult to grasp and act upon the essential premise of a humane globalization, which does not involve an escape from the old structures of power but does mean an attempt to devise new structures that must, of necessity, interact with those old structures and thereby transform them.

## Notes

1. Thomas Wolfe, *The Web and the Rock* (London: William Heinemann, 1947), 231.

2. Michael O'Brien, "Thomas Wolfe and the Problem of Southern Identity: An English Perspective," *South Atlantic Quarterly* 70 (Winter 1971): 103–4.

3. See Peter A. Coclanis, ed., *The Atlantic Economy during the Seventeenth and Eighteenth Centuries: Organization, Operation, Practice, and Personnel* (Columbia: University of South Carolina Press, 2005), and, especially, Peter A. Coclanis, "Globalization before Globalization: The South and the World to 1950," in *Globalization and the American South*, ed. James C. Cobb and William Stueck (Athens: University of Georgia Press, 2005), 19–35.

4. James L. Peacock, *Grounded Globalism: How the U.S. South Embraces the World* (Athens: University of Georgia Press, 2007); Jon Smith and Deborah Cohn, eds., *Look Away! The U.S. South in New World Studies* (Durham: Duke University Press, 2004); Scott Romine, *The Real South: Southern Narrative in the Age of Cultural Reproduction* (Baton Rouge: Louisiana State University Press, 2008); Suzanne W. Jones and Sharon Monteith, eds., *South to a New Place: Region, Literature, Culture* (Baton Rouge: Louisiana State University Press, 2002); Martyn Bone, *The Postsouthern Sense of Place in Contemporary Fiction* (Baton Rouge: Louisiana State University Press, 2005).

5. Deborah Cohn, *History and Memory in the Two Souths: Recent Southern and Spanish American Fiction* (Nashville: Vanderbilt University Press, 1999), 7.

6. Melanie R. Benson, *Disturbing Calculations: The Economics of Identity in Postcolonial Southern Literature, 1912–2002* (Athens: University of Georgia Press, 2008), 18.

7. One among many examples are the essays collected in Jane Elizabeth Dailey, Glenda Elizabeth Gilmore, and Bryant Simon, eds., *Jumpin' Jim Crow: Southern Politics from Civil War to Civil Rights* (Princeton: Princeton University Press, 2000).

8. Bone, *Postsouthern Sense of Place*, 252.

9. Michael O'Brien, *Placing the South* (Jackson: University Press of Mississippi, 2007), vii–xii.

10. Richard Gray, *A Web of Words: The Great Dialogue of Southern Literature* (Athens: University of Georgia Press, 2007), 5.

11. Romine, *The Real South*, 2.

12. Kathryn McKee and Annette Trefzer, "Preface: Global Contexts, Local Literatures: The New Southern Studies," *American Literature* 78 (December 2006): 678.

13. Smith and Cohn, *Look Away!* 9.

14. Leigh Anne Duck, *The Nation's Region: Southern Modernism, Segregation, and U.S. Nationalism* (Athens: University of Georgia Press, 2006), 4.

15. Benson, *Disturbing Calculations*, 17.

16. Bone, *Postsouthern Sense of Place*, 253.

17. Jennifer Rae Greeson, *Our South: Geographic Fantasy and the Rise of National Literature* (Cambridge: Harvard University Press, 2010), 2.

18. Peacock, *Grounded Globalism*, 162.

19. Saskia Sassen, *Territory, Authority, Rights: From Medieval to Global Assemblages* (Princeton: Princeton University Press, 2006).

20. C. A. Bayly, *The Birth of the Modern World, 1780–1914: Global Connections and Comparisons* (Malden, Mass.: Blackwell, 2003).

21. On this distinction, see Bruce Robbins, "In Public, or Elsewhere: Stefan Collini on Intellectuals," *Modern Intellectual History* 5 (April 2008): 172–73.

22. *A Guide to Naturalization* (Washington, D.C.: Immigration and Naturalization Service, 2010), 28.

23. http://travel.state.gov/travel/cis_pa_tw/cis/cis_1753.html (accessed 30 August 2010).

24. Hannah Arendt, "The Perplexities of the Rights of Man" (1958), in Peter Baehr, ed., *The Portable Hannah Arendt* (New York: Penguin, 2000), 31.

25. Sassen, *Territory, Authority, Rights*, 298.

26. Ibid., 280.

27. James Tully, *Public Philosophy in a New Key*, vol. 1, *Democracy and Civic Freedom* (Cambridge: Cambridge University Press, 2008), 156.

# Contributors

Daina Ramey Berry is associate professor of history at the University of Texas at Austin. She is the author of *Swing the Sickle for the Harvest Is Ripe: Gender and Slavery in Antebellum Georgia* and editor of *Enslaved Women in America: An Encyclopedia*. She is also completing a coedited collection of essays with Leslie Harris titled *Slavery and Freedom in Savannah*. The Ford Foundation, the American Association of University Women, the National Humanities Center, and the American Council of Learned Societies have supported her research, and she was just named a Distinguished Lecturer by the Organization of American Historians.

Martyn Bone, associate professor of American literature at the University of Copenhagen, is the author of *Where the New World Is: Literature about the U.S. South at Global Scales*.

James J. Broomall is assistant professor in the history department at the University of North Florida. Interested in the nineteenth-century South and questions of gender identity, James has both written about and presented on this subject in various forums. His essay in this volume is based upon a portion of his current project, "Personal Confederacies: War and Peace in the American South, 1840–1890."

David Brown teaches American history at the University of Manchester in the UK, where he is senior lecturer in American studies. He is the author of *Southern Outcast: Hinton Rowan Helper and the Impending Crisis of the South* and coauthor of *Race in the American South: From Slavery to Civil Rights*. He is currently completing a study of yeomen and poor whites in the South in the mid-nineteenth century.

Jennifer Rae Greeson teaches American literature and American studies at the University of Virginia. She is the author of *Our South: Geographic Fantasy and the Rise of National Literature* as well as numerous articles in journals including *African American Review, American Literature*, and *American Literary History*. She is editor (with Robert Stepto) of the *Norton Critical Edition of Charles Chesnutt's Conjure Stories* and (with Scott Romine) of the forthcoming volume *Critical Terms for Southern Studies*. She is presently at work on a book on the long eighteenth century titled *American Enlightenment: The New World and Modern Western Thought*.

Watson Jennison is the author of *Cultivating Race: The Expansion of Slavery in Georgia, 1750–1860*. He is associate professor in the history department at the University of North Carolina at Greensboro.

Susanna Michele Lee is assistant professor of history at North Carolina State University, where she specializes in nineteenth-century history and teaches the Civil War and Reconstruction. She has two forthcoming books: one on post–Civil War southern citizenship and another on civilians in Virginia during the Civil War.

William A. Link is the Richard J. Milbauer Professor of History at the University of Florida, a position he has held since 2004. His publications include *Roots of Secession: Slavery and Politics in Antebellum Virginia, Righteous Warrior: Jesse Helms and the Rise of Modern Conservatism*, and *Links: My Family in American History*. His current book project, a study of race and memory in Atlanta titled *Cradle of the New South: Race and the Struggle for Meaning in the Civil War's Aftermath*, will appear in 2013.

Michael O'Brien is professor of American intellectual history at the University of Cambridge and a fellow of the British Academy. He has written extensively on the intellectual culture of the American South, most notably in *Conjectures of Order: Intellectual Life and the American South, 1810–1860*, which won the Bancroft Prize and was a Nominated Finalist for the Pulitzer Prize in History. His most recent book is *Mrs. Adams in Winter: A Journey in the Last Days of Napoleon*, which was a Nominated Finalist for the Pulitzer Prize in Biography.

Scott Romine is professor of English at the University of North Carolina at Greensboro, where he teaches courses in American and southern literature. He is the author of *The Narrative Forms of Southern Community* and *The Real South: Southern Narrative in the Age of Cultural Reproduction*.

Peter Schmidt teaches U.S. literature and literary history at Swarthmore College. He has published books on William Carlos Williams and on Eudora Welty. His latest book is *Sitting in Darkness: New South Fiction, Education, and the Rise of Jim Crow Colonialism, 1865–1920*. He has also coedited the collection of essays *Postcolonial Theory and the United States: Race, Ethnicity, and Literature*.

Daryl Michael Scott is professor of history at Howard University, coeditor of *Fire!!! The Multimedia Journal of Black Studies*, and vice-president for programs of the Association for the Study of African American Life and History. He is currently working on a two-volume history titled *The Lost World of White Nationalism in the American South*.

Brian Ward is professor in American studies at Northumbria University. In addition to many journal articles and book chapters, his major publications include *The Making of Martin Luther King and the Civil Rights Movement* (coedited with Tony Badger, 1996), *Just My Soul Responding: Rhythm and Blues, Black Consciousness and Race Relations* (1998), *Media, Culture and the Modern African American Freedom Struggle* (2001), *Radio and the Struggle for Civil Rights in the South* (2004), and *The 1960s: A Documentary Reader* (2009).

Emily West is senior lecturer in American history at the University of Reading, UK. She is the author of *Chains of Love: Slave Couples in Antebellum South Carolina* and *Family or Freedom: People of Color in the Antebellum South*. She is now researching enslaved wet-nursing in the antebellum South.

# Index

www.ingramcontent.com/pod-product-compliance
Lightning Source LLC
Chambersburg PA
CBHW020237310525
27492CB00006B/464